MW01133993

handwritten notes:
Act naturally 120
114 / w Seed coffee ✓ 38
Yesterday

Scenes from

A

Diverse World

From

The International Centre

for Women Playwrights

COPYRIGHT NOTICE:

The individual authors retain ALL RIGHTS to the material in this anthology. Publishers, professionals, amateurs, teachers, and students should contact each author individually regarding additional permissions and per-performance royalties. It must be understood that no material should be performed in front of a public audience, paying or non-paying, educational or professional, without the expressed permission of the individual authors or their publishers or agents. Performance in closed classroom settings is considered fair use. The authors biographies and contact information can be found through the International Centre for Women Playwrights:

http:// www.womenplaywrights.org.

Published by the ICWP Press, Columbus, Ohio, United States of America

ISBN: 978-1480179332

Cover Artwork: © Mona Curtis, 2012,
www.famosapublications.com

A Jen Bendick, Margaret Flanagan,Chloe Sehr in BLOOD
SISTERS by Robin Rice Lichtig. DUMBO, New York. Photo by
Robin Rice Lichtig.

D *Lakota Woman*, photograph in the public domain, used in
association with GONE ASTRAY by Jennie Redling.

I Hyosun Choi in BECAUSE OF BETH by Elana Gartner. Photo
by Jason Specland.

V David Johnson and Eve Szapira in PILLOW TALK by Karen
Jeynes. Photo by Karen Jeynes.

E Gary Cowling in PATIENT HM by Vanda. Photo by Nat
Thorne.

R Partial cast of AVENGING ARCHNE: A NEMESISTER
FABLE by Alicia Grega. Photo by Professor Spats.

S Paul Caiola and Diane Tyler in PATIENT HM by Vanda. Photo
by Nat Thorne.

E Tatiana Godfrey and Jenny Donheiser in SPINNING by Elana
Gartner. Photo by Fabrefaction Theater Company™.

W Sharon M. Lewis, Helen-Claire Tingling, Mary Durkan and
Melanie Nicholls-King in CARRYING THE CALF by Shirley
Barrie. Photo by Shirley Barrie or Ken Chubb.

O Kelsey Painter and Nayab Hussain in PLAY NICE! by Robin
Rice Lichtig. Photo by Richard Day/Darla Photography.

R David MacInnis as Solo in THE SEED SAVERS by Katherine
Koller, Workshop West Theatre 2009. Photo by Russ Hewitt.
L NO SOCKS GANG by Shirley King, Produced by GAN-e-
meed Theatre Project. Photo by CJ Ehrlich.

D Kate Cottam in SPOTLIGHT by Kate Cottam. Photo by Zarene
Dallas.

FOREWORD

This volume was conceived in a discussion on the International Center for Women Playwrights' listserv about the dearth of publishers for drama by and about diverse theatrical voices -- "diverse" meaning the racial, gender, cultural and social minorities who contribute to the rich fabric of modern human culture. I volunteered to edit this book of scenes for theater students because I will never forget my exhilaration when my High School Drama teacher handed me a copy of *Waiting for Godot* -- and opened my eyes to artistic possibilities I never knew existed in the staid educational arena of drawing-room comedy. I also volunteered because I will never forget how angry I was when Samuel Beckett himself declined to allow my university theater program to present *Waiting for Godot* with a female cast. A similar exhilaration -- and anger -- lies at the heart of each one of these pieces, scenes from around the world by dramatists determined to express their vision without being constrained by gender, sexual orientation, race or culture.

This publication would not have been possible without the support of talented contributors from around the globe, and from countless volunteer readers, editors, artists and leaders in ICWP -- a diverse group who share a dream of theater without discrimination.

Karin Diann Williams

TABLE OF CONTENTS

UNCONDITIONALLY

By Bara Swain

CAST:
Sally Kolakowski, white female, age 18-21
Ernst Fletcher, Jr., black male, age 18-21
TIME: Present
PLACE: New York City park

AT RISE: *ERNST, dressed in a suit and tie,*
              passes out programs to the audience
              members. SALLY is seated on the
              end of a bench onstage center. SHE
              is dressed in a trendy but
              inexpensive party dress. While
              ERNST dashes around the theater,
              SHE tugs at her clothing and gazes
              about restlessly.

ERNST (ad libbing): Here you are, sir ... Thank you for
coming ... Yes, it's such a big turn-out ... Can you give the
lady next to you a program? ... Yes, we're just about ready
to start ... I'm afraid we're low on programs. Maybe you
can share with ... Thank you. I'd appreciate it ... ... You're
very welcome ... I'm sorry ... This is it!

(ERNST returns to the stage. HE takes a seat on
the opposite end of the bench. HE has the last
single program in his hand. SALLY is still
fidgeting. ERNST fidgets, too. Furtively, THEY
glance at each other. Suddenly, ERNST turns to
SALLY, reaches over, and hands her his program.)

SALLY: Thank you.

ERNST: You're welcome.

(Silence. SALLY opens the program, and SHE reads aloud.)

SALLY:
If you can love me
Unconditionally now
Then I'm yours always

ERNST: Haiku.

SALLY: No. It's Sally. Hi.

(SHE waves with her fingers, rises and sits on the bench. SALLY is fast-talking, disarming and quirky.)

ERNST: Are you …

SALLY: Sally Kolakowski.

ERNST: You mean you're …

SALLY: Kolakowski. Sally. Woo woo! That's cola, plus cow, plus ski. My mother's maiden name was Fruchtman, or she wouldn't have changed it to a beverage and a bovine and a dangerous sport. Have you ever been skiing?

ERNST: No.

SALLY: Me either. *(brightly)* But I spent Christmas break at Hunter Mountain on my 16th birthday, only we didn't go skiing. I mean, of course we didn't go skiing. You know.

ERNST: Excuse me?

SALLY: January 5, 1998, Silly! Mom wouldn't let anyone near a ski slope since January 5, 1998! That's when Sonny Bono died in Nevada. Hit his head on a tree. Skiing.

(ERNST doesn't appear to understand.)

You know. Sonny Bono? From the Sonny & Cher Hour?

ERNST: "I Got you Babe."

SALLY: Oooo, you're fresh! It's just "Sally." Just call me Sally, Silly. Or call me Silly Sally. Or ....   *(timidly)* Wow, I'm really nervous.

ERNST: Me, too.

SALLY: *(reading)*
Ronald James Kolakowski and Ernst Tariq Fletcher, Senior, consecrate their union as witnessed by family and friends in a Ceremony of Commitment, on Saturday, the twentieth of August, two thousand and seven.

ERNST: *(imitating SALLY)* Woo woo!

SALLY: Shhh.

(SHE reads)

If you can love me
Unconditionally now
Then I'm yours always

ERNST: Haiku.

SALLY: No. It's Sally. Hi.

ERNST: Are you putting me on, Sally?

SALLY: No! I'm already dressed!   *(SHE laughs hysterically)*
My dad thinks my sense of humor is one of my best qualities. When I was a kid, I couldn't remember my multiplication tables, but I knew hundreds and thousands and billons of Knock-Knock jokes. Honestly, I did!

(ERNST stares at her in disbelief.)
Why are you looking at me like that?

ERNST: Haiku.

(Before SALLY can interrupt)

Haiku. It's a poetic form. It's a type of poetry from the Japanese culture.

SALLY: It is? Knock knock.

ERNST: Haiku combines form, content and language in a meaningful, yet compact form.

SALLY: It does? Knock knock.

ERNST: Yes, and there's a pattern – 5, 7, 5. English haiku are traditionally separated into three lines that usually express a single mood or emotion. The first line is 5 syllables.

(HE holds up his hand, and ticks off on his fingers)

"If – you – can – love – me." And the second –

(Ticking off on his fingers)

"Un – con – di – tion – al – ly now" – 7 syllables. And the third line is –

SALLY: -- 5 syllables. "Then I'm yours always."

ERNST: Correct!

SALLY: *(after a moment)* Knock knock.

ERNST: *(reluctantly)* Who's there.

SALLY: Aardvark.

ERNST: Aardvark who?

SALLY: *(jubilantly)* Aardvark a million miles for one of your smiles. Woo woo!

(SALLY laughs. ERNST doesn't break a smile.)

Okay, Haiku Man. Who made you the know-it-all?

ERNST: I'm a creative writing major.

SALLY: So what? So they taught you how to write Haikus? Doesn't seem that hard to me.

(SHE ticks off on her fingers)

You – know – who – I – am
But – I – don't – know – who – you – are
Do – you – have – a – name?

ERNST:
Ernst – Flet – cher – Jun – Yer.
[Ernst Fletcher, Junior]
Af – ter – my – dad – Ernst – Ta – riq
[After my dad, Ernst Tariq]

(HE's pleased with himself. SALLY is stunned.)

SALLY: Your father is … Mr. Fletcher?! I mean, you're sitting there and you're telling me that your dad is my father's –

ERNST: *(counting)*
Lov – er. Yes. Sor – ry.

SALLY: Knock knock.

ERNST: Who's there.

SALLY: Leaf.

ERNST: Leaf who?

SALLY: Leaf me alone!
(SHE's very upset.)

ERNST: Oh, come on, Sally.

SALLY: Just give me a minute. I need a minute. Lemme think. Lemme think. Frank Sinatra!

ERNST: I didn't mean to upset you this way.

SALLY: Which way then, huh? Frank Sinatra! Frank Sinatra died two months after Sonny Bono. Ol' Blue Eyes, they called him, and my mom said he had style and he had guts! He did! And he was nothing like my dad.
(SHE retracts)

Okay, okay, okay! Except that they were both born in New Jersey …

ERNST: Newark.

SALLY: Yes! Correct! I mean, how did you know that?
(before HE can answer)
Never mind. And except that my dad has the steeliest blue eyes ever, I swear. Bluer than Sinatra's, you know? …

ERNST: Your eyes are also very beauti –

SALLY: *(barreling on)* … And then after Frank Sinatra died, Roy Rogers died and Linda McCartney died. And my mother said: "Famous or not, we all end up dead, Sally." But she was heartbroken, you see. Because … don't you get it? My mother was heartbroken and not because my dad wasn't well dressed, or fist-fighting or a swaggerer. Or because he couldn't sing – not even in the shower – not even Happy Birthday – not a single note. But because ...

ERNST: ... Because --

SALLY: Don't push me! I'm not as ... as arterial as you are ...
ERNST: *(gently)* Articulate.

SALLY: Articulate as you, okay?
(counting syllables)
I – did – not – go – to .... Oh, crap. College, okay?
I – barely – finished – high school. Okay?
(SHE tries again)
Because! ... because after my dad left my mother in 1998, she didn't have a Dale Evans with a trusty buckskin horse, or a Beatle. No! We had gerbils. Yes, we had pet gerbils – like rodents, with tails longer than a tampon string, only these kept multiplying and dividing and multiplying until we had three cages packed with ... with 15 generations of god damned gerbils! Until Mom let them loose by the East River, just over the footbridge that brings you to the park across the ... what's it called. It's called ... It's called ... Not the Henry Hudson Parkway.

ERNST: The East Side Highway?

SALLY: No. Yes, thank you. The East Side Highway, for crying out loud. But there's a point here. I'm getting to a point here. I have a ... an anthology --

ERNST: Analogy.

SALLY: An analogy here, okay? Because – pay attention! – because gerbils require very, very, very little care to thrive, okay? And ... and ... and ... and .... and ... and ...
(SHE takes a deep breath)
And for my mom, you know, there was only one man. And

when my dad left my mother in 1998 – she didn't have anyone. Anyone at all. Except for me.

(after a moment)
Not that my dad is dead, Mr. Ernst Fletcher Junior. Just to my mom.
(SHE ticks off on her fingers)
And – do – you – know – what? Else?
I – am – dead – from – the neck – down.

ERNST:
I – know – how – you – feel …
(using her name for the first time)
… Sally.

SALLY: You do?

ERNST: *(nodding)* It hasn't been easy. I never met your mother, of course, but … my mom has an English Toy Spaniel, a *Felis domesticus* --

SALLY: House cat?

ERNST: Oh, so you know Latin, too? The cat was named Fleming after my mother's hero, and…

SALLY: Peggy Fleming?

ERNST: Sir Alexander Fleming … the Scottish biologist who discovered penicillin. He shared the Nobel Prize for his work on it with … Let is suffice that he was a genius.

SALLY: Well, Peggy Fleming won an Olympic gold medal in 1968 in figure skating. And she married a dermatologist .

ERNST: Well, there you go then! He could be a distant relative.
SALLY: Ernst? I think you're … patronizing me. I know that word, Ernst.

ERNST: I'm getting to the point. The point is that I always knew that my father wasn't really happy. And ... I can still wish he'd been my mother's gerbil.

SALLY: You're not making fun of me ... *(timidly)*... Are you?

ERNST: Sorry, it's a metaphor ... gerbils are monogamous. And generally, they mate – for life! – in pairs. My father found his partner for life. He never stopped loving me. Not for one moment. And your dad – he loves you unconditionally. Look at me – you know that I'm telling you the truth, don't you. Nod your head, Sally.
(SALLY nods her head.)

That's right. Thank you.
(after a moment)
I think that everyone deserves to be loved. And I'm going to bear witness today to celebrate those old farts. Are you with me, Blue Eyes? Nod your head again, Sally.

(SHE does.)
That's right.

(ERNST picks up a program. Quietly, HE reads.)

If you can love me
Unconditionally now
Then I'm yours always.

SALLY: Haiku.

ERNST: No. It's Ernst. Hi!

SALLY: Nice to meet you, Ernst.

ERNST: The pleasure's mine, Sally.

End of Scene.

LIKE A METAPHOR

By Emily Cicchini

Characters:
SCOUT: A girl, 14 years old, who uses a wheelchair.
JAZZ: A boy, also 14, who is always listening to music.
RICKY: A kid who hangs around with JAZZ.
DONNIS: A guy older than SCOUT, Class President.

SCOUT: Before the accident, I took dance lessons, too. I loved to dance, hip hop, African, modern, even ballet. I thought maybe, someday, I'd be a dancer...maybe in videos, behind the lead singer...or commercials on TV...

(Music returns. She begins to dance with the music with her upper body.)

SCOUT: I could bust a move with the best of them, shaking my wild thang, feeling like I could slice the air like butter, I was a house on fire.

(She moves her head and upper body to the music, gracefully and full of meaning. DONNIS suddenly enters. The music changes to something slow)

DONNIS: May I have this dance?

SCOUT: Donnis - what are you doing in my bedroom? Am I dreaming?

DONNIS: Haven't you had this fantasy before?

SCOUT: Oh, yes - I guess I have.

(He walks towards her. She looks up at him. He reaches out a hand to her, as if to help her to her feet. She takes it, as if to stand up, right out of the chair. Just as she starts to:)

SCOUT (cont): Wait. Something...something's not right. *(She falls back in her seat. Donnis shakes his head, a little condescendingly. He squats down, as if he might try to pick her up)*

DONNIS: Get up. Get up on your feet and dance with me.

SCOUT: I...I can't, Donnis.

DONNIS: Don't say that. You can do anything that you put your mind to.

SCOUT: I can do a lot of things, just, not that.

DONNIS: I don't want to hear that kind of talk. You can get better again. They are making great progress with science. You will walk again, someday...

SCOUT: I don't want to spend my life waiting for someday. I don't want to feel like I'm not okay right now, just how I am...

DONNIS: Don't give up on yourself, Scout. You're so brave.

SCOUT: I'm not that brave, I get scared all the time.

DONNIS: It's not fair. I want you to be well again. You deserve to be happy.

SCOUT: I don't deserve to be happy any more than any other person, Donnis. I'm just a person. A person who uses a wheelchair,

DONNIS: Come on, now. Stand up!

(He tries to lift her to her feet. She struggles to get away, to stay down. He tries again, despite her protests.)

SCOUT: No! I can't walk Donnis. I don't even want to pretend that I can.

(He stumbles, and falls back)

SCOUT: I want to be okay with who I am right now, not who I used to be...even in my dreams.

(DONNIS exits. JAZZ music plays. Solo piano. New signs, maybe on a blackboard: DO, RA, ME, FA, SO, LA, TE DO; SPRING CONCERT TENTATIVE DATE: MAY 1. Jazz sits at a piano. It can be an electric piano or upright. JAZZ sits behind it, playing, totally engrossed in playing the music. SCOUT enters. JAZZ stops playing)

SCOUT: Don't stop. You're amazing. Unbelievable.

JAZZ: It makes me nervous to play in front of people.

SCOUT: But music sooths the savage beast, right?

JAZZ: I am not a beast.

SCOUT: I know, it's just another metaphor. And in this case, I'm the beast.

(RICKY enters)

RICKY: Huh. Oh. It's you again. Is she bothering you, Jazz?

JAZZ: No. She is not bothering me.

RICKY: Cause I'll get rid of her, if you want me to.

SCOUT: I won't be long. I was thinking of signing up for choir next year. I thought I'd talk to the teacher about it…

RICKY: There are risers in choir. Where are they going to put you, right smack on the floor?

SCOUT: Maybe, if they have to.

JAZZ: Ricky, why don't you just, go away, and get a life.

(SCOUT bursts out laughing)

RICKY: What? What's so funny?

SCOUT: Jazz! You just used a metaphor!

JAZZ: What?

SCOUT: When you said "get a life," you didn't literally mean that Ricky was dead. You meant he didn't have an interesting life. One of his own.

RICKY: Hey. Should I be offended by that?

JAZZ: I'm just saying, leave us alone.

RICKY: Fine, if that's what you want. No respect. I get no respect.

(RICKY exits)

SCOUT: See, I think your brain can handle more metaphors than maybe you've been letting on. And, Ricky's not the only one who needs to get a life. Maybe I do, too.

JAZZ: What do you mean? You're not dying, are you?

SCOUT: No. But I think I'm going to have to nip something in the bud.

(DONNIS enters)

DONNIS: There you are, Scout. I've been looking all over for you. I wanted to make sure that I'm prepared enough for the dance. I've ordered an accessible limo…

SCOUT: Donnis. Wait a minute. I want you to tell me something. And be honest with me.

DONNIS: Of course…

SCOUT: Would you be going to this dance with me, if I didn't use this wheelchair?

DONNIS: What?

SCOUT: Would you even know who I was if I hadn't have been in the accident?

DONNIS: I don't understand. What are you saying?

SCOUT: What is it, exactly, that you like about me.

DONNIS: Um (noticing JAZZ, who is still there, watching)…maybe this isn't the time or place…

SCOUT: Name one thing.

DONNIS: I don't know, I…

SCOUT: Can't you do better than that?

DONNIS: I think - I think you're a kind of hero, acting like it doesn't bother you.

SCOUT: Like what, like what doesn't bother me?

DONNIS: That you can't walk. That you'll probably never walk again. I mean, most people would fall apart, or get angry, or even want to die. I mean, it's a terrible, sad thing that happened to you, Scout. It's a tragedy. But you, you're still funny, even nice...

SCOUT: I'm not a tragic hero, Donnis. I'm just a girl who got in an accident. Don't you understand that? (pause) I really don't want your pity, okay?

DONNIS: What are you saying?

SCOUT: I think - maybe...we shouldn't go to the dance.

DONNIS: Are you...dissing me?

SCOUT: I'm sorry, Donnis. I just don't think it's right.

DONNIS: I don't understand. I'm just trying to help you.

SCOUT: See, I don't really need that much help. What I really need is a friend.

DONNIS: Okay. Fine. Have fun. Maybe you two freaks belong together.

(DONNIS exits)

JAZZ: Did he literally call us freaks?

SCOUT: Yes, he literally did.

JAZZ: I'm not sure I understand what just happened.

SCOUT: I think I just saved a mockingbird: me. You know what I've been thinking, Jazz? That your music, Jazz music, it's sort of like a metaphor. It's not all cut and dried and put together like a lot of music. It's more like emotion…it kind of goes all over the place, and it means many things at once.

JAZZ: People have so many emotions, and it's hard for me to know what they really mean when they talk.

SCOUT: I feel the same way sometimes. And I'm not even autistic. Jazz, do you still want to go to the Oasis?

JAZZ: Of course. But my parents…the Ladies' Choice Dance…

SCOUT: Listen. I want my Mom to take us. Both of us. This isn't a date or anything, we're just going to see some music. Do you think your parents would let you go then?

JAZZ: I don't know for sure. But I expect they would say yes.

SCOUT: So we'll do it.

JAZZ: Amazing. Unbelievable.

SCOUT: My mom needs to drive me someplace again. She hasn't done it since the accident. I take public transportation and a cab or get rides from other people. It's a big pain, and that needs to change. It will be good for her, and you'll get to see that quartet from Chicago…and who knows. Maybe I'll even dance a little.

JAZZ: But how can you dance? It's jazz…people can't dance to jazz…

SCOUT: Brother, watch me dance. I can dance like a mockingbird sings!

(JAZZ begins to play again. SCOUT moves her wheelchair back and forth with one arm, and lifts her other arm high in the air, moving it to his music. She moves more and more. SCOUT slips down, out of her chair, to the floor. She pushes the chair away. She is dancing abstractly on the floor, mirroring the highs and lows of the music with her arms and face, her legs still paralyzed, laughing. Jazz watches, and laughs, too.)

End of Scene.

PERSONA F

By Aiste Ptakauske

CHARACTERS:
SALOMEA – young poetess
PALMIRA – simply young

Two male voices:
a voice on the phone and behind the door
a voice outside the window

There are two rooms on the stage. Salomea lives in the left side room, and Palmira lives in the right side one. All the actions take place at both rooms simultaneously.

Scene 1
Salomea and Palmira are standing at both sides of the wall which is separating their rooms. There is a door in it. Salomea is boarding up the door with the hammer. Palmira is plugging up the handle hole in the door. Separate parts of the door handle are lying at the feet of Palmira and Salomea. Having plugged the handle hole, Palmira picks up a screwdriver and, with the help of it, starts nailing the door. Salomea is bolting the door with a bookcase. While she is moving the bookcase, a vase falls down from the top of it and breaks into pieces.

PALMIRA: It was mine, wasn't it?

SALOMEA: I'll get you a new one.

PALMIRA: That was a present from Japan.

Salomea is cleaning up the chips. Palmira is bolting the door with a hutch and putting her video and CD players onto it. She turns the CD player on. It starts playing Enrique Inglesia's "I can be your hero, baby…." Salomea takes earplugs out of her pockets, puts them into her ears and starts sorting the books in the bookcase.

Scene 2

Salomea's room: a writing table, a chair, a lamp, and loads of books on the shelves. Salomea is sitting on the chair and imitating a conversation of two people.

SALOMEA: You know... Speed!

(in a low voice): Of light!

She's laughing and staring in front of herself.

(reproachfully): Are you leaving?

She's stroking her leg hair with the tips of her fingers.

(in a low voice): You have nice hair.

(seductively): Bye, Sam.

(in a low voice): Bye, baby.

For a while Salomea sits on the chair and daydreams. Then she takes a sheet of paper and a pen, moves closer to the table and starts writing.

(loudly): It is so good to feel the moisture of your lips on my forehead

My bear feet imprison your huge foot

Your look is cracking in my glasses

And returning back to you

I am squeezing tea leftovers among my fingers

And my guts assonate with the sound

You promised to call me

And I lost myself in a navy blue teacup

I won't let anyone drink from it

So that only my lips can taste you

Scene 3

Palmira's room. There is a huge, wide bed in the middle of it covered with plush toys and jewelry. Palmira is lying in her bed and talking on the phone.

PALMIRA: I've got to study.

(voice on the phone): You can do that later.

PALMIRA: No, I can't. I've got a seminar tomorrow.

(voice on the phone): Nothing will happen if you skip it.

PALMIRA: Nothing will happen if I skip your date.

(voice on the phone): You'll miss a good match.

PALMIRA: I don't care about your match.

(voice on the phone): There was a time when you did.

PALMIRA: There was a time when you cared about me.

(voice on the phone): So I shan't come, shall I?

PALMIRA: No.

(voice on the phone): Your choice.

PALMIRA: I'm definitely not choosing you then.

She drops the receiver, waits for a moment, picks it up again and dials a number.

PALMIRA: Hi. That's me again. Do you have a minute? Good. Guess: who has just been calling me? No, not Enrique Iglesias. Who? Bingo! Wanted me to go to a match with him. I'm not interested. Of course I'm interested in the match. I'm not interested in him. And he dares to phone me. After two weeks of silence! As if nothing has ever happened. "You know, babe, I've already talked to all the chicks, and they're all busy. Fancy a match?" Let him go there alone now. Oh, but of course, he won't be alone... Oh he's such a jerk... A match... He doesn't even have enough fantasy to come up with something convincing. I wouldn't have been surprised if he'd asked what time it was. Asshole! Oh, no worries, of course, I'm taking it easy. There's nothing to be upset about. I just don't care about him any more. Who's playing, by the way? Really? Does that mean that this "heracles" is going to be there too? He might still remember me. Let's go! Oh, please, don't be a killjoy. We'll find someone for you too. Oh, trust the pro! In fifteen minutes. Right? See you!

Scene 4

Salomea is sitting at her writing table with a bunch of sheets in her hands. She is loudly reading, sometimes correcting mistakes with a pencil.
SALOMEA: You're sitting opposite to me

Having blurred with the hoarfrost

On the window

We're habitually silent

We never tell each other what we want to know

A hysterical female laughter comes from the other side of the wall. Salomea can hear voices: How much is that? Oh holly shit! No. That's just not possible... Low waist pants are out of fashion now. What? No, it makes me look obese. How much is that?

Salomea takes the earplugs out of her pockets and puts them into her ears. She scribbles something onto the sheet and goes on reading.

And the girls behind the wall are lively discussing pants prices

Our words,

Formless, wingless, faceless, meaningless,

Are melting together with the hoarfrost

And flow away out of our ears

(maybe this is why they're so sterile)

We're sitting opposite each other

And we're not together

A knock on the door. Salomea listens. The knock goes off again. Salomea approaches the door and leans onto it.

SALOMEA: What?

(voice behind the door): You're alone?

SALOMEA: Alone.

(voice behind the door): It won't take long.

SALOMEA: Good.

(voice behind the door): Fancy going to a match?

SALOMEA: I don't like soccer.

(voice behind the door): Soccer players are the most gorgeous guys.

SALOMEA: Not funny.

(voice behind the door): Then what about a tea?

SALOMEA: Not now.

(voice behind the door): Why?

SALOMEA: I'm sleeping.

(voice behind the door): I could keep you the company.

SALOMEA: Not funny, again.

(voice behind the door): So maybe in the evening?

SALOMEA: Maybe.

(voice behind the door): I'll come then.

SALOMEA: Yeah, whatever.

Salomea is listening to the vanishing sounds of male footsteps. Then she comes back to the writing table, grabs the pen and starts writing. Finally, she leans back in the chair and starts reading in irritation:

I'm melting together with this damned hoarfrost

You've broken the thread

With no hope to join it

It's hopeless! Can you hear me – just hopeless!

Leave the thread alone!

Scene 5

Palmira is lying on her bed and reading a magazine. A whistle outside the window. Palmira goes on reading. A whistle goes off again. Palmira closes the magazine. A whistle goes off one more time. Palmira approaches the window.

PALMIRA: Can I help you, Sir?

(voice outside the window): Is Margo with you?

PALMIRA: No, we haven't met today.

(voice outside the window): Will she come?

PALMIRA: Don't think so. We never talked about a meeting.

(voice outside the window): If she comes, tell her I was looking for her.

PALMIRA: Right.

(voice outside the window): I'm Martin.

PALMIRA: I'll tell her.

(voice outside the window): What's your name?

Palmira jumps into her bed and opens the magazine. A whistle outside the window. For two more times. Palmira again comes to the window.

(voice outside the window): Didn't hear your name, beautiful.

PALMIRA: It's definitely not Margo.

(voice outside the window): Do you like cinema, Miss not-Margo?

PALMIRA: Depends on a film.

(voice outside the window): Would you go to a good film with me?

PALMIRA: And what about Margo?

(voice outside the window): She's not here.

PALMIRA: Won't she get upset?

(voice outside the window): Trust me, beautiful.

PALMIRA: Well, if you really really nicely ask me, I might even go.

Palmira picks up the receiver, comes back to the window and talks in an emphatically loud voice.

PALMIRA: Guess: who has just paid me a visit? Some dandy has been looking for you. Wow, last action hero! Martin. He's OK. Wouldn't go for a "Cosmo" cover, but his V shape is really impressive. Who's he? Where? At your birthday party? Oh, the one who couldn't get his eyes off me all night? I didn't recognize him, honestly. So that was you who sent him? I knew it! Not bad, not bad. Nothing like Enrique Iglesias, but nice. And the way he looked at me... Of course, I'll go for it! It might work. You know I've even got a feeling it'll definitely work.

The sound of a low female voice comes from the other side of the wall: It's hopeless! Can you hear me – just hopeless! Leave the thread alone! *Palmira drops the receiver and turns on a radio:* I can be your hero, baby...

Scene 6

Salomea is lying on the floor in the middle of dispersed sheets of paper. She's rolling in the sheets, petting herself and reciting a poem.

SALOMEA: White nuts in black chocolate

Are cracking among your teeth

With every single nut you bite off a piece of my heart

Our feet are making love under the table

My heart is warmly bleeding

You bite again

And I'm falling into the wrinkle under your eye

And I feel so safe

As if inside the womb of my own

I'm being covered with your eyelashes

My heart is still limply bleeding

Salomea is suddenly startled by the sound of male footsteps in the corridor. She gets silent for a while.

SALOMEA: Coming. Already.

She comes to the door and leans onto it with her forehead. A knock on the door.

SALOMEA: Hi.

(voice behind the door): I've come for a tea.

SALOMEA: I don't have any tea.

(voice behind the door): You promised.

SALOMEA: Promises, promises...

(voice behind the door): Long time no see.

SALOMEA: Not that long.

(voice behind the door): It's only now that I've pulled myself together. It was not easy for me either.

SALOMEA: I see.

(voice behind the door): So why don't you let me in?

SALOMEA: I can't bear to see you.

(voice behind the door): I'm sorry.

Salomea says nothing.

(voice behind the door): Am I forgiven?

SALOMEA: It'll take time.

(voice behind the door): I see. Listen, I've got to go now. Can I call in later?

SALOMEA: What for?

(voice behind the door): We used to get along very well.

SALOMEA: We won't any more.

(voice behind the door): So you don't want me to show up, do you?

SALOMEA: Whatever.
Silence. Salomea is listening to the vanishing sound of male footsteps. Music is playing behind the wall: I can be your hero, baby... *Salomea gets her earplugs out of the pockets and plugs them into her ears.*

Scene 7

Palmira lies on her bed with a peeling mask on her face and reads a magazine. There are neatly folded clothes and black high-heels put on the edge of the bed.

PALMIRA: This week you may start a secret affair with a friend, a neighbor or a boss. If both of you are free, and especially if the feeling comes to you on Tuesday, on Wednesday don't try to escape from your happiness. But if you're thinking of a flirt with someone else or if you are married...

No, that's not for me...

By the way, the Black Moon is coming into your sign at this time of a year. Thus, you shouldn't rely on your usual seduction practices: good food and erotic out-fit may not work. The most important thing now is to create a secret and to become an unapproachable and nostalgic woman. If your relations have become blank...

That's not interesting...

On Monday avoid quarrels, drive carefully and beware of thieves and gossip. On Thursday all your plans concerning HIM may fail. Wait for something unexpected concerning kids.

Oh no, this is out of question!

Palmira puts away the magazine.

PALMIRA: So...

She takes all the clothes from the edge of her bed and drops them onto the floor. Instead, she gets a T-shirt and runners from under the bed.

Scene 8

The room is dark. Only a lamp on the writing table is switched on. Salomea is sitting at the table and writing.

SALOMEA: My sniveling trophy,

My umpteenth failure,

Have I told you

That you're just so damned convenient?

That's a pity,

That I fancy my acne

More than your blond curl

That's a pity,

That a growl of my water-tap

Is more exciting to me than your flirt

Put down another golden rule

Onto your narrow forehead:

I need a Verther only when there's

No Don Juan around me

The sound of a hair-dryer comes from the other side of the wall. Salomea holds on for a while. The hair-dryer goes on. Salomea comes to the wall and bangs on the boarded door. The sound of a hair-dryer shuts down. Salomea goes back to the writing table, rips the sheet with her poem, throws it away and takes a clean sheet of paper. A vacuum cleaner goes off at the other side of the wall. Salomea in irritation resumes her writing.

Scene 9

Palmira's room is vacant. There are loads of cosmetics and perfume bottles scattered on her bed. Voices outside the window.

(voice outside the window): You look great today.

PALMIRA: I feel great today.

(voice outside the window): It's good that you called me.

PALMIRA: It's good that you invited me to a good film.

(voice outside the window): Margo told me where you wanted to go.

PALMIRA: Did she tell you what else I wanted?

(voice outside the window): You're embarrassing me .

PALMIRA: Liar.

(voice outside the window): Let's go inside, I'll show you...

PALMIRA: Maybe next time... See you. Call me.

Palmira enters the room, grabs the receiver and dials the number.

PALMIRA: You know, he's really cute. Straight to the point. And the film was well chosen. Everything was just perfect. I think it's going to work. Well, you know: nice arms, long legs, soft lips. What else could I like in him? He hardly said a word. Maybe that's even better this way... Of course, we didn't... Well, yes, he did want it, but... I've got a plan: I won't call him now. Let him call me. If he does, it means he's serious. I have to check it somehow... Oh, no worries: he'll call. I know. He needs me. I'll just torture him a little bit and then... Everything's gonna be all right.

Scene 10

Twilight has already filled Salomea's room. Salomea is sitting at the lamp and reading. A party is taking place at the other side of the wall. Salomea can clearly hear banging music, hysterical laughter, tinging glasses and curses. She shuts her ears with her hands and starts reading a book in a screaming voice.

SALOMEA: Feminism started as protest to the worst ideas of European fascism and colonialism. No one before had in such a way spoken of power in relationship and difficulty in difference between violence and seduction, humiliation and resignation. On the other hand, a very negative image of radical feminism has been formed. That is a lesbian, who at once makes us raise a question of homophobia, and an utter destructor who does not belong anywhere. There is a destructive and negative image of a lesbian thriving in our society. Media portrays her as an all-men-castrating bitch. But why the most repugnant, dangerous and unattractive woman should be represented by a lesbian? Lesbians can be not only very beautiful and feminine, but there are also lots of them. All these images are nothing but political games. They prove how important it is for men to dominate. Thus, they project all their worst fantasies onto feminism. Thus, a fear of a castrating vagina and strong woman is embodied in all these mass images. In reality, these images are nothing but a fear of femininity, which gradually turns into an absolute negativity. Being feminists, we have to live with this and constantly deconstruct it and, of course, laugh at it, because if we take it too seriously, it will ruin our life.

Scene 11

Palmira lies in her bed with wet hair and a sour milk mask on her face. She speaks on the phone.

PALMIRA: Guess: who has been calling again? No, not

Enrique Iglesias. He wanted to explain everything. Who cares? Explanations… No one will listen to his explanations now. If he didn't want to do it earlier, it means he never really meant to do it. You saw him? When? Alone? I knew it! You know, he comes to see her too. He thinks I'm a complete idiot who doesn't see anything. No, there's nothing between them. I know, believe me. She doesn't even let him in. She doesn't care about men any more, you know. That's none of my business, anyway. No, of course, I stopped thinking about that. I just cannot bear when he phones me. What does he want? What does he want? What do you think he wants? Of course, it's over. I'm not a bloody masochist…

Scene 12

Salomea is sitting at her writing table with her jacket and shoes on. She's smoking and muttering to herself.

(in a low voice): I'm going to Rio.

SALOMEA: When?

(in a low voice): The day after tomorrow.

SALOMEA: Alone?

(in a low voice): No…

Pause.

(in a low voice): I'm taking Sue with me. Sorry. She looked so lonely. But I'm coming back. To you.

SALOMEA: Of course.

(in a low voice): I've got to go now. I'll bring you a candy. Bye, baby.

Salomea throws a stub into the corner and starts to undress. While doing so, she starts reciting.

SALOMEA: Bye-bye, baby!

Might see you again

If you behave yourself

I'll bring you a candy

You're constantly running away

I'm trying to catch up

And jumping over small corpses of my own

Hurdle-sex

I'll be chasing you

Till nothing but a wind-whirled thread is left of me

Then I'll twine round your neck

And strangulate your carotid artery

She throws all her clothes into the corner, crosses her legs and opens a book.

SALOMEA: The main tragedy of this era, this historical moment, is huge individualism. The current generation is being told: 'you can do it! You're smart, good looking, you can do it!' On the one hand, it is a great empowerment for a man because it makes one think that only the sky is a limit. On the other hand, it is an utter lie because it is just so obvious that nobody can do it alone. And it is especially well known for men who have the whole networks working for them. They have a society who takes care of their needs. Thus, women should similarly take care of their matters. They must realize the importance of a female network. Unless women help each other, no one else will do that. And the idea that 'you can do it!' only because you have a nice face is an utter lie. A woman can be successful only in that case if she is backed up by a team of other reliable women. Women, who will answer her phone calls, advise her on important issues and recommend her for other qualified women capable of taking good care of her.

A female laughter comes from the other side of the wall. Voices can be heard: Oh, come on! That can't be true! No… Well, I can see why he didn't… I wouldn't have come either. But of course! She's as scary as my life…

Salomea closes the book and throws it at the boarded door.

Scene 13

Palmira is sitting on her bed ready to leave. She speaks on the phone with an open magazine on her lap.

PALMIRA: No, he didn't phone me. Yea, that proves how much he needed me. No, I'm not upset. There's nothing to be upset about. Yes, it is a pity. I was waiting. I was sitting alone in that dirty bar among old smoking jerks and waiting. I told you we didn't make any appointment. But I thought he might… Doesn't matter. Oh please, don't call him! I'm sick of your kind help. OK, I'm perfectly OK. I told you. I know what I'm gonna do. I'll be just fine…

She drops down the receiver and goes on reading.

PALMIRA: You might feel a little depressed. But don't lose your dignity – the time when everyone appreciates your merits is coming soon. Remember that this is a hard time for you – the Saturn has come to your sign. You should take more care of yourself. No extra work or vain endeavor – everything must be purpose-oriented. Start following strict agenda: get up and go to bed early so that you can have time not only for a morning meditation and exercises but also for a quiet and substantial breakfast. Your weekend is going to be excellent – you won't lack either friendly attention or good luck. Don't start anything serious on Monday, make plans on Tuesday, but do not start bringing them to life.

Palmira closes the magazine.

PALMIRA: Fine. I'll be just fine. I should probably sit on a diet and everything is going to be fine…

Scene 14

Salomea is nailing a huge cardboard sheet onto the boarded door. Then she takes a piece of chalk, gets a squashed piece of paper out of her pocket and starts copying a text from the paper onto the cardboard.

SALOMEA: I've fallen ill with you

your sound

smell

smile

your hands on my breasts

your breath on my neck

the roughness of your palms on my thighs

I am hallucinating

you are a virus

you've penetrated me

my rattling daily rounds

my quiet festivals

my solemn solitary life

I took all necessary measures

I never touched you

I only watched you

I sometimes overheard you

now I can't throw you off of me

I talk to you when you're not listening

I caress you when you can't feel it

I make love to you when you don't know it

I have you

you are terminal

Salomea steps back from the cardboard. She looks at it for a while, sighs and starts cleaning the text off. A knock on the boarded door. Salomea goes on cleaning the cardboard in silence. A knock goes off again. Salomea stops cleaning.

PALMIRA: You still write, don't you?

No answer.

PALMIRA: I know you do. 'I have you. You are terminal'… Sounds very familiar.

SALOMEA: I don't eavesdrop on your personal conversations, do I?

PALMIRA: I don't on yours either. I just can't help hearing them.

SALOMEA: I'll try to be quieter.

PALMIRA: Won't help.

SALOMEA: Want a tea?

PALMIRA: No. Thanks. Got to go. Lots of business to take care of.

SALOMEA: As always. *(Pause)* Go then. I've got something on my to-do-list too.

Palmira moves away from the door and goes back to her bed. She starts loudly sorting her clothes and jewelry. Salomea gets a heap of books off the shelves and takes it to the writing table. Having messed around for a while, Palmira throws all her stuff back under the bed, takes her shoes off and sits onto the edge of her bed. She turns on her CD player: I can be your hero, baby… *Salomea gets her earplugs out of her pockets, plugs them into her ears and stares at a closed book.*

End of Scene.

BLIND SPOTS

By Colette Freedman

FRIEDA: ...and the president promises that he'll put a cap on the college's discretionary spending if violations aren't curbed in the public policy department.

GRETCHEN: What the heck does that mean?

FRIEDA: I guess if the public is making policy that doesn't involve the president, it's a violation.

GRETCHEN: He can't do that.

FRIEDA: Can't he?

GRETCHEN: It's conjecture.

FRIEDA: Actually, it's slander... but as soon as you put it down with your poison pen, it'll be libel.

GRETCHEN: I don't hate him that much.
They look at each other. Smile.

FRIEDA: Yes, you do.

GRETCHEN: Yes, I do.

FRIEDA: I'm tired of reading. Why do I always have to read?

GRETCHEN: Because I always have to write.

FRIEDA: But I had cancer--

GRETCHEN: --In your bladder.

FRIEDA: It makes it hard to read.

GRETCHEN: It was a small tumor, they took it out. You're fine.

FRIEDA: I'm a cancer survivor. I shouldn't have to read so much.

GRETCHEN: You love to read. And it has nothing to do with the cancer.

FRIEDA: See Dick write. See Jane read. Read Jane read. Write Dick write. I feel bad for people named Dick and Jane. They'll never escape the stigma of being objectified two dimensional idiots trapped in fifties counter culture literature.

GRETCHEN: It wasn't counter culture.

FRIEDA: It was to me.

GRETCHEN: Frieda.

FRIEDA: Yes.

GRETCHEN: Focus.

FRIEDA: If you want to teach children to read, don't give them Dick and Jane, give them Seuss. He at least approached education through the stomach... Though, in actual fact, who really likes green eggs and ham?

GRETCHEN: Cholesterol challenged goys.

FRIEDA: Don't do that.

GRETCHEN: What?

FRIEDA: Don't say 'goy'. You can't say goy unless you're Jewish. I can refer to you as a goy; however, you can't refer to yourself as a goy. It's tacky.

GRETCHEN" Who made up those rules?

FRIEDA: Jews.

GRETCHEN: Naturally.

FRIEDA: You're just being ornery to avoid the obvious-

GRETCHEN: Which is-

FRIEDA: You're going to miss me.

GRETCHEN: I am-

FRIEDA: Yes. Terribly.

GRETCHEN: Ah.

FRIEDA: Must I remind you that, come Sunday, the Woodward to your Bernstein is retiring. Moving on to greener pastures.

GRETCHEN: You sound like a cow.

FRIEDA: Cow's don't have stress.

GRETCHEN: Unless they're hamburgers.

FRIEDA: Come Sunday, you are going to be the official editor...Do you even appreciate that you're about to become the youngest editor-in-chief of this small town's top selling periodical?

GRETCHEN: I appreciate.

FRIEDA: Because, frankly, I don't feel as if you appreciate it. As a cancer survivor, I have learned the importance of appreciating every single moment--

GRETCHEN: I appreciate. I appreciate. And you're not retiring, you're being promoted.

FRIEDA: Yes, but retiring sounds so much more... enchanting.

GRETCHEN: Frieda.

FRIEDA: Yeah.

GRETCHEN: Enchant me.

FRIEDA scans the paper.

FRIEDA: ...blah blah blah blah blah blah... and the President welcomes all adversaries on his Commons Bill.

GRETCHEN: I'm an adversary.

FRIEDA: You are the queen of adversaries. Wait, which one is more powerful? The queen or king? Or is it the elephant. He slinks, right? Does he slink? Who slinks?

GRETCHEN: What's a Commons Bill? Oh, for Christ's sake, this isn't one of his "made up" names to accommodate an inane policy, is it?

FRIEDA: Why are chess pieces always black and white? If chess evolved from checkers, shouldn't they be black and red?

GRETCHEN: Who said chess evolved from checkers?

FRIEDA: I did.

GRETCHEN: Did it?

FRIEDA: Didn't it? *(SHE lays down the King)* Checkmate.

GRETCHEN: How many drinks have you had today?

FRIEDA: One. Okay, three. But Bloody Mary's shouldn't count, they're extremely nutritional. Whoa. Would you look at that.

FRIEDA points at GRETCHEN. Walks towards HER.

GRETCHEN: What?

FRIEDA: Your stress, it's materializing.

GRETCHEN: No, it's not.

FRIEDA: I can actually see your stress starting to pulsate.

GRETCHEN: It's not pulsating.

FRIEDA: Oh. It's pulsating. Definitely pulsating.

(Off GRETCHEN'S glare)

--Okay. Okay. The Commons Bill. Section two, paragraph four. Blah, blah, blah, blah,blah, blah... no same sex marriages on his campus.

GRETCHEN gets up, furious.

GRETCHEN: His campus? He's been Vassar's president for two months. And there have been thousands of weddings on the commons. We used to steal food from them as kids.

FRIEDA: He's not outlawing weddings in general. Just gay weddings.

GRETCHEN: Weddings are weddings. It doesn't matter if it's Dick and Jane or Dick and Dick.

FRIEDA: Or Dick on dick-- Sorry.

GRETCHEN: Oh give me a frickin break!

FRIEDA: And the pulsating is back, accompanied by profanity.

GRETCHEN: How can he propose a reactionary bill?

FRIEDA: His college, his rules.

GRETCHEN: He's a fricking fascist.

FRIEDA: Again with the fricking.

GRETCHEN: A Mussolinian Stalinist fascist.

FRIEDA: Now that's conjecture.

GRETCHEN: How can someone be a modern college president with such a myopic stance? Fucking bullshit. Thank you Nathan, you've just given me the perfect hook for my editorial.

SHE sits and begins to type furiously.

FRIEDA: You need me to proof?

GRETCHEN: Nope, job perk, I have an eager co-ed helping me.

FRIEDA: Your star freshman?

GRETCHEN: At Vassar they like to be called freshwomen. And she's a sophomore now. The pride and joy of the undefeated women's lacrosse team.

FRIEDA: Is it a feat to be undefeated in division three?

GRETCHEN: You are such a school snob.

FRIEDA: It's the curse of the overeducated. C'mon, I don't have to be anywhere 'til eight. Roger is taking me to the symphony.

GRETCHEN: Ah. The symphony.
(sings)
Da, da, da, da, da da da da da da.

FRIEDA: What's that?

GRETCHEN: I was being the tuba.

FRIEDA: You sounded more like an out-of-tune flute.

GRETCHEN: An hour of brooding violinists in black. I love the symphony.

FRIEDA: Two hours of Mendelssohn, Prokofiev and Bach in B flat major.
(Beat)

I'll pay you handsomely to get me out of it.

GRETCHEN: You need the culture.

FRIEDA: That's what Roger says. But how does he know?

GRETCHEN: You mix up your metaphors. You think elephants slink. Elephants plough over everyone in their path. It's the horse that moves gracefully, it prances.

FRIEDA: I thought horses trot.

GRETCHEN: On chess boards, they prance.

FRIEDA: Which is the one that moves diagonally?

GRETCHEN: The bishop. Or as you like to call him in your household.

FRIEDA: The goy.

GRETCHEN: The goy.

THEY laugh.

GRETCHEN: I'm fine. Go. I'll see you tomorrow.

FRIEDA: Brainstorming at two. Needless Markups at three.

GRETCHEN: I don't want anything.

FRIEDA: Want and need are two very distinct verbs.

GRETCHEN: Noun. My wants are few.

FRIEDA: Verb. You need a dress.

GRETCHEN: Can't I just--

FRIEDA: --No. You've been putting off this shopping trip for two months.

GRETCHEN: I have a black dress.

FRIEDA: You have twelve black dresses. Can you fit into any of them?
Silence.

FRIEDA: Have you tried to fit into any of them?

GRETCHEN: No.

FRIEDA: Fine. Try on your dresses. Show me one that fits, and we don't go shopping. And you're not doing that beaded jacket thing.

GRETCHEN: Beaded jacket--

FRIEDA: --Last year, Loehman's backroom. The beaded jacket? You looked like Bette Midler.

GRETCHEN: As in Beaches or The Rose?

FRIEDA: As in no one under the age of fifty should wear beaded jackets.

GRETCHEN: Fine, I get it.

FRIEDA: Do you?

GRETCHEN: Yes.

(Off HER look)
No beaded jackets.

FRIEDA: You're about to win an award--

GRETCHEN: --I may not win.

FRIEDA: --You must look nice when you go up to the podium to accept the award. When you go up to the podium to accept the award and to thank me.

GRETCHEN: I'm thanking you?

FRIEDA: I survived cancer. I'm an inspiration.
SHE pulls out a sheet of paper. And another. And another.

FRIEDA: I made a list.

GRETCHEN: That's a long list.
(Beat)
Why don't you just give me the highlights.

FRIEDA: *(Reads)*
"Ladies and gentlemen. My esteemed colleagues and confidantes. The gentle giants whose pearls of wisdom imprint themselves on the blank canvasses of--

GRETCHEN: --The highlights.

FRIEDA: I can rewrite the speech, you unappreciative swine.

GRETCHEN: You are really trying to get out of going to the symphony tonight, aren't you?

FRIEDA: Any way I can.

GRETCHEN: Whaddaya say you leave the accepting to me?

FRIEDA: Fine. Fine. You'll forget the little people soon enough.

GRETCHEN: Kiss Roger for me.

FRIEDA puts the acceptance speech on GRETCHEN'S desk.

FRIEDA: In case you need inspiration.

FRIEDA Exits. GRETCHEN goes to the stove to make tea.

End of Scene.

THINGS NOT SAID FOR A LONG TIME

By Natalya Churlyaeva
Translated by Jane H. Buckingham

CHARACTERS
EUGENE: Husband, in his 50s.
TATIANA: EUGENE's Wife.

*SETTING: The action takes place at a cottage of two
nouveau riches.*

TIME: The present.

TATIANA: *(surprised)* You have the keys to his
apartment?

EUGENE: Why does this surprise you? Smolin gave them
to me.

TATIANA: This is hard to believe! Again, you're pulling
my leg, Gene! Smolin wouldn't even let anybody near his
apartment, he was so afraid for his collection. Even his close
relatives couldn't just drop in. He's a very cautious fellow,
trusted no one.

EUGENE: *(sadly)* Yes...he was...cautious... Have to agree
with that...

TATIANA: Well, then! Why did he give you keys to his
apartment? For the sake of what?

EUGENE: We were friends.

TATIANA: So what? We have lots of friends all over the
world. Does that mean we'd give everyone keys to our
home?

EUGENE: We were very close friends.

TATIANA: What do you mean very close? I don't understand you. How close?

EUGENE: No one closer.

TATIANA: No, I definitely don't understand you.

EUGENE: We were very close to each other…closer than kin.

TATIANA: What? Closer than kin?

EUGENE: Closer.

TATIANA: How can that be? Who can be closer than kin?

EUGENE: Can't you guess?

TATIANA: I was always certain that only a love one can be closer than kin. For me it's the axiom.

EUGENE: Very true, the axiom for me too…

(Tatiana stares at her husband and slowly sits down.)

TATIANA: You want to say that...

EUGENE: Yes, that's right.

TATIANA: No, it's already too much for one day. No!

EUGENE: Yes Tanya, you understood me correctly.

TATIANA: No! It can't be! No! No!

EUGENE: Tanya, don't scream. What's there to hide now that he's no longer around…

TATIANA: So, you mean you and Smolin were... Oh Lord, what a nightmare! What horror! What shame...

EUGENE: Don't shout, Tanya. We loved each other. Try to understand this.

TATIANA: Loved? You said, loved.

EUGENE: Yes.

TATIANA: You want to say that you were lovers?

EUGENE: I told you that we loved each other. Why don't you want to understand this?

TATIANA: But how can it be? How could you? You...you're a normal guy!

EUGENE: Of course, normal...

TATIANA: In the sense that you're a MAN!

EUGENE: Well, a man, so? What else?

TATIANA: You're my husband! And suddenly you're raving!

EUGENE: Why have you decided that I'm raving? Because I cheated on you? And haven't you cheated on me? Not once, not twice...

TATIANA: There's no comparison!

EUGENE: Who told you this? Where exactly do you see the difference? Isn't it, in essence, one and the same?

TATIANA: *(confused)* Are you joking? You're really serious about this? How can it be the same? How is it not different? Of course, there's a difference! A big difference!

The difference is between a man and a woman...

EUGENE: You want to know what's the difference? The difference between us specifically? Fine, I'll tell you. Only first answer one question. Tell me, have you loved at least one of these, your, former...well, you know what I mean.

TATIANA: Loved?! You've got to be kidding! What love, I don't even remember them!

EUGENE: There, there, that's it, I thought so. But Smolin and I LOVED each other. Understand this, we were in love, and that's the difference... Yes, I loved him and don't know how I can live without him...

TATIANA: Oh God, again this blue love...what abomination! And since when...(Laughs spitefully.) did you change color?

EUGENE: *(screws up his face)* Stop. Don't try to offend me, else...

TATIANA: I'm not trying. Why should I offend you? I simply can't wrap my brain around it... You're not pulling my leg?

EUGENE: Now's not quite the time for it. I've told you the truth as it is.

TATIANA: Why tell me this truth? If it's the truth, then it's absolutely of no use to me... No, all the same I don't believe you. Holy cow, you're making it all up!

EUGENE: You don't have to believe me, but I didn't lie to you.

TATIANA: Yes, you're lying! You're lying! Well, fine, let's suppose I believe you, let's suppose it's the truth. Tell me, when did it start? Ah, you're silent! Can't think on your feet?

EUGENE: Do you remember how right after our wedding my father went to America?

TATIANA: To America?

EUGENE: Yes, when he went there for the first time, on business, remember?

TATIANA: When was that? During the Stagnation Era, perhaps? Well, what then? What does America have to do with you and Smolin?

EUGENE: Do you remember the stories he told when he returned from there?

TATIANA: To remember all kinds of nonsense! Where haven't we been to since then, what's America to us?

EUGENE: Still, you remember.

TATIANA: You know, only his silly stories about horror movies remain in my memory. That is, not about the movies but how he saw them there for the first time in his life, and he was so frightened that he almost peed in his pants. How he locked himself in his hotel room and didn't sleep all night, jumping from every little sound...

EUGENE: He didn't only watch horror movies there.

TATIANA: Well, clearly it wasn't only horror movies he saw.

EUGENE: Exactly, not just horror movies. Also didn't just bring home horror movie cassettes from there.

TATIANA: Cassettes? I don't remember anything about any cassettes.

EUGENE: Father told no one and showed nobody.

TATIANA: How then did you find out?

EUGENE: Wait. Do you remember that time he also brought me a leather coat?

TATIANA: The coat I remember. Remember very well. It was a very posh coat for the time.

EUGENE: Yes. Do you remember the cut of that coat?

TATIANA: Yes, vaguely.

EUGENE: That's it, Tanya. May even say it all began with that coat. Father bought it by chance, in a special store. A misunderstanding, certainly. How could he have known? Besides, those were times when we didn't talk about such things aloud. But Smolin quickly paid attention to it. He asked me once very discreetly, you know, why was I wearing such a coat? Was I looking for a friend perhaps?

TATIANA: Huh?! Did he really ask you that right away?

EUGENE: No, of course not right away. I would say it's all very low-key and under-the-table on his part.

TATIANA: What was your answer?

EUGENE: To tell you the truth, then I didn't even understand what he was hinting at. Later he advised me to look for magazines and cassettes that my father might have brought home. Smolin knew about such shops abroad and what's on sale in them.

TATIANA: And you searched your father's things! Papa raised a good kid, wouldn't tell a soul!

EUGENE: Away with you! What search? There was no search; I just came across the cassettes by chance. So, I found them and asked father to give them to me to watch with friends.

TATIANA: And father let you?

EUGENE: Why not? By that time, I was quite grown-up and already understood what's what; besides, married...

TATIANA: To me.

EUGENE: What "to me"?

TATIANA: Married to me.

EUGENE: Yes, well, true, married to you. Only this fact actually didn't play any role. You were pregnant then, and later were in the hospital for a long time. In short, we weren't intimate during that period...

TATIANA: What are you saying, Gene! Well, what are you saying! Are you at least aware of what you're saying?

EUGENE: I must say it openly, at last. Perhaps, for the first time in my life. At least, to myself...

TATIANA: Not to yourself but to me! And it's not speaking out you want but making excuses for yourself!

EUGENE: I'm not making excuses to you. I don't want to make excuses but to explain...

TATIANA: What do you want to explain to me? That I was a fool? That I was married to a pervert all these years?

EUGENE: I'm not a pervert!

TATIANA: And what are you if not a pervert? You need a

psychiatrist! He would assess you promptly, as needed! And would treat you at the same time, so that after treatment you… so that there wouldn't have any trace of homosexuality left in you!

EUGENE: Don't forget, Smolin was a psychiatrist. And highly respected too, by the way…

TATIANA: Highly respected, Indeed! As crazy as his patients! A man is known by the friends he keeps! A damn pervert, that's whom your beloved Smolin was!

EUGENE: Don't you dare speak badly of him!

TATIANA: What, do you think I should glorify him? Sing odes of praise in his honor for making my husband abnormal?

EUGENE: He didn't make me anything!

TATIANA: Aha, he didn't… Do you want to say that you were always like that? But didn't you say that you didn't even think of such things until you found your father's cassettes?

EUGENE: Yes…perhaps that's how it was.

TATIANA: So, you watch those cassettes there and they so influenced you that you…that you…heck, there's no word for it, how disgusting!

EUGENE: Don't, Tanya. It's not the cassettes. There was nothing much in them. At least, not much more than what they show on TV now. It's simply once at Smolin's place…

TATIANA: So it was at his place?

EUGENE: No. Simply once, I went to his place to have a beer. Well, we drank and drank and drank…fooling around, having fun, playing the movies a hundred times, and didn't even notice how the day passed. We finished all the beer, went out, got some more, and decided to continue. Only this time not at home but at the cottage.

TATIANA: Whose cottage?

EUGENE: Ours, of course. You know that Smolin had no cottage. At our old cottage, the one that burned down.

TATIANA: What the…

EUGENE: Yes. We just made the last train. Imagine, we were all alone in the car, darkness outside the windows, and they didn't announce the stops. In short, we missed the stop. Jumped out at the next one, ran back through the woods. It was so dark and terrifying at night that we didn't walk but ran! We ran at night through the woods, all alone, in the dark, with a case of beer! Can you imagine?

TATIANA: I can imagine…at least, no, I can't!

EUGENE: Tsk-tsk, you have a weak imagination. How we bolted back, ran and couldn't feel our legs! We were terrified then…and felt ridiculous. It was both funny and horrifying, all the time it seemed someone was chasing us.

TATIANA: Now this I can imagine very well. You're never noted for your bravery, Gene.

EUGENE: We ran to the cottage and saw that no one was there. No light in the windows and the door was locked. What to do? I've left the key at home! We went around, around, didn't want to break down the door. It was already getting cold. I said to him, "Let's go to the bathhouse, it's not locked."

TATIANA: To the bathhouse? At night?

EUGENE: What else could we do? Go back to town on foot? Well, then we got a fire going in the bathroom ... We had lots of beer with us... We felt so good...

TATIANA: Good? In what sense?

EUGENE: Don't interrupt. Can't you listen to me till the end? For me, it had never felt and will never feel so good with anybody else... We sat close together in the bathhouse, feeling relaxed with the heat and the beer, chattering about this and that...all over again about how we ran through the woods in the dark, scared... Little by little, we moved onto the movies we had been watching all day...started to recollect the details... I already don't remember how we started touching each other. It turned out to be so pleasant...surprisingly pleasant...

TATIANA: And then? What did you do after that?

EUGENE: What do people do in similar situations?

TATIANA: For how long?

EUGENE: Until we fell asleep.

TATIANA: What happened afterwards?

EUGENE: Next morning we felt somewhat uneasy...at least I did. Not a word was mentioned about what happened the night before. We drunk tea in silence, he left, and I after him. Immediately I was away on business. Thought somehow everything would be forgotten by itself. But no, I actually tried but could not forget. All the time I was thinking of Smolin...was suffering a lot. You can't imagine how much! At last, I was so exhausted that I went to a doctor. Wanted his advice but plainly couldn't explain anything to him. Not enough courage. He only understood from my words that I was having some problems with sex. He advised me not to worry, to wait for the birth of the child, and then everything would take care of itself.

TATIANA: And then? And then?

EUGENE: And then? You know how it was with us after that. After little Vanya's birth everything finally broke down between us...there was no more harmony in our intimate life.

TATIANA: Now I'm beginning to understand whose fault it wasn't.

EUGENE: It's nobody's fault. Simply that's how our life unfolded.

TATIANA: Our life?

EUGENE: Do you remember how after little Vanya's death we started to drift apart? They began to hint to me that you had someone else, then another. They pitied me and called you a bitch behind your back but it was already unnecessary. In fact, such a state of affairs suited me just fine.

TATIANA: Now I understand the reason for it... But Gene, did it ever occur to you that I had others only to get a bit of feeling out of you? At least show a little drop of jealousy!

EUGENE: In vain. You hadn't noticed how you had begun to acquire a taste for it. But others did. As for me, it didn't matter any more. Eventually Smolin and I became close friends, our relationship took shape, and everything suited me...and most probably you too. And if you weren't caught up by some absolutely mad thirst for money, then these our...

TATIANA: Then these unrepentant sins of yours would continue forever!

EUGENE: What unrepentant sins? There was no need to

bury treasures in the ground!

TATIANA: Aha, no need! Still tell me to give them to you for safekeeping!

EUGENE: It would have been safer at least!

TATIANA: So, you dug them out in order to hide them somewhere safer? Then where are they? Where? What haven't I seen them yet? Why don't you bring them here before it's too late?

EUGENE: We didn't dig them out on purpose! We just came across them by chance when changing the fence…

TATIANA: And decided to pocket them! Not even a word to your wife!

EUGENE: Not to pocket but to divide. I took the money and Smolin the necklace in order to sell to people he knew. Who could have known it would turn out like this? There was no need to bury them on the sly…nothing like this would have happened then…
(Sobs quietly.)   If you'd only told me…

TATIANA: Fancy that, how clever! Tell you…I didn't even tell Alex what we were burying! Though lately we're rather close enough. Had to fool him that I was burying money and some documents in case of a divorce.

EUGENE: Who cares why and whom you tried to fool, Alex or Malex. Now you won't be able to set things right, already too late…

(There are sounds of cars approaching. Headlights pierce the darkness.)

End of Scene.

COMMUNITY OF STRANGERS

By Catherine Frid

THE SCENE:
The action takes place in the woods in a Japanese internment camp in the interior or rural British Columbia, August 1945.

CHARACTERS:
VIVIAN, about 18
SHOJI, Japanese, about 18

(VIVIAN is fishing in the river, catching trout using a stick with a line of string. She shows finesse, hooking a fish and jerking the line. SHOJI is watching her, hidden in the trees. SHOJI shifts and a twig crackles. VIVIAN jumps, ready to run. When SHOJI sees VIVIAN is frightened, he steps into the clearing, embarrassed.)
VIVIAN: I thought you were a bear!

SHOJI: I was out walking.

VIVIAN: I didn't hear you. Once when my mother and I were fishing, a bear creeped up on us. She scared him away by hitting him with her fishing rod. That happens in berry season. Are you going to pick huckleberries? You don't have a bowl. Here, you can have mine if you want. I found a good fishing hole so I'm going to stay here today. See, the logjam up there moved with the big storm last week and the fish love this new spot under here. But don't tell anybody. Your best spots always have to stay a secret. I'm Vivian.

SHOJI: Shoji.

(VIVIAN starts to reach out for a handshake. SHOJI doesn't. VIVIAN withdraws.)

VIVIAN: Hi.

SHOJI: The fish are no good in this river.

VIVIAN: No good? They're great! River trout are the best fish there are. Everybody knows that.

SHOJI: You call them trout? They're ugly, black and bony and they taste bad.

VIVIAN: You don't eat those fish. Those are suckers. Nobody eats them. If I catch one I just use it as bait. You have to practice to catch trout. Suckers are easy to catch, they pretty much jump on to your hook. Trout are smarter. You have to dip your hook. Make it act like a bug. Then pull up to set it. You've never had trout?

SHOJI: I know how to fish. My father had a fishing boat. We caught tons of fish every week. Good fish, chinook salmon and halibut. We're not allowed to fish here. Even though the food's rationed, the RCMP patrols to make sure we don't fish. And the water's full of them. I tried one time, but all I caught were those black things.

VIVIAN: You can't fish? That's just dumb! Did you have to go to the Exhibition grounds in Vancouver? Before you came to New Denver.

(SHOJI stares at VIVIAN and then turns to leave.)

Shoji?

SHOJI: You're a real know-it-all, aren't you?

VIVIAN: I didn't mean….

SHOJI: You're like everybody else up here. "Let's look at the Japs!" "I've never laid eyes on one of you-lot before." You look at me and see a kamikaze pilot, happy to kill myself as long as I blow you up at the same time!

VIVIAN: I don't. I'm sorry.

SHOJI: I just wanted to get out of the camp for awhile. To think.

(Pause)
VIVIAN: You've seen the ocean? What's it like?

SHOJI: Big.

VIVIAN: Have you ever gone out so far you couldn't see land?

SHOJI: All the time.

VIVIAN: Weren't you scared?

SHOJI: No. On summer vacation I'd go out with my Dad. We stayed on the boat for days, laying the nets in the best spots. That's real fishing. They're big. Twenty-five pounds at least, not like these puny things. You don't pull a chinook out of the water with a stick. I've seen you before, at Joe's. The Ice Cream Parlour. You're Vivvy. You come there with Yukio and Sen. To dance. Jitterbug.

VIVIAN: They asked me to teach them and Joe's has the only jukebox in New Denver. I haven't seen you there, but I've seen --

SHOJI: I stay at the back. How did you learn to dance like that?

VIVIAN: My Uncle Bill. He'd drive for half a day to get to a dance, no matter what was happening on the farm. It drove my mom crazy. He taught me all the latest dances. The jitterbug's my favourite. But that was before he went away for the war effort. Maybe he's more serious now. His letters are so censored, it's hard to know what he's saying.

SHOJI: Why don't you go to the white dances in Silverton? You could get through the roadblocks, no problem. Why come out to Joe's on Friday nights, Jap night?

VIVIAN: I went once. I don't like the dances in Silverton. The boys there weren't nice. See, I'm not from here.

SHOJI: Nobody would dance with you?

VIVIAN: It wasn't that. *(beat)* The boys held on too tight. And the girls were ... mean. I was in the washroom and they were talking about me. I'm alone, here.

SHOJI: Where are your parents?

VIVIAN: My dad died, five years ago. I didn't really want to stay with Mom and Uncle Bill, on the farm.

SHOJI: Why didn't you want to stay? My father's in a work camp and we'll do anything to be altogether again.

VIVIAN: Your father's where?

SHOJI: They wouldn't let him come to New Denver with us.

VIVIAN: Mom told me she didn't want me in the house any more. Not even in the town.

SHOJI: You said you wanted to leave.

VIVIAN: After she told me that, I didn't want to stay.

SHOJI: What did you do?

VIVIAN: She sent me here to help my Dad's cousin Alice. She and her husband live out by the sawmill. That's where he worked, before the war. Now he's in England, waiting to be demobilized. They have four kids and the oldest, the twins, are nine. Boy, are they a handful. I've been here nearly three years, and they just get worse.

SHOJI: No, what did you do to make your mother ... you know.

VIVIAN: I turned Catholic!

(SHOJI looks expectant. Pause.)

She said it would kill my grandmother. And maybe it did.
SHOJI: Did you marry a Catholic?

VIVIAN: No. I was only 16.

SHOJI: Did you ... you know, have a baby?

VIVIAN: Of course not, Shoji! What would your parents do if you changed religions? Are they Catholic?

SHOJI: Why would they be Catholic? I don't know what they are. Nothing, I guess.

VIVIAN: You don't know?

SHOJI: Probably Buddhist. But we never went to the temple. For us, family is more important. Especially here, where the government considers us enemies.

(SHOJI pulls out a sheaf of newspaper from under the pail.)

Let me see your paper. Every edition has that ad for war bonds.

VIVIAN: My uncle used to say that people buy war bonds because there's nothing else to buy these days.

SHOJI: *(reading)* "Here you are free! Free from cruel decrees. Free from confiscation, from suffering, from wanton imprisonment without cause. Yes, you are free in Canada. Speed the Victory. Buy Victory Bonds!" Do you know they run these ads in the Japanese newspaper, too?

VIVIAN: No.

SHOJI: Who's free? We're stuck in an internment camp in the middle of nowhere, in shacks that the snow drifts right through. The hicks up here still use outhouses! We're getting out of here.

VIVIAN: There's nowhere to go. (pause) God is bigger than the government.

SHOJI: He's not doing much around here.

VIVIAN: It might look that way but that's because we have free will, which can lead us to go astray, sometimes into evil. But the sacred is in everything.

SHOJI: Sacred food rations. Sacred roadblocks.

VIVIAN: Shoji.

SHOJI: Sacred shhh-boxes. That's my favourite sacred thing.

(VIVIAN starts to pack up her things.)

VIVIAN: Stop it! Get away from me. Just go away. I gave up everything to become a Catholic and you have to make fun of it.

SHOJI: You shouldn't have done it. Your family's a lot more real than some religion.

(A branch cracks loudly in the woods. VIVIAN and SHOJI stand stock-still, prepared to run. Silence.)

Maybe somebody's coming. I should hide.

VIVIAN: Because you're Japanese?

SHOJI: You mean: because I'm yellow and you're white?
That, too. But we shouldn't be out here, alone.

VIVIAN: Why not? You may be a dope but you're not like
the boys from Silverton.

SHOJI: I don't want people to think badly of you.

VIVIAN: I'm more afraid of bears than people.

(They wait. Silence.)

SHOJI: Yes, it's a bear, looking for fish. And when he gets
closer and smells your stinky black sucker in that pail, he'll
run the other way: "Get me out of here! I'd rather starve than
eat that bony, smelly thing!"

*(VIVIAN grabs a fish from the pail and chases SHOJI with
it.)*

VIVIAN: Then the fish'll start chasing you.

*(VIVIAN slimes SHOJI with the fish. They grapple and laugh
and the fish slides away.)*

SHOJI: You stink!

VIVIAN: No, you do!
(They become awkward and move apart.)

SHOJI: Do you feel lonely here, Vivvy?

VIVIAN: Yes. Do you?

SHOJI: My grandfather lives with us here. He's going to

take us all back to Japan. We don't know what will happen to my father, and we can't even talk to him about it. We have to sign by the end of the week and by the time a letter from Angler gets through the censors, it takes three weeks or more.

VIVIAN: Angler? On Lake Superior? Is that where your father is?

SHOJI: Yes.

VIVIAN: That's where my uncle is.

SHOJI: What was he sent there for?
VIVIAN: He's working there. As part of the war effort. It's a work camp.

SHOJI: I know that. It's a work camp for POWs.

VIVIAN: Prisoners of war? Uncle Bill isn't a POW. He's a Canadian.

SHOJI: So is my father.

VIVIAN: Now you're trying to tell me my uncle's a prisoner of war? That means he'd be a traitor!

SHOJI: My father was sent there because he missed curfew one night, just after Pearl Harbour. We Japanese had a dusk curfew, but he was visiting my grandmother. She was very sick and when he came home that night the police caught him. That's when the rest of us were put in the Exhibition, as you call it. It was a cattle barn.

VIVIAN: Somebody once told me it was terrible in there.

SHOJI: It was. *(softly)* We were kept behind fences. Like dogs. Angler is a work camp. For prisoners of war. You don't go there to work. You get sent there. That's why their letters are censored. Every prisoner has a red circle painted on the back of his uniform. It's a target so the guards can shoot him, if he tries to escape.

VIVIAN: But Mom said he was doing this as part of the war effort. His contribution.

SHOJI: Are your mother's letters censored?

(VIVIAN shakes her head.)

You see?

VIVIAN: There was a man from Vancouver who rented our cabin for a couple of years before I left, even though he hardly ever stayed there. He said he wanted a place to rest when he passed through. But he was always asking about Uncle Bill. About his ham radio and where he got his money. Shoji, Uncle Bill couldn't have been a spy. Could he?

SHOJI: Just because he's in prison doesn't mean he did anything wrong. My Dad didn't.

VIVIAN: But he was sent there.

SHOJI: Yeah.

VIVIAN: And Mom didn't tell me. She was trying to protect me from the gossip. Maybe that's why she sent me away. Maybe it's not just because I'm Catholic.

End of Scene.

BULLETPROOF SOUL

By Jennifer Farmer

In Uganda, at a school for ex-child soldiers, Sol, a charity worker, tries to keep his rebellious 17 year-old sister Rena in line. Alice, a former soldier Rena's age, has seen and done worse than either of them realize. As friendship develops, so does the risk of betrayal.

If there is no dialogue after a character's name, this indicates an active silence between the characters. This is where characters can also take a moment to make a transition.

Scene 2
Schoolhouse, Uganda

The schoolhouse is an old disused building; an empty shell of a space. As yet, there are no chairs, tables or desks.

Sol is unpacking second-hand textbooks and supplies. Rena sits on an unopened box, fanning herself. Sol, struggling with a load of supplies, drops a stack of pencils and they scatter everywhere. Rena laughs maliciously as Sol bends down to pick them up. As he does so, he drops a ream of paper that he is holding. Rena laughs even harder.

SOL: You could help.

Beat. Rena kicks the pencil nearest her over to Sol. Beat.

RENA: The word is 'thank you.'

SOL: If you hadn't kept bunking off school, you'd know that's two words, actually.

Rena gives Sol the two-fingered salute.

Charming.

Sol continues to collect the scattered pencils and paper.

(to himself) This is for Mum, this is for Mum, this is for Mum.

RENA: What, picking up paper off the floor? *(beat)* Come off it, bruv. We both know that I could've crashed at one of my spars'.

Sol is busy counting the pencils.

I could've, man. I just wanted to vex you by coming out here. *(beat)* I did. And Dad, well he thought it would be good for me to get away for a bit. Coz Dad knows the kind of stress I've been under lately. And the only reason Dad didn't come to the airport was coz he's not one for tearful goodbyes.

Rena watches as Sol remains engrossed in his task.
You know, you shouldn't crawl on the floor like that, getting your trousers dirty. But then again, what do you care that Mum and Dad didn't pay for a first-class education so you can wear second-hand clothes.

Pause; Rena knows Sol's heard her. Rena walks over to the doorway, stepping on sheets of paper and breaking several pencils in the process. Sol tries to get as much stuff as he can out of her path.

SOL: What the hell are you doing?!

RENA: They were in my way.

SOL: Do you know how precious this is?!

Rena shrugs.

RENA: Just look like pencils and paper to me.

SOL: These donations will have to last the whole year.

RENA: Better keep them off the floor then.

Sol shakes his head in disbelief and continues to gather everything up.

What these Africans need to be learning about is air con, man. I mean, I thought we were making poverty history! What was Live 8 for, then? It ain't like there wasn't like millions of us watching the show. You think with all the help we gave them, cancelling debts and all that they'd be grateful enough to buy some kind of cooling system. You'd think they'd—

SOL: Rena?

RENA: What?

SOL: Please be quiet.

RENA: What, can't I state my opinion?

SOL: No.

RENA: Why?

SOL: Because no one wants to hear it, okay?

RENA: Fascist.

SOL: Oooo, big word for you, Rena.

RENA: I've got an even bigger one: prick. *(beat)* Where the fans at?! I can't buy a breeze up in here.

SOL: You don't even realize when someone is doing you a favor, do you?

RENA: Na-uh, unlike your savage charity cases, I don't need your handouts.

SOL: No? Your 'spars' wouldn't even let you kip on their floor. Now what's that say about you?

Oscar enters.

OSCAR: I hope this is where all the fun's happening. That Kate, she's doing my head in with all that admin.

Oscar holds out his hand.

Oscar Parsons—Wait, I remember you. I've worked with you before, right? Where was it? Tibet?

A stunned Sol scrambles to stand up, pencils and paper still in hand.

SOL: Palestine.

OSCAR: Palestine, that's it. *(beat)* Youngblood, right?

SOL: Sol. Walker. *(beat)* Youngblood. That's what you called me.

OSCAR: May forget a place, but I never forget a nickname. How's it going?

Oscar shakes Sol's hand vigorously.

SOL: Okay, I guess. I didn't, I didn't expect to see you again.

OSCAR: No one ever does in my case.

SOL: Thought Palestine was to be your last gig.

Oscar grunts.

OSCAR: Thought I'd make Uganda my last shout. I'm really too old for this shit.

SOL: Yes, Uganda—what a coincidence.

OSCAR: If you believe in that sort of thing. And I don't. You just arrive?

SOL: Two days ago. You?

OSCAR: Just over three weeks ago. Hitched my way from Kampala. Just wanted to have a look at the country before we got stuck in. *(to Rena)* And who is this?

SOL: Uh...

RENA: Rena.

OSCAR: Pleasure's all mine, Rena. Oscar.

RENA: I heard.

OSCAR: So Rena, are—

SOL: Long time since Palestine. What three years?

OSCAR: Yeah, about that. I remember now. Israeli tanks didn't put you off humanitarian aid, I see. *(to Rena)* First time I laid eyes on Youngblood here, he was standing in front of a bulldozer about to raze the school to the ground.

SOL: You know...

OSCAR: It worked; the school was left standing. So where did you two meet? It's not unheard of for romance to blossom over anti-malaria tablets.

RENA: What?! No, no, no, no, hell no! Man, he's my brother.

OSCAR: Ahh. *(beat; to Sol)* So is this the sister?

Oscar clicks his fingers, trying to remember something. What is it? What is it? *(to Rena)* Menia zovut Oscar. Rad s vamee poznakomit'sya.

Pause as Oscar waits for Rena to respond. Sol is about to say something but realizes it's too late.

Did I get that right? I didn't, did I? Here's me trying to blind you with the only bit of Russian I know. Learned it from a girl I was working with in Guatemala. So, how would you say 'Which writers have captured the zeitgeist of the nation?'

RENA: How should I know?

Oscar laughs, thinking Rena's made a joke. He quickly realizes that she hasn't.

OSCAR: When Sol mentioned you studied in Moscow, I assumed you'd be fluent in the native language. Anyway, please tell me you find Dostoevsky overrated. I say that, people think I'm mad.

RENA: I can see why.

OSCAR: I'm a Pushkin man, myself. Who do you like?

Silence as Oscar waits for Rena to respond. The waiting becomes uncomfortable.

Gogol? Tolstoy? Turgenev? Don't say Chekhov, everyone says Chekhov.

RENA: What are you on about?

OSCAR: Don't be modest; I hate people that are modest—it's a waste of time. A scholar of Russian literature is what you are.

RENA: Nah-uh. I ain't studied Russian anything, mate.

OSCAR: Really? You sure?

Rena shakes her head.

Sol said he had a sister that studied in Moscow.

RENA: I bet he did.

OSCAR: I thought that might be you.

RENA: Nope.

OSCAR: Sorry. Must be of your other sister, then.

RENA: There ain't no other sister.

Oscar looks at Sol.

Oscar:

Sol:

Rena: Just me.

Beat.

OSCAR: I'm sure it was Youngblood that—sorry, I must've gotten the wrong end of the stick.

RENA: Uh huh.

OSCAR: Uhm, anyway, pleased to meet you, Rena. How are you liking Uganda so far?

RENA: I'm not.

SOL: What she means is that the lack of infrastructure…I mean by the civil war and …she's overwhelmed.

OSCAR: Yeah, is a bit of a mess, isn't it? So, where else have you been on placement?

RENA: Place—

SOL: This is Rena's first time—in a placement abroad.

OSCAR: Well enjoy it. *(beat)* So Youngblood, fill me in. What else you been up to? What other civil unrest are you causing?

SOL: Well uhm, there was a demo against the Terrorism Act a few days ago.

OSCAR: Good turn-out?

Beat.

SOL: I, uhm, I missed it, actually.

OSCAR: From what I remember, you're not one to miss a demonstration. As I recall, you were always organizing one.

SOL: Family troubles. Our mum, she had a stroke.

OSCAR: Oh, I'm sorry. I'm very sorry to hear that.

SOL: She'll be fine; our Dad's there. Rena's with me to give Mum some space.

OSCAR: It must be a comfort to have a good lad like you.

Rena rolls her eyes.

Bet you had your heart set on that demo, huh?

RENA: Not—

SOL: Rena doesn't get caught up in politics.

OSCAR: Really? That's a surprise.

RENA: Actually Oscar, I've been—

SOL: But she's starting to get an awareness.

OSCAR: It's never too late to get your political bearings. I didn't sign my first petition until I was at uni.

SOL: I was eight.

RENA: Of course you were.

Oscar laughs.

OSCAR: Has he always been so head-strong?

RENA: If that's what you wanna call it, then yeah.

OSCAR: Always the provocateur.

RENA: Always the—

SOL: I just try to do what I can when I see an injustice.

RENA: Oh God…

SOL: I think this will be a real eye-opener. For all of us.

OSCAR: I must admit even I'm feeling a bit—

RENA: Hot?

OSCAR: Apprehensive. And I've seen some shit. But these poor kids. That's sounds so patronizing, I know. But…fuck me, did they ever get to be children? Did they get to have a childhood?

SOL: Childhoods were stolen from them by corrupt governments and authorities; people who should have known better.

OSCAR: Right?

Oscar looks at Rena, who shrugs.

RENA: I haven't a clue as to what you're on about.

OSCAR: The students.

RENA: What students?

SOL: The ones we're here to teach.

RENA: What about them?

OSCAR: The fact they used to be soldiers.

RENA: What?!

OSCAR: You didn't know?

RENA: Nah-uh.

SOL: I told you before we left London.

RENA: Like I listen to you. *(to Oscar)* For real? They used to blatt, blatt, blatt?

Rena mimes shooting a gun. Beat.

SOL: Yes.

RENA: They really killed people?

SOL: Yes.

RENA: Straight-up gangsta.

SOL: Rena, please.

RENA: Hopefully some of the blokes'll be fit.

SOL: Rena!

RENA: Wait a minute—I ain't about to get my head blown off am I?

OSCAR: There is still fighting in some parts, but we are relatively safe here.

RENA: Relatively?! *(beat)* So how old are these killing machines then?

Beat as Oscar looks a bit unsure at her choice of phrase.

OSCAR: Some in their teens. A few are 20, 21. Some might be twelve or even younger.

RENA: What, 12?! How can they join the army if they're 12?

SOL: Don't you watch the news?

RENA: Not really.

SOL: Not really.

OSCAR: The rebel army's illegal, that's why they can have children fight.

SOL: If you paid attention to what goes on in the world, you'd know this.

RENA: What I do?

SOL: Nothing; that's the problem.

RENA: You can have a go at me, but at least I ain't got nobody shot up. *(beat)* Well, not that I know of.

SOL: They are not silly kids playing at 'keeping it real.' These are victims, Rena. Victims of corruption and manipulation who—

RENA: Who killed people and that's not right. Is it, Oscar?

OSCAR: No, it's not, Rena.

RENA: *(to Sol)* And you said I wasn't into politics.

SOL: You—

RENA: Oscar, did you know I've even been arrested; for protesting? Exercising my freedom of assembly.

OSCAR: Alright, Lil' Sis.

SOL: Well—

RENA: A political prisoner, me. Just before we came out here. Sol ain't the only Walker that can organise a 'demo'.

Oscar shakes his head.

OSCAR: And they say young people are apathetic.

RENA: It was well worth it, getting banged up.

OSCAR: No shame in getting incarcerated in the name of your beliefs.

RENA: True that.

OSCAR: Sometimes, that's the only way us little people can be heard.

RENA: Exactly.

OSCAR: Because when we break down the walls of that cage they call a prison cell, the whole world will hear our cry.

RENA: Let the church say 'Amen!'

OSCAR: So what was the cause, warrior?

SOL: It was nothing, Oscar.

OSCAR: *(to Rena)* What were you fighting for?

SOL: Rena doesn't—

OSCAR: Sol, let the woman speak.

RENA: Yeah Sol, let the woman—let me speak. *(to Oscar)* Me and my spars, right, we was getting pretty vexed about the whole Somali situation.

OSCAR: Oh man. It's so good to know people are looking beyond the racism and xenophobia of the media.

RENA: You what? Nah, we was protesting that the asylum seekers is taking over. You can't move for all them foreigners. What about our housing and our benefits? Our jobs? Who's looking out for us? Don't seem like the council was listening, so we decided to get the message across ourselves. They heard us that time.

OSCAR: Sorry?

RENA: We threw stones at them freeloaders. You shoulda seen it, yeah? Black and White kids together. A few Asian lads. Fighting for our country, innit.

Beat.

OSCAR: You were chucking rocks at the Somali kids?

RENA: Believe.

OSCAR: At other Black kids?

RENA: No, we're Black; they're Somali. *(beat)* Nobody got hurt. Not hurt bad, anyway. We was the ones that came out of it worst. You shoulda heard what them lot was calling us. They gave just as good as they got. Now they know not to be using our community centre.

OSCAR: Your community centre?

RENA: We were there first! And don't go giving me that mouthful about them fleeing war and poverty. Man, I seen war! At the post office, you try staying too long at the window on giro day! A bloodbath!

Rena laughs.

OSCAR: I've got work to get on with.

Oscar walks off.

SOL: Let me give you a hand, Oscar.

Sol exits. Rena calls after them.

RENA: Nah, but you don't wanna hear that, do you?! You don't wanna hear our side of things!

Rena is left on her own. She walks around the empty schoolhouse and steps on an already broken pencil that Sol missed—crushing the pencil further. Rena picks up the pencil and tries to connect the broken ends, but the pencil is beyond repair. Rena becomes frustrated with trying to make the ends fit so she breaks the pencil into as many smaller pieces as she can.

End of Scene.

UNICORN

By Cecilia Copeland

FATHER
DAUGHTER
MOTHER

SCENE 1:

FATHER and DAUGHTER are sitting in chairs facing the audience. The chairs are set up to indicate that FATHER is driving and DAUGHTER is in the back seat. When FATHER speaks to DAUGHTER he does so using the "rearview mirror".

FATHER: I don't like Jenny. Jenny is a snotty little bitch. Yes, I said bitch. Jenny prances around and plays dress up all day. She doesn't think of anyone else's feelings. She isn't a nice person. She's selfish. Jenny is stuck up, and she has an ugly face. Her face is always in a nasty scowl. She thinks she's better than everybody else. My daughter wouldn't act like that. Are you listening to me?... Hello?... God you're callus. You know what callus means? You what a callus is? It's a place that has been rubbed and rubbed until the skin is thick and it's numb. You are numb. Nothing gets in does it?... You don't feel anything do you?... What do you have to say for yourself? Say something... You are no better than anyone else on this planet you understand me! No better... Say something. What's the matter with you? SPEAK!

DAUGHTER: What do you want me to say?

FATHER: Just acknowledge me. Acknowledge that you even hear what I'm saying to you. It's like you just tune out. Earth to Jennifer. Earth to Jennifer. What do you have to say for yourself?... You are going to answer me before you get out of this car. You might be able to get away with murder at your mother's house, but not with me. Don't stonewall me. I can read your face like a book. I can see in your eyes exactly what you think. You're a terrible liar. You can't keep anything secret... You didn't want to write that letter just because you are lazy. Your grandmother is not gonna live forever, and you can't take five minutes and write her a goddamn letter? What the hell is wrong with you?... You flipped the page back on that notebook, you flipped it like you were some kind of queen and I was making you do something loathsome by writing to your grandmother. Jenny acts like that, not my daughter. Jenny can't take a few minutes to write a letter to her grandmother for her birthday. You are turning into your mother more and more by the minute.

FATHER stops the car.

FATHER: Don't even think about it. You need to listen to me. Jenny is not real. Jenny is some stripper's name. Can you imagine a president Jenny? No, of course not. Jenny sits around with Brittany and Buffy and plays tennis all day. Jenny is not my daughter, she doesn't look like my daughter, she doesn't speak like my daughter, and I don't like her.

DAUGHTER: I'm sorry dad.

FATHER: Thank you Jennifer. I love you daughter.

DAUGHTER: I love you too dad.

DAUGHTER gets out of the car and crosses to MOTHER. Lights dim on FATHER in the car and come up on MOTHER.

MOTHER: Hey sweetheart!

DAUGHTER: Hi mom.

MOTHER: How was it?

DAUGHTER: Great. Dad was great. It was really fun. He took me horseback riding, and then um... we... we went to Barnes and Noble and he got me the new Anne Rice Vampire novel in hard back, but I have to leave it at his place... He said he's coming to my dance recital next week, and he can't wait to see me dance, and he's gonna bring flowers cuz he forgot last time... And he took me out for pancakes this morning. And he listened to me. He laughed and he thought I was really funny. And he said he was really proud of me. He said I'm turning into a fine young woman. He said... he said I'm the best daughter in the whole world, and I know it's true because I have the best dad in the whole world.

MOTHER: I know he can be hard to deal with sometimes, but he does love you, in his own way. Nobody's perfect, and those TV dads don't exist. They're made up. Nobody has one those magical fathers who says all the right things and does all the right things.

DAUGHTER: I do. My dad's a unicorn.

End of Scene.

20/20

By Anita Chandwaney

CAST OF CHARACTERS

*KALI DESAI 55. Born and raised in the U.S. of Indian
parents. No trace of an Indian accent.
DEVI DESAI 20. KALI'S daughter. Born and raised in the
U.S. of Indian parents. No accent
SID O'CONNOR 20. DEVI'S half-Indian half-Irish
boyfriend. No accent.*

SETTING
*The action takes place in an upscale town-home in the
upscale neighborhood of Lincoln Park of Chicago.
Casting Note: The playwright realizes it may be difficult to
find actresses of Indian heritage. If this is the case, Kali and
Devi may be cast using Hispanic, Mediterranean or other
dark-haired actresses. The important thing is that there be
no discernible ethnic accent.*

*KALI enters. She is put together in tailored separates. SID
follows. He wears multi-ethnic layers.*

KALI: Here it is, Sid. This is where my Devi spent her
creative playtime. We shared many moments of joyful
discovery here.

SID: And you kept it like this for all these years. Far out!

KALI: So, how long have you two been dating?

SID: Long time now, beginning of the semester.

KALI: Ah. Young love. You both have years to figure out who you are and what you want. The world is your oyster.

SID: It's funny, Devi and I feel a connection like nothing we ever felt our entire lives.

KALI: All twenty years of your entire lives?

SID: I know it sounds whacked Kali but -

KALI: - Mrs. Desai.

SID: Really? But a name like Kali? She's the most revered and prominent Hindu goddess. Mother of the universe, the source of all being, the ultimate reality.

KALI: Mrs. Desai will do.

SID: Your call. Sid's short for Siddhartha. My mom's Indian but not my dad, ergo Siddhartha O'Connor. I guess Devi being Indian just added to our bond. But it's not like she reminds me of my mom or anything. That'd be weird.

KALI: Yes Sid, it would. I knew I noticed some South-Asian features in you. It's your chin, and your knuckles.

SID: Wow. I been told it's my soulful 'Gandhi-esque' eyes.

KALI: Have you? *(beat)* Devi's been in the powder-room a while. I'll go see.

SID: It's probably 'cause we had Indian food last night.

KALI: Her stomach's not used to those spices. I never cooked that.

SID: Why not?

KALI: Overcooking destroys all the live enzymes.

SID: But food is how culture and traditions are kept alive from generation to generation.

KALI: Yes, well, I don't do yoga or wear a dot on my head either.

SID: That was my next question.

(DEVI enters, dressed in ethnic layers.)

Here she is with her itty bitty bladder, so cute, I love you.

KALI: Sid here says you've been dating since the semester began.

DEVI: I've been wanting you to meet for the longest time. Oh my God, my backpack! Remember how I'd hide your hair clips so you'd tickle and kiss me?

KALI: How could I forget?

DEVI: That was my most favorite game. Mom, guess what? Sid's short for Siddhartha!

SID: The P's were humungo Herman Hesse aficionados. That's how they first hooked up. The university library storage room. They still go at it -

KALI: We get the picture.

(beat)

SID: Mrs. D, Danny and Meera love Devi like she was their own. This is really going to rock their boat.

KALI: This?

DEVI: We want you to come to Sid's parents house tonight.

KALI: Tonight?

DEVI: We're both really happy.

KALI: Sweetheart, you're in love. I know, it's a beautiful thing. Am I preventing you from any of this? No. Would I prefer you take your time and make the most of your opportunities? Yes.

DEVI: Mom, I want different things than you do.

KALI: Why don't we sit down and talk about this later.

DEVI: No.

SID: Our souls immediately recognized that we're destined to go through this life together, as a couple.

KALI: I'm sorry?

SID: All this tension will be water under the proverbial bridge when we're one big happy family.

KALI: Family?

DEVI: The civil ceremony is next weekend.

(beat)

KALI: You wait till now to tell me this?

DEVI: You would have tried to talk us out of it.

KALI: I put aside my pain so I can be mother and father to you-

DEVI: - I know but -

KALI: - Did you need or want for anything, even after Dad passed?

DEVI: No. But we're doing this with or without you.

KALI: I see. My feelings, I, mean nothing to you.

DEVI: How can you say that?

SID: You know Mrs. D, that's just a fear. F.E.A.R, a Fantasy Expectation Appearing Real.

DEVI: You'll see, you'll love Danny and Meera. And his other Mom.

KALI: Other Mom?

SID: My DNA-mom.

DEVI: When Sid was growing up they told him he had two moms.

KALI: That's ridiculous.

DEVI: Mom!

SID: *(to DEVI)*

Not everyone's heard about this stuff.

(to KALI)

You see, Danny and Meera had a different kind of journey to have me. So I got my birth-mom, Meera, and an egg donor, my DNA-mom.

KALI: But there's only one mother.

DEVI: Mom!

SID: It's okay sweetie, let her process.

(to KALI)

One birth-mother, but sometimes there's also a birth-other, or two. A birth-mother who may or may not be the genetic mother; a genetic mother who may or may not be the birth-mother; an intended mother who may or may not be the genetic mother or the birth-mother. And of course the old-fashioned way where the intended mother is also the genetic mother and the birth-mother, not to mention -

KALI: - Please, just stop.

DEVI: Sid's only here thanks to his DNA-mom's generous gift.

KALI: Those girls get paid thousands of dollars. They go shopping.

DEVI: Or put themselves through school.

SID: You'll meet 'Sita-Mom' at the wedding.

KALI: Who?

SID: 'Sita-Mom'. My DNA-mom's name is Sita, and Meera's favorite prayer chant is "Sita-Ram", so 'Sita-Mom'. Inside joke.

DEVI: Mom doesn't listen to chants.

SID: *(to KALI)*

'Sita-Mom' comes to all the big occasions. She's family.

(to DEVI)

Hon, she's painting us a canvas for a wedding gift!

DEVI: Really? I lover her stuff!

(beat)

KALI: This Sita is an artist?

DEVI: She even put herself through art school.

KALI: Really. Where?

DEVI: Art Institute.

(pause)

KALI: Sid, will you excuse us?

DEVI: Why?

KALI: I need to talk to you.

DEVI: Whatever you want to say to me, you can say in front of Sid.

KALI: This is between you and me.

DEVI: Then it involves Sid. He's a part of me now.

KALI: I know but this is private.

DEVI: No. We're going to be together forever.

KALI: Well, you can't do that!

DEVI: I'm over 18, I'll do what I want.

KALI: He's not right for you.

DEVI: You don't know what I want or -

KALI: Don't!

DEVI: - or who I am!

KALI: *(slowly)* Don't say that to me!

(beat)

DEVI: Mom, what's wrong?

(pause)

KALI: I grew your body and your mind and your heart and your soul.

DEVI: I know...

KALI: I gestated and birthed you into this world.

DEVI: Okay...

KALI: I am your Mother.

DEVI: So?

KALI: I am, but not...genetically.

DEVI: What?

KALI: I'm sorry...

DEVI: I have a DNA-mom?

KALI: Yes...

(beat)

DEVI: How could you not tell me this?

KALI: I didn't know when...or how...or what...

DEVI: You find a way!

KALI: We lost Dad and then all the sorrow...and pain...

SID: You know what? Better late than never. We'll invite your DNA-mom to the wedding party and get both DNA-moms on the dance floor. We'll do some *bhangra,* it'll be great.

KALI: You can't be together!

DEVI: You keep this huge thing from me, and now you want to keep me from Sid?

KALI: Please...

DEVI: Over my dead body!

(beat)

KALI: It's not just a DNA-mom! It's the same one, as Sid.

(beat)

SID: 'Sita-Mom' is Devi's DNA-mom too?

KALI: Yes.

DEVI: Oh my God.

KALI: I'm so so sorry...

DEVI: This is who I am and where I come from.

KALI: You came from me.

DEVI: And Sita-Mom.

SID: So, Devi's my half-sister?

DEVI: Oh my God.

KALI: I worked so hard to have you. The doctors and injections and retrievals and transfers. You were my baby, from day one. We had to move forward...as a family. You don't know what that's like.

(beat)

DEVI: Well in about six months, I will.

KALI: What?

SID: We're pregnant.

(pause)

KALI: You're...going to have it?

(silence)

But you're both...

DEVI: *(simultaneously)*

Yeah...

SID: *(simultaneously)*

Yeah...

Fade to black

End of Scene.

ENOUGH

By Pat Montley

SYNOPSIS
Using various methods of persuasion and intimidation, the
destitute ZERO requests/insists that the well-off RAY share
his wealth and power.

CAST OF CHARACTERS

ZERO: any age, race, sex; a shaman from a poor country;
(possibly Siberian or African or Native/Pre-Columbian
American. Or a New Yorker?)
RAY: any age, race, sex; wealthy, accustomed to power,
smug

SETTING: A surrealistic crossroads in a distant place of
metaphor/nightmare.
         or
A street corner in the U.S.
Time out of time…or
The Present. (or Past…or Future.)
Optional: in background—a slide of the Twin Towers before
9/11.

AT RISE: RAY, dressed in a suit, works an I-Phone (or its
futuristic equivalent) as he waits. ZERO, whose clothing,
though not indicative of a specific time or place, suggests
poverty, beats a small drum with his hands. His battered
backpack and hat lie next to him. He stares at RAY, who
notices and grows increasingly uncomfortable, until
finally…

RAY: What? *(ZERO stops playing, continues to stare.)*
What?!

ZERO: I suffer.

RAY: I see.

ZERO: Will you help?

RAY: *(Unnerved.)*Well…I guess…yes…of course. Not to help would be selfish, wouldn't it? *(Extracts a dollar bill from wallet, drops it into ZERO's hat. Waits for "thank you." Then, sarcastically.)* Don't thank me. It's my...moral obligation.

ZERO: Yes, that's true.

RAY: You're welcome.

(Beat.)

ZERO: I need more.

RAY: More?

ZERO: I still suffer.

RAY: Well, do something about it.

ZERO: What?

RAY: Pick yourself up by your—

ZERO: I have no boots.

RAY: Is that my problem?

ZERO: Yes.

RAY: Why?

ZERO: Because you have many.

RAY: Which I worked very hard to get.

ZERO: No harder than I.

RAY: Then why don't you have—?

ZERO: Poor soil. Drought. Flood. Famine. War. Unemployment. Bad government.

RAY: Get rid of it.

ZERO: I tried.

RAY: Look, I sympathize...

ZERO: Show me.

RAY: Oh, all right. *(Gives ZERO two more bills.)* Now will you leave me alone?

ZERO: You are the one free to leave.

RAY: I'm meeting someone here.

ZERO: I see.

RAY: Look, I've been more than generous.

ZERO: You have given from your excess.

RAY: What do you expect?

ZERO: More.

RAY: Why?

ZERO: The same sun shines on me that shines on you.

RAY: So what? What gives you the right to—

ZERO: To live?

RAY: To live off me?

ZERO: No one should have more than enough...while others have less than they need.

RAY: Says who?

ZERO: The moral philosophers.

RAY: Bunk!

ZERO: It is written.

RAY: Where?

ZERO: In the hearts of the just.

(Beat. RAY puts two more bills in ZERO's hat. ZERO does not look at them, but continues to stare at RAY.)

RAY: Just how much do you want?

ZERO: As much as I'm entitled to.

RAY: And what would that be?

ZERO: Give until you reach the level of marginal utility.

RAY: The what?

ZERO: The level at which, to give more would cause as

much suffering to you as would be relieved in me.

RAY: Where did you get that wacko idea?

ZERO: John Stuart Mill.

RAY: Well, he's mad. And so are you.

ZERO: *(With controlled anger.)* I have reason to be mad. I am hungry and cold and sick while you are warm and healthy and... smug.

RAY: Are you seriously suggesting that I empty my wallet into your hat until the amounts in each are the same?

ZERO: And your bank accounts. And your stock portfolios.

RAY: What do you take me for—a lunatic saint!

ZERO: It's your...what did you call it?...your "moral obligation."

RAY: Why should I believe you would stop at half?

ZERO: I wouldn't need more.

RAY: But you'd want more.

ZERO: Only if I were as deluded as you.

RAY: It's human nature to be—

ZERO: Compassionate.

RAY: *(Sarcastic.)* Right. So—if the shoe were on the other foot?

ZERO: My feet would be warm.

RAY: Enough! You're starting to piss me off.

ZERO: *(Stands.)* "Smug" cannot last forever.

RAY: Neither can "naïve"—which is what you are. Apart from greedy.

ZERO: I'm not the one with the excess.

RAY: Don't you understand? My stocks multiply. And if I don't have enough of them multiplying, I can't have this— *(Whipping bank card out of wallet.)* and...I can't afford to give you anything.

ZERO: *(Grabbing card.)* What do you buy with this?

RAY: *(Tries to grab it back but ZERO pulls it out of reach.)* Stuff.

ZERO: What kind of stuff.

RAY: Stuff that I deserve.

ZERO: *(Circling RAY menacingly, waving card at him.)* Designer stuff? Frivolous odoriferous stuff? Super-sized, motorized stuff? Obscenely ridiculous conspicuous stuff...moronic, electronic stuff...extra-deluxe, big-bucks stuff... *(Puts card in pocket.)*

RAY: What are you doing?

ZERO: Equalizing. You don't need all that stuff. None of you do. Get rid of it. Stop buying and selling it.

RAY: That won't work.

ZERO: Why not?

RAY: I got my money by selling stuff.

ZERO: Well?

RAY: If nobody buys the stuff I sell, I won't have any money to share with you.

ZERO: Then sell something else. Or make something. Or grow something. Something essential. Food. Blankets. Medicine. Art.

RAY: But that wouldn't keep everybody here...employed.

ZERO: So? Work less. Enjoy your family.

RAY: If I work less, I'll have less.

ZERO: True.

RAY: Which means you'd have half of less.

ZERO: Which is a lot more than I have now.

RAY: Then what if somebody else came along with nothing—would I have to give that person half of my remaining half?

ZERO: Of course.

RAY: And you?

ZERO: *(Taking card from pocket, offering it to the hypothetical person.)* Would do the same.

RAY: Sure, sure. This is ridiculous. How would it end?

ZERO: In the…equalizing of power. In justice!

RAY: Ha! The line of paupers would go on forever.

ZERO: *(Waving card.)* On the contrary. It's the only way to eliminate poverty.

RAY: *(Reaches for card, but ZERO pulls it back out of his reach. Frustrated.)* This is unreal.

ZERO: What?

RAY: This situation. This conversation. It can't be happening. I must be dreaming this. It's a...nightmare!

ZERO: Let's hope it ends in a wake-up call.

RAY: Is that a threat?

ZERO: That depends.

RAY: On what?

ZERO: On whether you're listening.

RAY: I don't like what I hear.

ZERO: Then do something about it.

RAY: What you propose I do will cost too much.

ZERO: Not as much as not doing it.

RAY: I don't like your attitude.

ZERO: Well...you could try walking in my shoes...if I had any.

RAY: Equal distribution of wealth? It's a preposterous idea. It can't be done. I mean people just don't behave that way—sharing everything they have. It's unnatural.

ZERO: Greed is unnatural.

RAY: I'll bet you can't find one person on earth who behaves that way.

ZERO: And if I do?

RAY: What?

ZERO: What's the bet?

RAY: You won't.

ZERO: *(Shaking card.)* Will you give this away ?

RAY: To you?

ZERO: To everyone in need.

RAY: Humph. What do I get when I win?

ZERO: Don't you already have it all?

RAY: Then why should I bet?

ZERO: I don't know. You're the one who suggested it.

RAY: It was a figure of speech: "I'll bet you can't find one person..."

ZERO: Oh.

RAY: *(Gesturing to audience.)* But do go ahead and look.

ZERO: *(Tosses card back at RAY, who catches it.)* I think I will. *(Sits and takes up drum, looks hard at audience.)*

RAY: At least it's a way to get rid of you.

ZERO: Maybe...not. Maybe I'll turn up where you least expect me...to collect on our wager.

(ZERO starts to drum. The drumming gradually intensifies—and is enhanced by sound effects—as the lights fade up on him and down on RAY. ZERO throws back his head and closes his eyes as the drumming reaches a climax and light becomes blinding. Then: blackout.)

End of Scene

WHY'D YA MAKE ME WEAR THIS, JOE?

By Vanda

Cast of Characters:
Charlotte (Charlie) Kelly- a working class young
woman. She speaks with a Brooklyn accent.
Aubra Westgate- an upper class woman who lives in a Fifth
Avenue townhouse, a talented musician.
Joe O'Brien- Charlie's working class boyfriend. He speaks
with a Brooklyn accent. He's getting ready to ship out to the
South Pacific.
Lieutenant Philip Atwood-Aubra's fiancé. He's getting
ready to ship out to the South Pacific.

Synopsis
Why'd Ya Make Me Wear This, Joe? is about two women
who fall in love with each other while their men are in the
South Pacific fighting in World War 2
Act 1, Scene 1

Time: 1944

The lights come up on Joe wearing an Army Air Corps
uniform. HE enters with his girl, Charlotte. He has a piece
of paper that he keeps referring to as he looks for the right
number. Charlotte wears her hair and clothes in the style of
the mid forties. She is less than graceful on her high heels.
She pulls at her dress that doesn't seem to fit right and at the
hat that appears to itch.

CHARLOTTE: Oh, Joe, why d'ya make me wear this?

JOE: *(More concerned with finding the right house)*

You look good in it. It should be up here a ways. Will ya
get a load of this neighborhood? I thought Fifth Avenue'd be
classy but this-- Not one bit a garbage nowhere. And ain't
them trees pretty?

CHARLOTTE: I look like a horse.

JOE: But a very pretty horse. Look at all these townhouses!

CHARLOTTE: Joe! I can't go in looking like this.

JOE: Well, ya gotta! This Lieutenant is important to our future. He's got big bucks, connections and he likes me. And you don't look like a horse in that dress. Ya look like—like Loretta Young coming down a long staircase like she's floating. We're gonna have a good life, Charlie. You'll see. And ya had a good time at the concert tonight, didn't ya?

CHARLOTTE: Oh, Joe, wasn't she wonderful? And I heard one lady saying she can sing opera too. I wonder why she stopped playing right in the middle of that song and made us all leave.

JOE: Look, there goes a Caddy!

CHARLOTTE: Before that she played with her whole body.

JOE: You stick with me, kiddo. We're movin' up in the world. Here it is.

He knocks

CHARLOTTE: Oh, Joe, that music was so, so...

Charlie, about to explode, having run out of words, bursts into a pantomime of passionate piano playing, complete with sound, her hair bouncing.

JOE: Charlie, Charlie, someone might see you. This ain't Flatbush, ya know.

CHARLOTTE: Oh. I'm sorry.

JOE: Here. Put your hat on. Now, listen, I'm gonna be calling you Charlotte tonight, okay?

CHARLOTTE: But I hate that name.

JOE: Yeah, I know, but they ain't gonna understand a girl being called Charlie. We don't want them thinking yer mannish.

LIEUTENANT PHILIP ATWOOD comes to the door in his uniform. As Joe enters he takes his hat off.

PHILIP:

Shaking hands with Joe

Joe! Come in. Come in. I'm so glad you could make it.

To CHARLOTTE

And this must be...

JOE: Lieutenant, this is my girl, Charlotte.

PHILIP: Well, it's a pleasure to meet you young lady. Joe has told me so many nice things about you. Do you still volunteer to make bandages?

JOE: She's at the church every Monday and Wednesday. And Tuesdays she sells war bonds.

PHILIP: I think that's wonderful. Just wonderful. Uh, Miss Westgate's feeling a little sensitive about becoming under the weather in the middle of the concert so she may be a little testy. She doesn't mean anything by it. Come into the living room.

They enter the living room. AUBRA WESTGATE sits on the couch wearing an attractive full-length gown.

And this is the star of the evening—my fiancée, Miss Aubra Westgate.

CHARLOTTE: Oh, Miss Westgate you were terrific. I can't believe I'm standing this close to you. I've never heard anyone play with such, such…!

JOE:

Trying not to be too obvious

Charlotte.

CHARLOTTE: Huh?

Joe gives her the signal to reign herself in

Oh.

JOE: Yes, Miss Westgate, you were very good.

PHILIP: Oh, Aubra, this is Joe O'Brien and Charlotte— Charlotte?

JOE: Kelly.

PHILIP: Well, sit down. I'll get the drinks. Joe, what are you having?

JOE: Oh. Uh, uh…Whatever you're having.

PHILIP: A martini. That all right for you?

JOE: Yeah, fine.

PHILIP: How about you, Charlotte?

JOE: She'll have the same.

PHILIP: And Aubra are you having your usual Pink Lady?

AUBRA: Yes, dear, thank you.

Philip moves to the bar to get the drinks.

I'm so sorry I couldn't finish the concert. But you, enjoyed it, Miss Kelly, what there was of it.

CHARLOTTE: Oh, yes, very much!

AUBRA: Oh? And do you go to a great many concerts?

CHARLOTTE: No. I listen to records. This was my first time.

AUBRA: Well, I'm honored to be your first. *(Beat)* But tell me, Miss Kelly, what do you do with your time when you're not listening to concert records.

CHARLOTTE: I'm a projectionist.

AUBRA: Projectionist? I don't understand.

PHILIP: That's the person who runs the film in movie theatres, dear.

AUBRA: Really? Well, how fascinating.

CHARLOTTE: The job itself isn't all that interesting, but I get to see all the movies. The projectionist joined the army and they gave me his job. I'm the first girl in Flatbush to ever have that job.

AUBRA: Then you're a real groundbreaker.

JOE: She's just doing her bit for the war effort. It's not very feminine, but when the war's over she's gonna have a more important job to do.

AUBRA: Really? And what's that?

JOE: Being my wife.

Joe and Charlotte almost overlap

CHARLOTTE: Making movies!

JOE: Stop joking around. You know girls don't make movies.

PHILIP: Drinks for everyone.

He hands Joe and Charlotte their drinks.

PHILIP: And for you, my dear. Well, we should have a toast. To the ending of the war, may it be soon, and to new friendships.

They all sip their drinks. Joe and Charlotte gag on theirs, Charlotte a little louder than Joe. They exchange glances.

CHARLOTTE: Uh, Miss Westgate, do you like movies?

AUBRA: Well, this is going to sound strange, but, uh... I've never seen a talkie. The last movie I saw was Mary Pickford in My Best Girl.

CHARLOTTE: That was practically before I was born! Why?

JOE:

Chastising

Charlotte.

AUBRA: That's quite all right, Mr. O'Brien. I don't mind answering. It's because I hadn't been out of this house for fourteen years before tonight. Philip arranged for the concert tonight. Through some of his friends. Oh, but I did so enjoy watching Mary Pickford. Did you know, Mr. O'Brien, that Mary Pickford produced most of her own films?

JOE: No. I didn't.

AUBRA: Well, she did.

CHARLOTTE: She did?!

(To JOE)

See? *(Beat)* Oh, Miss Westgate, you have to come with me to a movie soon. I can get us free passes. If you haven't been to a movie since—wasn't that 1927?-- that means you didn't see Now, Voyager, with Bette Davis. That's my all-time favorite so far. Oh, Miss Westgate, what a story! Wow!

JOE:

Whispering.

Charlotte.

CHARLOTTE: And Bette Davis is so, so... You see, in this movie, Bette Davis has this really mean mother and...

JOE:

Whispering

Charlotte.

CHARLOTTE: ...and so Bette, well, her name is Charlotte in the movie, like mine, but I'm nothing like her, so this Charlotte is this fat, ugly spinster lady who nobody wants. Especially not a man. Which has gotta be the worst thing in the whole wide world. And then there's this psychiatrist—played by Claude Rains...

JOE:

Louder

Charlie!

CHARLOTTE: Oh. I'm sorry.

AUBRA: Did you do something?

CHARLOTTE: Oh, sometimes, I go on and on and Joe...

Joe forcing a smile, signals her to be quiet.
I mean, uh...
AUBRA: But, I was enjoying your story, Miss Kelly.

CHARLOTTE: You were?

AUBRA: Yes, I'd like to hear more of it

Directed at Joe

if I may.

CHARLOTTE: You would?

PHILIP: Hey, Joe, why don't you and I go out on the balcony and have a smoke.

JOE: Okay.

PHILIP:

To AUBRA

You'll be all right, dear?

AUBRA: Oh, yes, I'll be fine. Miss Kelly, won't you come and sit by me. I wouldn't want to miss a single word.

CHARLOTTE: All right.

The men move to the balcony taking their drinks.

JOE: Look at that view!

JOE lights a cigarette

Hey, ya want a Lucky?

PHILIP:

Lighting HIS pipe

No, thank you. I have this. The girls are really getting along quite well. Don't you think?

JOE: Yeah, sure. That's Central Park down there, ain't it? But what building is that over there.

PHILIP: Aubra doesn't usually make friends so easily. Joe, I invited you over tonight because I really wanted to have a talk with you about something.

JOE: Sure, Lieutenant.

PHILIP: Joe. Charlotte, she-- she's everything you said she is. Maybe more.

JOE: Yeah sure, Charlotte's a swell kid. Living here must cost an awful lotta dough. You think someday I could afford a place like this? If I work hard.

PHILIP: I don't see why not. Uh, Joe, about Charlotte…Aubra isn't as strong as your Charlotte.

JOE: *(Bitter)* She sure seemed plenty strong to me.

PHILIP: That's the kind of impression she makes, but now with the war…

JOE: Isn't this war swell? I was so scared the whole thing'd be over before I even got outta high school. That's why I quit. I'll go back later, but I wouldn't wanna miss this war for nothing. And when it's all over I'm gonna make ya so proud. Your help won't be wasted on me.

PHILIP: Joe, you and I will be taking off for the South Pacific next week. Who knows when we'll get back. I suppose there's even a chance that we—I—won't come back and…

JOE: Hey, can that kinda talk. The two of us are coming back and we're gonna shake up the whole darn world.

PHILIP: Of course. But while we're away. Don't you worry about Charlotte? How she'll manage without you.

JOE: Nah. She's got a pretty good job at the Regency and her volunteer work keeps her busy. And she lives with her parents so I don't see why…

PHILIP: Yes, of course, her parents. I forgot about them. A girl should live with her parents. I guess I'll have to speak to them.

JOE: You wanna talk to Charlotte's parents. Why?

PHILIP: Well, Aubra doesn't have parents to depend on like Charlotte and with me away she'll be quite alone. Alone in this big house. And when I'm not here she fires all the servants so...

JOE: You have servants?!

PHILIP: Just a couple of girls to help around the house. Nothing elaborate. Aubra and I like our privacy.

JOE: Oh, sure. I can understand that. But I sure wouldn't mind having some servants.

PHILIP: I know it's a terrible imposition and I barely know you, and I have to talk to her parents, but Charlotte seems to be such a cheerful person, she may be able to cope with Aubra's dark moods. I know it's a lot to ask, but do you think Charlotte would come here to live. As Aubra's companion. Just while I'm away. I could pay her.

JOE: Live here?! Are you kidding? Charlotte would love to live here.

PHILIP: She would? Then, you'd talk to her parents, smooth the way?

JOE: Don't you worry about it, Lieutenant. I'll take care of everything. Charlotte'll move in the day we board that train for San Francisco.

PHILIP: Thank you, Joe. Thank you so very much.

Shaking Joe's hand. The men return to the living room.

CHARLOTTE: So this woman's all dressed up in a tuxedo, top hat and all. You've never seen anything like it. And she's singing, "After the Ball" and....

PHILIP: You ladies seem to be having a good time.

AUBRA: Oh, yes. Lovely.

CHARLOTTE: Oh, I know! I'll take a picture.

JOE:

Chastising

Charlotte.

She looks at Joe and hesitates

AUBRA: I think that's a wonderful idea. A memento of our burgeoning friendship.

CHARLOTTE:

(Taking flash brownie camera out of purse)

Joe got me this for graduation. Joe's very good to me. I like pictures because no one ever gets old or sad in them. They stay the same. Happy. Like now, Miss Westgate.

AUBRA: What a lovely thought.

CHARLOTTE: Now Joe, you go over there and stand next to the Lieutenant. Lieutenant you stand behind Miss Westgate. That's good, only closer together. A little more. Yes, yes, that's it. Don't move.

Charlie takes the shot. There is a big flash. They freeze as if they have become the photograph.

End of Scene

TO BE CONFIRMED

By Cheryl Games

CHARACTERS:
PRIEST, male, off-stage voice
MARGARET MARY CLAYTON, age 13, Marilyn's younger sister
HUNCHA (ANNIE) SOKOL, age 32, Marilyn's and Margaret Mary's aunt
MARILYN CLAYTON, age 16
LOU SOKOL, mid-50s, the grandma, Huncha's and Paulette's mother, Marilyn's and Margaret Mary's grandmother
PAULETTE CLAYTON, age 34, Marilyn's and Margaret Mary's mother
DANNY CLAYTON, age 35, Paulette's ex-husband, Marilyn's and Margaret Mary's father
RICHIE GILLESPIE, age 19, church friend of Danny's, recently returned home from the war

PLACE
Youngstown, Ohio and vicinity
The action takes place in two locations: 1.) the front porch of Grandma Lou's house which is in the city limits near the steel mill, 2.) about a hundred miles away, the small yard outside the trailer home of Danny Clayton.

TIME
Summer

Lights up on the trailer. MARILYN clears away the dishes from the cookout. DANNY and RICHIE are at the table. MARGARET MARY enters from the house with the pie.

RICHIE: I don't really like to talk about it too much. And there's only so much I can talk about.

DANNY: Of course.

RICHIE: Again, I'm just grateful that good Lord gave me the will and the, well, the passion to serve this great country of ours. I know there's been lots of talk about the boys – and women, we have lots of fine young women serving. But the troops, you know, we signed up to do a job, to serve. And whether you like it or not, I mean, whether you agree with why we're there or you don't, well, it doesn't make one bit of difference in my book. For me, and I can speak only for me, although I'm pretty typical, but, for me, it's a matter of doing what you say you're going to do. You know, it's keeping your word. And I made a vow to God first, country second, a vow to do whatever I'm able to help others and to serve God. I'm blessed that God gave me an able mind and an able body to do those things. To help and to serve.

MARGARET MARY: I'm thinking about becoming a soldier myself.

RICHIE: Really? Well, it's a very rewarding and honorable –

MARGARET MARY: Not that kind of soldier. A soldier of Christ.

RICHIE: Oh?

DANNY: Margaret Mary's considering making her Confirmation.

MARGARET MARY: Do you consider yourself a soldier of Christ?

MARILYN: Of course he's not. That's a Catholic thing.

MARGARET MARY: But he's a soldier, right? And everything he does is for God, a.k.a. Jesus, a.k.a. Christ. So, literally, he's a soldier of Christ.

RICHIE: I guess I do then, Margaret Mary. I am a soldier of Christ.

MARGARET MARY: So is Marilyn. See, she got confirmed back in the seventh grade.

MARILYN: Shut up, M&M.

MARGARET MARY: You guys have a lot in common. Only her "army" doesn't go around killing anybody.

DANNY: All right, that's enough, Margaret Mary.

MARGARET MARY: My dad doesn't think I should get Confirmed 'cause he hates Catholics.

DANNY: I do not hate Catholics.

MARGARET MARY: He hates anything having to do with the Catholic religion.

DANNY: I just think you should be open to other ways of worship before making such a commitment.

MARGARET MARY: Right, you want me to be open to joining your church. My grandma, of course, wants me to do it, but she can't give me a good reason why, other than "that's what good Catholics do." My Aunt Huncha thinks it's all a bunch of baloney – she didn't actually say baloney, but since we're having a nice, Christian lunch, I'll keep it clean. And my sister, here –

MARILYN: Dad, make her shut up!

MARGARET MARY: What? I'm just saying you're not giving me any help in my decision.

MARILYN: I didn't know it was my job to help you make your decisions!

DANNY: Girls, stop it!

MARGARET MARY: So, what do you think, Richie? Think I should do it or not?

DANNY: Margaret Mary, don't' bother Richie with this.

RICHIE: It's all right, Mr. Clayton. I don't mind. Margaret Mary, I'd say you should get advice from the only One that matters. And that's God. Listen to God. He'll reveal the answer to you. Pray about it, and God will give you the answer.

MARGARET MARY: Um, okay, sounds good. Dad, could I have another piece of pie?

MARILYN: What happened to your diet?

MARGARET MARY: I'm not on a diet.

MARILYN: You were supposed to give up pop.

MARGARET MARY: That's pop, this is pie.

MARILYN: You've been drinking pop, too.

MARGARET MARY: No sir!

DANNY: Girls! Neither one of you is getting another piece –

MARILYN: I don't even want another piece.

DANNY: Richie's gonna take it home – what he doesn't eat here.

RICHIE: No, that's okay. The girls can have it.

DANNY: The girls don't need it. You're taking it with you, and that's final.

RICHIE: Can't argue with that, Mr. Clayton. Thank you.

DANNY: Margaret Mary, help me with the dishes.

MARGARET MARY: What about Marilyn?

MARILYN: I cleared.

RICHIE: I can help.

DANNY: Nonsense. You eat your pie and relax, son. Marilyn'll keep you company. Margaret Mary, inside.

(MARGARET MARY follows DANNY inside the trailer.)

RICHIE: Sure is good pie. Don't you think?

MARILYN: I'm not a big pie lover.

RICHIE: I'm a big pie lover, and a small pie lover. Any size pie –

MARILYN: Hot or cold.

RICHIE: That's right, hot or cold. . .

MARILYN: Sorry about my sister.

RICHIE: For what?

MARILYN: For being such a smart-ass – I mean, aleck.

RICHIE: Aleck?

MARILYN: Smart-aleck.

RICHIE: It's okay.

MARILYN: No it's not. She's rude.

RICHIE: I mean, it's okay that you cuss. I don't mind.

MARILYN: What?

RICHIE: It doesn't offend me.

MARILYN: That's not why I –

RICHIE: God knows, I'm as human as the next person.

MARILYN: It's my father. He doesn't like it when I swear.

RICHIE: You don't have to clean up your act on my account.

MARILYN: I wasn't.

RICHIE: Did you get some sun?

MARILYN: What?

RICHIE: Yeah, you did. Your cheeks are red. The sun must've been hot today.

MARILYN: Sort of.

RICHIE: So, your dad tells me you're going to be a senior.

MARILYN: Yeah.

RICHIE: You excited?

MARILYN: I guess.

RICHIE: Yeah, I know what you mean.

MARILYN: What do I mean?

RICHIE: Everybody thinks senior year is supposed to be so great.

MARILYN: Isn't it?

RICHIE: Just another stepping stone.

MARILYN: Stepping stone? To what?

RICHIE: I didn't get off on the power of being a senior. You know, being the top dog, supposedly, in the school.

MARILYN: I don't think I'm going to be any top dog.

RICHIE: You probably think it's a strange way for me to think, me being in the military.

MARILYN: You're in the Army?

RICHIE: I'm home for a couple of weeks, then back to Virginia.

MARILYN: Virginia?

RICHIE: That's where I'm stationed.

MARILYN: I don't know anything about the Army. Or the war.

RICHIE: I can't really talk about what I did there, Marilyn.

MARILYN: Fine by me.

RICHIE: But, no, if you really wanted to know. . .

MARILYN: If I wanted to know, I would know.

RICHIE: How long are you staying here with your dad?

MARILYN: End of June. Then I'm going back home to Youngstown. That's where I'm stationed.

RICHIE: I know about more things than just the Army and the military, by the way.

MARILYN: Good for you.

RICHIE: I mean, you know, things that maybe you're interested in.

MARILYN: I'm not interested in anything.

RICHIE: Nothing?

MARILYN: Nope.

RICHIE: How about sunbathing?

MARILYN: Yeah, I'd like to get a tan this summer.

RICHIE: So, yeah, we could talk about that.

MARILYN: What's to talk about?

RICHIE: I'm sure there's lots to talk about – lots of things to consider and plan for. If you want to get the best tan possible, you know, meet your tanning goals –

MARILYN: I don't have tanning goals.

RICHIE: Well, you should. You definitely should set goals for anything you want to accomplish. I could help you with that. I'm very good at devising plans to meet goals. Strategic thinking is one of my strong points.

MARILYN: I'm just gonna lay out when the sun's out.

RICHIE: Oh, but there's so much more to consider!

MARILYN: Like what?

RICHIE: Well, like, what's the best time of day to lay out? What's the best lotion to use? How often should you turn over? Things like that.

MARILYN: I don't need a plan for that. I just do whatever I feel like doing.

RICHIE: Well, that's a strategy too. I call that the intuitive strategy. See, there's so much to go over – I don't know if we're going to be able to cover it all in two weeks.

(DANNY and MARGARET MARY enter from the trailer.)

DANNY: Ready for me to take you home, Richie?

RICHIE: Yes, Mr. Clayton. But first, I'd like to ask your permission for something. . .

DANNY: Permission? Don't you know it's easier to ask for forgiveness than permission, son.

RICHIE: Sir?

DANNY: You don't need to ask my permission for anything, Richie.

RICHIE: Permission's probably not the right word. I just –

DANNY: Let's talk about it in the car. I want to get back to watch the Indians. You like the Indians?

RICHIE: Yes, yes I do.

DANNY: That a boy! Say goodbye, girls.

MARGARET MARY: Bye.

RICHIE: Goodbye, Margaret Mary. See ya, Marilyn.

MARILYN: Yeah, bye.

(DANNY and RICHIE exit.)

MARGARET MARY: Oh my God! How many things can the good Lord bless one person with? He's a freak! Isn't he? Don't you think he's a freak, Marilyn?

MARILYN: I don't know. . . yeah, no, he is . . .

MARGARET MARY: I'm telling you, he is. That's why I don't want to dad's church – freaks like him. What a creep. But, the good news is, the good Lord blessed me a great idea. . .

(MARGARET MARY gets the lighter fluid, holds it up to show MARILYN)

Lighter fluid! Come on, before dad gets back.

MARILYN: What?

MARGARET MARY: My uniform.

(MARGARET MARY runs into the trailer. After a beat, MARILYN slowly exits into the trailer. MARGARET MARY returns with her uniform in hand.)

MARGARET MARY: Marilyn? Marilyn! Come on! You're gonna miss it!

End of Scene.

REVOLUTIONS PER MINUTE

By Rebecca Nesvet

Characters:
KALI   Female, 20s. A South Indian railway driver. She is disguised as a man, in the uniform of the railway drivers. In reality, the first known female South Indian train driver was first employed in the late 1990s.
HARI   A 12-year-old South Indian boy. He is in the process of coming out as gay.

Place/Time:
The state of Tamil Nadu, South India, 1987.

(Bare stage. KALI enters. She holds her driver's hat.)

KALI: Sahibs and Memsahibs! Ladies and Gentlemen! The 2621 Up Tamil Nadu Express is ready to depart this station. All aboard for Vijayawada Junction, Warangal, Nagpur, and points in between, and beyond. I shall be your driver on today's journey on, if I may say so, one of the most scenic routes in all of India. I received my Senior Driver's certification six months ago, in June 1987, and I assure you all, you'll find my sense of direction and timeliness as irreproachable as that of the god Krishna when he drove the chariot of Prince Arjuna. You do know the story? Yes? No? Well. A long, long time ago, Krishna drove Arjuna from the ending of one age, to the beginning of another. From the ending, it has been said, of one universe to the beginning of another. Of course, Arjuna did not know it was the god holding the reins. This was because, to avoid raising any astonishment, or alarm, Krishna cleverly disguised himself...

(puts on the hat)

... as a mortal man. So I will take you on a journey like that.

Not the journey that was written, precisely, but we shall stop in a few of the same places. A very few. This is, after all, the express service.

(HARI enters, sneaking.)

Hey! What do you think you're doing?

HARI: Nothing.

(as KALI grabs him)

Let go!

KALI: That's no answer, little boy.

(Turns him upside down.)

HARI: Nooo!

KALI: Tell me the truth!

HARI: I... I wanted to drive the train!

KALI: My train.

HARI: Yes! I'm sorry!

(She puts him down, but keeps her hold.)

KALI: Why do you want to drive my train?

HARI: To run away.

KALI: Ah. You don't like it here in Madras?

HARI: My family's here. I can't stay with them any more.

KALI: I'm sure that's not true, little boy.

HARI: It is so. I need to run away.

KALI: With a whole train? And all the people riding it?

HARI: They know where they're going. It's on a track.
They bought tickets.

KALI: That doesn't mean they know where they're going.
Especially if you're the one at the controls.

HARI: I know lots about trains. My father and grandfather
are in the railway industry. I know all the models: steam
trains and the new electric.

KALI: Is that so.

HARI: I'll show you.

KALI: You're a little boy, who knows nothing of the world.
And anyway, who ever really knows where they're going?
Especially when they seem to be on a track?

HARI: That makes no sense. You're crazy.

KALI: Am I, little expert? Let's see what you know about
trains.

(Opens door of a mimed locomotive ['engine'].)

HARI: The driver's seat?

KALI: Yes, but hush-hush. This is completely against
regulations. Now, you see this dial?

HARI: Uh huh.

KALI: Do you know what it is?

HARI: The speed?

KALI: Not quite. It's a tachometer. It tells your RPM. You know how many this engine does?

HARI: What?

KALI: RPM. Revolutions per minute.

HARI: What does that mean?

KALI: You don't know?

HARI: Not exactly.

KALI: And you think you know about trains!

HARI: I know other things about them.

KALI: About trains that go nowhere, maybe. RPM is a unit to describe the rate of rotation of a body, or, how much topsy-turning-over happens in a span of space-time. How much changes, that is. In the engine.

HARI: The engine changes?

KALI: No, silly. Everything does. The landscape, as it flies by. And soon, when all the trains run on electric...

HARI: It doesn't change enough.

KALI: What doesn't?

HARI: Everything. The railway's getting electrified, all right, but nothing that matters changes. I could help you drive the train. I want to be a driver.

KALI: Then go back to school. Now get down, and get lost.

HARI: Are you going?

KALI: No. This train is. Whatever I say, she just refuses to travel alone.

HARI: Please, let me go with you. I can't go back. I've done something awful!

KALI: Buy a ticket.

HARI: I can't. And I can't go home. Please let me on!

KALI: What have you done?

HARI: I'll say when we get to Nagpur.

KALI: Say now.

HARI: Why?

KALI: Because I don't give free rides except in cases of genuine emergency. So you'd better let me know right now how bad things will be for you if you're left where you are.

End of Scene.

WITNESS

By Helen Shay

*MILES BROSGELL (SOLICITOR, 50) IS AT HIS DESK,
LISTENING TO THE FRIGHTENED VOICE OF SELIMA
ON A TAPE. A COURT WIG, TELEPHONE, AND WAD
OF PAPERS, WITH ANOTHER CHAIR TO THE SIDE.*

V/O TAPE: You run and run, because you know what they
do to you. Looking for safety, searching. *(BEAT)* But
everywhere you run, is only fear. And so -

MILES REWINDS THE TAPE.

V/O TAPE: You run and run, because you know what they
do to you. Looking for safety …

MILES STOPS THE TAPE AND PUTS ON THE WIG.

MILES: *(TO AUDIENCE)* Ladies and gentlemen of the
jury.

MILES: *(TO AUDIENCE, TRYING LIGHTER STYLE)*
Ladies and gentlemen of the jury.

MILES STANDS ON HIS DESK

MILES: *(TO AUDIENCE, LOUD AND SOLEMN)* Ladies
and gentlemen of -

*KNOCK AT THE DOOR INTERUPTS. MILES SIGHS AND
LOOKS RESIGNED.*

MILES: Come.

ENTER KIRSTEN, STARTLED TO SEE MILES ON DESK.
HE'S SURPRISED TO SEE HER.

MILES: Good afternoon.

KIRSTEN: Weren't you expecting me?

MILES: *(BEAT)* Of course.

MILES CLAMBOURS DOWN.

MILES: I was just *(BEAT)* practising.

MILES SITS, GESTURING KIRSTEN TO THE OTHER
CHAIR. KIRSTEN JUST STARES.

MILES: I'm Miles Brosgell. The Brosgell of Messrs
Brosgell, Snell and Pace.

KIRSTEN: I was looking for the Snell.

MILES: But I can help you. *(PROUDLY)* Senior partner.

KIRSTEN: I made an appointment. Am I in the wrong
place? There was no name on this door.

MILES: You are in exactly the right place. And I can help
you.

KIRSTEN: Can you?

MILES GESTURES TO THE CHAIR. KIRSTEN SITS
DOWN.

MILES: Now don't tell me. Polish? No, Czech. That's it,
isn't it? I was in Prague in the early eighties. Did a lot of
dissidents. Are you a dissident?

KIRSTEN: I am eighty years old.

MILES: And still fighting the system. Wonderful! I haven't had a Czech, since the wall fell.

KIRSTEN: I'm not Czech, I've lived in Britain most of my life and I'm here to make a will.

MILES: Where there's a will, there's a way, dear lady. Don't worry, I won't let it happen. You've received a letter, haven't you?

KIRSTEN: *(SUSPICIOUSLY)* I have actually.

MILES: Wait until the papers get hold of this. Home Office tries to deport eighty-year old Czech woman, after living in Britain all her life.

KIRSTEN: It wasn't from the Home Office, I'm not Czech and I want a will.

MILES: Hungarian?

KIRSTEN: *(PROUDLY)* German.

MILES: Well, I can still help you. The power of words, in the mouth of a good lawyer. Words can set you free.

KIRSTEN: The bible says the truth sets you free.

MILES: Ah, you're religious.

KIRSTEN: Catholic.

MILES: That'll do. You're being persecuted?

KIRSTEN: *(UNDER BREATH)* Only by my son.

MILES: Well, I can definitely get you a Visa. Maybe even a work permit.

KIRSTEN: Work permit?

MILES: Definitely. I've a brilliant track record as a solicitor. I know what you're thinking.

KIRSTEN: *(UNDER BREATH)* You do?

MILES: We've all seen the headlines. `Bogus Asylum Seekers', `Soft Touch Britain.' But don't worry. I'm no soft touch. I'll have them eating out of my hands.
(ADDRESSING AUDIENCE) Ladies and gentlemen of the jury.

KIRSTEN: Are you allowed to wear that wig? *(BEAT)* You being just a solicitor.

MILES: Just a - ! Miles Brosgell was never `just a solicitor'. And yes. I'm a (BEAT) solicitor-advocate. Lot of them about, these days. All wearing wigs.

KIRSTEN: Then I apologize, Mr. Brosgell. Only, well, I thought.... a small practice in Denby Dale. Anyway, about my will. Do I need tax planning?

MILES: I thought you needed asylum.

KIRSTEN: Perhaps I do. *(SIGHS)* My son has written to me. *(TAKES OUT A LETTER FROM HER POCKET)* I've never heard a thing from him, since he dropped by on his way from prison to relieve me of the contents of my purse. *(MIMICS GERI)* `I'm all right. Honest.' Honest? *(LAUGHS)* My Geri. Oh, you should meet my son, Mr. Brosgell. Still, it seems a nice letter. 'The power of words', you might say. *(KIRSTEN READS, MIMICKING GERI)*`Dear Mum, How are you?' *(ORDINARY VOICE)*

Translation – Mother, are you any nearer to dropping dead yet? That house must be worth a bit. *(READS, MIMICKING GERI)* ' I've been too busy to write before. In fact, I've opportunity to get in on a sweet little business deal, if only I can raise the capital.' *(ORD VOICE)* Translation– if you won't obligingly drop dead, then loan me a few thousand *(BEAT)* Well, this time, no!

MILES: I'm sure your son means no harm.

KIRSTEN: I intend to make a new will. His share can go to the Refugee Council. *(MIMICS GERI)* 'Bring you one step closer to heaven,' he'd say to taunt me.

MILES: Dear lady.

KIRSTEN: I'm not a dear lady. I'm Kirshteen Morris.

MILES: Mrs. Morris. Kirsten.

KIRSTEN: Kirsht-een!

MILES: But do you have a visa?

KIRSTEN: What?

MILES: I know these home office bastards, let me tell you.

KIRSTEN: *(SARCASTICALLY)* Yes, all the cases you've won.

MILES STARTS PACING AROUND AGITATEDLY.
KIRSTEN SIGHS.

MILES: You must believe me. I've saved lots of people. My words. I saved -

MILES SWITCHES THE TAPE ON.

V/O TAPE: ...searching *(BEAT)* ...

MILES: her!

V/O TAPE: But everywhere you run, is only fear.

MILES STOPS THE TAPE AND SLUMPS DOWN.

KIRSTEN: Something wrong? *(BEAT)* Can I help you, Mr. Brosgell? Who-? *(BEAT)* Is she one of your clients? A witness statement?

MILES: You might say that.

KIRSTEN: Someone you helped? Czech, Pole?

MILES: Somalian.

KIRSTEN: Ah. You must forgive me, Mr. Brosgell, only I thought ...

MILES: Who'd come to pathetic little solicitor's practice in Denby Dale, seeking asylum?

KIRSTEN: Well, you must admit...

MILES: *(TAKES OFF WIG)* I admit. *(BEAT)* None of them. The nearest I've got to a big case is in the books, I surround myself with. My sanctuary of words. I can't even do you that will, dear lady.

KIRSTEN: Kirshten.

MILES: Kur-er-sh-tee-een. Anyway, you'll have to see Snell for that. I'm family. Strictly domestic violence, divorce and custody battles. Roll up for a Brosgell special. A quickie decree nisi, plus discount if you make it absolute. *(BEAT)* A lifetime, behind a desk, making a living out of everyday misery. Putting it down on paper, sanitising it into words. You don't have to go to a war zone to find suffering.

KIRSTEN: *(SCREWS UP HER LETTER)* No. *(BEAT)* But the girl on the tape?

MILES: Selima. She came here. Sat where you are, pleading. Such eyes. *(BEAT)* It wasn't easy for her to get to England, but she did it for the child.

KIRSTEN: Ah. To be a mother in a foreign land, that is not good, Mr. Brosgell.

MILES: But worse for her to go back. She feared repercussions in her homeland. God knows why she came to me. Hardly the crusading lawyer, hardly the hero. But those eyes. Pleading. I'd witnessed so much tragedy, here in this room, taking depositions, preparing affidavits. Words are never enough.

KIRSTEN DROPS HER LETTER.

KIRSTEN: No.

MILES: But if I could just save Selima. Act. Really act for her. Not sit complicit, bearing witness, *(BEAT)* keeping safe on my side of the desk. *(BEAT)* What is it, they say about the life of a single sparrow?

KIRSTEN: That's in the bible. But someone *(BEAT)* a Jewish boy I knew once, told me the Talmud puts it a different way. `He, who saves one, saves the entire world'.

MILES: I saved Selima. Me. Paunchy old Brosgell of Messrs Brosgell, Snell and Pace. I pulled a few strings at the Legal Services Commission, and won her appeal.

KIRSTEN: So she stayed? You can do it, you know. A young woman in a foreign country.

MILES: I gave her a job. And a little flat, where I could visit. Even gave her a new name.

KIRSTEN: You look after her?

MILES: So innocent. Guess the one she chose? Jordan! I ask you. Saw a picture in a magazine. `Pretty girl,' she said. `Is she an actress or a singer?' I could hardly disillusion her. Shame it wasn't Charlotte Church though.

KIRSTEN: Jordan?

MILES: Selima Jordan. Deed poll. I can do deed polls. It's just the wills, I leave to Snell.

KIRSTEN: That name? Jordan?

MILES: She worried about repercussions. Thought 'they' might come after her. Change of name made her feel safe. 'Good river too,' she said. You'll know, from your bible.

KIRSTEN: Selima Jordan? I'm sure, I've read that name. That statement. When was it made?

MILES: I saved her.

KIRSTEN: Then why does she sound so scared? *(BEAT)* There was something in the papers.

MILES: I gave her a new life, taught her more English. I taught her lots of things.

KIRSTEN: `Girl hangs herself in Railway station cloakroom'. Wasn't that the story? *(BEAT)* Just who was she running from? When she had a little flat, where you could visit?

MILES: No, no! I saved her. I loved her.

KIRSTEN: I know about such love. My son's an expert on it. Some call it 'exploitation'.

MILES: I wouldn't do that.

KIRSTEN: But I read about her death in the papers,

MILES: If you won't believe me, believe her.

MILES TURNS ON THE TAPE.

V/O TAPE: And so, I decide I must stop running. You are good man, Mr. Brosgell, like father to me. But nowhere is safe. I leave this tape here, like when I was doing witness. Only now to say goodbye.

SILENCE AS TAPE ENDS.

KIRSTEN: Was that just before she killed herself?

MILES: You wanted to know who she was running from.

MILES THROWS THE WAD OF PAPERS IN FRONT OF KIRSTEN, WHO SIFTS THROUGH.

KIRSTEN: Letters? *(READING)* `Go back where you belong, coward!'

MILES: At first, she thought it was spies from her homeland.

KIRSTEN: *(READING)*`Leave British jobs to the Brits, scrounger!' No signature. Poison pen?

MILES: These were just the ones that came to the office.

KIRSTEN: `We'll fix you, you dago cun -.' Oh, I can't say that word, Mr. Brosgell.

MILES: God knows, what she received at home. More threats and intimidation. So much for asylum in the land of the free.

KIRSTEN: BNP?

MILES: Who knows? I promised her she'd be safe.

KIRSTEN: My son could have so easily written these. *(BEAT)* Yet he was taunted like this once, for having 'a Nazi for a mum'. What does that do to someone? Despair? Anger? *(BEAT)* So you didn't take advantage of her?

MILES: I saved her. *(BEAT)* Like all those others. You must believe me. Power of words. If I can save them all, then she'll see it's safe and come back .

KIRSTEN: She can't come back, Mr. Brosgell.

MILES: But I'm a good lawyer.

KIRSTEN: You're a good man.

MILES: And aren't you a religious dissident? I can save you. Especially if you're Czech.

KIRSTEN: I came here for a will, remember?

MILES NODS, PICKS UP THE PHONE, DIALS, THEN HANDS IT TO KIRSTEN.

MILES: Snell on the internal line. He'll sort it out for you.

KIRSTEN: *(ON PHONE)* Hello, Mr. Snell. *(BEAT)* Yes, it's Mrs. Morris. In the wrong office. *(BEAT)* Mr. Brosgell's, yes. We've been having an *(BEAT)* enlightening conversation. *(PAUSES, LOOKING AT MILES)* Oh, now I understand.

KIRSTEN PUTS DOWN THE PHONE. SILENCE.

MILES: Are they coming?

KIRSTEN: Mr. Snell says they'll be here soon. But he says you can still come back, when you need to. To your old office. He knows it helps you sometimes.

MILES: It's the tape. I like to hear her voice.

KIRSTEN: Only Mr. Snell did say to remind you, of what he said about not talking to clients.

MILES: Oh, dear. Did I forget that bit?

KIRSTEN: I'm glad you talked to me, Mr. Brosgell.

MILES: Ker-sh-teen!

KIRSTEN: That's right.

MILES: Snell will do you that will. Next left down the corridor.

KIRSTEN: I don't think I'll bother now. I've decided to go see my son instead. It starts here, doesn't it, Mr. Brosgell? The life of a sparrow.

MILES: I did win her appeal. That bit was the truth.

KIRSTEN: Yes. But perhaps the truth doesn't always set us free.

MILES PUTS HIS HEAD IN HIS HANDS. KIRSTEN TOUCHES HIM GENTLY.

KIRSTEN: Look, all that was before your breakdown, caused by her suicide. 'Vicarious trauma', Mr. Snell says.

MILES: `Rescue fantasies', they say.

KIRSTEN: I'm sure the psychiatrists there are highly trained. They'll take you back soon.

KIRSTEN RISES. MILES SHAKES HER HAND.

MILES: We are all asylum seekers, you know.

KIRSTEN: I know.

EXIT KIRSTEN. MILES REWINDS THE TAPE.

V/O TAPE: `.... you run and run, because you know what they do to you. Looking for safety, searching....'

End of Scene.

MOONTANNER GIRLS

By Cecilia Copeland

CAST:
JENNY   Teenager
CARLEY Teenager

SCENE 1

JENNY and CARLEY are sitting on a sleeping bag partially under it with a magazine. They have a flashlight. They are flipping the pages together looking at the magazine.

JENNY: I think he's hot. I'd sleep with him.

CARLEY: Yeah. He's cute, I like him better.

They flip the pages of the magazine.

JENNY: What about him?

CARLEY: No way.

JENNY: Right?

CARLEY: I don't why he's even in here. He's not even cute at all.

They flip more pages.

JENNY: He's hot.

CARLEY: Totally. I'd for sure sleep with him.

They flip the pages.

JENNY: What about her? She's pretty. Don't you think she's pretty?

CARLEY: Yeah. She's beautiful.

JENNY: Would you sleep with her?

CARLEY: I don't know.

JENNY: I would. I think she's beautiful. I'd sleep with him too.

They flip more pages.

CARLEY: He's hot.

They flip more pages.

JENNY: What about him?

CARLEY: He's okay. She's prettier.

JENNY: Totally.

They flip more pages.

JENNY: I think you're pretty.

CARLEY: I think you're pretty too.

JENNY leans in and shyly kisses CARLEY.

CARLEY: You have really soft lips.

JENNY: So do you.

CARLEY: You kiss way better than Tommy.

JENNY: How does Tommy kiss?

CARLEY: Like this.

CARLEY kisses JENNY and presses her lips against JENNY really hard until JENNY almost falls over.

CARLEY and JENNY laugh.

JENNY: Shhhh.

CARLEY covers JENNY'S mouth with her hand.

CARLEY: You shhhh. We can't get in trouble again. We won't get to go to the end of camp dance.

JENNY takes CARLEY's hand off.

JENNY: You have soft hands too. Why don't boys know how to kiss?

CARLEY: How did you learn how to kiss?

JENNY: I don't know. I just... I mean... Well... It's not like... I don't know.

CARLEY: Was I a good kisser?

JENNY: Yeah. For sure.

CARLEY: Do you open your mouth when you kiss?

JENNY: You mean French kiss?

CARLEY: Yeah.

JENNY: Sometimes. Well... twice.

CARLEY: Is it gross?

JENNY: You wanna try it?

CARLEY: What if I'm bad?

JENNY: Why would you be bad?

CARLEY: Are you gay?

JENNY: I like boys, but I like girls too. Girls are pretty.

CARLEY: Have you kissed a lot of girls?

JENNY: No. Just you.

CARLEY quickly kisses JENNY.

CARLEY: Good night Jenny.

The flashlight goes out.

JENNY: Good night.

CARLEY: Hey, Jenny?

JENNY: Yeah?

CARLEY: When I go back home…. will you be my facebook friend?

JENNY: As long as you promise to be a Moontanner with me next year.

CARLEY: I promise.

End of Scene.

FRITTERS AND FURLOUGHS

By Christina Cigala

Evelyn Bender: Nineteen years old. A freshman at John Bowls Baptist University. Attractive, but not pretty. Loud, impulsive, peculiar, invasive, bold.
Brandy Holsmith: Evelyn's pretty, conservative roommate. Has a Southern accent.

Time: October 1988. Before the Bush Sr./Dukakis election.

At Rise

EVELYN is in the middle of the first semester of her freshman year at John Bowls Baptist University.

SCENE II. BRANDY IS IN THE DORM ROOM HER AND EVELYN SHARE.

LEANING AGAINST THE WALL NEAR HER IS A LARGE WOODEN CROSS WITH WHEELS ON THE BOTTOM. EVELYN ENTERS. SOMEONE HAS WRITTEN GRAFFITI ON THE CROSS WITH MARKER, AND BRANDY IS SCRUBBING IT OFF.

EVELYN: Hey lame-o, I actually met a decent… *(Notices cross)* Brandy. What the hell is that?

BRANDY: *(A little embarrassed)* Oh, it's nothing. Just something we're doing for Baptists for Christ.

EVELYN: *(Horrified)* Are you going to nail someone to it?

BRANDY: Shut up, Evelyn.

EVELYN: Then what on earth are you doing with it? Is it for a skit or something?

BRANDY: No, we just take turns carrying it around, to remind people of Jesus' suffering.

EVELYN: You carried it to CLASS?

BRANDY: Yeah, Ev, it's not that big of a deal.

EVELYN: *(Notices Graffiti. Delighted.)* Did someone write...?

BRANDY: Yes! Okay! Someone wrote "eat shit and die" on it!

EVELYN: *(Surprised)* You just said shit!

BRANDY: It's okay if you're repeating someone.

EVELYN: Oh, silly me.

BRANDY: You always make fun of me, Evelyn.

EVELYN: Brandy, it's easy. And then you give me props.

BRANDY: You can be so smug.

EVELYN: *(Sees that Brandy is upset.)* Not always, I was just about to tell you about a guy I met until I saw your new vehicle.

BRANDY: Well tell me anyway, my day's been hard enough. This thing weighs like 100 pounds.

EVELYN sighs. She begins helping BRANDY clean the graffiti off the cross.

EVELYN: *(Whispers)* I don't know if they told you this, Brand-o, but Jesus didn't have wheels.

BRANDY: I'm not saying I'm Jesus.

EVELYN: Well, I'd hope not. Good Lord. I think I'm getting hives. You can talk to people about your religious views without props, Brandy.

BRANDY: I don't want to talk about this. We're just going to argue.

EVELYN: What is there to argue about? You have a portable crucifix in our dorm room. I don't need to discuss it any further.

BRANDY: *(Sighs.)* Just tell me about the boy.

EVELYN: *(A bit giddy.)* Fine, fine. Okay. So his name is Clarence.

BRANDY: That's a real faggy name.

EVELYN: That's a terrible word, Brandy. Jesus wouldn't approve of all that hate.

BRANDY: I wasn't talking about the homosexuals, Evelyn. It's an expression.

EVELYN: Well so is 'eat shit and die,' do you want people to write it on your cross? No. Anyway, people call him Butch here.

BRANDY: Butch Blake?

EVELYN: Yeah, I think that's it.

BRANDY: You like him? That's surprising. He's really normal.

EVELYN: I didn't say I was buying him a promise ring. I

said he was attractive. And I'm totally normal when I'm not in the crotch bulge of the Bible Belt.

BRANDY: Gag me!

EVELYN: So do you have to hand off the cross to somebody? Is it like a relay race?

BRANDY: I don't know, I got harassed so much I doubt any of the other kids will want to carry it.

EVELYN: *(Snidely)* Did you get a parking permit for it?

BRANDY: It folds up and fits in the car, Evelyn.

EVELYN: *(Considers this for a moment)* You are a sweet girl and everything, but this is insane.

BRANDY: You shouldn't talk like that. It's not ladylike.

EVELYN: And I'm so concerned with being ladylike.

BRANDY: *(Sighs)* It's your life. I talked to my mom about you today. She said she used to do the same things as you, before she was a Christian.

EVELYN: What things?

BRANDY: Go to parties, curse, fornicate, whatever. But she changed. You will too.

EVELYN: I will not. And why do you assume I'm fornicating?

BRANDY: I don't know, I just did.

EVELYN: Well maybe I don't.

BRANDY: Okay. Well that's good.

EVELYN: I said maybe I don't. It's just not your business.

BRANDY: I guess I just didn't think you'd have any reason not to.

EVELYN: So because I'm not you, I don't have any morals?

BRANDY: No...I... we just see the world in different ways.

EVELYN: *(Under her breath)* Yeah, I know it's not flat.

BRANDY: What?

EVELYN: Nothing.

BRANDY: Don't talk down to me, Evelyn.

EVELYN: Don't talk down to YOU? Brandy, every word you speak to me is an assertion of your holiness.

BRANDY: That is not true.

EVELYN: "My mother was like you, before she was a Christian." Do you know how that sounds?

BRANDY: Well, you're not a Christian.

EVELYN: How do you know that? I've never told you my religious beliefs.

BRANDY: Ok. Well, are you a Christian, Evelyn?

EVELYN: No. Not really.

BRANDY: See?

EVELYN: But that does not mean I'm morally reprehensible!

BRANDY: Maybe not reprehensible, but still wrong. But that doesn't mean I don't love you.

EVELYN: That's it. I'm taking your cross.

BRANDY: *(Defeated)* Take it. I can barely push it anyway.

EVELYN: Oh my god, let's recycle it!

BRANDY: *(Hesitantly)* Is that bad?

EVELYN: No, it's totally what Jesus would do. Wanna wheel it with me?

BRANDY: Sure, why not. Let me get my cardigan.

They get the cross and walk out the door.

EVELYN: You're lucky I'm a nice person, or I'd make fun of you for owning a cardigan.

End of Scene.

GHANDI MARG

By Anita Chandwaney

CHARACTERS: NOTE: ALL CHARACTERS ARE BORN OF EAST-INDIAN PARENTS; EXCEPT VINOD, WHO IS HALF-IRISH

SHARDUL KAPADIA   34; MUSICIAN/SINGER/SONG-WRITER BORN IN THE U.S.; MARRIED TO SHANTI FOR A MONTH.

SHANTI KRISHNAMURTHY-KAPADIA 24; BORN IN THE U.S.; MARRIED TO SHARDUL; PRACTICAL.

BINA KRISHNAMURTHY 35; SHANTI'S SISTER; A PERFECTIONIST.

MITUL SHAH   34; SHARDUL'S FRIEND FROM HIGH SCHOOL; AN INFORMATION TECHNOLOGY WORKER.

RANJAN KAPADIA 34; SHARDUL'S 3RD COUSIN; IMMIGRATED TO THE U.S. WHEN HE WAS 16; HAD AN ARRANGED MARRIAGE TO JAYA 11 YEARS AGO IN INDIA.

JAYA KAPADIA 33; HAPPY AND CONFIDENT MOTHER OF 3; RAISED IN INDIA.

VINOD O'DOUL 33; SHARDUL'S HALF-INDIAN, HALF-IRISH DRUMMER AND FRIEND.

THE SETTING: THE ACTION TAKES PLACE IN THE FRONT "YARD" OF SHARDUL AND SHANTI'S APARTMENT BUILDING, AND INSIDE THE APARTMENT ITSELF. IT IS A SMALL ONE-BEDROOM ON ROSEHILL STREET, WHICH IS PERPENDICULAR TO DEVON AVENUE BETWEEN WESTERN AND CALIFORNIA, ON CHICAGO'S FAR NORTH SIDE, AFFECTIONATELY KNOWN AS "LITTLE INDIA".

SCENE SIX

Crossfade to JAYA sitting in the 'yard' wearing a shawl separating mint leaves. BINA enters with two rolling suitcases.

BINA: Do you speak English?

JAYA: I am here eleven years now.

BINA: Does Shanti Krishnamurthy live here?

JAYA: Who are you?

BINA: Bina Krishnamurthy. Her sister.

JAYA: I didn't even know she had a sister.

BINA: You didn't?

JAYA: Were you at the wedding? Just City Hall but still.

BINA: I was in India. Our mother's ashes.

JAYA: Shanti told me, sorry huh? You're a good daughter, you should teach Shanti. She is Shanti Krishnamurthy-Kapadia now.

BINA: What?

JAYA: I know. My in-laws would have died if I did that. After killing me.

BINA: Kapadia?

JAYA: Krishnamurthy-Kapadia. These modern girls. Did you also do this with your name?

BINA: No.

JAYA: You are married no?

BINA: No.

JAYA: But you are...older, no?

BINA: Yes.

JAYA: So you do a job?

BINA: Daycare.

JAYA: That's a good job for ladies. It's in our nature. This way men will know. In this country ladies are too busy, go-go-go all the time. And that Manhattan is too much, my God. But you're from Jersey City, it's better there.

BINA: We grew up in Princeton.

JAYA: Shanti told me she came from Jersey City.

BINA: After our father passed we moved ... there.

JAYA: Family is big help at those times.

BINA: It was just us three.

JAYA: You should guide Shanti better. Coming here so soon after your mother. It doesn't look good.

BINA: Is she here?

JAYA: She's at Shardul's band rehearsal.

BINA: Shardul?

(pause)

Shardul Kapadia?

JAYA: Yes.

BINA: He's a musician?

JAYA: He does singing and guitar. Not sitar, but guitar.

BINA: But he's from Chicago.

JAYA: He moved here long ago. Soon after I was married. Ay, from Jersey City, like you and Shanti! You want tea?

(silence)

You want tea or no?

BINA: No.

JAYA: Oh ho! You must be saying, "this lady's a stupid idiot making me stand outside." Come we can sit in Shanti and Shardul's unit. I'll make you tea. It's okay, my in-laws own the building.

(JAYA uses a master key. They each roll a suitcase into the apartment.)

They are crazy. For one-hundred dollars more they could be in two-bedrooms. There was one on the second floor. I told them and told them but finally I got fed up.

BINA: You know, I have a terrible headache. Maybe I'll just take a nap till Shanti gets back.

JAYA: Here, use this cushion.

(hands BINA a cushion)

We sell these in our shop, Kapadia's Groceries. But it's not just food so if you need anything go there. I'll give the cashier your name so you get a discount. It's no problem. Even shawls like this. Nice, no?

(places her shawl on BINA's shoulders)

BINA: No, please --

JAYA: - It's okay, I have so many. I'll tell Shanti you're here. It's no problem, Mitul's garage is across the street and my friend Shilpa is across his alley. I'll use her food processor. She and I have known each other twenty-two years, from India. That's something isn't it?

(she exits)

(BINA wanders around then crosses to the window. She slowly slides the shawl off her shoulders and stops when it's almost off. She remains transfixed.)

SHANTI: *(enters the yard)* 'Didi'!

BINA: Shanti.

(SHANTI enters the apartment)

SHANTI: Didi!

(hugs BINA)

It feels like I haven't seen you in so long.

BINA: Two months is long.

SHANTI: Sorry I wasn't in when you got here. We were expecting you later.

BINA: I caught an earlier flight.

SHANTI: Welcome to my new home. I'm married, can you believe it?

BINA: I got the e-mail in India. You eloped.

SHANTI: I wanted to call but the time difference.

BINA: I left you messages after I got back.

SHANTI: I've been so busy. I got a job at a bank.

BINA: I got back and had to deal with Mom's friends telling me how the funeral was all wrong and it's a crime she didn't see me married and that her soul will have no peace --

SHANTI: - Ignore them.

BINA: One side of their mouth they're all 'God this' and 'God that' with their 'puja's' and 'aarthi's' and fasting. "Oh thank God", "oh please God", while the other... Their God can kiss my ass.

SHANTI: It's not that much different around here.

BINA: Your landlady was all over me with "You want tea, come I'll make you tea."

SHANTI: Her chai-masala rocks.

BINA: 'Guju's' have their tea masala -

SHANTI: Shard's Gujarati.

BINA: The minute Mom passes you come here and shack up with a 'Guju'.

SHANTI: Bina.

BINA: The ashes were still warm.

SHANTI: I waited three weeks for the mourning period.

BINA: Good of you.

SHANTI: We couldn't afford for both of us to go to India. Why shouldn't I come out for this year's festival?

BINA: He's the one you met last year. The one you were so excited about.

SHANTI: I invited you when he came to J.C. for last year's gig.

BINA: Had I known --

SHANTI: - I know what you're thinking.

BINA: No, you don't.

SHANTI: He's a musician and there's no money in it --

BINA: - Now that you mention it.

SHANTI: He wants to move people and make them connect to their inner core of true feelings.

BINA: And if I followed my true feelings, what would've happened to you and Mom?

SHANTI: Was there someone special back then?

BINA: What would you and Mom have done?

SHANTI: What am I supposed to do, not live my life?

BINA: Should I have lived my life?

SHANTI: You can now.

BINA: It's too late for me.

SHANTI: You're only thirty-seven, that's the new twenty-seven.

BINA: Maybe I should have run off when I was your age.

SHANTI: Are you okay?

(beat)

I'll go upstairs and ask Jaya for some Tylenol.

BINA: Sure, just go.

SHANTI: I'll be right back.

(SHANTI seats BINA and places the shawl on her shoulders)

BINA: No!

(SHANTI exits the apartment)

(BINA slides the shawl off her shoulders then stops)

BINA: No.

(she throws the shawl to the floor and lays down staring at the shawl)

End of Scene.

SPANGLISH - UNDER SEIGE

By G.L. Horton

"Spanglish" transliteration was contributed by Anna Gonzales, the Counselor who inspired the play.

(Setting is a counseling cubicle at a Women's Health Clinic. In the original production, Emily and Sally were played by African-American actresses.)

THERESA, the patient, mid 20's wears heels and a bright skirt and blouse.

EMILY, early 20's is the newest counselor at the clinic.

ALLISON, a bit older, is the counselor Emily most admires.

SALLY, is the most experienced, and the clinic's head counselor.

The counselors all wear white coats over business attire.

EMILY: I see your name is Teresa?

TERESA: *(nods)* Si. Teresa. (Spanish pronunciation)

EMILY: *(tries to correct)* Uh-Teresa. I'm Emily. I'm here to answer your questions, if I can. Is there anything you particularly want to ask about?

TERESA: *(frustrated)* No. Si. I wish--

EMILY: *(baffled)* I'll try to help.

TERESA: *(mimes)* About ... planificacion.... to stop babies.

EMILY: *(understands!)* Birth control?

TERESA: Si! Si!

EMILY: *(consults chart)* What birth control. *(TERESA nods)* For a married woman 26 years old, the recommended birth control is the pill. Do you want to take the pill? Pill-- *(mimes)*

TERESA: Pildora! No...no puedo. I can't.

EMILY: *(pantomimes)* You can't take pills? They make you sick? Nausea?

TERESA: No. No. No puedo. I-- *(she is very upset)*

EMILY: Teresa, do you understand English?

TERESA: Si. A little. Un poco.

EMILY: Well, I have less than un poco Spanish. Would you be more   comfortable with a counselor who speaks Spanish?

TERESA: Si. Yes. Gracias.

EMILY: *(into intercom)* Sally? Is Alma with a patient right now? ... What about Allison Would you ask her if she could come to room four, please? *(to TERESA)* Allison's going to come and take over for me. She's not as fluent as Alma, but I think you'll find it a lot easier to talk to her. In Espanol.

TERESA: Gracias. *(they sit, awkwardly, alternating smiles)*

ALLISON: *(enters)* Emily?

EMILY: *(hands over chart)* Allison! This is Teresa.

ALLISON: Hello Teresa, my name is Allison. I'm going help out your counselor Is that OK?

TERESA: OK? (confused) Espanol?

ALLISON: Hablo un poco de espanol.

EMILY: She has some concerns about birth control.

ALLISON: Preguntas?

TERESA: Si, about...planificacion?

ALLISON: Well, que clase quieres? Pildora?

TERESA: No, no puedo.

ALLISON: Nausea, mareos?

TERESA: No puedo.

ALLISON: Y la diafragma, o condones y espuma?

TERESA: No eso, es imposible.

ALLISON: Por que?

TERESA: Tiene algo secreto, una inyeccion para que nadie
sepa?

ALLISON: *(looks at chart)* Algo secreto? Teresa, que
pasa? Tu esposo, el..?

TERESA: No. Mi senior. El dice que la planificacion es
mala. El es muy catolico, y es un pecado. Pero tenemos
cinco babies.

EMILY: Five babies?

ALLISON: *(points to chart)* And it says here, four

abortions. Teresa, tu esposo, el piensa que la planificacion es mala, pero il aborto no?

TERESA: No, no. El no sabe nada de los abortos. Dios mio, me mata!

EMILY: Mata?

ALLISON: *(to EMILY)* He'll kill her. De verdad?...Teresa, el te maltrata?

TERESA: *(nods)* Quando encuentra mis pildoras, me pega. Y quando digo "tenemos que usar un condon" tambien me pega, y me llama "puta, prostituta". *(crying)* Yo se que el aborto es un pecado. Dios me va a castigar..ire al infierno. Pero que puedo hacer?

ALLISON: *(to EMILY)* He beats her when she tries to use contraceptives. *(to TERESA)* Yo conozco una consejera, Hispana, una mujer bien buena. Te gustaria hablar con ella? En privado, para ti, para no tener que estar sola.

TERESA: Si, por favor. Me gustaria.

ALLISON: *(writes name and gives)* Llamala. Ella es muy buena gente...Vas a estar OK?

TERESA: Si.

ALLISON: Buena suerte, Teresa. Y, mira, se me necesitas, llamame, OK?

TERESA: OK. Gracias, mija.

ALLISON: Cuidate.

(TERESA goes out, EMILY and ALLISON pause to talk)

EMILY: What happened?

ALLISON: I gave her the name of a Puerto Rican friend, an ex-nun. She'll help her get a tubal ligation.

EMILY: Thanks. I was in over my head.

ALLISON: No problema. Why'd they give her to you?

EMILY: I don't know. I had Spanish in high school, enough to read maybe the headlines in a newspaper.

ALLISON: If you want to brush up to use it here, you need the kind of newspaper they sell in the supermarket. A Spanish version of the National Enquirer.

EMILY: Where can I get one? Does it have the words for birth control?

ALLISON: You're really interested? I'll get you some. The words it doesn't have, I can teach you. But I've got to dash, now. Sally's going to "remind" me: Patient waiting. *(exits)*

EMILY: *(calls after ALLISON)* Thanks again!

SALLY: *(comes up to EMILY)* Emily? You have a problem?

EMILY: A patient who didn't speak English.

SALLY: Damn! Was she Portuguese?

EMILY: Hispanic.

SALLY: I thought you spoke Spanish. Your application said so.

EMILY: I said I took it. But not - I can't deal with any problem   more complex than the menu in a Mexican restaurant.

SALLY: Shoot.

EMILY: Did I give you the impression that I was bilingual? Oh God--. That wasn't the reason you hired me?

SALLY: No. No, of course not. I probably read it wrong because that's what I was wishing. And when Allison leaves-

EMILY: Oh, no! Allison's leaving?!

SALLY: She hasn't said so, but I know she's applied to graduate school. I wrote her a recommendation.

EMILY: She told me she's not sure-

SALLY: Well, I'd love to keep her. But I've got to be realistic. If the clinic paid Allison what her education says she's worth, nobody could afford to come here!

EMILY: She offered to help me brush up.

SALLY: That's a kind thought. *(laughs, turns to leave.)* You know, you could take a course in "conversational", at night. Allison would!

(EMILY watches SALLY exit)

End of Scene.

TURN A BLIND EYE

By Hindi Brooks

CHARACTERS:
Young Malka, 19, very pregnant.
Hershel, 20, her husband.
Two SS men.

SET: A dark street in Cologne, Germany, in 1938.
In 1964, Shelly and her blind mother, Malka, reflect on what
happened to Malka in 1938, in Nazi Germany. This scene is
what Malka remembers of one day on a street in Cologne.
MALKA'S VERSION
OF THE COLOGNE INCIDENT - 1938
The dark street is empty and the alley coming off it is darker
and foreboding. We hear footsteps of someone running
clumsily. Then Young Malka's SOTTO VOCE bounces off
the walls echoing:

YOUNG MALKA: *(O.S.)* Hershl...Hershl, wait for me!

YOUNG MALKA, 19, appears stage right. She's eight
months pregnant and beautiful. She walks/runs with a
waddle, and stops near the alley to catch her breath. Then
she calls again, a bit louder:

YOUNG MALKA: Hershl?

HERSHL, 20, an intense young radical, steps out of the
alley.

YOUNG MALKA: *(Startled)* Oh!

HERSHL: Sha!

YOUNG MALKA: You frightened me!

They both speak SOTTO VOCE, now.

HERSHL: I told you to stay home.

YOUNG MALKA: It's too dangerous for you to go there alone.

HERSHL: You're making it dangerous by holding me back.

YOUNG MALKA: I can keep up with you.

HERSHL: You can barely walk, Malka. Go home.

YOUNG MALKA: *(louder)* Everyone else in the Gruppe will be at the station. Trudi and Moishe and Yossef and Lisl and -

HERSHL: *(Whispering harshly)* Sha! Someone will hear you.

YOUNG MALKA: *(Softer)* I want to see it, too.

HERSHL: *(embracing her)* I know. And I wish you could.

YOUNG MALKA: I want our baby to see it.

HERSHL: Leibchen, if anything happened to you -

YOUNG MALKA: If anything happened to you - ... Whatever happens, Hershl, let it be to both of us.

HERSHL: And to the baby?

YOUNG MALKA: *(Giving in)* ...You'll be careful, won't you?

HERSHL: I promise.

YOUNG MALKA: Don't try to be a hero.

HERSHL: I'm trying to be a father.

(kisses her gently)

Now, go home.

YOUNG MALKA: You'll come right back after it happens and tell me about it.

HERSHL: Of course.

YOUNG MALKA: If I'm sleeping, wake me up.

HERSHL: I will. Now, go home.

He kisses her again, and hurries off, stage left. Malka watches for a moment then turns stage right to exit - and stops, hearing the CLOMPING approach of boots. She freezes. Looks back for Hershl. He's gone. She starts to run - and is face to face with two SS men.

SS 1: So, Fraulein. Where are you going in such a big hurry?

YOUNG MALKA: I -... I - ...I'm trying to get a taxi. To take me to the hospital.

SS 2: And why isn't your husband taking you?

YOUNG MALKA: He's working. He had to work late.

SS 1: Doing what?

YOUNG MALKA: His work.

SS 1: And that work is?

YOUNG MALKA: ...He works for the police. At the

Polizei Beamt.

SS 2: Why didn't you go there? To get him.

YOUNG MALKA: I was going to, but I'm already in labor -

She fakes a contraction.

Oh! Please. Help me find a taxi.

SS 2: First your passport.

YOUNG MALKA: I...I don't have it. The labor came on so suddenly -

(fakes another contraction)

Oh! It's coming. Please, let me go to the hospital.

SS 2: After we see your passport.

YOUNG MALKA: No! There's no time! It's too far away! I have to - I have to find... Oh!...a taxi.

SS 2: We will take you to the hospital. After we take you home to get your passport.

Young Malka tries to run. The SS grab her.

SS 1: *(to SS 2)* What do you think?

SS 2: Obvious. Jew.

They drag her off.

End of Scene.

LEMON DROPS

By Vivien Jones

Meelya is a fifteen year old kid in care, a talented dancer who dreams of fame for herself but more deeply, of the reconciliation of her family, shattered by the depressive illness of her mother and her parents' subsequent divorce. She has a conscientious social worker in Madge, with whom many of the central issues of the play are explored. Madge feels that Meelya needs to be real and her efforts are aimed at helping Meelya confront her new circumstances, but reality for Meelya is painful, and all her efforts are poured into various lines of escape. Her central escape is into a romantic vision of dance which possesses her entire being from time to time. Madge constantly tries to gently disentangle Meelya from this fantasy.

Developments in both parents' lives present Meelya with further difficulties. A tentative recovery of her mother which would allow her to resume partial care for Meelya's young brothers but not the difficult Meelya, cause her distress. Her father's imminent re-marriage to a woman with a daughter much like Meelya, threatens her precarious relationship with him. Meelya must decide whether reality is possible, desirable or acceptable for her.

Characters :
Amelia Delaney, always called Meelya : a fifteen year-old girl in care
Madge Davis: her social worker
Victoria: Meelya's mother
Thomas : Meelya's father

SCENE ONE : AUTUMN EVENING IN THE CITY
THE FLAT ROOF OF AN INSTITUTIONAL BUILDING. BREEZE BLOWING. TRAFFIC SOUNDS FAR BELOW. MEELYA IS ON THE PARAPET, HUMMING A TUNE FOR DANCING ('Aquarium' from Saint Sean's Carnival of Animals) A VOICE CALLS.

MADGE: Meelya ! Meelya!

*DOOR OPENS. MADGE STEPS OUT ONTO THE
ROOF.SHE IS SHIVERING.*

MADGE: There you are ! We've been looking for you
everywhere. Everyone wanted to congratulate you. Look at
you, you'll freeze up here. Shall we go and fetch your coat ?

MEELYA: I'm fine. I lost my earring.

(SCRATCHING SOUNDS.)

The lemon one that my mum gave me. Who wanted to speak
to me ? Anyone interesting ?

MADGE: Well I didn't actually spot the Hollywood
producers in the audience but I know that Charlie was well
impressed.

MEELYA: Charlie ! He's easily impressed, man, he's a
Hearts supporter. And a sad git ! Running a children's home,
what sort of job's that ? What did he say ?

MADGE: He said a bit more of that spirit and he'd take you
off report.

MEELYA: Big deal ! What did you think ? Was it what
you expected ? Did you like the music ? I got it off a tape in
the library. Saint-Saens Greatest Hits. It's called 'The
Aquarium'.

Meelya hums the tune again.

MADGE: I was surprised. I think everyone was. I knew you
love to dance and I knew you're a good dancer. I've seen
you at parties and discos but I've never seen you move like
that. Where did you learn that dance ?

MEELYA: *laughs broadly* I made it up myself. Well, I learn the steps and arms ages ago when I did ballet, when I was at home with mum, but I made the dance up myself listening to the music. I practiced at night in the kitchen at the home. It's got a lovely big floor when the chairs are up on the table. I took my wee Sony down. Wee Jerry told me heard noises in the night so I told him the home was haunted. He shat himself.

MADGE: Meelya, how come you manage to turn everything into an carry-on ? Now, seriously, you'll have to cut that out, being up at night. You'll get into more trouble. But if Charlie's going to take you off report you can go to dance classes again after school. If you go to school. Shall we go back down now ?

MEELYA: *Angry* I don't want to go to dance classes again. It's all stuck-up bitches with proper tu-tus and mummies in Range Rovers. Shit dancers ! I want to dance on my own.

MADGE: That's a bit negative. You've only been twice. *firmly* It's half-past eleven and well past your bed-time and getting to mine. I want to take you back and then go home myself. We'll speak in the morning. Come on now.

MEELYA: Can you smell anything ?

MADGE: What ?

MEELYA: Perfume. Off my mum. Last Christmas. *Shuffles in the gutter again.* I must find that earring. My mum gave them to me last time we went. She'll be upset if I've lost one. When can I see her again ? I'll need to tell her about this. It'll help, won't it ? Won't it ?

MADGE: Yes, it might help. This is useless, we'll never find it in this light. Look, I'll check it out with Charlie and get the key and I'll bring you in daylight, before school tomorrow.

MEELYA: *quickly* Oh that was a cute one. Who says I'm going to school tomorrow ?

MADGE: *caught out, embarrassed* No it was not cute ! You know perfectly well you have to go back to school sometime, and tomorrow might be a good time, on the back of this. They'll still all be talking about you, but in a good way.

MEELYA: It won't last though, will it ? And they won't all know. Alison Foster won't know and she won't care either !

MADGE: Well it's true it might take more than your dancing skills to make up for you having broken her nose. Have you apologized yet ? You did promise the meeting.

MEELYA: *wriggling* I did phone last week but her brother answered and he told me to piss off. I can't go round. He said he'd batter me if he saw me. Have you seen the size of him ? I'll do it when I see her at school....

MADGE: *quick* And how do you propose to do that without going to school ?

MEELYA: You didn't answer my question. When can I see my mum ? I need to tell her about tonight. It'll help, it will......oh, don't look at me like that, I know it was bad last time, but it wasn't my fault. I was trying to help. I thought it would help.....

MADGE: *gently* I know, but I thought I'd explained. I thought you understood. She can't cope with you talking about the past yet, especially when you romance it. They're just not nice memories for her.

MEELYA: What do you man, romance it ? It was brilliant, me and her and dad and the boys in our wee house. Going to the park, Christmas, my wee bedroom, my birthdays. I was there, I know what it was like. When dad took me to the park he used to push me on the swings high enough to see over the bar and then we played army games around the pavilion.....stalking and hiding......it was brilliant. Madge, why does it make her cry ?

MADGE: Your dad said he used to take you to the park when your mum was upset. It was the only thing that calmed her. She wasn't having the fun, Meelya.

MEELYA: But everything upset her, not only me. She was always crying. When the washing–up liquid ran out, if Dad was late home, no letters for her when the postman came....I tried to help, I did the shopping, I put the boys to bed, I made her cups of tea but she just found something else to cry about. It was like I was the mum. *suddenly flooded* Why'd such a dumb thing have to happen ?

MADGE: *making a decision* Ok. I'll try and fix a visit very soon. Now, young lady, let's get off this roof before you freeze and I fall asleep.

THEY LEAVE THE ROOF, SHUT THE DOOR, TRAFFIC SOUNDS AND FADE.

Scene Three

The meeting room of a residential institution...pale, tidy, impersonal. Madge and Meelya enter. Madge sits. Meelya inspects the room, restless, and knocks an ornament off a shelf. She looks anxiously at Madge.

MEELYA: Sorry. Didn't mean to. She picks the pieces off the floor.

MADGE: It's ok. I know you're nervous. But come and sit down. Your mum won't be long....Mrs. Blyth has gone to fetch her. Now, remember the meeting saying I have to stay? Just in case. I won't listen to what you're saying, I can sit over there and I brought a book to read.

MEELYA: I want you to stay. I was really scared last time when she broke the window. You could listen, I don't mind, you might stop me saying something to set her off. I wrote a list this morning [*she pulls the list from her* pocket] see, no happy stories, no asking for cuddles, no asking when we can get home again, no crying (that's me, not her). Ok ?

Meelya hands the list to Madge. She's reading it when the door opens and Victoria and Belle, a nursing assistant, enter. Victoria is in day clothes, her hair brushed and her face clean. She moves widely around Madge and Meelya to take a seat. Belle smiles a question at her and she nods. Belle silently shows the panic button to Madge and leaves.

MEELYA: *leaning forward, speaking as to an invalid.* Hello Mum. Nice to see you. I'm wearing the perfume you sent me at Christmas. Can you smell it ? *she offers her wrist to Victoria. Victoria doesn't respond.*

VICTORIA: *smiles, but holds onto arms of her chair* Meelya. frowns Has something happened ? Are you all right?

MEELYA: *leans further forward* Yeh, brilliant ! That's why we're here. Thought you'd like to know…I'm a star !

VICTORIA: What do you mean ? *looks to Madge, agitated* Has something happened to her ? Has she done something ?

MADGE: *shakes her head* No, Victoria, really. Let her tell you.

MEELYA: *grinning broadly* Last week at the community centre there was a show to raise money for poor kids somewhere. I did a dance, a kind of ballet dance of my own,

on my own, a solo.....and I was brilliant. Wasn't I, Madge ?
Meelya gets up and twirls round, then sits again.

MADGE: *nodding vigorously* Yes, indeed, she was. And quite beautiful.

VICTORIA: *warily* Meelya. Beautiful ?

MEELYA: Mum ! I was, I was. I had a frock made of voile, so it was light and flowy, pale, pale lemon and my hair up and primroses in my hair, and my ballet pumps and sparkle on my face.

VICTORIA: Nice. Where did you get a dress like that ?

Madge perks up to listen, Meelya mumbles something incomprehensible. Hurries on.

MEELYA: But it was the dance that was brilliant. I chose the music and made it up myself... at night...... in the home. Remember my dance classes when I was wee....you took me to Madame Gilbert's in the High Street, you and dad.......?

Madge clears her throat loudly. Meelya looks over at her in alarm. Victoria looks panicky.

MEELYA: Doesn't matter....I just made the dance up. Is there a tape recorder in here?

She gets and looks inside a very old-fashioned radiogram unit

I brought the tape. I could do it for you. It's real classical music, the stuff you like. Everyone clapped for ages.........

VICTORIA: *still wary* I don't listen to music..........I might be leaving here.

Meelya freezes, quite still.

MEELYA: What ? She moves closer to Victoria. *Madge listens closely.*

VICTORIA: There's another place. I could have a flat. I could have the boys sometimes. Maybe.

MADGE: *looking at Meelya's suddenly glowing face. Very firmly* That'll be something for the future, Victoria. It's not in your care plan.

VICTORIA: *sulkily* Yes it is ! I talked with Dr. James and Belle and Mr. Ames this morning. Yes it is !

MEELYA: And me, mum, and me, mummy.

VICTORIA: *looking away* No.

Meelya gasps, throws a drowning look to Madge. Madge crosses to her.

MADGE: This isn't the right time to be speaking about this. Meelya, they won't have decided anything without letting us know. Victoria, it's best not to speak about this right now, not in front of Meelya.

VICTORIA: *coldly* Why not ? She knows why I'm here. She knows how I got here. She knows why her dad left.

MEELYA: *deeply stung* It wasn't my fault ! Madge, tell her ! She can't say that.

VICTORIA: Ring for Belle. I want to go in the garden.

MADGE: *ringing bell, speaking to Meelya.* I want you to stay as calm as you can. Your mum's upset and it's certainly not your fault. Have you got that, Meelya, emphatically it's not your fault. *Victoria slumps in chair. Meelya hangs onto Madge's arm.* Your mum is ill, Meelya, just like we talked about before. Understand ?

MEELYA: *completely deflated* Yes.

Belle returns, takes one look at Victoria, and takes her out of the room. Madge enfolds Meelya in her arms. Still holding the list in her hand she drops it.

MADGE: You can cry now, pet.

Scene Six

Back on the roof of the community centre. Meelya sits as before but dressed in jeans and sweat-shirt, hair pulled back harshly from her face. The door opens and Madge comes out on the roof, bagless. Madge is breathless.

MADGE: *visibly calms herself, not immediately successful.* Thought you might be here. Favourite spot is it ?

MEELYA: Just wanted to think. I never found that earring, you know.

MADGE: I'll just need to phone the home, *she takes out her mobile* tell them I've found you. *Madge moves the mobile about at arm's length.* I'll need to go over there for a signal. Back in a minute.

Madge moves out of hearing. Meelya gets up and does a half-hearted dance. She sits again when she hears Madge returning.

MADGE: It's cold up here. How about we go downstairs for a hot chocolate while we wait for Charlie ? He says he'll come as soon as the Transit's free.

Meelya smiles

MEELYA: Who was that woman the other night ? The one who came with you ?

MADGE: Just a friend. Helen.

MEELYA: She didn't stay long. Was she watching me dance ?

MADGE: Yes, she thought you were lovely. Maybe, next year the Council budget will stand you some dancing lessons at her school.

MEELYA: Not this year ?

MADGE: No, sorry.

MEELYA: Next year's a long time. Do I have to be good ?

MADGE: 'Fraid so.

MEELYA: Of course......Can you smell anything ?

MADGE: *sniffs deeply* Only you and the ciggie you put out five minutes ago. Now then, how long are you going to stay up here this time ?

MEELYA: *dreamily* Forever. Just me and you, Madge. *suddenly sharply* Madge, Do you ever feel you're invisible ?

MADGE: *looks ruefully at her large frame* Not much chance of that, would you say ?

MEELYA: No, really. I wanted to know because I do. Feel invisible.

MADGE: How ?

MEELYA: I know I'm here. I'm always here but, sometimes, no-one else knows it. I say things. I ask for things. I bug people. I know I do. I came up here so you would come for me, and you came. Then I'm visible again. That's why I would like it to be forever.

MADGE: You'll soon get bored with just me.

MEELYA: Well I don't have anyone else, do I ? My brothers are miles away, my mums in a nut-house and my dad's in Sierra Leone. In Sierra Leone, but not a-lone. He sent me a letter. He's getting married.

MADGE: When did this happen ?

MEELYA: It was waiting for me when I got back from seeing mum.

MEELYA: *she takes out a letter which she reads stiffly to Madge.* "Dear Amelia, (that's me) this is to inform you that I have met a fine woman out here and we are going to be married. Her name is June and she, like me, is a divorcee. She has a daughter about your age and guess what – she's a brilliant dancer too. Perhaps one day you could dance a duet. There's a beautiful park near June's home with a bandstand for such purposes. I hope all goes well with you and that you are being good. I enclose a small gift. Please spend it carefully, from your loving father." He sent a fiver.

MADGE: *letting out air* Well, that might be very nice......
some time. We could certainly look at the possibility of a visit

MEELYA: I was thinking. Apart from you, there's no-one in charge of me. My Gran's too old, my mum can't, my dad won't. And you do it because it's your job...no. no, don't interrupt, I know you sort of like me as well. But I can't risk loving you because you could be moved on anytime. I could lose you as well. Isn't that true? If they knew we were close, they'd move you ? *Madge shrugs* Ah well, better confess, you know that dress, the one I danced in, well it was my bedroom curtains...the ones I made you buy when we did my room at the home....I just tied them together and put a ribbon round the waist......Alma never noticed. I had them back up the next morning.

Pause, then serious again. So I thought I should make the decisions about myself. So I have. Can you smell anything?

MADGE: *sniffing* Like what ?

MEELYA: Like the bonfire I lit downstairs.

MADGE: *immediate alarm, looks around, looks over the edge, back at the door, sniffing hard now.* Meelya, this isn't funny. I can't smell anything but if you've done that, you'd better say and I'll...well, I'll ring 999 and *she drops her mobile and fumbles for it......*oh, you silly girl !

MEELYA: Yes, that's about it. Story of my life. Silly girl. She looks over at the frightened Madge. Stop fussing, Madge, I wouldn't do that to you. There isn't any bonfire. What is it they said on my report " attention seeking"? Just a bit of attention seeking.

MADGE: Ok. What now then? You have my attention.

MEELYA: You know what now. Another meeting. Another bunch of people understanding why I get into bother. Another sanction. Another care plan. How come I end up here each time? Oh, Madge, I'm so tired of trying to stay visible. I'm fifteen and I feel about a hundred and fifty. Why is life so shit?

MADGE: Hey, funny-face. Remember that daft game we used to play? From that song on the old record ? Count your blessings? That always helps.

MEELYA: And another trouble shared ? One day at a time? Every cloud has a silver lining ? *Wearily* Oh Madge, save it for the dumb kids.

I've had enough.

She leans outward, brushing a curve in the air with her arm. The curve deepens and gets faster. Madge moves closer. Meelya turns quickly to look at her, stops moving. Madge freezes.

No....that's not right.

Meelya begins the movement again, looking down far below, dipping her body with the curve.

I can't get enough.

Madge makes a pleading gesture. Meelya looks at her again. She re-energizes the movement which starts her whole body rolling, close to the edge.

MEELYA: *shouts.* Because there isn't enough.

MADGE: *dry-throated, moving in tiny, slow movements towards Meelya.* Meelya. You're going to have an accident if you don't stop that. Please stop it. Now.

MEELYA: *continuing to roll, enjoying the rhythm.*

Did you know I can sing as well ?

She sings rawly.

"Rock a bye baby

On the roof-top

When Meelya rolls,

The penny will drop"

She looks back at Madge.

MEELYA: Are you going to catch me, Madge? Better run, there's five flights of stairs. That'll do your ankles in. See you at the bottom, then.

She swings her legs round to sit over the drop, looking down.

MADGE: Meelya ! For Christ's sake ! *she lurches forward, still short of Meelya*

MEELYA: Well, catch me then ! *she leans further out, no longer quite in control of her balance.*

Wow…this is a new one.

Bit like dancing.

Bit like flying.

Catch me Madge !

Meelya gracefully moves her body forward, past her balancing point, looks back at the frozen Madge, and lets go. She rolls off the roof, silently.

Lights down

End of Scene.

THE REFRACTION OF LIGHT

By JEAN KLEIN

Joe Taylor, an African-American WWII Vet
Nettie French, his girlfriend
Rose Beauchamp, an older white woman who has been Joe's mentor

Time: 1940's

JOE: I got that GI bill and all and I just figured out what I want to do with it. A lump sum of money to put down . . . .

NETTIE: Oh, Joe! A house! Joe? *(beat)* You talking about this house?

JOE: Only one I'd think of buying in this town. At least for you . .

NETTIE: Oh, Joe, I don't believe it! You and me . . . But . . . But this house — I don't think we'd be welcome.

JOE: Things are changing, Nettie. They have to. This war changed a lot—

NETTIE: Don't see that many changes in Berkley. You see them?

JOE: Maybe not too many. Not yet. But I got some cousins just moved over on Whitehead Street. Nobody said nothing about that.

NETTIE: "Anything"

JOE: Now, don't you go getting uppity on me. Just because I'm buying you a new house and marrying you and all . . .

NETTIE: I was afraid you were going to leave that out. The marrying part. *(beat)* I got to be uppity if you want me to live in this house. *(beat)* I don't know, Joe. You don't know how much I just want to say "yes" and be happy—

JOE: Then do it! Things are just waiting to happen, Nettie. More and more people like us come back. Carrying medals from the war—

NETTIE: And then some man makes you step off the sidewalk so he doesn't have to walk around you? What you think then?

JOE: I learned in this house I was just as good as anybody else. Stepping off the sidewalk today doesn't mean I'm gonna step off tomorrow. I think one day that man's gonna see me different. Like when I own this house!

NETTIE: *(Shaking her head)* They're gonna see you and a house that they think you don't belong in.

JOE: If anybody belongs here, we do. We spent half our lives growing up in this house. I learned about the Straits of Magellan there. And how I was going to cross them one day. And that window? That was more than light bending in a prism. This is it, Nettie!

NETTIE: Oh, Joe, I hope you're right. This isn't just for you, you know.

JOE: I know. I'm making a stand for all of us. Even for Harry. I never saw the camps. But I saw some refugees. They'd just gotten off a train. Don't ask, Nettie. Don't ask. All of those people. So thin. Secrets in their faces they'd never be able to tell. *(beat)* I don't want to think about that! It's about us, now, Nettie. You and me. Okay. I told you my secret. It's your turn, now.

NETTIE: Things just don't work out that easy for me. I was the last child, brought into a tough world. You wouldn't want to bring a child into a tough world, would you, Joe? You'd want things nice. Easy. You've got a big laugh. Like my dad. That's what you'd want a child to hear. Every day.

JOE: Hey, we got time for that. Take one thing at a time. I get us a house. We get married... you let me take care of you.

NETTIE: That's the last thing I remember my dad saying to me. The next day, we put his body on the train to go home to Georgia.

JOE: You hear any whistles? See any tracks? Okay, then,

(We hear the sound of the teapot whistling. NETTIE looks at JOE.)

JOE: That's a teapot, Nettie.

NETTIE: Maybe to you.

(ROSE enters with the tea tray and puts it on the desk.)

ROSE: I made us some tea. Sit down, Joe. Those old timbers can wait for a while. I wanted to show you something I saw this morning in the paper.

(ROSE hands him the newspaper. He takes it and looks through it.)

ROSE: It's right there on page four. You can see what it says. It talks about all the boys who came back to Berkley from the war. What they've been doing.

JOE: Funny nobody asked me what I've been up to.

ROSE: I guess they couldn't ask everyone. And I never

gave you a proper celebration when you got back. *(To JOE)* You stayed so busy! All those newspaper articles and everything. And some of them even mentioned you.

JOE: In the Journal and Guide.

ROSE: In the white paper, too, not as many times, but... *(She puts the cups out on the desk.)* I thought we could have this right here. Around my desk. Where we used to do our times tables.

(She draws up chairs. JOE and ROSE sit. ROSE motions to NETTIE.)

ROSE: You, too, Nettie. I brought three cups. I made your favorite tea cakes this morning. You haven't been eating right lately and I thought you might be able to eat these.

NETTIE: *(Looks at cakes.)* Thank you. Really. It's just . . . Sometimes the thought of food . . . . Let me clear this tray away.

(She quickly clears away the tray and exits to the kitchen.)

ROSE: I swear, I can't get that child to sit down for a minute. Thinks about everybody but herself. You treat her right when you get married.

JOE: You know about that?

ROSE: Anybody who looks at the two of you knows about that.

JOE: I want to make a good life for her.

ROSE: She deserves it, if anyone does. And you can do it. I can still remember you sitting at this table with the afternoon sun streaming in. And now you've been to Italy. You've never said much about that. Did you get to Florence? To Rome? Did you see the Sistine Chapel?

JOE: Miss Rose, I went to a lot of places in Italy. Problem was, I always had a gun or grenade in my hands. No one offered me a guided tour.

ROSE: Of course. Your Italy and mine must be two different places.

JOE: Must be. Not this room, though. This is always the same place. Whether I'm sitting here or imagining it.

ROSE: We had the light coming through that window to track the progress of the afternoon.

JOE: Making triangles and circles on the desk. Like it's doing now.

ROSE: While we talked about what you were going to do when you grew up? How you were going to change the world.

JOE: So far, it always ends up changing me.

ROSE: There are lots of opportunities out there for young men coming out of the service.

JOE: I was just talking to Nettie about some ideas I had.

ROSE: About Nettie. I don't mean to speak out of turn...

JOE: Don't you worry about her. I'm not leading her on. Miss Rose.

ROSE: I'm glad to hear that. I know young men like you mean well, but . . .

JOE: I have it all figured out. I'm going to marry Nettie . . .

ROSE: That's what I'm afraid of. I hope you're not forgetting about college... You have a mind! A capital M mind that buzzes like blue lightning! You take to ideas like a frog takes to flies.

JOE: To most people, no matter how I croak, I'll still be a frog.

ROSE: Not the way you've learned to speak. Why, I've heard you sound like Winston Churchill when you get going. You'd make a good lawyer, Joe. You could always get me to believe up was down.

JOE: I'll go back to school, I mean, part time with my GI Bill. If I stay here in Berkley, I can afford to do all that.

ROSE: But Virginia State's not going to be opening a campus here for at least a couple of years. You don't want to lose it, Joe. The momentum. The energy.

JOE: But timing's important. I learned that in the trenches. Your head has to pop out of the foxhole just after you hear the whine of the bullets. Sometimes, you just got to grab a moment or you lose it forever. *(beat)* The war got me thinking about how life could change in a single instant. I reached over to tie my boot. A bullet whizzed over my head. A single decision meant life or death. And we're always dodging bullets whether we ever see them or not. *(beat)* I want to buy this house.

ROSE: This house . . .

(JOE crosses and gets the sign.)

JOE: You're selling it, aren't you?

ROSE: Well, I hadn't . . . that is, not really . . .

JOE: You told me the other day that it'd gotten too much for you.

ROSE: But I still manage . . .

JOE: You ask me to change the light bulbs in the ceiling.

ROSE: I just wanted to see—

JOE: To see what?

ROSE: How it felt—

JOE: How what felt?

ROSE: Selling the house. Leaving it behind. I'm just putting out some queries to help me make up my mind. I may not sell for a long time.

JOE: I can wait.

ROSE: No, Joe, don't wait. Find a school, a good one. Then come back . . .

JOE: Just what do you see me doing with this college degree you seem so hot on me getting?

ROSE: Well, I really didn't think that far ahead—

JOE: Miss Rose, you've always been thinking three steps ahead of anyone else I know.

ROSE: Joe, don't wait. Just find a good school. Get what's coming to you. Then come back.

JOE: You'll sell me the house then?

ROSE: Why, I might not even be alive!

JOE: That's not what I asked. Would you sell me the house then?

ROSE: By that time, you probably wouldn't even want an old house. With your degree and all. Who knows where you'll want to go once you have that piece of paper in your hand.

JOE: And what if I still want to be here?

(They look at one another. Pause.)

That's what I thought.

ROSE: It's not that—

JOE: Of course not.

ROSE: It just never crossed my mind that you—

JOE: I can see how it wouldn't.

ROSE: I never thought about—

JOE: Well, I have. I thought once I had that piece of paper in my hand, everyone would look at me differently. You made me believe that.

ROSE: And it's true!

JOE: It's not even true for you, Miss Beauchamp. Teaching and preaching. That's about what's out there for me, don't you think.

ROSE: Those are honorable professions—

JOE: I study, work hard, and graduate. What do you and everybody else see? A colored man with a piece of paper in his hands. If I'm lucky and work real hard, maybe I can get to be head porter on the Southern and Western Railroad.. Oh, wait a minute. If I've got a degree, I don't need to be a porter. I could probably get a job in the circus. "Step right up, ladies and gentlemen. For just one thin dime, you can see the colored man recite from memory. He adds. He subtracts. He makes change for a ten dollar bill!"

ROSE: The Joe Taylor I used to know wouldn't have talked like that

JOE: The Joe Taylor you knew is missing in action. That Joe Taylor didn't try to buy a house from you. When you get right down to it, you're not much different than the rest of them. I tried to buy my nephew a little paddle ball down at the five and dime the other day. Stood there 'til every white man in the place got what he wanted. Had to step off the sidewalk so three white teenage boys could walk through. I want to live in this house. Miss Rose. I want you to tell me I'm good enough to live in it.

ROSE: You are.

JOE: Then let me buy it. Let me own all the memories I have here. Bring my own into it. Bring the memories of my mother cleaning that window. Let them live here. With me and Nettie. Let us be part of this history.

ROSE: But you're part of it already...

JOE: Not until we own a piece. I want our pictures on the front pages of some of those scrapbooks, my babies sitting in front of that window. I can make the down payment by the end of the week. Is that soon enough for you?

ROSE: I'm just not ready!

JOE: For what?

ROSE: For you, Joe. For the man who came back from Europe. Walking differently. And talking differently. And you're not the only one. Young Negro girls walking down the sidewalk bumping right into me, as if I weren't there or didn't count. Sometimes I think they snicker at me behind their backs. And no one wears gloves any more. I never went to town without my gloves.

JOE: From where I sit, Miss Beauchamp, some changes were needed.

ROSE: But think of it. Other feet walking on these floors when mine are gone. New furniture in here? A Frigidaire in place of my icebox? I'm not selling to anyone! I'll die in this house like my husband did. But there won't be anyone to find me. Let me rot here just like everything else. There are houses for sale all over Berkley! Nicer houses.

JOE: Closer to the color line.

ROSE: Yes! You might be up to facing people down in the street, but Nettie isn't.

JOE: You look at me and tell me the only reason you don't want me in this house is because of Nettie. *(pause)* Can you tell me you don't shudder at the idea of my big feet moving into your sitting room? My dark babies crying in the night? Can you tell me none of that bothers you? Have you washed every spoon I've used twice? No, don't even answer that. I always counted on you for the truth. You were like a compass. A moral magnetic north. And now I have no idea which direction you're pointing. There's nothing here for me in Berkley. Goodbye, Miz Beauchamp.

ROSE: Please. Don't go. I'm very ashamed. I'll say it. What about Nettie?

JOE: She can come with me. We'll manage somehow. We'll both work . . . .

ROSE: Then buy the house. I want you here, you, and Nettie.

JOE: You want to sell, sell to Harry. Give him his wedding and take back the mortgage.

ROSE: I want you playing magic lanterns under the window in the afternoon sun. I don't want strangers here, reading your books, standing in your sun.

JOE: A long time ago, I would have believed you but the sun doesn't belong to people like me. I once almost got blown up by a sniper who walked right up to me with a smile on his face. I learned to look behind smiles.

(NETTIE enters with a tea towel in her hands.)

NETTIE: What's the matter? Why are you shouting?

JOE: There's nothing wrong here. What could be wrong in this house? We grew up here. We're just like family, at least almost.

ROSE: *(To Nettie)* I just wasn't ready. . .I didn't expect ... Oh, Nettie, talk to him. I'm sorry and he won't believe me.

NETTIE: Sorry about what?

ROSE: Joe asked . . .he asked . . .and I. . .Oh, tell him I know I was wrong, but I just can't . . .couldn't . . . *(She collapses in tears and exits.)*

End of Scene.

ANOTHER PARADISE

By Donna Spector

CHARACTERS
BIRDIE MAE: Early 60's, She speaks with a thick,
uneducated, back-woods Kentucky accent.
NEVA: 15, daughter of BIRDIE MAE, her accent is slightly
more refined

SETTING
Paradise, Kentucky, 1916

SYNOPSIS
Set in Paradise, Kentucky, ANOTHER PARADISE is a
memory play narrated by two women, Birdie Mae Tyler and
her daughter Neva, both on a journey of self-discovery. The
play's action, called forth by these women's narratives, runs
from Birdie Mae's marriage in 1903 to Hiram Tyler until
Neva's marriage in 1924 to Aaron Greenberg.
Although the events which Birdie Mae and Neva describe
are the same, their points-of-view throughout the play are
conflicting. Birdie Mae tells a simple, honest story of her
difficult marriage and family life in backwoods Kentucky.
Neva, a would-be writer and early feminist who is ashamed
of her background, embroiders her story, making it into
"elegant literature."

BIRDIE MAE: *(To audience.)*

One day Neva come home in a tatty ol' dress, cryin' an'
cryin'. She curled up on her bed under the covers an'
wouldn't talk to no one.

(Moves to bed, sits on edge. To NEVA, gently.)

What's the matter, honey?

NEVA: Nothing.

BIRDIE MAE: Somethin's the matter.

NEVA: No.

BIRDIE MAE: Why you hidin' under them covers?

NEVA: I don't feel so good.

BIRDIE MAE: I'm sorry, honey. Lemme boil you up some tea.

NEVA: No.

BIRDIE MAE: A little warm milk an' molasses?

NEVA: No. *(Whimpers.)* Ma?

BIRDIE MAE: Yes?

NEVA: *(A tiny voice.)*

Ma, will you give my pink dress to Alvira?

BIRDIE MAE: What fer, chile?

NEVA: She always liked it.

BIRDIE MAE: But it still fits. An' looks real good on you.

NEVA: And give my books to Percy?

BIRDIE MAE: But you ain't finished with 'em.

NEVA: And, Ma... bury me under a white rose bush.

BIRDIE MAE: Bury you?

NEVA: I'm dying!

BIRDIE MAE: Dyin'? What you dyin' of?

NEVA: Oh...

BIRDIE MAE: *(Feeling NEVA's forehead.)* You ain't got a fever. You got pains?

NEVA: Yes.

BIRDIE MAE: Where yer pains?

NEVA: In... in my stomach.

BIRDIE MAE: Food poisonin'? You got food poisonin', Neva? You eat somethin' to school made you sick?

NEVA: No.

BIRDIE MAE: Mebbe you got a little flu.

NEVA: It's worse than flu.

BIRDIE MAE: I better send Ben fer the doctor.

NEVA: Don't get the doctor!

BIRDIE MAE: I ain't lettin' you die.

NEVA: I won't let him see me.

BIRDIE MAE: It's jes' ol' Doc Wilkins.

NEVA: He can't come in here!

BIRDIE MAE: Is there somethin' else wrong you ain't tellin' me?

NEVA: *(Pulls covers over her head.)*

Go 'way, Ma. Don't talk about it.

BIRDIE MAE: Lemme see.

NEVA: Don't touch me!

BIRDIE MAE: Neva!

NEVA: I'm bleeding!

BIRDIE MAE: Bleedin'? Where?

(No response.)

You got a bad cut?

(Silence.)

You fall down an' hurt yerself?

NEVA: *(Rocking back and forth under covers.)* No, no, no...

BIRDIE MAE: You gotta lemme see.

(Gently loosens NEVA's hands and pulls back covers. NEVA turns away.)

What you doin' in that ol' dress? Where's yer white silk skirt?

NEVA: Oh, Ma... I buried it. Over at Annie's house.

BIRDIE MAE: Why'd you do a thing like that fer?

NEVA: *(Sobbing.)* It had blood all over it, Ma. And I loved it so.

BIRDIE MAE: *(Beat.)* Honey. Yer jes' havin' women's bleedin'. It's a most natural thing.

NEVA: What do you mean?

BIRDIE MAE: Look at me. Lift up the pillow.

(NEVA does. BIRDIE MAE wipes her tears with the bedclothes.)

Women all bleed when they grow up.

NEVA: *(Shocked.)* They do?

BIRDIE MAE: Uh-huh.

NEVA: *(Whispers.)* Why?

BIRDIE MAE: Well... it's how the Lord punishes women fer eatin' the apple, like it says in the Good Book. Ain't nothin' to worry about.

NEVA: *(Sits up, very angry.)* Damnit, Ma, you should've told me!

BIRDIE MAE: Neva! I ain't never in all a my life heard a gal say "damnit"!

NEVA: Damnit, damnit, damnit!

BIRDIE MAE: You ask the Lord to fergive you fer them bad words to yer pore ol' ma.

NEVA: Damnit!

BIRDIE MAE: Gal, yer teeterin' on the edge a damnation!

NEVA: I don't care! If the Lord's going to make me bleed all the time for something I didn't even do, then I hate him!

BIRDIE MAE: *(Drops to her knees.)* She don't mean it, Lord. Fergive 'er. Fergive my baby.

NEVA: Ma! Get up off your knees and talk to me!

BIRDIE MAE: She ain't feelin' right, Lord. It's 'er time. Please fergive 'er.

NEVA: Ma! Quit that!

(She melodramatically falls halfway off the bed.)

BIRDIE MAE: *(Takes NEVA in her arms.)* Now, honey, you jes' calm down.

NEVA: No!

BIRDIE MAE: *(Rocking her gently.)* Rest yerself.

NEVA: No.

BIRDIE MAE: The Lord fergives you.

NEVA: NO!

BIRDIE MAE: You ain't gonna bleed all the time. Jes' once a month.

NEVA: *(Sits up, looks at BIRDIE MAE.)* Once a month?

BIRDIE MAE: When it's yer time. That's the way it is with women.

NEVA: Not with Annie or Bessie. They would've said.

BIRDIE MAE: Mebbe it ain't their time yit.

NEVA: Ma, why didn't you tell me?

BIRDIE MAE: I guess I didn't think 'bout it.

NEVA: You should've.

BIRDIE MAE: I figgered to tell when it happened.

NEVA: That's too late. You better tell Alvira right now. And poor Sal Henry.

BIRDIE MAE: I'm sorry, honey.

NEVA: Men don't bleed?

BIRDIE MAE: No.

NEVA: Why not?

BIRDIE MAE: It's a special burden the Lord give to women.

NEVA: That's awful.

BIRDIE MAE: You grit yer teeth an' bear it a few days each month.

NEVA: And the pains always come too?

BIRDIE MAE: Most always.

NEVA: Seems to me the Lord hates women.

BIRDIE MAE: He don't. Ain't His fault Eve sinned. He give 'er a chance.

NEVA: Oh, that's nonsense.

BIRDIE MAE: You doubtin' the gospel?

NEVA: I didn't sin!

BIRDIE MAE: We all sinned, honey. Ain't jes' you.

NEVA: I don't believe it! We didn't all sin!

BIRDIE MAE: It's the Holy Word.

NEVA: We're no worse than men.

BIRDIE MAE: *(A final and perfect justification.)*

But men cain't have children.

NEVA: So?

BIRDIE MAE: Bleedin's a part a havin' children, the first part. You gotta start in bleedin' 'fore you can have babies.

NEVA: That's disgusting! I won't bleed any more, and I won't have children, either! And you can tell the Lord next time you're having one of your little talks!

(Runs off stage.)

End of Scene.

THE TEMPLE OF THE SOUL

By Rebecca Nesvet

Characters:
DOCTOR Portuguese Jewish refugee. Personal physician to
Queen Elizabeth I.
SARA An English-born Jewish woman. The Doctor's wife.

Place/Time:
London, circa 1590: the era of Shakespeare.
(The DOCTOR'S home, night. SARA, the DOCTOR's wife, is
packing a travel trunk. She folds a heavy black coat in a
boy's size.)

SARA: So that is it. Our son.

DOCTOR: He is only going to school.

SARA: But why must he go to Winchester? London has
schools.

DOCTOR: Winchester is different, Sara. The Queen herself
suggested it.

SARA: She hasn't been to school.

DOCTOR: Of course she hasn't. Ambrose will go in as the
son of "Doctor Lopez", but come out as a Winchester Man.
He will find that useful.

SARA: And so will you?

DOCTOR: So will we, yes. He won't need that coat.

SARA: For winter.

DOCTOR: In the south, Sara, the climate is different.

SARA: It's very far, then.

DOCTOR: Nonsense.

SARA: Far enough to have a different climate.

DOCTOR: When I went to Salamanca, Sara, that was a different climate. Another country. When I arrived, I knew five words of Spanish. "Yes", "No", and "Christ save you." Our Ambrose will have a much easier time of it.

SARA: His sisters will miss him.

DOCTOR: Tell them, he'll be home at Hilary.

SARA: That won't help any.

DOCTOR: Then they must learn patience. It's a virtue.

SARA: They don't know what it is.

DOCTOR: Patience?

SARA: The Feast of Saint Hilary.

DOCTOR: Still?

SARA: I haven't had a reason to tell them.

DOCTOR: Sara, they were born in a Christian country. So were you.

SARA: Not in a Christian house.

DOCTOR: There is a world, Sara, beyond this house, and this neighbourhood.

SARA: I know. In it, we are still Jews.

DOCTOR: Of course, but we are also English.

SARA: The English are Christians.

DOCTOR: Sara, I am an English denizen, you are a native-born subject, and the children are ours, not wards of the state. Does Ambrose know what Easter is?

SARA: Maybe.

DOCTOR: You haven't discussed it?

SARA: No.

DOCTOR: The Lord's Prayer.

SARA: Of course he knows that. They all do.

DOCTOR: Does he know what the words mean? "Thy kingdom come?"

SARA: I don't think so, no.

DOCTOR: I see. Why doesn't he?

SARA: Because it's wrong.

DOCTOR: The Lord's prayer?

SARA: The kingdom to come. There's no Rabbi will tell you how to get there, the way the ministers and priests do. You haven't forgotten?

DOCTOR: No.

SARA: My father worries that the children will. If we tell them about saints and festivals, and they get… mixed up… my father would die. Or kill me.

DOCTOR: I'm sure he won't.

SARA: You're right. He wouldn't kill me. He would kill you.

DOCTOR: Don't even say that, Sara. It's not amusing.

SARA: My father says, don't tell them two stories that don't agree, or they'll get confused. They'll forget how the world really is.

DOCTOR: I see, Sara. Your father knows "how the world is," and I am confused.

SARA: You don't know which world to live in.

DOCTOR: There's only one. Some people—the Grand Inquisitor, the King of Spain, and your father wish us to persuade us otherwise. I won't let them limit our son's chances.

SARA: They run everything.

DOCTOR: Now they do, Sara, but I promise you, they won't for long.

SARA: The Messiah will come?

DOCTOR: No, Sara. The anatomists will, and the navigators, and the astronomers. They're finding that the earthly questions are important, because, when we solve them, we find solutions to grander mysteries. When the average man and woman are as familiar with the workings of their bodies, the extent of the seas, and the motions of the stars as they are with the design of a water-wheel or the floor plan of their parish church, then the petty distinctions will crumble away, like the walls of Jericho before Joshua's musicians.

SARA: Petty distinctions?

DOCTOR: Precisely. But in the meantime, we must teach the children some false superstitions it is useful for them to know, and dangerous not to.

SARA: But there's no need. In this country, we are safe.

DOCTOR: That, Sara, is what my father said about Portugal. I was wise enough not to believe him. In the morning, speak with all the children. Before Ambrose goes.

SARA: You can tonight.

DOCTOR: No, I can't.

SARA: Why?

DOCTOR: Duty calls.

SARA: A patient.

DOCTOR: The Queen.

SARA: I hope she's not ill.

DOCTOR: No. Thank Heaven. There are some things she requires me to explain to her. She likes to learn about things she doesn't know.

End of Scene.

NORA

By Inkeri Kilipinen

CHARACTERS
Husband
Wife
Nora
(all about 40 years old)
A Boy's Voice
Custodian's Voice
Radio Voice

(January to April in the 1980's)

SCENE FIVE
(A March evening in Nora's apartment. She is wearing a light robe. Husband is dressed casually. Music from the preceding scene gradually fades away)

NORA: Every morning the sun rises a minute earlier. Wonderful, even if it is still winter! How can March be so frigid?

HUSBAND: We've known each other for two months, the only two months I've been actually alive.

NORA: Yes, I do call that living! Do you remember the Greek epic where the heroes not only eat and sleep and wake but relish their dreams, revel in the fresh spring water, marvel at the mountains? Well, I want to experience everything at a fever pitch. I always did work too much.

HUSBAND: For what?

NORA: For my goals and for my mother. Yes, for her. I wanted to fulfill her hopes, make my accomplishments match the ambitions she had for me.

HUSBAND: Do you really have to go away tomorrow?

NORA: Yes. I must attend a conference and several company meetings, plus I also promised to attend a friend's award banquet.

HUSBAND: You sure do have lots of friends!

NORA: Yes, I know many people.

HUSBAND: Nobody ever visits … at our home, I mean.

NORA: Why not?

HUSBAND: Never seemed to get into the habit. What with your career and your friends, there's no way I'll fit in.

NORA: Oh, but you will! Actually, most of my so-called whirlwind existence is merely a substitute for love. Love is the most important element of living.

HUSBAND: Not everyone finds love.

NORA: True. When I was young, the other girls were busy living while I was busy getting ahead. They cheered and chatted while I took exams. The professors nodded their heads at me and said, "Bright girl." Then one girl after another got married, some by chance and some by design, but the bright girl always kept to herself.

HUSBAND: Didn't you even want to get married?

NORA: Not really. Or…to tell the truth, I did dream of some man who would seize me by the hair and drag me off to his cave. Most girls studied how to trap men while I dreamed of how a man might trap me – a great bear of a man.

HUSBAND: Club in hand! Grrr! (pretending to be a caveman) Grrr! *(a wild embrace)* Here I am. Name, Kontio The Bear!

NORA: *(in mock fright)* A beastly bruin! Help! What do you do with your grizzly paws?

HUSBAND: Pounce on runaway Noras.

NORA: Did you pounce on your wife, too?

HUSBAND: *(brief pause)* No, she's the one who snared me, but these days she endlessly accuses me of being involved with other women.

NORA: Where are you supposed to be right now?

HUSBAND: On overtime.

NORA: What if she telephones your office?

HUSBAND: The company PBX is shut down. There's no direct line.

NORA: Could she have followed you?

HUSBAND: No.

NORA: Then we can feel secure?

HUSBAND: Yes.

NORA: Absolutely?

HUSBAND: Yes.

NORA: But what if she has...

HUSBAND: She hasn't.

NORA: May I pour you a drink?

HUSBAND: No thanks. I don't want to miss a thing while we're together, certainly not a thing due to mere alcohol.

NORA: I agree. How did you two get together?

HUSBAND: Through my youthful ignorance and stupidity. During my first semester I drank too much. Then my friend Olli, the one who runs the factory now ...

NORA: The blond fellow?

HUSBAND: Yes, Olli, the one who climbed the company ladder via the bedroom and got to be the boss. When we were still just students, he invited me to his May Day party, and that's where it happened. Stopped my studies. Then Oli got me my job at the plant, so it turned out I didn't need a degree.

NORA: Did you first meet your wife at the party?

HUSBAND: Yeah, sure.

NORA: And the two of you hopped right into bed?

HUSBAND: Well, onto the sofa. A trap well baited!

NORA: And so she fell into a good marriage?

HUSBAND: And I fell into a lifelong cage. Company housing and the boys. Lord knows, there's nowhere else for me to go now.

NORA: *(pause)* Tell me a little about the boys.

HUSBAND: Great kids. Younger one's a chip off the old block, sharp as a tack. The older one's blond, dilatory in school. He was a preemie, maybe that's why. Favors his mother's features.

NORA: What does your wife want out of life?

HUSBAND: Who knows? I've no idea of what'd become of her without me.

NORA: What does she do?

HUSBAND: She starts! First she starts one thing and then another! She starts writing, she starts studying, she starts singing, she starts painting, she starts studying languages. Now she want to start making wine at home. She starts, starts, and starts but never finishes anything.

NORA: I see.

HUSBAND: Now, for the very first time, it's my turn to start something, namely, my life. *(brief pause)* I won't give you up, Nora. We've got to think of something.

NORA: What do you have in mind?

HUSBAND: Not much, but the two of us ought to be smart enough to figure something out.

NORA: Just what is it that you see in me?

HUSBAND: The real question is, what do you see in me?

NORA: I see great potential. You're different from everyone else I know. Potentially you have great integrity, but it may be as dormant as your libido used to be.

HUSBAND: Can it be reawakened?

NORA: I believe so.

HUSBAND: I've been living as though I were sleepwalking. I never had the freedom of many choices but always felt pressured into making premature decisions.

NORA: I must have been sleepwalking, too. Until I met you, I could never have been a woman, a wife, a mother.

HUSBAND: But you at least had a chance to choose your career! I was planted at the factory as though I were a tree. And at home I don't know what to do, what a man's role ought to be, maybe because my mother raised me by herself after the divorce. (rising and walking agitatedly back and forth, then becoming calmer and approaching Nora) But with you I do know what to do, perhaps intuitively. But in all seriousness, Nora, do you really want children, what with all the care they need?

NORA: You have to experience genuine loneliness before you can truly appreciate the kind of happiness a man and a woman can provide each other. At that point you have to decide to pay the price. No man has ever touched me so deeply.

HUSBAND: I touch you?

NORA: Yes, profoundly.

HUSBAND: And I can prove that you touch me in a special way! You see, I've embarked on a self-improvement program. Just finished Ibsen's "Doll's House." (removing a book from his pocket) Seems to me that Ibsen's Nora was pretty foolish.

NORA: And her husband a hypocrite! Why would you consider her foolish?

HUSBAND: First, because she forged her husband's name on a loan application...

NORA: *(interrupting)* In order to get money for his medical treatment.

HUSBAND: Then she expected him to take the blame for it. *(opening the book and reading)* "A man might sacrifice his honor for his wife's sake because hundreds of thousands of women have sacrificed their honor for their husbands' sake."

NORA: But Nora was prepared to commit suicide so that her husband's innocence would eventually come out.

HUSBAND: What kind of logic is that?

NORA: A woman's logic is often a mystery to a man.

HUSBAND: Then what kind of mystery's behind her last outburst? In the final act, Nora leaves her husband and children to find herself. In her own words, "So that our life together might become a marriage."

NORA: Yes, yes!

HUSBAND: Then why did she leave by herself? And that's not all. The husband's as dense as she is. They should have left together if making a marriage was their real goal But was it, actually?

NORA: But you must admit that for thousands of years men have enjoyed privileges.

HUSBAND: What do you mean, privileges? Take my privileges for example. I work as hard as I can, then carry my paycheck home, only to hear that it isn't enough and that I'm a good-for-nothing. Is that what you mean by "privileges?" (happening to glance at his watch and slapping his forehead) Oh, Christ!

NORA: *(concerned)* What is it?

HUSBAND: I forgot!

NORA: Forgot what?

HUSBAND: Damnit! I promised the boys we'd buy a pellet gun today.

NORA: Do you have to leave immediately?

HUSBAND: No, the stores're already closed. May I use the phone?

NORA: Of course. Use the one in the kitchen.

HUSBAND: *(dialing a number)* Hi. This is Dad … Well, yes, well … had to get the job done … look, we'll go tomorrow, tomorrow afternoon … Mama's not at home? … Where? … Didn't say? … You go to bed now. Yes, I'm sure she'll be there soon. And so will I. Yes, yes. We'll talk about it tomorrow … yes, yes, tomorrow, for sure … I'll be there real soon, so you go to sleep now so's we can get this thing taken care of tomorrow. *(hanging up)* 'Bye now.

(A pregnant pause. For the first time Nora sees him in his role as a father and husband. It embarrasses her. She is also embarrassed for him to hear that his wife is not at home. He sits, face pressed into his hands)

HUSBAND: *(continuing)* Nora, give me one reason why I, Jorma Kontio, exist. And tell me what I'm striving for. What chances do I really have?

NORA: *(speaking thoughtfully while putting on a record)* Those are questions that only you can answer.

HUSBAND: What's the truth and what isn't? To be or not

to be? The other day my younger son asked me, "What did Abraham want from God, being willing to sacrifice his son Isaac?" I couldn't explain it to him. Can you?

NORA: Abraham wanted to be obedient to God, no matter what the cost.

HUSBAND: What a cruel God! Ordering a man to sacrifice his only son! And what a selfish father, being willing to do so for his own sake!

NORA: Both the Old and New Testaments are steeped in suffering and cruelty. The far-eastern religions seem much more advanced, going beyond mere suffering. Have you read Siddhartha? It contains the most beautiful description of life's fulfillment.

HUSBAND: What?

NORA: *(taking a book from the shelf and reading)* "And when Siddhartha had listened reverently to the river's thousand-voiced song and heard in it neither pain nor sorrow any longer, and when he did not cleave his soul unto any voice ..."

HUSBAND: *(interrupting)* And then?

NORA: Then, "when he did not cleave his soul to any voice nor unite it within his being but listened to all of them, he realized totality, unity. The great song of a thousand voices consists of a single word which is 'Om,' fulfillment."

HUSBAND: And what then? That's a mood, not life itself. I don't see that it solves anything.

NORA: No, it is simply one of world literature's most beautiful descriptions of peace of soul.

HUSBAND: But is that a solution for ordinary people like me who are looking for solutions?

NORA: What solutions?

HUSBAND: Answers to the problems of living. What will become of us, of the boys, of the family? I certainly can't give you up.

NORA: Sometimes you do go right to the heart of the matter! And I refuse to give you up. You have brought such joy into my life.

HUSBAND: It's hard to imagine my bringing joy to anyone.

NORA: You liberated the joy in me. I knew all along it was hiding there inside me, chained to dungeon walls. I longed for that joy like a madwoman. Tagore says that a wondrous joy is born when infinity finds finiteness. I found infinite joy in your finite embrace. I only wish I could only explain to you what that means to me!

HUSBAND: And what it means to me! But what about the others...

(The music becomes harsher. Desperate, he rises as though torn between two worlds. He embraces Nora, clinging to her as though his life depended on her. As he begins to remove her robe, the music suddenly stops and the doorbell rings stridently once, twice, three times. Someone is at the door, has heard the music, seen the light, and knows someone is at home. The faces of Nora and Husband reflect their apprehension)

End of Scene.

TIMBERWOLVES

By Christina Cigala

CAST OF CHARACTERS
TED, a young gay man in his 20s. He has recently moved to
New York with his best friend, T-Anne. They live in TAnne's
grandfather, JACK'S, house in Brooklyn.
MARTY, T-Anne's uncle. A converted Mormon sports
hypnotist.

Setting: JACK'S living room. Totally worn out, timberwolve
memorabilia as well as dream catchers decorate the living
room. Cat toys hang from the ceiling on string. The wall-
paper is peeling off.

SCENE I.

TED IS WATCHING "BROKEBACK MOUNTAIN" ON
THE TELEVISION, INTENTLY. MARTY ENTERS AND
STOPS AT THE DOOR, SURVEYING THE SITUATION.
TED DOES NOT SEE HIM. (THERE DOES NOT
ACTUALLY HAVE TO BE A TELEVISION ON STAGE, IT
CAN BE SUGGESTED.)

MARTY: Hey bud. Whatchya watchin?

TED: A cowboy movie. How are you?

MARTY: I'm good. Real busy. I'm a real busy man. I'm
very successful, I don't know if T-Anne has told you that.

TED: No, but you mentioned it before.

MARTY: Have I? What did you say this was?

TED: A western.

MARTY: Looks kinda... artsy fartsy.

TED: Artsy-fartsy?

MARTY: Yeah. You're one of those artsy-fartsy types, aren't you? I can tell

TED: I don't really care much for art, actually.

MARTY: Oh. You into sports then?

TED: No. Not really.

MARTY: Not sports? Well what?

TED: Drugs.

MARTY: If my father catches you doing drugs, I'll---

TED: I was joking. I don't do drugs.

MARTY: Oh... I ... um... what church do you go to, Ted?

TED: I don't, Marty.

MARTY: Well what is it that you do exactly?

TED: I decorate.

MARTY: *(sarcastically)* You've really spruced this place up.

TED: I took down some of the cat toys.

MARTY: Don't tell my father that.

TED: The cat is dead.

MARTY: So is my mother, that doesn't mean he can just throw away her things!

TED: I don't think it's the same thing.

MARTY: I do. Whiskers was a part of the family.

TED: Oh. Well, I'm sorry for your loss.

Pause.

MARTY: You and Ken are always welcome at my church, you know.

TED: Thanks for that. I don't think Annie's into Joseph Smith, but maybe I'll go one day.

MARTY: She doesn't know what he's into. She wanted to be a priest when she was little.

TED: She told me she wanted to be Madonna.

MARTY: She's Catholic and idiots listen to her. In her mind it's the next best thing.

TED: I think she's into Kaballah now.

MARTY: Sad.

TED: Why is that sad?

MARTY: Because it's a lie... You can't watch this in my dad's house, Ted.

TED: I bought this TV so we could watch what we want.

MARTY: Well you're not even family, and I'm here taking care of Daddy...

TED: Taking care of him?

MARTY: Yes. You don't know anything. You just live here for free and watch....

TED: What?

MARTY: Fag porn is what. This is disgusting.

TED: I can turn on straight porn if you want.

MARTY: You wouldn't be into it.

TED: Oh, who knows, I'm artsy.

MARTY: I could kill you you little asshat. I was the state wrestling champion in 1979.

TED: You wrestled? And you think this is homoerotic?

Marty makes a move for Ted. He gets tangled in a cat toy.

TED: Annie!

MARTY: Don't get her involved. This is between us. Man to man.

TED: There is nothing between us, Marty. Except for three urine stains and a half-dozen cat toys.

MARTY: My father loves animals! That is a gift!

TED: Your father shouldn't be living alone. That is neglect.

MARTY: He is as sharp as a tack!

TED: He fell on Thursday.

MARTY: No he didn't.

TED: We had to take him to the hospital.

MARTY: Why didn't you call me?

TED: Annie did. You didn't answer.

MARTY: On Thursday? I was busy with work.

TED: Is that why your boss called here looking for---

MARTY: My life is none of your business!

TED: Well neither is mine but you sure told your whole family about it.

MARTY: I don't even know you.

TED: Yeah.

MARTY: I didn't want a gay man living with my father.

TED: Annie--

MARTY: Annie is a soft-hearted girl and doesn't see you for what you are.

TED: I'd like it if you left.

MARTY: This is my house.

TED: Actually, it's not. Annie and her father made that very clear to me. I don't want to have to bother Gary at home with this.

MARTY: What the hell does he do? Use big words and drink? Effing alcoholic.

TED: I didn't know Mormons cursed so much.

MARTY: I'm human.

TED: Oh really? Because the way you talk about yourself, I thought you were God.

MARTY: You don't know the first thing about God.

TED: You're right. He speaks directly to smarmy adulterers, but I'm way out of his league.

Mary does not know what to say. HE walks out. Ted continues watching Brokeback Mountain. After a moment, Marty Re-enters, with a pellet gun.

MARTY: You listen closely to me.

TED: What the he---

MARTY: You are not a good listened, Ted. You don't remember what neighborhoods I tell you to live in, or my daughter's name, or that I told you not to put away my freaking trophies!

Ted and Marty stare at each other for a moment. Ted quickly gets up, grabs the pellet gun nearly effortlessly from Marty's hands, and sits back down on the couch. He is quiet for a moment.

TED: No, Marty. I'm a very good listener. I listened when you borrowed 16 thousand dollars from Jack and said it was for the baby. I listened to Gary talk about what loser you are, long before I ever met your ugly, fake-Mormon face. Now TAnne is asleep, and I'd encourage you not to wake up, because she will call her father, who will promptly fly from Texas and break your one real kneecap, if I don't put a pellet into it first, and Gary might even know about that money you stole from that poor old man... I might even write a real artsy showtune about it.

Marty reaches for the gun. Ted plays keep-away from him, holding it in the air. He sings to the tune of "Cabaret."

TED: What's good about being a giant has-been?

MARTY: You mother effing faggot!

TED: Come here the idiot say!

MARTY: I'LL KILL YOU!

TED: I know you hire prossssstitttutes.

Marty stops dead in his tracks.

T-ANNE: *(from upstairs)* What's going on down there?

Marty leaves very quickly

TED: Nothing!!

Ted sits down, still holding the gun. He turns up the volume on the TV.

TED: *(sings very softly)* Come to the cabaret.

End of Scene.

THE CONQUEST OF MEXICO

By Steven Schutzman

Times: The present. The year 1519.

Settings:
In the present: mayoral campaign office; in a car at a MacDonald's drive-thru; a hotel room; all in the same large American city.

In 1519: the tent of Hernando Cortes near Tabasco on the East Coast of Mexico; the private apartments of Montezuma in Tenotchtitlan, Mexico; sacrificial temple in Tenotchtitlan.

Characters:
Bernard - also Cortes
Paul - also Montezuma
Dona Marina - also Marina
Old Teacher - also Hunchback
Astrologer
Quetzalcoatl
Female companion of Quetzalcoatl

Scene 3

(The Present. A few days after Scene 1. PAUL at MacDonald's drive-thru speaker.)

MARINA: *(OVER SPEAKER)* Welcome to MacDonald's. May I please take your order. *(Beat. Beat.)* May I please take your order.

PAUL: *(Butchering the Spanish.)* Dos fajitas, por favor.

MARINA: *(OVER SPEAKER)* Algo mas, Pablito? Algo mas?

PAUL: Uhh...?

MARINA: *(OVER SPEAKER)* Is that all?

PAUL: Yes, si.

MARINA: *(OVER SPEAKER)* Two ten is your total.

PAUL: I...yes...si.

MARINA: *(OVER SPEAKER)* First window please, Paul.

(PAUL pulls up. MARINA gets in car.)

MARINA: Vamanos.

(PAUL drives.)

PAUL: You saw me?

MARINA: On my TV screen. That's my job. Was my job. It cost me five hundred dollars. The brokers. Fake I.D. broker. Job permit broker. Job broker. Rateros. Thieves. Bastards. I am their slave. I curse them with a slave's curse.

PAUL: Slouch down.

MARINA: What's this slouch?

PAUL: Get low in the seat. If someone sees us, I could lose everything.

(MARINA slouches.)

MARINA: If you lost everything, you would soon have it again. My people who have nothing to lose but their lives, lose them all the time for nothing. Very cheap lives, no?

PAUL: So that means stealing is okay.

MARINA: The coins are for you only.

PAUL: What do you mean for me?

MARINA: The first time you appeared on my screen, I decided to give you one, a lucky coin from my unlucky home.

PAUL: Why?

MARINA: Because of who you are and what you are. And here you are.

PAUL: That's crazy.

MARINA: Many things are crazy but they also still happen.

PAUL: Can't argue with that.

MARINA: You came in secret, Mr. Mayor, so I needed a secret way to bring you back. And you came, three times more.

PAUL: I'm not mayor yet.

MARINA: Your position is of no importance.

PAUL: Here. Look. I saved them all.

(PAUL shows coins.)

MARINA: Hello, little messengers.

PAUL: I was going to pay you with them today as a signal to get you to stop stealing.

MARINA: So you needed a secret way also.

PAUL: I'm running for mayor. *(Beat)* How old are you?

MARINA: Nineteen.

PAUL: No way.

MARINA: Seventeen, and I need your help.

PAUL: Help? How?

MARINA: I need your power.

PAUL: I have no power yet.

MARINA: Not the power of being mayor. Your strength as a man. What was in your blood from the beginning. I wouldn't care if you were a beggar. I need a man of power, and you are that man.

PAUL: Why?

MARINA: To do what I have to do.

PAUL: And what is that?

MARINA: To bring my friend back from the terrible journey she's on. I need a man of power to help me fight demons. A week ago, her husband committed suicide by putting a rifle in his mouth and blowing the brains out of his head. They called him Loco and he was. A small, beautiful man with yellow eyes and jet black hair who could not stay still, who is very still now. It seemed to us Loco never slept. He used to go out late at night. That's when he would borrow the eyes of an animal and climb in people's windows to slip bills from their sleeping wallets like a boy stealing pesos from his father to buy sweets. Just enough so they wouldn't miss it, a dream you forget in the morning.

PAUL: You are beautiful…

MARINA: They called him Loco and he was. He was an artist who could capture someone's face in three blinks of their eyes. After he drew someone that person would touch his face to make sure it hadn't been stolen. Once the police sent Loco to jail and he captured the face of every thief and junkie in there. He was going to have an exhibition of those sad, hard faces and become famous but he left the window open one night and they got soaked by a storm. And other pictures got stolen. That was how it went a lot. Some days he would set up his easel on the street and he would draw faces for a dollar but Loco couldn't do what he asked his subjects to do. Stay still.

PAUL: You are fantastic.

MARINA: They called him Loco and he was. Some say he was bipolar and one day the bottom opened. Loco said he wanted to be a painter with brushes and everything. His friend the pencil was no longer enough. No one pays any attention to anything done with a pencil, said Loco. He began to paint pictures of the aerials, elevator shafts and satellite dishes of the tenement roofs with laundry hanging and chili peppers drying, and the clouds behind them. Everyone thought it was a change for the better. The trouble was the light wouldn't sit still for Loco. Unlike the face of a person who will live many years, each separate day ages quickly. Loco wanted perfect stillness but the light kept changing as light does and he kept painting over what the light first showed him to capture what the light was showing him now. His paintings wound up thick messes like scabs on the canvas. Nobody saw it coming. If we knew we would have gone up on the roof and pulled the painting off his easel and said there it's done, it's great, and sold it for a thousand dollars. But I don't think it would have done any good. My friend was the one who found him in their bedroom, all messed up like that. The police who couldn't find his brain put in their report that it had flown out the window to be eaten by crows or dogs but it wasn't true. My friend had picked the brain up and put it in her son's Leggo box. Up Loco's loco brain went to the top shelf of my friends' closet and it's still there. She had loved that crazy man and wasn't going to give his mind up, talking to her with the voices of mirrors, dolls and parrots. My friend, she acted normal, answered all the police's questions, even went down to the corner with me for a soda that night. I should have stuck needles in her feet. When someone acts normal after such a thing happens, it is the worst possible sign. The next day she woke up as someone else and has been waking up as a different person for two weeks now. They are not good people. They are the people from the bad news headlines who kill their own children and blame it on a stranger or say god told them to do it. I have to rescue her before it's too late and that involves a ceremony for which I must be very strong.

PAUL: You are electric. What a story.

MARINA: I am a poet who doesn't write her poems down but says them out of her mouth. I have won many poetry slams in clubs in my second language. I can also free-style your face off. I will be famous one day.

PAUL: I believe it.

MARINA: Now I must be strong for the magic. Take me to a hotel, fill me with your male strength and I will be able to do it. Magic is a way of thinking like a bird and a bird needs two wings not just one to fly. So what do you say, Pablito?

(Fade to black)

End of Scene.

MI CORAZON

By Lojo Simon

Characters
Skye, a teenage girl (Caucasian)
Gabby, a teenage girl (Mexican)
Nurse, an adult male (Texan)

In GABBY's hospital room. The NURSE wheels in Gabriella in a hospital bed. Attached to the bed and to GABRIELLA are an IV pump and a heart monitor that beeps.

SKYE: Hey.

GABRIELLA: Don't look at me. I look like crap.

SKYE: Pretty much. Is that your heartbeat?

GABRIELLA: Yeah.

SKYE: Cool.

NURSE: Are you comfortable?

GABRIELLA: I guess.

NURSE: Holler if you need anything.

SKYE: Is her heart beating OK now?

NURSE: If you like the two-step.

SKYE: Huh?

NURSE: Don't you know the two-step? *(He demonstrates.)* The heart's got a rhythm – bah-bum, bah-bum – same on the downbeat as the upbeat. When someone has hypertrophic cardiomyopathy, like Gabby here, the muscles in the heart wall lose their elasticity so they don't pump regular like they should. The rhythm is off beat – one, two, three-and... one, two, three-and... -- like the Texas two-step.

GABRIELLA: I told him it's salsa, but he insists it's two-step. Stuck-up Texan.

NURSE: You get well enough to dance with me, and I'll prove it's a two-step.

GABRIELLA: Fine.

NURSE: Thatta girl. Now remember, push the button if you're desirous of a cowboy. *(tipping his imaginary hat to Skye.)* Nice to meet you, Miss.

NURSE exits.

SKYE: He's funny.

GABRIELLA: They put the best nurses on pediatrics. Humor is supposed to make you get better faster.

SKYE: How long do you have to be here?

GABRIELLA: Until I'm 18, I guess. Adults are on a different floor.

SKYE: I mean, when can you come home?

GABRIELLA: I don't know.

SKYE: I'm gonna die if I have to face Mr. Trotter without you.

GABRIELLA: If you died in his class, he'd probably put you in vinegar so he could use you for dissection.

SKYE: Gross.

GABRIELLA: You have to do that if you go to medical school. On dead people. Texas said he did it once.

SKYE: I could never be a doctor.

GABRIELLA: They talked to me about the heart transplant.

SKYE: What'd they say?

GABRIELLA: They keep the heart beating even after the donor is dead.

SKYE: You mean brain dead.

GABRIELLA: Yeah.

SKYE: That's gross.

GABRIELLA: It has to be kept alive the whole time or it won't work. And when they're ready to do the surgery, they cut out the heart and pack it in a cooler like the kind you put beer in.

SKYE: I never really thought about the details.

GABRIELLA: I think about it a lot, even though I don't mean to. I mean, it's weird to think that there's someone out there right now who's living a normal life and then they're gonna get hit by a car or something, and some doctor is going to harvest their organs and transplant them into other people.

SKYE: And there are all these people walking around who have parts inside them that they got from dead bodies.

Long beat.

GABRIELLA: Skye, are you still having that premonition?

SKYE: You don't keep having a premonition. You just have it once.

GABRIELLA: Do you still think it's going to come true?

SKYE: How am I supposed to know? It's not like I've died before.

GABRIELLA: I don't want it to.

SKYE: But you need a transplant.

GABRIELLA: Still, I don't want to take advantage of another person's tragedy. I don't want anyone to die.

SKYE: What if the donor died by suicide? Then you wouldn't be benefiting from someone who died by accident.

GABRIELLA: Just promise me it won't be you.

SKYE: Don't ask me that.

GABRIELLA: If anything happened to you, more people would be hurt.

SKYE: I just want to take care of you.

GABRIELLA: Then promise me you won't die.

SKYE: Don't you want to live?

GABRIELLA: Yes. But that's my responsibility, not yours.

SKYE: I don't want to live without you.

GABRIELLA: If you die for me to live, then I'll have to live without you. That's just as bad.

SKYE: I can't believe you've got me in a Mexican stand-off.

GABRIELLA: A what?

SKYE: A Mexican stand-off. Didn't you ever see a Western? Two cowboys. Both of them have their guns drawn. And both know if they shoot, the other one is going to shoot back and kill them.

GABRIELLA: So no one shoots.

SKYE: Or they both shoot. Either way, the fate of one is the same as the fate of the other.

GABRIELLA: Why is this thing called Mexican?

SKYE: Who cares?

GABRIELLA: I was just wondering.

SKYE: Why are you being so stubborn?

GABRIELLA: You're the one being stubborn.

SKYE: I'm just trying to help you.

GABRIELLA: Well, you can't. You can't. And Tia can't. And the doctors can't. No one can unless some poor kid out there like me dives into a shallow swimming pool and kills himself. And then only if his parents say it's OK for the doctors to cut him open and remove his heart and put it on ice while it's still beating. How do you – how do you think that makes me feel waiting for some kid to die so I can live?

SKYE: Well, you're not being very grateful for what you have.

GABRIELLA: I just think it's – it's loco to give me your heart.

SKYE: Just forget it, OK.

GABRIELLA: Promise me you won't die.

SKYE: I already made a promise.

NURSE enters.

NURSE: Sorry, hon, your time is up.

SKYE: How can you say that to her?

NURSE: I was talking to you. Doc's on his way to do an exam.

NURSE starts to wheel away GABRIELLA in hospital bed.

GABRIELLA: Skye – no one's going to die today.

NURSE and GABRIELLA exit.

End of Scene.

ALL THINGS BEING EQUAL

By Faye Sholiton

This scene takes place in a classroom in Liberty Falls, Ohio, as BERTA FREEMAN, a black teacher 30, teaches a class on Social Justice, and her friend and colleague CARRIE BRAUN, 34, looks on.

BERTA: *[To her class]*...Tomorrow, we're going to talk about one of those places the Constitution didn't reach: the U.S. Military. How many of you have heard of Port Chicago?

It's not in the textbook, children. Port Chicago was a naval installation on the Sacramento River. On July 14, 1944, something happened on the docks. The Civil Rights Act of 1964 was enacted, in some part, because of what happened that night. Look it up. This, too, is American history.

(BELL RINGS. CHAIRS SCRAPE. Then silence.)

CARRIE: You gonna give me a hint?

BERTA: There was an explosion.

CARRIE: ...with racial implications.

BERTA: Well, who do you think was doin' all the grunt work? You know, I don't think you ever told me what your daddy did during the war.

CARRIE: Is that what all this is about?

BERTA: I'm asking for a reason.

CARRIE: Fine. He was in the Army. Quartermaster Corps.

BERTA: I see. ...An officer?

CARRIE: Captain. Why?

BERTA: Then you know that his Negroes were nothing more than slaves in uniform.

CARRIE: No. I don't. I mean, he never ...

BERTA: No, I don't suppose he did. Well, my daddy was Quartermaster Corps, too. Only Navy.

CARRIE: ...He was at Port Chicago?

BERTA: They got one, maybe two days of so-called "training" before pulling ammo duty. And when they didn't work fast enough, passing the bombs hand to hand, they were ordered to toss them, in the air...

CARRIE: How many died?

BERTA: Three hundred twenty-some. Hundreds more injured. And the ones who survived? Sent right back to work, ten days later. Except some of them made a stand. Got themselves sentenced to 15 years' hard labor.

CARRIE: My God.

BERTA: Oh, they were released after 16 months. But with dishonorable discharges. And you know who defended them? (...) Thurgood Marshall. ...I told you there was a link.

CARRIE: How come you never mentioned this when we were planning the unit?

BERTA: I just get weary hearing about your mama this and your mama that. It's time we talked about your daddy.

CARRIE: There's nothing to tell. He managed properties. …In the city.

BERTA: Properties.

CARRIE: …Near downtown. That's all. End of story.

BERTA: I see. And as Captain Rice...

CARRIE: Actually, it was Captain Reisenfeld. And he requisitioned supplies.

BERTA: And he never spoke of the men under his command?

CARRIE: Hill's right. You do have an ax to grind.

BERTA: Did he talk about his buddies? Go to any reunions?

CARRIE: It's not as if he landed on Omaha Beach, for God's sake!

BERTA: …Show you photographs?

(The light dawns.)

CARRIE: …They were all black.

BERTA: Uh-huh.

CARRIE: Look. His point of reference back then was the silver screen. Negroes dug ditches. Indians carried tomahawks.

BERTA: So your sainted mama married Archie Bunker.

CARRIE: Like I said. He was a product of his time.

BERTA: So was she.

CARRIE: They divorced in 1962. And he's been dead for seven years, okay? Could we talk about something else?

BERTA: Carrie. Honey. When are you gonna take off those Pollyanna braids? In case you haven't noticed, we're different.

CARRIE: If you're talking about race,

BERTA: Well, somebody should.

CARRIE: That's what the whole Civil Rights Movement was for! To make sure it didn't matter!

BERTA: Perhaps it has to matter before it doesn't. Sooner or later, race always rears its ugly head. Somebody launches a grenade and we retreat to our "bunkers." We're wired that way. And pretending we're not won't get us diddly squat.

CARRIE: Well, if we haven't been talking about race these last few months, what the hell have we been talking about?

BERTA: Damned if I know. But I got this feeling, keep asking myself, "What does this woman want from me?" …Tell me, Carrie. How many black people in your address book? I'm not talking about your old housekeeper, either. I'm talking heart-friends. Peers.

CARRIE: Well, how many white people in yours? Or don't you have any "peers"?

BERTA: What we just experienced was a moment of pure, unadulterated honesty.

CARRIE: I was merely trying to prove a point.

BERTA: Which was…

CARRIE: …I have no idea.

BERTA: Lord, I wish you'd stop trying so hard.

(Pause)

CARRIE: Have you ever had your mouth washed out with soap? …When I was in tenth grade, I wrote this amazing essay about the end of civilization. How we had already proven ourselves capable of pushing the nuclear button. My teacher entered it in a citywide competition and told me it was almost certain to win. …Well, she failed to mention she'd entered another girl's essay, too. A black kid who wrote about fair housing – about the office my mom had co-founded! …Well, the day they announced the winner, I have to say, I got a little steamed. I had already planned where I was going to spend the prize money. …Unfortunately, my mother was passing through while I was venting to a friend. …I can still taste the soap.

What's so funny?

BERTA: What that black girl was probably saying about you.

CARRIE: If I'm to be your heart friend, what the hell am I supposed to be doing?

BERTA: One day you will enter my world.

CARRIE: I've been waiting for an invitation.

BERTA: When you get there, I'll need you to hold it together.

(Pause.)

CARRIE: Does this have anything to do with why I've never met your husband?

BERTA: You've never met him, because he's been in the hospital.

CARRIE: Oh. ...Oh, God! You can't imagine what I thought.

BERTA: About a black man who abandoned his wife and baby. Let me guess.

CARRIE: I'm an idiot.

BERTA: He's at the V.A., Carrie. ...It's where I go on Sundays.

CARRIE: ... I'll be damned.

BERTA: What.

(BELL RINGS.)

CARRIE: You know, you can be a royal pain in the ass.

BERTA: You have no idea.

End of Scene.

THE PICNIC - WEST OF THE THIRD MERIDIAN

By Trina Davies

Cast:
One Female Larisa (mid to late 20s)
One Male Petro (mid to late 20s)

Notes on Scene IV The Picnic:
Ukrainian accents are used in this scene.
Notes on pronunciation, background, and meaning:
* *Shier=Shy-er*
* *perishke is a type of bread, with cottage cheese, dill and cream that is baked, and studnats is a type of headcheese – both of these are special dishes and take quite a lot of labour*
* *Slouhe means "listen!" (pronounced 'slew-hjeh')*
* *Oi Bozhe mean "oh god" (pronounced Oi B'je)*
* *Oi Marta Boje means "oh mother of god" (pronounced Oi Marta (rolling r)B'je)*

In West of the 3rd Meridian the two actors in the play become malleable ghost figures, who take on the characterization of the different characters as the moments/scenes materialize. The style of the piece is similar to mask technique – in this case the 'masks' are pieces of clothing that the actors take on to 'become' the various characters. The movements involved with the 'slipping on' of character should be evocative of the sad, eerie and haunting feeling that ghost stories create.
meri'dian: n. & a. circle passing through celestial poles and zenith of any place on earth's surface; corresponding line on a map; point at which sun or star attains highest altitude; prime, full splendour.

West of the third meridian is a physical location. Rural sites on the prairies in Canada are identified with a series of locators, one of which is the site's relation to the meridians. This particular location is firmly placed in my home

*province of Saskatchewan. The meridian is also the
pinnacle, the best, the highest point of a star. This play is
populated with characters that haunt a location full of raised
and lowered expectations and who find softness in falling
just a bit short.*

Scene IV

*Late 1920s, Late Spring, Afternoon. The house plays Eastern
European accordion music through a gramophone.*

*Petro comes into the kitchen through the screen door. He is
wearing a flat cap. He is beaming with pride. He takes a
deep breath and looks around, then realizes that he is alone,
and exits the screen door.*

*Petro reappears carrying Larisa, who is obviously pregnant,
and is holding a large picnic basket and looking concerned.
After Petro carries Larisa over the threshold, he sets her
down, and enters past her into the room. Larisa clutches her
basket as if it is the last piece of the world. She pauses, looks
at the room, then turns quickly on her heel and exits through
the screen door. Petro quickly follows.*

*Petro escorts Larisa back through the screen door and into
the room. Larisa stands by the door, while Petro goes to the
cupboard to try and show off the features of the room,
opening the doors, showing the interior. The house squeals
with happiness.*

Larisa clutches her basket and begins to cry.

LARISA: Petro It's. I...

*Petro goes over to Larisa and tries to embrace her. She is
stiff. He helps her to sit in the chair near the table.*

PETRO: You'll get used to it. It really isn't that bad.

Larisa glares at Petro.

PETRO: Here.

(he takes the basket from her and sets it on the table. He removes his cap and sets it on the table)

Let's have our first meal in our new home!

LARISA: It's not my home.

PETRO: Larisa, I was lucky to get it. It's not forever. *(pause)* It's the best I could do, Larisa! It's good land, it's a good start!

Long Pause. There is a noise – floorboards creaking in happiness.

LARISA: What was that?

PETRO: Nothing.

LARISA: Rats! There's rats!

PETRO: There aren't any rats.

LARISA: You've found a place with rats!

PETRO: There aren't any rats! *(Cupboard doors fly open. Petro is startled, but thinks he must have opened them.)* See? None. No rats. *(beat)* I built this house myself...do you know how long, how hard...I put every piece of this place together *(he notices her drifting off)*...never mind. We'll just make the best of it.

LARISA: You told me they had everything here. You told me it was just like home, but better...better land, better everything.

PETRO: There are good things/

LARISA: "Come over right away, sweetheart", you wrote, "we'll have a little place all our own, there will be a little rose garden for you, where you can pick flowers all day long."

PETRO: I never said that/

Larisa pulls out a letter from her bodice or sleeve and smoothes it out.

LARISA: *(reading)* "We will have an orchard, where we can pick our own fruit, and have parties for all our new friends. It will be better than your father's house. It will be better than anything you've seen before."

Larisa looks at Petro and raises her eyebrow. She folds the letter and puts it back where she found it.

PETRO: Alright. So I exaggerated a little. I wanted you to come.

LARISA: Well you got your wish, didn't you.

Ernie's image walks by with his crate of dishes. Long pause. Petro starts to unpack the picnic basket. Larisa watches out of the corner of her eye.

PETRO: Let's have some picnic lunch. Well, let's see what we've got here. I sure am starved. Well, this looks…this looks good!

Pause as Petro looks at the mushy bread that he has pulled out of the picnic basket a little dubiously.

LARISA: I wanted…I wanted to make you studnats, as it's Sunday and all, and perishke…but Mrs. Johnson, she says that "we just can't have what we want any old time we'd like it." So, I got us a chicken instead. She wasn't laying anymore, so Mrs. Johnson said I could have it.

PETRO: Well, I'm sure this is just fine. I haven't had perishke for a long time.

LARISA: And there's some bread…and some vegetables…

PETRO: Yes, I see…

Long pause. Petro looks into the basket.

LARISA: I know that it's not very good.

PETRO: No, no, I never said that. I can hardly wait to try it! What should we have first? *(pause)* Hm. Where to start…

Petro hesitantly breaks off some bread and brings it slowly to his mouth, trying to take the longest amount of time before it reaches there. Larisa turns a little and watches. Petro stops short of taking a bite.

LARISA: Aren't you going to eat it?

PETRO: Maybe later. I'm not sure I'm that hungry just now.

LARISA: I thought you said you were starving.

PETRO: Well, I was. I guess it's just…well it just passed me by, I guess. I'll have some a little later. *(pause)*

LARISA: It often "passes by" with the hired men, when I'm making eggs for breakfast, or roast for supper. Those men will eat anything…except for what I cook.

PETRO: I'm sure they're just bashful in front of such a beautiful girl.

Larisa throws Petro a withering look.

LARISA: Oi Bozhe! Why am I doing this at all? Why, Petro? I never said that I could do any of these things. Never once! I don't know how to make this food...these 'puddings' and 'kippers' They all just turn their backs, and sigh and roll their eyes/

PETRO: They just forget sometimes, they forget what it's like at the start/

LARISA: Start of what? Beginning of what? I can't do this anymore.

Larisa goes to leave the kitchen, Petro blocks her way.

LARISA: Slouhe! Are you listening to me? Are you listening to what I'm saying to you? I can't do this.

PETRO: Listen, this isn't the way I wanted things either. It wasn't supposed to be like this, I really thought that... *(pause)* well, we just have to make the best of it, that's all.

LARISA: I want to go home.

PETRO: Larisa, this is home.

Petro guides Larisa back to her chair at the table.

LARISA: It's not. You can have it if you want. I want to get back on that boat and go home.

PETRO: I thought you were sick on that boat.

LARISA: I was. But if I'd known what was at the end of it...I'm no good at this, Petro. I don't know what we were thinking/

PETRO: Ridiculous! We can do anything. You can do anything. Mrs. Johnson/

LARISA: Mrs. Johnson thinks I'm useless. She's been telling all of the ladies in town what a stuck-up I am, and how I can't even pluck a chicken/

PETRO: Larisa, you're exaggerating/

LARISA: And she's right. She's right. I don't know how to make this odd food! How did this happen…how did I end up here…I'm the daughter of a/

LARISA: A Kulak, yes. You never forget that do you?

LARISA: I had my own servants, Petro. We had our own girl to clean and cook. Now I'm that girl.

PETRO: Larisa, it's not forever.

LARISA: I don't want to be at the Johnsons, Petro. I came to be here with you. I came to be here with you, and I get off the train and the first thing I see is you in one of these…these caps (she picks it up off of the table). And I see John Shier in a big sheepskin coat walking down the boardwalk, and a loose piece of board comes up and just hits him in the shoulder. And I thought…where have I come to…

PETRO: Larisa/

LARISA: AND then you tell me that I can't even stay on the same farm as you, cause we're not married, and then we do get married - with not a single person I know at the ceremony - and I think, "well, finally, we can live together"/

PETRO: Listen, this is what/

LARISA: But we CAN'T live together because we have no

home… so I have to keep staying with the Johnsons, and they seem to think I know how to do all of these serving girl things/

PETRO: Larisa!

LARISA: And then I get pregnant! Pregnant!

PETRO: I didn't know that you'd/

LARISA: That I'd what?

PETRO: That…it would happen so quickly…

LARISA: Yes…so lucky…so fortunate they all say…I just keep getting bigger and bigger and I've got no space of my own, no home of my own, have to waddle around while they all stare at my belly AND you're fifteen miles away!!

PETRO: Larisa, that's what I mean. Things are changing. We'll have our own place now.

LARISA: Oi Marta Boje!! How is this going to be better, Petro. How!?

PETRO: Larisa what do you want me to do?

LARISA: My father told me this would happen.

PETRO: Your father! Not again with your father!

LARISA: My father is a smart man!

PETRO: Yes! Your father knows that I'm not good enough for you, doesn't he.

LARISA: Maybe he was right!

PETRO: You can keep blaming me forever if you want to, but it's not going to make anything better here, is it? I try and smile and be happy for you, and I try to get you what you'd like, your own house, your own kitchen…

LARISA: And this is what I get?

The house protests. The argument comes fast and furious.

PETRO: What else can I do for you? What else am I supposed to do? Tell me, because I really don't know.

LARISA: I don't know/

PETRO: Everything went into coming here, and getting you here, and getting this place/

LARISA: How could I end up here…

PETRO: What can I do for you Larisa? Tell me and I'll do it!

LARISA: Did you know that Mrs. Johnson told me that you can be snowed in for days here in the winter? Days! How much snow is that?

PETRO: What does it matter? We'd never have got a place like this back home.

LARISA: You wouldn't have got a place like this back home/

PETRO: What does it matter how much snow there is, or how many days we don't see other people. I thought you didn't like them anyway.

LARISA: That's not the point.

PETRO: Then please. Please tell me what the point is!

LARISA: I'm better than this.

PETRO: Better than me you mean!

LARISA: We're better than this.

PETRO: No, it's me who isn't good enough, isn't it? Isn't it? Why didn't you say that at the start, why didn't you/

Petro throws a piece of the picnic lunch on the floor for emphasis. Larisa looks at the food on the floor and slaps him. He slaps her back hard and she falls. Larisa pulls back. The house screams. They're both taken aback. Long pause.

PETRO: Larisa, I...

He reaches for her, she pulls away, as if expecting to be hit again.

PETRO: I...I didn't mean...it was reflex, if you hadn't...

LARISA: glares at him.

PETRO: You do deserve better than me. Much better. That's the truth.

Larisa pulls herself to her feet. Petro tries to help, she refuses.

PETRO: I'm sorry...I...Is the baby...?

Larisa leans against the house. The house makes a "there, there" sound to comfort her.

Petro takes the cradle and places it at Larisa's feet. Pause.

PETRO: I...made this. For the baby. I thought maybe...you would like it.

Petro rocks the cradle to demonstrate.

Larisa starts to cry softly.

PETRO: Larisa...no...please...I'm sorry...so...

He reaches for her, she flinches. Long pause. He pushes the cradle further towards her. Larisa continues to cry quietly.

LARISA: How can this happen? I imagined it so differently...so...

PETRO: Imagined?

Petro moves towards her, she moves back.

LARISA: So happy. My first child...my family, my mama...how am I supposed to do this without my mama...without anyone...

PETRO: You have me.

LARISA: You don't want me.

PETRO: Oh...Larisa...I do...I do...you're my heart. I...don't know how I could...I didn't know I could ever...(beat) Are you alright? Did I hurt... I don't know what to say. I wanted you with me, to live your life with me so badly...I love you so much.

LARISA: This is love...

PETRO: This is my stupidity. And my hope. For us.

Both of them look at the piece of food on the floor. There is a moment of quiet.

LARISA: You didn't have to throw it.

A pause. Petro sheepishly goes to pick up the piece of food, wipes it on his pantleg, and then sets it back on the table.

PETRO: I'm sorry, Larisa. I didn't mean/

LARISA: Now you have an excuse not to eat it.

PETRO: No! No, I'll eat it anyway, watch...

Petro goes to bring the piece of food to his mouth, slowly. He hesitates, but

Larisa is watching, so he takes a bite.

PETRO: *(unconvincingly)* Mmmm.

LARISA: You're not fooling me.

PETRO: *(slightly more over-the-top than before)* MMmmm.

A beat, and then Larisa laughs just a little.

PETRO: Come here.

Petro holds out his hand to Larisa. She takes it cautiously. Petro begins to slowly dance with her.

PETRO: You'll see. You'll see Larisa. This is the beginning for us. This is it.

As Larisa becomes comfortable she rests her head on Petro's shoulder. A moment passes. Silence.

LARISA: I'm scared.

PETRO: Whoa… whoa, there's nothing to be scared about, now.

Pause

LARISA: I miss…everyone. I miss them terribly. Will I ever see anyone again? My sister? My father?

PETRO: Of course/

Larisa looks at Petro intently

PETRO: *(pause)* I don't know, Larisa. Maybe. *(pause)* Would you still have come if you'd known?

LARISA: I don't know, Petro. Maybe.

PETRO: This is a good start. We'll make something of this. Something great. You'll see. And with any luck…maybe the children will have that rose garden, eh?

Pause. Larisa pulls away and goes to look out the screen door.

LARISA: We're crazy. How are we supposed to do this. You worked in a factory for shoes and I'm the daughter of a Kulak. How are we going to farm?

PETRO: How hard can it be? *(he shrugs)*

Petro goes over to Larisa. He tentatively reaches out to touch her back.

PETRO: I'm sorry I exaggerated.

LARISA: *(not turning around)* You lied.

PETRO: Alright. I'm sorry I lied. *(pause)* But I love you. We have to hope.

LARISA: For how long?

PETRO: Until we can't anymore. Until it's gone. And then we start over and build it up again. Yes? *(pause)* Come here, Mrs. Melnychuk. See out there? That's where we'll bring in the crop from the field before we take it to town and sell it for enough money to keep us comfortable till we're old. Over there? A little vegetable garden where you can grow whatever you like, whatever we need. And there? Maybe a swing? For our baby...

Larisa nods.

PETRO: Come this way. I have a picnic lunch prepared just for you.

Petro puts out his arm as an escort, and accompanies Larisa to the table, where he sits her down in a chair, playing butler. He removes some of the things, snaps the tablecloth and lays it out nicely. Then he begins to set out the dishes and food.

PETRO: We have some chicken, some... *(pause as he tries to recognize one of the items)*...some vegetables?...Well, it's a good menu.

Petro dishes out food onto Larisa's plate, then sits at his own. He pours himself some coffee and then notices that Larisa is staring intently at her own plate. He watches her for a moment.

PETRO: What's the matter?

(pause)

LARISA: I...I don't want to eat this.

PETRO: You don't want to eat this?

LARISA: No.

PETRO: But you want me to eat this.

Larisa shrugs. Petro steels himself and takes a bite of his food, trying not to make a face while Larisa watches intently.

LARISA: I'll get better at it, I promise.

PETRO: Tell you what, Mrs. Melnychuk. How about for today we pack up this lot and head into town and have a nice dinner at the café. I'll even throw in some pie. How's that for a deal?

LARISA: Alright.

PETRO: Alright then. *(packing up the picnic basket)* Let's go. I'm starving.

LARISA: *(standing, looking around the space)* In a minute.

Pause, Petro looks at Larisa. He takes up the picnic basket, then goes over and touches her arm.

PETRO: I'll be waiting outside.

Larisa walks around her new kitchen, idly touching surfaces, inspecting, claiming the space as her own. Petro leaves the stage. Larisa is silhouetted looking out of her upstage window.

The actors slip out of Petro and Larisa. They leave the stage.

End of Scene.

SOFA SURFERS

By Felicity McCall

Carly is just 18 and in her final year at school, bright and hard working. An only child, since her birthday she has been the official 'carer' for her mother who suffers long term clinical depression; her parents divorced six years ago after a four year separation and she has little contact with her father. Effectively she has been caring for her mother since the age of twelve, and running their house. She can't get out much and because of this her house has become an unofficial home-from-home for a number of 'sofa surfers'- school friends who for a variety of reasons don't stay with their own families most of the time. She supplies a roof over their head, space to study, and food; they supply the young company she needs. Her mother has home helps and nurses to call while she's at school but for the rest of the time she depends on Carly; although her medication leaves her sleeping 14 hours a day dozing in between, and generally subdued. Carly will have the qualifications to go to college but knows it'll have to be in her hometown. She tries to hide the fear that she'll never have a life of her own....

Two of her regular visitors are Stacy and Danny.
Stacy is 17, pretty and young looking, the youngest of a big family who have gone their separate ways apart from her next eldest sister, Chelle. Stacy and Chelle's Mum has acquired a new 'boyfriend', a loud-mouthed, fairly ignorant man whom they dislike; they also find him 'creepy.' Chelle moved out a few months ago and Stacy hopes to join her.... she's naïve and immature, and her standards, hopes and dreams tend to be defined by celebrity magazines and reality TV.

Danny is 18, mad about drama and performing arts, and quite gifted. He does little work at college and dreams of being 'discovered'- not unlike Stacy. He trusts Carly

because she knows his family background- his father, a
macho, homophobic layabout, has not time for the son he
regards as encapsulating the total opposite of himself, the
total failure of his ambitions for a son.

SCENE TWO
STAGE AS BEFORE EXCEPT THE TABLE HAS BEEN
MOVED TO THE CENTRE FRONT WITH A CHAIR ON
THE LHS SIDE OF IT. STACY, WEARING CARLY'S
DRESSING GOWN, IS SPRAWLED ON THE BED, DANNY
LIES ON THE FLOOR. A COUPLE OF CELEBRITY MAGS
ARE LYING AROUND, TELEVISION HAS BEEN ON, /IS
ON, EMPTY CHIP WRAPPERS AND CANS OF COKE
ETC. THE DRAWERS OF CARLY'S WARDROBE ARE
PULLED OUT AND CLOTHING IS STREWN WHERE
STACY HAS BEEN TRYING IT ON.THE CURTAINS ARE
STILL DRAWN EVEN THOUGH IT'S 4PM. NEITHER
LOOK AS IF THEY HAVE REALLY GOT UP OR DONE
ANYTHING MUCH THAT DAY. DANNY GETS UP,
SWITCHES OFF THE TELE AND REACHES FOR A CAN
"" STACY GIVES A YAWN, STRETCHES AND OUT ON
THE BED.
STACY: She is pure class.

Danny looks up quizzically STACY

Cheryl Cole. She is so gorgeous. Wouldn't you just love to
be her?

DANNY: What, and ride big Ashley ?

Gives her a look Stacy throws the cushion at him

STACY: Shut up. You know what I mean. She's just
gorgeous, like she has everything she wants.

Points out pix in the magazine

STACY: Did you see her there, that's her when she was

fourteen, she's way better looking now.... and that's her after she did Pop Stars- The Rivals.

DANNY: Hope for us all then Stace? Is that what you're saying? With the wonders of plastic surgery-

STACY: *(interrupts)* She's never had plastic surgery

DANNY: *(quizzical again)* Sure. None of them have.

STACY: She hasn't. I read it-somewhere.

DANNY: Buy the dream, Stacy

STACY: You're just hateful and jealous

DANNY: Jealous? Moi? Of that airhead?

Stacy huffs and buries her head in the mag. But a minute later she looks up.

STACY: See if there's anything good on. Is Americas next top model on the day? DANNY (lifts the remote) I can't change channels. The remote's broken. Remember the back came off it when you threw it at me?

STACY: Carly will go mad-

Enter Carly, stage R, wearing school uniform, carrying a bag and files, which she sets down. She immediately goes into action, pulling back the curtain, switching off the television, lifting wrappers and cans, as Danny mutters dissent.

CARLY: Carly will go mad at what? Look at the state of this place! What did you do today anyway? *(To Danny)* I thought you were going into class?

STACY: I felt sick this morning. I stayed over at Laura's and their dog stinks. Their whole house stinks. Laura was going up the town but I'd no money. I texted Danny to see what he was doing and he was still here- so I came round.

DANNY: I stayed off to keep her company

Pause

DANNY: So what? We keep you company don't we when you can't leave your Ma? Lighten up would you?

CARLY: Thanks for the big favour. What state 's the kitchen in? And how many days have you missed this term?

Danny shrugs.

DANNY: I made us toasties, that's all. I'll tidy it later. But- right now, I'm getting ready for tonight- we both are. Aren't we, Stace?

STACY: *(Fawning)* Carly Go on let us borrow your dress. Your red one

CARLY: The new one

STACY: Aye.

CARLY: It'd be too big for you.

STACY: It's kind of OK – I could get a belt for it...

Carly sees it lying on a heap in the floor where Stacy has been trying it on. Picks it up, looks disgusted.

STACY: *(defensively)* I was going to text you in class to ask if I could try it on. But Danny said not to disturb you.

CARLY: Thanks Stacy *(not getting it)* It's all right. I need something really good for tonight. Danny said he told you about me having to meet Chelle's boyfriend about-

CARLY: *(cuts her dead)* Tell me later. And you two keep the noise down. I have to study

(Turns her back)   *Lights down.*

SCENE 3

When the lights go up again, Carly is sitting at the table, working on her books. Danny has gone. Stacey has a towel round her head and is applying tan to her legs.

STACY: So will you lend us it then?

CARLY: What *(distractedly)*

STACY: Your red dress. The one out of Top Shop. *(Pause)* The one you got for your interviews. Just for tonight. I'll give it straight back to you. Promise.

Carly looks up, her face a picture of disbelief

STACY: Honest to God, I will. I won't let Chelle borrow it or anything. Go on, Carly, please. I've nothing to wear.

CARLY: *(Getting involved, now)* Does it matter? What you wear to meet your husband to be?

STACY: Shush! You weren't taking me on, were you? I told you. Chelle says I won't have to see him until the registry office. It doesn't matter what I look like

CARLY: Well, then-

STACY: It's not for him. It's for Elliott. And his mate. It's like an interview to see if I get the job. And you said this was your interview dress.

CARLY: Different type of interview, different type of job

STACY: They're both going to be in Phaedra's tonight. They're the ones who decide whether I get to do it. *(Pause)* Chelle told them I looked eighteen. *(Pause)* They're going to get me a birth certificate and all; that says I'm eighteen.

CARLY: And your name is...

STACY: What?

CARLY: Your name. The name on the birth certificate. And the name of the fella you're ''marrying.'' Where you're supposed to be living. You've a lot more to worry about that whether you can borrow my dress.

STACY: Danny says he'll help me out. He's good at learning lines. He promised he would.

CARLY: That was the promise of a very drunken Danny who, let's not forget, wants a piece of the action himself.

STACY: And you wouldn't? For a grand?

CARLY: That's right, I wouldn't.

STACY: Aye. Sure. It's well seeing your Ma gets you everything you want- for all you cry about her- I'm sorry...

CARLY: It's all right...

STACY: What's your problem anyway? Like Chelle says, your Ma never drinks and she doesn't have a creep of a boyfriend hanging round the place like he owns it...

CARLY: I said it's all right! OK!

STACY: I just meant-like- well, your Ma, it's not like she's an alky or anything, she just gets depressed,

CARLY: Let's just leave my Ma out of this, shall we? She walks away, lost in thought.

Embarrassed silence.

CARLY: She'll be grand. Mammy, by Tuesday or so...she always is, it just takes time-

STACY: How is she now?

CARLY: She's sleeping. *(Seeing Stacy about to interrupt)* Yeh. Still. *(Forced)* It's the best thing for her.

STACY: *(stands up and starts brushing out her hair.)* What are you doing this weekend?

CARLY: It depends.

STACY: Depends on what?

CARLY: Yes, it depends on Mammy. Probably not a lot. Why? Are you staying with Chelle?

STACY: Dunno. It depends.

CARLY: On what?

STACY: They might want a bit of space. Her and Elliott

CARLY: So he's moved in has he? What's his other name?

STACY: How do I know? What does it matter? I was wondering, like. See tonight.... I'll not be that late in, maybe, two.... you could lend me a key.

CARLY: No. Non-negotiable. No

STACY: Suit yourself.

CARLY: I will. Mammy likes to know where our keys are. *(Faces Stacy)* It makes her anxious if she thinks anyone has a spare key. OK? And no, before you ask, I will not lie to her. She doesn't need any more worries. And she doesn't need you coming in blocked.

STACY: *(Mutters)* She's dead to the world, she wouldn't hear me.

Carly leans across, and lifts Stacy's magazine....

CARLY: You are tragic, wee girl...

STACY: Shut your mouth. *(mimics Carly)* I'm studying .

CARLY: What, exactly?

STACY: What theme I want for my wedding. Like, Fairytale Princess or Tropical paradise

CARLY: *(On her feet)* I do not believe this. This is not real. Stacy. Listen to me. You-are-not-getting-married. You are taking part in a criminal act with a man who needs an Irish address and an Irish bride which means he has, come on, -a passport to an Irish passport-understand? Good. So he can stay here. Permanently. And why do you think he might want to do that? Cos he likes the climate? No?

STACY: Maybe he's ...an asylum seeker. Maybe they're going to put him in jail if he goes back home. Or shoot him

CARLY: Maybe he's a drug dealer with a ready market? Maybe he has a criminal record? And he's on the run? Think about it. Why would he be happy to pay out big wads of cash for a marriage of convenience? What if you get caught?

STACY: Chelle says just to let on we didn't know.

CARLY: I see. You used a fake ID to go through a marriage ceremony with a man whose name you'll probably not be able to remember. For money. And you'll tell the police you didn't know who he was, or why he did it.

STACY: I'll say it was a mistake. *(Pauses, floundering)* How else am I going to make a grand? It's all right for you..

CARLY: So you always say. Look, I know what it's like for you living with your Ma and her- boyfriend...

STACY: No you don't. You only think you do. I will not stay in the house when-he's there. No way. He's a creep, he-

CARLY: Then do something about it! What exactly has he done?

Stacy falls silent

CARLY: I do believe you. Even I can tell he's a creep. But if it's more than that

Stacy switches on the hairdryer

CARLY: You have to tell somebody....

Carly realizes she's drowned out by the dryer. She walks off, stage R. Stacy brushes through her hair, lifts the crumpled dress and key plus some cash that's lying there, pockets it, and starts on her makeup. Carly comes back in

CARLY: She's still asleep. Stacy, you have to get Chelle to clean up her act. Danny said she was in a bad way last night. Again. Maybe your Ma's boyfriend has a point-sorry, sorry. But if she's keeping well, then you can move in with her- that's if she really wants you...and it's not just her slobbering on when she's out of it....

STACY: Shut your mouth! She's my sister; of course she wants me- we're blood-

CARLY: Like your Ma wants you? When there's no man about?

There's a frozen silence as Carly realizes she's gone too far.

CARLY: *(Goes to put an arm round Stacy)* I'm sorry. I shouldn't have said that.

STACY: *(Shrugging her away)* No, you shouldn't.

Another silence. Stacy gathers up her things, ties back her wet hair.

CARLY: Look, Stace...I said sorry...it's just, well, it's true...isn't it... she's still using, and she'll end up getting put out of that flat, like the last one.... who is this 'Elliott' anyway?

STACY: *(Turns to go)* Forget the dress.

CARLY: Take it.

STACY: Don't want it. I'll get one off Chelle. And don't even think of turning up at the club tonight, mouthing off, you hear me? I don't want your advice. Stop meddling. Mind your own, for once. If you want to "sort people out," start a bit nearer home-with your Ma.

Walks off stage left. Carly pauses, and then slowly begins clearing up.

End of Scene.

THE DATE

By Joan Lipkin

SETTING

The present. It is late. Somewhere in urban America. The entire scene takes place in front of Pun's door.

Pun and Zak, two gay men, are at Pun's door. They've just had their first date.

PUN: So now what?

ZAK: Now I kiss you good night…

PUN: Yes?

ZAK: I kiss you good night, and you thank me for a lovely evening…

PUN: Yes?

ZAK: And I say, I'll call.

(Beat)

PUN: Oh. And will you?

ZAK: Will I what?

PUN: Call. Will you call?

ZAK: Sure.

PUN: When?

ZAK: I don't know. When I do?

PUN: Right. *(Beat)* You won't call.

ZAK: I won't?

PUN: No. No, you won't. But the thing is, you know, you really should get it right. What you really should say is, I'll call tomorrow.

ZAK: Oh?

PUN: Yeah. See, that's better than saying, I'll call. Because if you say I'll call you tomorrow, then I only have to feel like shit until, say, the day after tomorrow. The day after tomorrow when you don't. But if you say I'll call...whenever...it's purgatory, see? And purgatory stretches on. As purgatory will. *(Beat)* I'm Catholic.

ZAK: I gathered.

PUN: It doesn't work too well with the gay thing but I'm managing. They have their version, and I have mine. And I still think God loves me although lately, he must be pissed because I haven't had a date like this in so long. Hell, I haven't had a date...And then you come along and you're cute and funny and smart. And then you say, I'll call. You say I'll call.

ZAK: Well, maybe I will.

PUN: Uh huh. See? See, that's what I mean.

ZAK: Maybe I just wanted to think about it.

PUN: Right.

ZAK: Right.

PUN: I can't believe I'm saying all this, but what the hell. I'm tired of being, you know, polite and going through the motions because this is our lives. Right? There's an epidemic. It's hard.

ZAK: I know.

PUN: So I just decided, I decided after Jamie died that I wouldn't put up with the games, anymore. No more games. No more bullshit. I may be a big queer, but at least I can be an honest one.

(Beat)

ZAK: I'm sorry.

PUN: Uh huh.

ZAK: Really, I'm sorry.

PUN: Forget it. It's late. I don't know what I'm doing.

ZAK: I'm sorry I hurt your feelings.

PUN: Right. Look, I'll see you around. Okay?

ZAK: Will you?

PUN: Sure.

ZAK: When?

PUN: When I do.

(Beat)

ZAK: You're going to drive me nuts. You know that?

PUN: Ooh, careful now. You're speaking in future tense.

ZAK: I know. I said it, didn't I?

PUN: So, say it again.

ZAK: What? You're driving me nuts?

PUN: No. No, not past tense or present tense but future. Say it in the future tense.

ZAK: How can there be a future if you can't keep your pants on long enough to see? You see, I was going to call.

PUN: Were you?

ZAK: Yeah. How does it go? Soon enough to seem interested but not too soon to look pushy.

PUN: So not tomorrow then?

ZAK: No, probably the day after, the day after tomorrow.

PUN: Oh.

ZAK: Not that I didn't want to call you tomorrow.

PUN: You didn't?

ZAK: No, I didn't. I didn't. No, I mean, I did.

PUN: You did? *(He looks at his watch.)* It is tomorrow.

ZAK: So it is. Hell, it's the day after tomorrow somewhere.

(Beat)

PUN: Right. So call me.

ZAK: What?

PUN: Call me now.

ZAK: I don't have your number and this is really…

PUN: *(Overlapping)* You wrote it down on the…

ZAK: You want me to call you?

PUN: Yeah, I really do.

ZAK: Now? You want me to call you now. *(Beat)*

(Zak pulls out a cell phone from his pocket and dials. The phone rings in Pun's pocket.)

ZAK: *(Into phone)* Hello?

PUN: *(Into phone)* Hello.

ZAK: Um, is Pun there?

PUN: Speaking.

ZAK: Pun, this is Zak. *(Beat)*

PUN: Oh. Hi.

ZAK: Hi.

PUN: How are you?

ZAK: Fine. And you?

PUN: Good, I'm good. So what's up?

ZAK: I had a really nice time with you last night.

PUN: Me, too. *(Beat)* Go on.

ZAK: Um, I liked the restaurant? I always wanted to try that place?

PUN: Uh huh. Go on.

ZAK: This is silly.

PUN: Is it? Well, silly is ok. Don't you think? I mean, sometimes.

ZAK: It's just that you're making me do all the work.

PUN: Am I? I think I just did a ton.

ZAK: You did?

PUN: Well, what do you think? So, go on.

(Beat)

ZAK: I, um…

PUN: It's okay. Go on.

ZAK: I, um, I think you're really funny and sexy and I want to see you again.

PUN: Good, that was very good. So, when do you want to see me?

ZAK: Now.

(Beat)

(They slowly kiss and hang up the phones.)

(Beat)

PUN: Hi.

ZAK: Hi.

PUN: God, I hate being a fag sometimes. You know? How are you supposed to date someone when you meet them at the Club Baths?

ZAK: Date. An interesting question. Is that what we're doing?

PUN: I don't know. We're talking. We had dinner, and we're talking.

ZAK: We're talking alright. We're talking so much, I feel like a goddamn lesbian.

PUN: Careful, you.

(He kisses Zak.)

ZAK: What? Was it the goddamn? Or the lesbian thing?

PUN: Shhhh.

(They kiss again.)

ZAK: God, it's late. I really need to get going.

PUN: It's beyond late.

ZAK: Yeah.

PUN: Yeah. So stay.

ZAK: What?

PUN: Zak.

ZAK: I don't know.

PUN: Really. It's okay.

ZAK: It's just that I really like you.

PUN: And I like you. And this is a bad thing?

ZAK: Are you sure?

PUN: About staying? Sure.

ZAK: No. I mean, sure that you like me.

PUN: I'm positive. You big nut. *(Singing)* Sometimes you feel like a nut, sometimes you don't ...

ZAK: Pun. Pun?

PUN: Oh, sorry. Am I tired or what? So, you gonna stay?

ZAK: I don't know.

PUN: Aw, come on. I thought we had it settled. I want you to stay. Really. I'm positive.

ZAK: No. *(Beat)* I'm positive. *(Beat)*

PUN: Oh.

ZAK: Yes. Oh. *(Long beat. Pun opens his arms and embraces Zak.)*

PUN: So, now we begin.

ZAK: We begin?

PUN: Yes. Really. Now. *(He embraces Zak.)*

End of Scene.

SEEING RED

By D. Stirling

Cast of Characters
Nathalie (Nat): 20's, a heroin addict trying to go straight.
Charlotte (Charley): 30's, her lover, works as a cocktail
waitress. Used to work in IT for an investment bank.

Scene: London. A flat in Stockwell

Time: Friday evening, October 3rd, 2008

Charlotte and Nathalie's living room. It's a mess.
NATHALIE is lying asleep under a quilt on the sofa. There is
a sick bowl nearby on the floor. She is in the latter stages of
heroin withdrawal.
CHARLOTTE enters with a hot water bottle. She's wearing
an outdoors coat that's long enough to conceal her uniform
for work. She picks up some sweet wrappers from the coffee
table and puts them in a waste paper bin. She retrieves a
discarded hot water bottle from the floor by the sofa and
places a fresh one under the quilt after first checking that it
is securely sealed. She rearranges the quilt and sits beside
Nathalie, who's having a bad dream. Charlotte strokes her
hair. Nathalie starts to wake up. She's exhausted from lack
of sleep but this soon changes to extreme agitation when she
doesn't get what she wants.

CHARLEY: It's alright, honey. I'm here.

NATHALIE: Will you rub my legs for me?

CHARLEY: OK. But I have to go to work soon. Did you
get some sleep?

NATHALIE: I had another dream.

CHARLEY: Same one?

NATHALIE: No, a different one. But I was still using.

CHARLEY: You're going to get those. You know that.

NATHALIE: Someone was doing something horrible to me.

CHARLEY: How are you feeling?

NATHALIE: I was sick again. And I've still got the shits.

CHARLEY: That's my girl. Always the lady.

NATHALIE: This fucking sucks. Why does it always have to be so hard?

CHARLEY: Is that helping? Am I doing it right?

NATHALIE: Yeah, that feels nice... I'm just crawling all over. My skin-

CHARLEY: I know, honey, I know. I'll look after you.

NATHALIE: Charley, I just want a little baggie. A ten spot to take the edge off. Then I'll be OK.

CHARLEY: You know it doesn't work like that. And I have to go work now. I'd love to stay and rub your legs all night if that would help, but you know I have to go.

NATHALIE: Please, Charley. Just call Red.

CHARLEY: No, darlin', I'm sorry. I'm not picking up for you. I'm not calling Red, and I'm not giving you money.

NATHALIE: Charley, please! I'm fucking dying here.

CHARLEY: No, darlin', you're not. You're just sick. It's almost three days now. Not much longer. It'll get better soon. You just have to remember that.

NATHALIE: I can't do this. Please, Charley, just pick up the phone and call him.

CHARLEY: No, Nat, I'm sorry-

NATHALIE: You're not sorry-

CHARLEY: I promised I'd help you do this. But that means no shit and no money. You know how this works as well as I do.

NATHALIE: What d'you want me to do? Go out and suck some old fucker's dick? I can hardly get to the fucking toilet. But I'll do it if I have to. I'll fucking do it. You know I will.

CHARLEY: I know.

NATHALIE: You want me to do Red? You know he wants me to. He told me. Any time I want a freebie.

PAUSE.

CHARLEY: Use a condom.

NATHALIE: Fuck you, Charley! Fuck you!

CHARLEY THROWS OPEN HER COAT TO REVEAL HER UNIFORM.

CHARLEY: I'm working for tips in a lap dancing club. And I'd doing it for you. Hold the front page, Nathalie. I lost my job. HBOS, Lehman Brothers- they're all gone. The party's over. There's no more bonuses coming in. I'm serving drinks to sleaze bags. If you want to suck dick I can bring you some home, 'cos I get plenty of offers.

NATHALIE: You're not going through this. My stomach's fucking killing me. And all I need is a little gear so I can get some sleep. And then I'll be fine, I promise.

CHARLEY: And then this all starts again from the beginning. You want that, you go ahead. 'Cos you'll do whatever you want to do. We both know that. You want to get clean, you'll get clean. Not much longer and you'll start to feel better. You can do it.

NATHALIE: You don't get this. You smoke blow but you don't get hooked... And you still do coke. You've got some right now but you're going to do it at work.

CHARLEY: No, I don't and you know that. I've stopped. I quit because of you. To help you. And that other shit just doesn't do it for me. Maybe that makes me lucky. I don't have all the answers, Nathalie. I wish I did.

NATHALIE: JUST CALL FUCKING RED!

CHARLEY: No, I'm going. There's some jelly in the fridge if you-

NATHALIE: I don't want fucking jelly. I want you to call Red. If you don't call him, I will. And you know what that means 'cos I don't have any money and you won't fucking give me any.

CHARLEY: I wish I'd never given you money. But I thought that- Maybe I made it too easy for you. God, Nat, sometimes I wish we'd never met but we did. And I love you. You're my little angel. Remember what you used to call me?

NATHALIE: You're my gift from God.

CHARLEY: A gift from God. Well, maybe I don't believe that any more. Maybe I made it all too easy for you and you're not ready to turn it around. Maybe you haven't sunk low enough. I think you've got to know what rock bottom feels like so you don't want to go there again. Maybe I should leave you. Maybe that's what it takes. But please don't make me, Nat. I couldn't bear it. Please don't sink any lower than you have to because you might not make it back. And you're my angel... You can do this. I know you can. Just a little longer that's all.

CHARLEY MAKES FOR THE DOOR.

NATHALIE: Please, Charley. Just get me some valium. Some pills, fucking anything... If you loved me you'd do it.

CHARLEY STOPS. SHE LOOKS AT NATHALIE. SHE TURNS AWAY AGAIN AND EXITS.

End of Scene.

DREAM MUSIC

By G. L. Horton

CAST

NADIA is a dancer from Eastern Europe

KENJI   is a musician from Japan

NADIA and KENJI are a colorfully dressed couple in their mid thirties or older, serene and accomplished. The couple is at a New Age gathering in the USA, and they talk to the audience as if it were one or more of their new American friends. No set is necessary. The characters may sit on the ground or on a bench or platform, and the piece should incorporate bits of Kenji's music and Nadia's movement. Kenji's "ideal" instrument is probably an electronic keyboard that makes otherworldly as well as traditional instrument sounds, but a production where he uses something else is fine. Musical and bodily expressions accompany and slow down the verbal dialogue, as if the couple is speaking in several "languages " at the same time. Begin with Kenji's playing and Nadia's wordless singing,

NADIA: We met at a festival in Greece.

KENJI And we knew at once that we were meant to be together.

NADIA: We had no common language.   I'm Romanian.

KENJI: I'm Japanese.

NADIA: A few words of Greek, a few of English.

KENJI: But we had music. *(plays a little)*

NADIA: We had dance. *(moves)*

KENJI: Nadia had dance. I had lost touch with my body. But she taught me, and then we had dance. *(moves with Nadia)*

NADIA: We decided both to learn English.

KENJI: With English you can be the most free, travel the most of the world.

NADIA: I started out as a potter. Then, the dance was just for health, for exercise. You get all stiffed up, sitting hours at the potter's wheel.

KENJI: Her pots were very beautiful. They remind me of Zen pots, the oldest and simplest and most valuable.

NADIA: They were beautiful. But so heavy! You know? The weight of the earth.

KENJI: I could see that Nadia was my opposite-- my complement. Earthly. Grounded.

NADIA: Grounded is good. But you know, a potter can never be free. A potter is so heavy, bound not just to the clay, but the wheel and the tools and the kiln. A pot is real and useful as well as beautiful--

KENJI: Grounded. Real and useful.

NADIA: But so many of them! Every new pot a burden, a heavy thing to be guarded from breakage, carried to market, stored. I began to feel that I was building my own tomb.

KENJI: While I was building nothings. Structures in the air: mathematics, philosophy.

NADIA: I went out less and less, so busy making and storing. People were distractions to me-- to me, who as a child was always laughing and playing and singing and dancing with friends!

KENJI: Human beings began to seem very small, very far away. One day I looked up from my studies and realized: I was lonely.

NADIA: Me, too. Lonely. I realized. I looked up an old friend, a dancer, and went to visit her.

KENJI: I went down into town, and passed a wine bar where some musicians were playing. I walked in and listened for a while to this trio. Their music. Some of it sounded familiar, but I couldn't put a name to it. Later, I realized that their music was like the music I always heard in my dreams. Not the same, only like.

NADIA: My friend was going to this festival in Greece.

KENJI: Isn't that strange? The trio made me think: what about music? Music was in my dreams. What is it for?

NADIA: One of my friend's dance students was supposed to go with her, do small parts and help with the equipment. But the student got sick. My friend asked me to take her place, to go with the dancers to Greece.

KENJI: When I went back to the wine bar the trio was gone. But there was a poster of them-- they were going next to play at the Greek festival.

I decided to go there to hear them again. Something called me. All this time, music in my dreams, and never had I paid attention.

NADIA: I had not danced since I was a child!

KENJI: Since I was a child I had not played an instrument. I found my old violin, and took it with me.

NADIA: It brought us together.

KENJI: When I began playing again, I didn't get out my old music. I played what was in my dreams. *(plays)*

NADIA: When I heard it, I had to come and dance. *(dances)*

KENJI: So many years I didn't pay attention. Always I had the music in my dreams. And so did she! Same music! We discovered!

NADIA: I don't always, not like Kenji does.

KENJI: But when she does-- sometimes it's the same music! We discovered!

NADIA: My dream was his dream.

KENJI: Music is a sound wave is the butterfly wing that changes the whole universe!

NADIA: Not so unusual to dream music. Many people do, I think. Kenji's though--- when I dream it, I don't feel that it is my music. It's coming from somewhere else, beyond my understanding. But for him, it is his own... composed or at least as the material for composition as it comes in his dreams.

KENJI: Always. I wake up and write down, or try to but forget. But Nadia remembers for me!

NADIA: Not always, not even most. But if I had heard his dream....

KENJI: I come to the part that is missing, and Nadia has it!

NADIA: I can sing it, or dance it for him.

KENJI: Or even beat it on the drum. I write it down, and the rest comes flooding back to me. In the night I would use a notebook and flashlight, but now I use a recorder, a tiny recorder, under my pillow. It is so easy, I don't even have to wake up, but I can put it into my recorder as part of the dream. *(closes his eyes and sings da-da-da melody as if into recorder)*

NADIA: But it is not always there when you wake up? Is it?

KENJI: No. Usually, but not always. Sometimes I have only dreamed that I have recorded it. *(they laugh)*

NADIA: We travel to bring this all over.

KENJI: We do workshops.

NADIA: I teach dance. People are my pots now, bodies my clay. I ground them, I mold them, but they are not heavy. I shape them for music, for soul, so they can fly.

KENJI: Most people come to this country for the economy. *(playing through to the end)*

NADIA: Even artists.

KENJI: They teach for the money and the fame. They make their art a commodity.

NADIA: Not us.

KENJI: Money is of no interest to us.

NADIA: We come for the spirit. The freedom.

KENJI: Places like this, where people gather, we are home.

NADIA: The air-- you can smell it.

KENJI: The way people walk and sit and listen. *(to audience member)* Like you!

NADIA: With their souls.

KENJI: All over the world there's the longing.

NADIA: Wherever we go, we find it.

KENJI: People trapped in themselves, but ready to be free.

NADIA: We unwrap them, we give them wings.

KENJI: Wherever we go, butterflies.

(If it is possible to invite the audience to dance and sing with the cast, this is ideal!)

End of Scene.

AT THE CENTRE OF LIGHT

By R. Johns

This excerpt of the play looks at how Mary deals with her family's burden of poverty and how she escapes the ties of her family in order to follow her life work.

Time: Late 1850's

Characters :
MARY MACKILLOP - in this excerpt is a teenage girl. She is torn between wanting to please her father by rescuing her family from poverty, or finding a way to follow her own dreams.
ALEXANDER MACKILLOP- Mary's father is easily angered, easily frustrated and at times so optimistic that when his plans fail he gets very depressed.

Stage directions US - Up stage, DS - Down stage. PS - Prompt side of stage (stage left),OP - Off prompt(Stage right) CS - Centre stage.

The two actors are tied through most of the scene with a length of cord rope, so that wherever one goes, the other must follow. The father carries on his back the burden of debt, which can be symbolized by either a large puppet or a big bundle that weighs him down.

There is a small bench and wash bucket. The set has an inner circle of five large stones which represent the Southern Cross. The actors have to navigate their way through and around the stones.
Mary's hair falls to her shoulders like that of a young girl. She speaks to the audience.

MARY: Poor Papa was a dreamer

His head so full of schemes

He wanted those around him

To realize their dreams

But in debts he went under

And that's the way it stayed.

Alex enters. He wears on his back the creditor puppet (or a very big cloth bundle marked "debts"). The weight of it makes him almost bend double. It has a black rope attached to it. Alex has a broad Scottish accent

ALEX: They took the land off the blacks for strings of beads and bric-a-brac .Swindled them! And now they've swindled me. Leeches sucking our blood. We've lost our home and money.

Mary picks up washing bucket. She takes from it an apron which she puts on. She has a small piece of white cloth - she uses this in a movement sequence as if hanging sheet after sheet on a line.

ALEX: Mary...my bairn.... The creditors are after me. We've so many debts. I'm bent double with the burden. I can't go on. This creditor here demands payment.. and we've nothing left! Except to kill your animal!

MARY: Bloric..you want ..Bloric?

ALEX: I know she's your pet cow. But we all have to die sometime.

MARY: Pawn her then. And so we can get her back, chain the creditor to me. I'll work harder.

Mary ties the black rope of the puppet to her waist. So now when she moves she pulls Alex and the puppet with her. Mary kneels by the bucket and washes faster and faster

Poor Mama's hands are stiff hard from all the washing we're taking in I can wash faster than her. Make more money.

ALEX: Washing! Pah! That won't satisfy the creditors!

Alex moves away dragging Mary after him as she attempts to hang the washing up, so the black rope becomes taut like a washing line.

Now you're a big girl I've found you a situation. You're going to serve ladies and gents at a stationer's. You have to sell envelopes and paper, till the debts are paid off. We'll get an advance from your new employer.

MARY: But Papa. It's not my calling.

ALEX: And what is your calling?

Mary wraps the sheet around her face like a veil

MARY: To join an order of nuns.

ALEX: Ah that old dream!

MARY: But I saw Our Lady. She came to me. It wasn't a dream.

ALEX: Mary lass, forget it. You are doomed to worldly pursuits. But I won't have the education I've given you wasted. You'll not be a washerwoman. You can dream about the amiable and lovely perfection of God in the whir of the printing presses as you hand the ladies their stationary.

MARY: It is an occupation that is revolting to me. But I'll do it for you and Mama.

ALEX: If I could work I would. But no-one'll give me a job. And I'll fight every last bigot, who dares call me a bankrupt Papist who's the scum of the earth.

MARY: Don't upset yourself Papa. We'll manage.

ALEX: You must give me your wages. Your mother, bless her heart, is an incompetent manager of money.

Mary in ritualized movement hands out envelopes and places money inside the mouth of the puppet on her father's back. Alex holds out his hand for payment that never comes.

Where's it gone? Who took it?

Alex attacks the creditor puppet.

You scurrilous fraudster! You've cheated me enough. Made my life futile and empty!

MARY: Calm down Papa. Before you burst something.

She sits him on a bench DS OP. They sit side by side

ALEX : You could try work as a teacher? Or maybe I could teach!!! Amo Amas Amat. Which of us will it be? We're like the ass starving, can't choose between the two bales of hay. You must do it. I'll help. Take the burden and me with you Mary.

MARY: Situation after situation.

Mary steps out. She moves in varied directions around the circle with puppet and father hanging on.

ALEX: Amo Amas Amat Amamas Amatis Amant
(throughout movement sequence as Mary spins him around as she moves faster and faster around the circle)

MARY: Relatives children. Friend's children. Squatters children. Richmond, Western District, Penola. Then somewhere new.

Alex and Mary DS PS arms around each other's shoulders. They look out at the audience.

Portland Victoria. Where no one knows us. Become part of a school. Salary paid by the headmaster.

She turns her back and chalks on imaginary wall and then turns again front and directly addresses the audience as if they are children.

Portland. Who can tell me what is special about Portland?

Alex mimes whales in size and spouting air

Yes! Seals on the rocks!

ALEX: The whalers thick with blood! Whales... Harpoons stuck in their throats!!!

MARY: Maybe we could sing the carol we learnt. I saw three ships a'sailing .

ALEX and MARY:*(sing)* Come sailing by on Christmas day in the morning.

Mary and Alex link arms and dance a jig. Then Mary chalks again upstage as if on a school board teaching the children. Alex glares at the bench, and the schoolmaster he sees in his mind, sitting there

ALEX: I wouldn't have a clear conscience. If I didn't fight the Headmaster here. *(He starts to spar with an imaginary opponent ducking and weaving)* Stand up. Fight like a man. You're a cheat headmaster. The outside examiner comes in to judge your school. So you take Mary's class for the day and pretend it's yours because her children are drilled so lovely. You leave her with your little beasts an' brats who canna' spell nor read. How dare you make a fool of my daughter? Why you're no better than Shakespeare's Bottom become a Donkey! HEEHAW!

Alex swings a boxing blow then falls backwards.

MARY: *(runs to him)* Papa are you hurt?

ALEX: I can't get off the ground. All this is killin' me.

MARY: I've been sacked. Portland is sending us packing.

ALEX: Why?

MARY: Oh Papa!

ALEX: Because of that cross-eyed cheat. Mary, love, I had to do it. To help you! *(To audience)* I went up high street yellin' what are all you stupid fat lazy prize idiots going to do about it.

MARY: *(looking at audience apologetically)* Excuse me. *(She helps him up and takes him off to one side)* Nobody will do business with us anymore. Only Dr. Rodriquez will help.

ALEX: But he's the Blacks Doctor! I don't want his rose oil on my bruises/

MARY: He told me he had a strange dream.

ALEX: Stinks of garlic/

MARY: Miss Mary, you in brown habit. You're a nun. This army of nuns follows you. They cry. Weeping like someone died. The Pope makes the sign of the cross and all peaceful.

ALEX: He's even poorer than us. What would he know?

MARY: Is a true dream, Miss MacKillop.

Alex leads Mary to the bench. They kneel side by side DS OP. The bench now becomes a pew in the church.

ALEX: Mary love, a religious life is a hard one. How are you ever going to be a nun? I wanted to be a priest. But it was a sacred state I felt unqualified to fit.

Mary whispers to him

MARY: There's a priest. He wants me to teach at a school for him. He says he can pay our debts.

ALEX: Pay our debts?

MARY: I go to him without you and Mamma.

ALEX: Who is this priest?

MARY: The one who writes to me.

ALEX: Oh him! Father Woods! He's an embarrassment to the name of priest. What sort of a priest trains for a year here and there. He's a second rate sort of priest. I did the years in Rome. I studied for years. All or nothing. That's what makes a first rate priest. Not Father Woods.

MARY: I'm going. It's the only option left.

Mary gets up and walks upstage however as Alex and puppet still attached to her by the rope, she moves in different directions without success.

ALEX: Are you deaf? He won't do well by you.

MARY: I've struggled and struggled. I've tried to keep you happy but it never works out because we're not obeying what God wants for us.

ALEX: How can ye split the family?

MARY: We struggle on and struggle on. Mama is always afraid. The young ones all farmed out to relatives year after year.

ALEX: We depend on you Mary.

MARY: We do our best but times always turn bad - the arguments and the feuding.

ALEX: Don't leave us Mary. I beg you.

MARY: It's killing all of us.

ALEX: What will become of me?

MARY: You have my heart Papa because Jesus gives me his.

Mary kisses his forehead and slowly unties the black rope that binds her to him. She holds the rope out to him

But to do my work I have to have my soul and my body so I can labor for him in this world. With love.

ALEX:I won't let you go. You're breaking my heart.

He refuses to take the rope which drops

MARY: Your way we'll both go under.

(She steps away from him DS OP. Her eyes fill with tears but she keeps her face turned away from him)

MARY: I have to be free.

ALEX: All my life I've chased the will' o the wisp of freedom. And I lost everything. Even you.

Mary still is turned away as her father stands upstage of her.

If you must go, I canna' stop you.

Mow harshly almost bitterly.

May the Lord bless you and keep you.

He turns back to look at Mary in a last effort to get her to look at him

ALEX: And remember whatever happens. You're a survivor. You're a MacKillop.

She doesn't look so he exits unaware Mary has now turned to watch him leave bent double with the burden. She , heartbroken, puts her hands to her face, to stop the tears.

End of Scene.

THE LAST OF THE KENTUCKY GLENROW PAPER DOLLS

By Molly Hagan

*The lights come up on two young girls – JUDY and HANNAH
RAE, wearing bathrobes. Hannah Rae sits at a vanity
applying make-up as Judy walks the room. Behind the two
girls is a rack holding two dresses – one an enormous,
white and frilly wedding dress and the other a gaudy blue
gown.*

JUDY: Mama said you met a new man, said she heard you talkin' about him on the phone.

HANNAH RAE: That's a lie!

JUDY: That's not what Mama said. Says you always talk about the men over there – says you can't get 'em outta your head, but you won't tell her anything. Don't worry! I won't breathe a word to Bobby, you're still with Bobby aren't you, Hannah Rae?

HANNAH RAE: I brought him today, didn't I?

JUDY: It's only natural for a girl to keep her – options open. He's a bit of child though, don't you think? Something a little too cute about him, in his face it's –

A knock at the door.

BOBBY: *(Offstage.)* Hannah Rae? Judy? You girls in there? Can I come in?

HANNAH RAE: *(Looking at Judy.)* You can come in, Bobby.

BOBBY enters.

JUDY: ...And I just told the man at Macy's, I said, blue, blue for my baby sister, she's always looked so pretty in blue. And only nineteen! A perfect little doll, my Hannah Rae! Then I told him, the man at Macy's. Ted. I believe was his name. Anyway, I told Ted, I said - I haven't seen my poor baby sister in twelve whole months – a year! She is comin' all the way from Iraq (pronounce "EYE-RACK") for my wedding day! Well. Ted just about had to dry his eyes and he said to me, Judy, that is the nicest thing I have ever heard. And then he sold me the dress half-price, you like it?

HANNAH RAE: Sounds nice. Don't you think he sounds like a nice man, Bobby?

BOBBY: Sure does, sure does. How are y'all doin'? Ready for the big -

Judy moves to the hangers at the back of the stage, holding up her wedding dress like a grail.

JUDY: Help me with my dress, baby? I can't wait another second.

Judy brings the dress to her sister.

JUDY: I'm so nervous I could pee. Bobby, will you make sure to tell Tommy not to come in here? Good. He better not see me in my dress before the wedding or I will not be spreading my virgin legs tonight - I told him that just yesterday. Can you believe it?

BOBBY: *(Blushing.)* No, I cannot.

JUDY: I couldn't either. I blush just thinking about it.

BOBBY: I think I'll go tell Tommy now, but I don't think he'd wanna come in here anyways.

BOBBY exits.

JUDY: HANNAH RAE:

Bye, now. Bye, Bobby.

HANNAH RAE: You didn't have to do that, Judy.

JUDY: I don't know what you mean. Do you think I would strip down in front of that boy? I don't care how young he is-

HANNAH RAE: Judy!

JUDY: I just hope you finally met a real man in the army. You're still a virgin, aren't you, Hannah Rae? Good, it's better that way – God's way. Dress me, baby?

She undoes her robe letting it fall to the floor. She wears a silk, white slip. She holds her arms out to her sides, smiling radiantly. Hannah Rae begins to dress her in silence.

JUDY: I sense that you have no desire to talk to me at this particular moment, which is a shame considering that it is my wedding day. *(Pause.)* So I shall continue to speak for both of us. I feel weightless, like a doll, like a little paper doll. Make sure to fold back those tabs, Hannah Rae, close those zippers! I don't want anything falling out in front of the baby Jesus and everybody when I walk down the aisle.

HANNAH RAE: God this, baby Jesus that – you sound like Mama.

JUDY: No problem with a girl soundin' like her mama, Hannah Rae. It is the proper way of things. A girl will become her mama someday she will become a lady. You will understand when you get married, when you're no longer a child.

HANNAH RAE: Is that what you think, Judy?

JUDY: Look at that boy, Hannah Rae! Just look at him.

HANNAH RAE: This isn't about Bobby! If anyone is acting like the child, Judy, it's you.

Hannah Rae zips up the back of Judy's dress and fastens the clasp.

JUDY: Excuse me for being blunt, baby, but we've let you run wild – we let you join the army and pretend to be a boy, but now it is time for you to settle down. It is time for you to settle down and meet a good man – become a woman, a lady. Now, how do I look in my wedding dress?

It was Mama's – all the women of the Glenrow line have worn it. And one day, baby girl, it will be your wedding dress too.

The two sisters examine Judy's appearance in the mirror.

HANNAH RAE: You look just like Mama.

JUDY: Don't be ridiculous. I am much prettier than Mama was. Now, let me dress you. Let me dress you like a little paper doll.

HANNAH RAE: Absolutely not, I am perfectly capable of dressing myself.

Judy retrieves Hannah Rae's gaudy blue bridesmaid's dress from the rack.

JUDY: Don't be silly. Let me dress you. Let me dress you, so you can tell me all about this man you met in the army.

HANNAH RAE: I told you – there was no man!

Judy removes Hannah Rae's robe. She wears a thin slip.

JUDY: You're telling me no man has seen this pretty little body? Pick up your arms – and smile! It's my wedding day.

Judy begins to dress her sister.

JUDY: Look at you! Skinny as a twig – probably only weigh about a hundred pounds. Rounding out in the thighs and the breasts, though – you're practically a grown woman! Men were probably droppin' their guns at the sight of you!

HANNAH RAE: That is none of your business.

JUDY: You are my baby sister. Everything is my business. Now, hold out your arms! Aren't soldiers supposed to have better posture?

HANNAH RAE: That's enough, Judy!

JUDY: I told you, if you want to become -

HANNAH RAE: All that talk about bein' a lady. I bet you've spread your "virgin" legs more times than you've prayed to the baby Jesus.

JUDY: Hannah Rae Glenrow Stevens. You take that back right this second! What if Tommy hears you! You are an absolute liar. A liar and a – a fornicator!

Hannah Rae spins around to look at Judy. For a moment she doesn't speak.

JUDY: I knew it! I could see it in the way you move – full of sin. Who's the liar, now, Hannah Rae? Who was he? I know it wasn't Bobby. Was he attractive? An officer?

HANNAH RAE: What if I said he was an officer, an older man?

JUDY: Hah!

HANNAH RAE: What if I said that I was ashamed of it –
every second of every day - and I wish I had never been
born? What if I said I was a liar, a fornicator and killer?
What would you think of me then Judy? You think I'll ever
be a lady?

*Judy falls silent. Hannah Rae's voice becomes softer now,
like an adult speaking to a child.*

HANNAH RAE: You can have your paper dolls and your
pure, white wedding, Judy. But for me, this body's all I got
left.

*A loud KNOCK at the door takes both girls by surprise.
Long pause. Another knock.*

JUDY: Tommy, what did I tell you about coming in here?
Don't make me tell you again.

BOBBY: *(Offstage.)* It's Bobby. What's all that yellin' in
there?

Pause.

HANNAH RAE: Nothing, Bobby. Just excited that's all.

Bobby, a boy wearing his father's tuxedo, enters.

BOBBY: Walkin' by, ya'll about nearly gave me a heart
attack. Why are my two favorite little ladies so upset? Dress
don't fit, or something?

JUDY: No, Bobby, fits like a dream, like it was cut out for
me. What do you think? How do I look, Bobby? Don't I
make a pretty bride?

BOBBY: Sure do, Judy, you look real nice. *(Beat.)* Hannah Rae, baby, what's the matter? You cryin?

JUDY: You know how we girls are – gettin' sad over nothing.

BOBBY: *(To Hannah Rae.)* I think you look real sweet.

JUDY: *(To Hannah Rae.)* What do you think, baby? Do you like it? I want you to like it.

BOBBY: You ready, pretty girl?

JUDY: Wait! Your zipper's come undone. Let me fix it – make sure that nothing falls out in front of the baby Jesus, nothing we wouldn't want him to see. There! How do you feel now, pretty baby?

HANNAH RAE: Same as you, Judy. Weightless, just like a little paper doll.

Judy and Bobby laugh. Bobby clasps Hannah Rae around the waist and they exit. Judy returns to sit at the vanity where Hannah Rae sat at the beginning of the play. She sits, lost in thought, playing with the folds of her dress and waiting to walk down the aisle as the lights fade out.

End of Scene.

GOOD SOLDIERS, BRAVE COMRADES, LOYAL CITIZENS

By Toni Press-Coffman

MEL is a young Japanese American soldier in the first Iraq war whose grandfather was incarcerated in a re-location camp during World War II. IRINI is a 19 year old Arab exchange student who lives next door to MEL's grandfather. The scene takes place on IRINI's patio.

MEL: Let me take you out someplace tonight.

IRINI: I like this hat.

(MEL takes off his baseball cap and puts it on her head.)

IRINI: Now I wish we could go to baseball.

MEL: I'll take you to a basketball game instead.

IRINI: Stanford has a game I think.

MEL: You can't get tickets to a Stanford game.

IRINI: I will get them because I am a student. *(beat)* Was that the phone?

MEL: No, Irini.

IRINI: I am going crazy with this bombing.

MEL: But it's far away from Morocco, right?

IRINI: It is Arab people, therefore it is not so far. My father especially must be besides himself.

MEL: Beside.

IRINI: Beside himself. Thank you. I think my father will not allow me to go home. He is a - *(she laughs)* like you say, a bull.

MEL: A bully.

IRINI: Yes.

MEL: Mine too.

IRINI: When I was a child our house was very different with and without my father. We were much more - dignified - when he was at home, but when he was not, Ya Ya, my mother and my father's sisters and me suddenly would be very silly. We would sing together and we would be very wild. We would cook dinner with no clothes on.

MEL: What?

IRINI: Yes, we would be nude cooks. Secretly my father loves this wild part of my mother. Really, he is so much in love with her and so he should because she gave up so much for him. She gave up Greece and it is a lot to give up your country.

MEL: My dad's nuts about my mom too, only I guarantee you she hasn't got a wild bone in her body.

IRINI: No?

MEL: No.

IRINI: You do?

MEL: I don't know.

IRINI: Mr. Rudy does.

MEL: He does?

IRINI: Oh, yes.

MEL: You want to help me throw a little party for him tomorrow?

IRINI: Yes. His birthday, yes?

MEL: 70 years old.

IRINI: Yes I want to.

MEL: Just the three of us.

IRINI: He'll like that better. He is a - he enjoys to be alone.

MEL: He's a loner.

IRINI: Yes. When my father visited last year, this is also what they called his rented car.

MEL: They're spelled differently. *(IRINI looks at him questioningly.)* Those two words. They're spelled differently.

IRINI: Yes, but then why does one pronounce them identically?

MEL: *(shrugs)* I'm stumped.

IRINI: You are stumped. *(beat)* Strange language. *(pause)* Why are you in the Army?

MEL: I joined up right after school because I didn't want to go to college and I didn't know what else to do. I figured it would give me time to think.

IRINI: But you didn't settle it?

MEL: No.

IRINI: Well, what do you like?

MEL: I guess I should know by now but I don't.

IRINI: You do. Baseball?

MEL: Yeah, baseball.

IRINI: What else?

MEL: I like to work out.

IRINI: Be strong?

MEL: Yeah.

IRINI: Be a big man?

MEL: Yeah.

IRINI: You look good.

MEL: Thanks.

IRINI: *(beat)* You want to be like your grandfather? A sumo wrestler?

MEL: *(a laugh)* No. Well. I want to be strong like him, have a strong body. *(beat)* His family really got screwed by this whole re-location thing. You know, the orchard just went to seed during the war when they couldn't care for it. My mother told me when they went home to the Sacramento Valley her grandfather tried to revive it singlehandedly. Now this guy was gigantic. My mom makes this guy out to be like Samson or something, grasping a grapevine barehanded where the tops had died but the roots were good so the suckers would come up, digging into the earth and cutting the trunk and putting new buds into that and then covering it over. Can you imagine that? Sometimes she looks at me and I know she's thinking about him, because - well, you know, she says I look so much like him. Anyway, even though her uncle lost a leg in France, he and her father tried to help. But it was just too much for them. Her grandfather died in that orchard. One day he tried to get up after lunch and he just keeled over and he had to be lifted up and carried out of there. Big old guy. He was the sumo champion of Northern California - he was undefeated. He was paralyzed. He lay in bed for a couple years, but really he died that day in the orchard.

IRINI: Maybe before that.

MEL: Yeah.

IRINI: All big strong men in your family.

MEL: They loved their land. They loved to labor and make things grow in the earth. So does my Mom.

IRINI: So do you?

MEL: Yeah. (pause, he puts his arms around her) I'd like to kiss you but I kind of feel like you're my sister or cousin or something.

IRINI: I am not.

(They kiss, then again, again and again. Then the phone rings.)

IRINI: Oh.

MEL: Shit.

IRINI: Yes.

(She starts to go, turns to him.)

IRINI: I will come back.

(She exits quickly to her bedroom)

End of Scene.

GONE ASTRAY

By Jennie S. Redling

CAST:
Warren O'Mally, Irish American, 40-50
Winston O'Mally, Warren's son, deaf, mentally handicapped,
obese, 22
Abbie Firewing: Lakota Sioux, 20

TIME: Present

PLACE: A small town in the eastern Adirondacks

AT RISE: Winston sits before a battered upright piano
wearing a set of earphones unconnected to anything. Having
just transported the piano from an upstairs room, Warren is
staring with wonder at his biceps. Abbie has just returned
from searching for clues in an effort to find Warren's
daughter, Raven, who has been missing for nine years.

WARREN: Somethin come over me, never felt like that,
even liftin parts at the shop.

ABBIE: Those tracks? Looked to me like they could have
been from a mountain lion.

WARREN: Mountain lion? Never saw one a those fifty
years I lived here. Musta been a big dog or somethin.

ABBIE: The mud dried around them, they were pretty clear.
I'm a little worried.

WARREN: How about a beer? You know, it's just a hobby,
collecting beers. Winston? why don't you play for Abbie?

ABBIE: He's sleepy. I'll fix your bed, Tahca Ushte.

WARREN: Ever hear of Polar beer from Venezuela? I ordered it from a catalog.

(Abbie opens the sofa bed. Warren rises and makes his tipsy way off. Winston lays his cheek beside the piano and presses a key.)

ABBIE: Mr. O'Mally, if it's okay, I'm gonna sleep down here tonight. (*She turns to see Warren gone.*) Tahca? I have something for you. (*No response*) Lame Deer?

(Clapping her hands) WINSTON?

(Still no response. She removes the earphones from his head, listens to them, hands them back.)

You can't hear a thing, can you?

*(Winston smiles, automatically moves his hand from his ear to HIS mouth, then touches his chest [**Deaf**].)*

ABBIE: Lame Deer, have you ever seen a man with a beard outside anywhere?

(Frightened, he moves away from her and into the sideboard, knocking the posters to the floor. He gapes at them, then scrambles to the sofabed, cowering. Abbie lifts a poster, stares at it. Shaken, she sets it aside.)

Don't——don't be afraid, little brother. I'll find him.

(She opens her back pack, removes something.)

But if anything happens to me and you need to talk to the spirits, you burn a little of this sage bundle, you understand?

(Winston accepts the small bundle, sniffs it, looks at her and nods.)
(Low, urgent) Tahca, where did your sister used to go on the

mountain, do you know? (*Articulating clearly*) Up on the mountain? Where is that camp?

(*Winston places his hands side by side in front of him, palms toward his chest and fingers pressed together, then springs open his fingers and crosses his hands over his heart [**Afraid**].*)

Maybe my grandfather was right, Tahca. We might need to make a sacrifice.

WARREN: What sacrifice?

(*Abbie whirls around. Warren appears in the doorway with an open bottle of beer, a pillow and pair of pajamas.*)

Whatcha gonna sacrifice?

ABBIE: Uh, nothing, I was just, you know, telling Winston about different ceremonies and stuff.

WARREN: Come get in your jammies, Winston.

ABBIE : I think he's been having dreams about my people.

WARREN: What makes ya say that?

ABBIE: He mentioned Drinks Water.

WARREN: He mentioned what?

ABBIE: See, I have this old book. (*Taking a book from her backpack*) It's got interviews with chiefs and people like my grandfather and it mentions Drinks Water.

WARREN: (*To Winston*) Whatsa matter, baby?

(*Winston snatches the pajamas, begins clumsily to undress.*)
ABBIE: He was a Lakota holy man who dreamed about

how this strange species would weave a spider's web around my people and how we'd live in a wasted land and we'd starve.

WARREN: Sure, Winston, go ahead——you can do it by yourself. Go on.

ABBIE: Mr. O'Mally, those tracks? They come pretty far down in this direction—and I know your wife doesn't want to understand the truth but——

WARREN: Ah, don't hold nothin' against Ker, okay? She's sweet underneath, if you ever heard her sing, she's got a voice like one a heaven's birds——hasn't sung a note in years but once you bring Raven back——

ABBIE: I can't bring Raven back.

WINSTON: DAD-DY.

WARREN: Well, well, will you look at you, Winston? Look, he got his jammies on— just let Daddy fix the buttons.

WINSTON: Dreem...

WARREN: Good job, Winston. Come on now, in to bed we go. What a big boy, getting dressed and undressed all by himself. That's right, fella. Close your eyes. That's my boy. (*Turning off the lamps.*) Ready? Now I lay me down to sleep, I pray the Lord my soul to keep. If I should die before I wake, I pray the Lord my soul to... (*Pause*) to...

(*Warren suddenly buries his face in his hands. Winston stares at Abbie then speaks something only she hears.*)

WINSTON: Ay-chana ninck-inck-day. You are going to die soon.

(Abbie freezes. Warren raises his head to see her grab her backpack and head for the door.)

WARREN: Wait—where you goin?

ABBIE: I can't talk to spirits—okay, Mr. O'Mally? I never did any of this stuff before last year—I'm sorry if I stirred her up, I didn't mean to——

WARREN: Don't be sorry——this here's the closest I felt to Raven in I can't say how long——since that ceremony you did——

ABBIE: I was just pretending with that ceremony—

WARREN: So? I pretend alla time——I go up and take holy communion——I know it's just a bingo chip made a puffed rice, but I pretend it's God and it is. You're no fake, you're a sweet kid——

ABBIE: I'm not sweet—at fifteen I was turning tricks for booze——I was the biggest joke on the Res——I was a drunk like you. She's dead——okay? What you whites call dead. I have to go.

WARREN: *(Stopping her)* Hold it——I know you were arrested. Okay? We know all about it. It don't matter to me. The police still looking for you? That what you're afraid of?

ABBIE: No, and if your wife went on line to check me out she'd have seen those charges were dropped——that son of a bitch cop just wanted to get me alone. Goodbye, I'm sorry, I should never have come.

WARREN: Then why did you? Why, if you were just gonna give up after making us hope? You know what it's like? It's like living half a sneeze, half a heartbeat, waitin for the other half, expectin, never sleepin. Why the hell did you come if—? Forget it. Go. Just go. Get the hell out of here.

(Abbie doesn't move. She turns to where Winston lies asleep. Warren sees the one unopened beer bottle on the table, lifts it, gives the cap a twist but Abbie places a hand on his arm and lowers it.)

ABBIE: Last year on the Res things started getting sick——trees—— animals——pets——then a baby I was caring for died. And another. It was on the news, you must of seen it——disease control people said it was a bacteria or something, but the old grandmothers——they blamed me. So my grandfather held a ceremony. He said a spirit strayed into our midst——vengeful spirit. I wanted to get back at the ones who blamed me, who were saying how I was a disgrace, how I dishonored my grandfather so I boasted I was as good and as brave as any blood and that I'd kill it——the dark spirit. I thought it was all bull but I went through the motions anyway cause I was so mad. I prepared, made it through inipi——the sweat lodge——and I cried for a vision, for a dream——three nights, no water, no food, no sleep, full moon like this, I hear it——somebody crying. Sobbing. Someone yelling, I see a car. I see a man, beard, long hair. And a girl. A little girl. Ten...eleven— *(Grabbing the poster) This* little girl.

WARREN: Last month? But Raven, was——she'd be twenty years old.

ABBIE: The car was an old model silver Camaro——believe me, visions don't lie, I know that now——she must have been dead for years——

WARREN: No, you're her, aren't you? Your name is "Raven." You're my daughter. You just don't remember.

ABBIE: Raven's my Indian name and maybe that's why she picked me, I don't know, but she——your daughter——I think Hicks killed her out there by the Res and she showed me in dreams how to get here. I thought she was trying to lead me to the bastard who poisoned our water or whatever but now...

now there's some fierce hungry force out there that Winston can feel and I think it might be *her*.

WARREN: Who?

ABBIE: Raven! I don't know what she wants but she's freaking me out.

WARREN: If Raven's really dead like you're saying, then prove it
to us. That's all I ask——prove it! Once and for all, make it clear as a bell so Kerryn can see. Clear. Clean. Goddamn it, can't you just make it all clean again?

(Abbie stares at Warren. A long pause.)

ABBIE: That... could be it.

WARREN: What?

ABBIE: Yeah. That... that could be what she's after.

WARREN: What're you talkin about?

ABBIE: Sure. Why else would she kill the babies? That must be it. She's hungry for a clean spirit. A niya.

WARREN: A what?

ABBIE: A child's spirit. An innocent one. In exchange for hers that was slaughtered.

WARREN: What the hell does that mean? *(Grabbing her)* Give me a straight answer you goddamn little——

ABBIE: Let me go, Mr. O'Mally—there's nothing I can do anymore—I think she's coming after your son.

End of Scene.

MEASUREMENTS OF A MURDERER

By Lucy Tyler

Characters:
Nona: A young woman, incarcerated at 14, now 19.
Ana: A young woman incarcerated at 16, now 19.

Scene VII

Two chairs CS. The Beauty Pageant banner is perfectly hung US. The balloons are unpopped.
ANA, is stood on one chair, naked or scantily clad. Throughout the scene she dresses in the Greek Goddess costume. NONA is kneeling at her feet, hemming. She is wearing a boiler suit.

ANA: I wanted to be Jesus Christ.

NONA: You are.

ANA: Here used to be heaven because it's irrelevant.   This is all because a wolf won't eat wolf.

NONA: Excuse me, I have love for you. A. Men. A. Men. A. Men.

ANA: It's a contrary teaching.

NONA: But I'm sure it's nearly a truth.

Nona stands.

The truth is I. Do. Love. You.

ANA: I try not to love myself. But I can't stop.

NONA: I. Love. You.

ANA: *Uncomfortable pause.* We should love each other. These are the rules I know. What else is there? Not a lot. Besides freedom. Listen.

We must love ourselves. If we don't, we'll never be free.

Nona climbs onto the other chair to be face to face with Ana.

NONA: *Shaking Ana.* Yes but I. Love. You. You. You alone and devotedly. You as husband, you as wife and you and me in front of God.

ANA: I don't want a husband.

Nona forces herself against Ana.

NONA: But I'm your reflection, your truth made flesh.

Holds Ana tight.

Ana allows Nona to hold her for a moment. Nona's back is to the audience, Ana's eyes are wide with fear facing the audience.

Do you remember that outside, they call this communion?

Ana pulls herself out into the shape of a cross

And when you bleed, to me, it's the blood of Christ.

ANA: Holy blood?

NONA: Yes!

ANA: I'm not Christ.

Disturbed, Ana sits down.

NONA: No?

Nona sits, tries to kiss Ana. Ana won't let her.

ANA: I'll love myself and eventually be free. Anyway, my crucifixion has never meant love. A community did. And family. My family. Faith and community and children and marriage.

NONA: Never. We're connected. We renew each other, like bleeding; it's something only two women have innate understanding of.

Takes Ana's hand.

It unites us.

ANA: Let's just say we have an understanding and leave it there.

Ana exits. Nona stays stood on the chair. Faces audience.

NONA: No.

Blackout

Scene VIII

Fade to Nona still standing on the chair. The lights dim. There is a boiler suit on the floor in front of her. She provocatively removes her own boiler suit.

Holding the two boiler suits as far apart as she can manage, she looks from one to the other.

NONA: During the day, we've become so reformed, so conscientious and citizenly. Ana loves me.

But with polite diffidence.

At night? In the dark? The rooms fill with every crime.
Every selfish desire. And mine is the biggest of all.

*Frantic, she stands down and winds the two boiler suits
together. She lies them on the floor.*

Never leave me alone, never leave me alone in the dark.

*She replaces one of the boiler suits in the union, and
entwines herself with the other.*

Into your hands I go. I've commended my spirit, so love me.
Love me closer. Light me. You've warmed the cold from
my heart, now lick this dirt from my soul. Let me take the
hunger from my mouth and taste your freedom, your body,
your blood, your love. *She strokes the boiler suit, kisses it
all over.* The heat of you in this cold is undeniable and
essential.

She lies next to it, holding the sleeve like a hand.

Iamnameless&empty&cold&hungry&criminaldespicable&n
othing&nothing except to you. We've shared a bed and a
common prayer for twelve years. Until now.

*Fade to ANA who is kneeling SR in front of Innovator and
Warden, as close to audience as possible.*

ANA: Bless me. I have sinned. Twelve years since.
You've punished me accordingly. And I understand now. I
value life now, and I promise, I understand the value of love.
I do love you. I do, do love you. I love you. Amen. But
not enough. I want my freedom.

Lights dim. Fade to Nona

NONA: They flung us out of the world together. It didn't matter, it was better: jostledaboutjiggledupamongeachother, finding the rest of ourselves in someone else.   Our reaction: to love

Some boiler suits fall to the stage; others stay suspended and huddle closer together.

NONA: and survive together.
Waiting&wilting&wasting&tested until nothing is sacred but the knowledge that we are in communion; tightlytightlyunited.

Nona suddenly holds the boiler suit very tenderly.

Please Ana, take me as your comfort: a kiss as recompense. You must love the measurements of a murderer's body.

Her mood changes

Until now.

ANA: I can't. I can't love you. I want a husband and children, to fall in love over a long summer, and for the sky not to change colour over me. I'm there now. So I won't love you. And I'm leaving without you.

Ana exits

Nona remains silent in shock. Suddenly she tears viciously at the boiler suit. It tears. She bites it and screams and tears and tears. There is silence for a long time. Nona reacts to the sight of the torn boiler suit as if she has understood for the first time.

Immediate blackout. Nona screams a long scream in the dark.

End of Scene.

MADRIGAL IN BLACK AND WHITE

By Pat Montley

SYNOPSIS
A chance encounter between two young women—one black, one white—escalates into the beginning of a relationship, despite their own awkwardness and the warnings of their uncensored alter-egos.

CAST OF CHARACTERS
Liz: mid-to-late 20's, white
Shadow Liz: Liz's uncensored, wise-cracking alter-ego; any age, white
Cleo: mid-to-late 20's, African American
Shadow Cleo: Cleo's uncensored, wise-cracking alter-ego; any age, African-American

SETTING
The street in front of Liz's suburban house.
The present.

PRODUCTION NOTES
Liz and Cleo can be played realistically. But the performances of the Shadows should be stylized. They are less the ominous Jungian "evil twin" than they are the sometimes humorous, always embarrassing Turret's-twin. Non-realistic costumes and stylized movement might serve them best. The Shadows generally talk to their respective Persons, but the Persons—although they hear these comments—speak only to each other. The "car" can be represented by a two-dimensional cut-out frame, or simply by chairs.

SCENE: Bright sunlight. Sound effect: lawn mower. LIZ is (miming) mowing the lawn. CLEO is sitting in the driver's seat of a car whose headlights are on. SHADOW-CLEO is in the car with CLEO. SHADOW-LIZ accompanies LIZ.

LIZ stops mowing, crosses slowly towards the car, squinting into the sun, but   within a few feet of it, stops abruptly.

LIZ: Oh! Sorry. I didn't see anyone in the car. I, um...

SHADOW-LIZ: You didn't see her because she's black.

LIZ: The sun! The sun was in my eyes.

SHADOW-CLEO: *(To CLEO.)* You're invisible.

CLEO: The sun? *(Turns to look out the back window.)* Oh. The sun was...in your eyes.

LIZ: *(Finishes sentence with her.)* In my eyes. Yes. *(Self-consciously pointing and squinting.)* West. *(Gesturing to the lawnmower she left behind.)* I was, uh, mowing the lawn and I...saw the car sitting here.

SHADOW-LIZ: A car you didn't recognize, on your dead-end street—

LIZ: And I wondered—

SHADOW-LIZ: What it was doing in front of the Johnson's driveway.

LIZ: —why the lights were on.

CLEO: Oh. I didn't realize they were.... *(Turns lights off.)* Thanks.

SHADOW-CLEO: Neighborhood Watch at work. They'll all sleep safer tonight.

LIZ: I was going to turn them off. I mean if no one was in the car. So the battery...

SHADOW-CLEO: She was going to rifle the glove compartment for crack.

CLEO: Tricky business.

LIZ: *(Misunderstanding.)* What? No, really. I was only thinking that the battery would—

CLEO: No, I didn't mean—I meant you always feel...a person always feels—

SHADOW-CLEO: A black person always feels—

CLEO: You always feel funny about doing that to another person's car.

SHADOW-LIZ: Doing what?

CLEO: Reaching in the window.

LIZ: Right! Or opening the door to—

CLEO: Yeah. So you make a big deal of it. Or look around the parking lot for an accomplice so you can say: "Should we try to turn the lights out in that car before the battery—"

LIZ: Exactly! And you think the cops are going to pull up just as you put your hand on the switch.

(LIZ and CLEO laugh.)

SHADOW-CLEO: They wouldn't arrest you, Sweetheart.

SHADOW-LIZ: So ask her what she's doing here.

SHADOW-CLEO: Better tell her what you're doing here.

CLEO: I'm waiting for my brother. *(Gestures to the house next to LIZ's.)* He's in there.

LIZ: Oh.

SHADOW-LIZ: Didn't know the Johnson's were having any work done.

SHADOW-CLEO: She thinks he's robbing the place.

CLEO: His car's in the shop.

SHADOW-CLEO: Tell her he's a financial adviser. American Express.

SHADOW-LIZ: Wait. They did talk about getting a new roof. Remember they asked us about recommending—

CLEO: So I'm giving him a lift.

SHADOW-LIZ: In the getaway car.

LIZ: Who says siblings can't be nice?

SHADOW-LIZ: She's probably got twenty of them—raised by a single mother who worked herself to an early grave cleaning white women's houses with carcinogenic chemicals.

SHADOW-CLEO: Tell her he's a doctor making a house call. *(Realizing no one would believe it.)* Nah. Forget that.

CLEO: I was just admiring...your house.

SHADOW-LIZ: Lock up the silver.

SHADOW-CLEO: Good move. Now she'll go right in and lock up the silver.

LIZ: Did you want to come up on the porch while you wait. Maybe have a cold drink.

SHADOW-CLEO: Your big break, Girlfriend! Sit on the plantation veranda, sipping mint juleps and watchin' the darkies pick cotton.

LIZ: I was just ready for one myself.

SHADOW-LIZ: Calm down, Sister. Next you'll be telling her your grandmother marched in Selma.

CLEO: I...I brought some work to do. *(Lifts papers on her lap.)* But thanks. Thanks anyway.

SHADOW-CLEO: Now you've gone and hurt Miz Scarlett's feelin's.

LIZ: Oh. Sure.

SHADOW-LIZ: Don't look so disappointed. It's embarrassing.

CLEO: I think I would like to stretch my legs though. *(Gets out of car.)*

SHADOW-LIZ: *(To LIZ.)* Nice legs, eh? We need to spend more time in the sun, you know. Promise me.

LIZ: *(Noticing parking sticker on windshield.)* Ah. University sticker. You a student there?

SHADOW-CLEO: O, Sweet Sojourner! This is my favorite part!

CLEO: I'm a teacher.

SHADOW-LIZ: Whooooa! Great White Liberal puts foot in mouth.

LIZ: Hey! Me too. What do you teach?

SHADOW-CLEO: Ease her conscience. Tell her we teach remedial reading to the phonetically challenged.

CLEO: Shakespeare.

LIZ: Wow!

SHADOW-LIZ: Don't act so surprised.

LIZ: I'm...impressed.

SHADOW-CLEO: I wonder why.

CLEO: In the English Department.

SHADOW-CLEO: And all this time she thought Shakespeare was physics.

CLEO: What do you teach?

LIZ: Music.

CLEO: Really?

SHADOW-LIZ: Tell her it's gospel and she'll have a drink with you.

LIZ: I'm at the City High School for the Arts. *(Thrusts her hand out.)* Liz Trotter.

CLEO: *(Shakes hands.)* Cleo Harris.

LIZ: For Cleopatra?

SHADOW-CLEO: Here we go.

CLEO: My mother was a fan.

LIZ: Of Shakespeare?

CLEO: Of Cleopatra Jones. *(THEY laugh.)* What kind of music?

LIZ: Choral. I conduct the concert choir. And the madrigal group.

CLEO: That's great.

LIZ: Do you sing?

SHADOW-LIZ: Why not ask her if she does the Watusi?

CLEO: No. But I did my dissertation on Shakespeare's love songs.

SHADOW-LIZ: Uh-oh—bombs bursting in air.

LIZ: What!?

CLEO: The songs in Shakespeare's plays. You know... "O Mistress Mine"... "How Should I Your True Love Know"... "Where the Bee Sucks, There Suck I"....

SHADOW-CLEO: Stop it!

SHADOW-LIZ: She's making this up.

LIZ: So...you're an authority on—

SHADOW-CLEO: Sucking.

LIZ: —Shakespeare's songs. That's...terrific.

SHADOW-CLEO: You should be ashamed—flirting with this white trash. *(Imitating outraged Southern black preacher.)* What are our fine Negrah women tah do in the face of this desertion by our best and brightest?

LIZ: You know, I've been thinking it might be fun to have the madrigal group do some songs from Shakespeare.

SHADOW-LIZ: Oh yeah. How long you been thinking that?

LIZ: I mean using the music that would actually have been used in the Globe. It would be a great history lesson for the kids.

SHADOW-LIZ: Going for Selfless-Teacher-of-the-Year Award?

SHADOW-CLEO: *(To CLEO.)* Say "No" before you get into trouble.

LIZ: I wonder if you would be willing to help me find...

SHADOW-LIZ: Stop! What are you getting into here?

SHADOW-CLEO: Tell her to check out the Shakespeare Variorum. It's got to be in their school library. Probably on the damn Internet by now. Or let her download the stupid songs from MP3. She doesn't need your help.

CLEO: Well...I could suggest a few places to look...

SHADOW-CLEO: Don't do this!

LIZ: Maybe we could meet for...

SHADOW-LIZ: *(Seeing the handwriting. Going for the lesser of two evils.)* Coffee. Just coffee.

LIZ: For coffee...at... *(Starts to gesture towards her house behind her.)*

SHADOW-LIZ: At Borders.

LIZ: For cappuccino at Borders. I could bring my list of the songs I'd like the group to sing, and we could put our heads together and...

SHADOW-CLEO: And then our knees...

SHADOW-LIZ: And then our hands...

SHADOW-CLEO: Eyes...

SHADOW-LIZ: Lips...

SHADOW-LIZ & SHADOW-CLEO: THIS IS A BAD IDEA!!

CLEO: Sounds like plan.

SHADOW-CLEO: A plan for disaster!

SHADOW-LIZ: Look, this doesn't work out, and we'll be the ones accused of racism.

SHADOW-CLEO: *(To CLEO, accusing.)* You think you have enough in common because you're both teachers?

SHADOW-LIZ: *(To LIZ.)* You're worlds apart. Solar systems. Galaxies.

SHADOW-CLEO: Hasn't your family stretched to its limit already?

SHADOW-LIZ: You think your liberal friends are ready for this? They'll smile and make nice—

SHADOW-CLEO: And wait—without even knowing it—

SHADOW-LIZ & SHADOW-CLEO: for her to screw up.

LIZ: So...

SHADOW-LIZ & SHADOW-CLEO: And so will you.

LIZ: So...should we...set a time?

CLEO: Um. Sure. *(Pause.)* Or I could just...

LIZ: Just what?

CLEO: Just...send you the list of sources. *(Gestures to house.)* I mean, I...know the address.

LIZ: *(Beat.)* Yeah. I guess we could...we could do it that way...if we want.

CLEO: Might be...easier.

LIZ: Right.

CLEO: Or...

LIZ: Or...

CLEO: Or...

LIZ: Or you could come to my house for dinner Saturday night.

CLEO: I could?

LIZ: I mean...you know the address.

CLEO: That's true. Yes. Well, then. What can I bring?

LIZ: It's not a potluck. I'll cook dinner. What's your favorite?

CLEO: Roasted quail with mead-and-chestnut dressing.

LIZ: Piece of cake.

CLEO: *(Correcting her.)* Trifle.

LIZ: Of course.

CLEO: OK, I'll bring the candles.

LIZ: And the music. Don't forget the Songs....

CLEO: "How should I...

LIZ: "...your true love know."

LIZ and CLEO: Right.

(THEY smile. SHADOWS moan. Lights.)

End of Scene.

STARS

By Evan Guilford-Blake

The complete *Stars* is published by YouthPLAYS. To request information regarding obtaining the rights to perform the complete play, please contact YouthPLAYS at www.youthplays.com

CHARACTERS:
JEN: 16. White or Asian. A romantic who is intellectually sophisticated but not especially mature. There is a fragility about her.
TINA: 16. Black or Hispanic. Charismatic. She has always been mature for her age. Having spent her early childhood in the projects, however, she is streetwise, a little cynical and sometimes a little "tough"; and she is capable of bouncing back and forth between the two "personas" at will.

TIME: Approximately the present. About 10:00 p.m. on a late summer evening.

SETTING: A hilltop on the outskirts of a still-developing suburb of a major American city.

Stars, they come and go

> They come fast or slow

> They go like the last light

> > of the sun, all in a blaze

> > and all you see is glory...

---Janis Ian

For Janis Ian and Barbara Cook

AT RISE: JEN is seated alone as if on a hilltop, memorizing from a book, with a small flashlight as her illumination. NIGHT SOUNDS are heard.

JEN: "...Thou art more lovely and more temperate. Rough winds do shake the darling buds of May, And summer's lease hath ---"

TINA: *(Entering)* Hey, babe; how you doin'?

JEN: Oh; hi. Okay. How 'bout you?

TINA: Yeah, I'm fine. Writin' poems?

JEN: I was memorizing one, actually. Shakespeare.

TINA: Shakespeare? Jen; man...

JEN: Hey, Tina: He's cool.

TINA: Yeah, right.

JEN: He is.

TINA: I said: right. Okay?

JEN: Okay... Nice sky, huh.

TINA: Yeah.

JEN: *(Beat)* So, you, um, what d' you think about it now?

TINA: 'Bout what?

JEN: Here. Living here, I mean.

TINA: I'm gettin' used to it.

JEN: Yeah. *(Small laugh)*

TINA: What?

JEN: It's only been four months. Feels like longer. Like I've known you longer, I mean.

TINA: *(With a laugh)* It feels like you been makin' yourself my personal welcome wagon.

JEN: I don't, I mean, it's just I like you. You're interesting.

TINA: Hey -- you are too. It's cool. I just wish you could shoot a basketball.

JEN: *(As THEY both laugh)* I'm learning.

TINA: Yeah. Yeah. *(A long beat, while THEY listen.)* Man, you c'n hear ev'rything out here. *(Whistles)* And you were sure right about seein' things. Really bright out tonight.

JEN: Yeah; this is my - private spot. You're the first person I ever asked to come.

TINA: Not some boyfriend? Not even your brother?

JEN: Unh-uh.

TINA: I guess I'm honored.

JEN: I guess you should be.

TINA: Shee-it.

JEN: I really do love it here. You can see everything.

TINA: All those stars.

JEN: That's the 'burbs for you; you can see 'em 'cause there's so few streetlights. In the city everything gets washed out.

TINA: Now, what do you know about the city? 'Specially at night.

JEN: I've been there. Sometimes.

TINA: Um... This's somethin' else, though. Reminds me of the woods or somethin'.

JEN: You've never been in the woods!

TINA: Sure have.

JEN: *(A challenge)* When?

TINA: Three years ago. My folks rented this cabin, by this lake; spent two weeks there.

JEN: That's not the woods.

TINA: Yeah, it was. Four 'r five miles off the road, practically nobody else around; fished for our supper. Even had to pump water, from a well.

JEN: Yeah?

TINA: Yeah.

JEN: Sounds - neat.

TINA: "Sounds neat"; shee-it.

JEN: Never mind. Tell me.

TINA: 'Bout the woods?

JEN: Yeah.

TINA: Well... the coolest thing? it was at night, after they both went to bed. First night we were there, I snuck out and I just - sat, in the back, lookin' at the water; and the stars. There was a million of 'em and I could see every one, bright and clear and shining, like they were angels or somethin'.

JEN: Maybe they were.

TINA: What?

JEN: Maybe they were; angels, I mean. There's this legend I read, from the Incas or somewhere: Every human soul becomes a star.

TINA: Yeah?

JEN: When we die. That's why the universe is endless: There're all these souls up there that've turned into stars, everyone who's been born since the day God made the world, and every moment, this one ---... Just look; you'll see it.

TINA: What?

JEN: Just look, Tina.

TINA: *(Pause; then)* I don't see anything.

JEN: Keep looking; every second another star is being born.

TINA: *(Still looking)* That's - weird.

JEN: No, listen: It's great. I mean, think about it: Some day, you'll be up there and a couple of people sitting down here'll - look up and see you and one of 'em'll say: God, look at that star, how it - sparkles. It must be really special.

TINA: *(Beat)* Shee-it.

JEN: *(Putting an arm lightly on TINA's shoulder)* No; I mean it. *(Softly)* Really special.

TINA: *(Pause; still looking at the sky)* See that one?

JEN: Which?

TINA: That one. See? Looks like it's sort of red?

JEN: Oh. Uh-huh.

TINA: Who you figure that is? Lenin?

JEN: Yeah. And the one next to it's Marx.

TINA: And they're sayin': "Stars of the world unite; you have nothing to

TINA and JEN: Lose but your gas."

(THEY laugh)

TINA: *(Puts her hand on JEN's shoulder)* Girl, how'd you do that, figure out what I was gonna say.

JEN: Oh, it ---... *(Slowly)* It's not that difficult when you, uh, um...

TINA: When you what?

JEN: *(Shrugs)* I don't know.

TINA: Hey, babe; when you what.

JEN: When you...

(Short beat)

Close your eyes?; just for a second?

TINA: Close my ---

JEN: Just for a second.

(TINA does. JEN just sits there, uncomfortably at a loss.)

TINA: *(After a pause)* W'll, c'n I open 'em?

JEN: *(Quickly)* No!; I mean, not yet.

(Clears her throat)

Can, um, can I read you a poem?

TINA: With my eyes closed?

JEN: It's short.

TINA: Sometimes you are weir-eird. Go 'head.

JEN: "Shall I compare thee to a summer's day? Thou art more lovely and more temperate: Rough winds do shake the darling buds of May, And summer's lease hath all too short a date. Sometime too hot the eye of heaven shines, And often is his gold complexion dimm'd; And every fair from fair sometime declines, By chance, or nature's changing course, untrimm'd; But thy eternal summer shall not fade, Nor lose possession of that fair thou owest; Nor shall Death brag thou wander'st in his shade, When in eternal lines to time thou growest; So long as men can breathe, or eyes can see, So long lives this, and this gives life to thee."

(Long beat)

You like it?

TINA: Sounds pretty. What's it mean?

JEN: It means, it means...

(With difficulty, SHE kisses TINA.)

TINA: What the ---, hey: Cut that shit out.

JEN: I'm, I'm...

(SHE buries her head in her arms.)

I'm...

End of Excerpt.

WE'RE ALL A LITTLE F***ED

By Jessica DiGiacinto

ACT II. SCENE I.

*Lights fade up on Cole (16), Peter (16), and Nate (16)
 sitting in Cole and Peter's room, playing a video game.*

All three boys stare at the television.

PETER: Hey! Stop shooting me from behind!

NATE: I'm a terrorist, brotha. That's what I do. Shoot you
in the back when you ain't looking.

PETER: Cole, get over here and cover me!

COLE: I've got the Russians and the entire Middle East after
me! Take care of yourself!

They continue to play.

PETER: No!

NATE: I'm gonna carbomb your ass so hard...!

They keep playing.

COLE: You guys want a coke?

No answer.

COLE: Nate, did you drink that entire liter or what?

*Cole looks at Nate, Nate is concentrating too hard on the
game.*

COLE: Hey, we could -

PETER: Screw everyone!

Peter throws down his controller and looks at Nate.

PETER: That was low, dude.

NATE: You know the terrorist code: no mercy for the infidels!

Nate laughs. Cole puts down his controller and rubs his eyes.

PETER: You alright?

COLE: Yeah. Sometimes the screen...it's hard hold back the massive amounts of numbers, I guess. Count this, count that...

NATE: Hard to hold back.

Cole looks at Nate, Nate won't look at him.

PETER: I gotta take a dump. Don't go crazy while I'm gone.

Peter pushes himself up and walks out of the room.

Nate continues to stare at the glowing TV screen, even when it's obvious Cole is looking at him.

COLE: Hey.

No answer.

COLE: It's been a week and you haven't said anything.

NATE: And I'm gonna continue to not say anything. So you can stop freaking out.

COLE: I'm not freaking out.

NATE: My lips are sealed. Do whatever.

COLE: Thanks.

NATE: No one would believe me anyway. I lie a lot.

COLE: I hadn't noticed.

NATE: You don't know me well.

The two boys sit in awkward silence.

NATE: You know what's weird? How in this game the terrorists are always the bad guys.

COLE: They're kind of the bad guys in life.

NATE: Not really. I mean, sometimes they do pretty messed up stuff, but wouldn't you do the same things if you had the chance?

Cole stares at Nate.

COLE: Like driving a plane into a building? Blowing up busses filled with women and children?

NATE: That's the messed up stuff. I said they did messed up stuff. But like...imagine people just being assholes to you all your life, and everything sucks for so long, and then one day, someone tells you there's a way to get back at everyone. Wouldn't you at least consider it?

COLE: I wouldn't do the things they do.

NATE: That's because you're rich. Rich people are stupid when it comes to the capacity poor people have to hate the world that made them that way.

Nate looks at Cole.

NATE: I think about it. I'd probably never do it. But I think about it. What does that make me?

COLE: Angry?

Nate almost smiles.

NATE: That's a clean way to put it.

Peter comes back into the room. He sits down.

PETER: What'd I miss?

NATE: Richie Rich over here is diagnosing me as "angry".

COLE: Shut up. You were fishing for an answer.

PETER *(to Cole)*: Don't let him get under your skin to bad. He rides that poor kid label into the ground every single time.

NATE: I am poor, moron.

PETER: And you're also a student at a top tier prep school. So quit complaining.

NATE: I'm stating facts. Facts neither of you will ever have to deal with. People like me clean the bathrooms of your family's' private yachts.

PETER: Screw off. My family doesn't own a yacht.

COLE: I don't even have a family.

Nate and Peter look at him.

NATE: What?

COLE: My parents are crazy. Like for real. Got a rich uncle who likes sending me away for years at a time. So…

Pause.

COLE: Everybody's got their own crap.

NATE: I'm destitute, you're an orphan, Peter's got an ugly face –

PETER: Screw you –

NATE *(to Cole)*: The one thing you do have, Richie Rich, is a smoking hot teacher girlfriend.

The room goes silent. Nate realizes he's said too much.

NATE: I mean –

PETER: What?

COLE: Nothing –

PETER: What about a smoking hot teacher girlfriend?

COLE: Nothing…it's nothing. Nate thinks Ms. Stevens has a crush on me. That's all.

Cole looks at Nate.

COLE: Right? That's all.

NATE: Yeah. Right. That's all.

Peter looks back and forth between his two friends.

PETER: What am I missing?

Nate stands up.

NATE: Check you guys later.

PETER: Where you going?

NATE: I'm bored, man. You rich kids bore me.

Nate walks toward the door.

PETER: What's with all this rich, poor crap? You never used to bring it up.

NATE: Yeah well, I never used to be surrounded by a kid who got everything.

He leaves. Peter looks at Cole.

PETER: What's his problem?

Cole is already standing up.

COLE: He wants to be a terrorist.

PETER: What?

Cole leaves without answering.

PETER: What do you mean he wants to be a terrorist?

No answer. Peter looks around the empty room.

PETER: Why would anyone want that?

End of Scene.

HUMANS REMAIN

By Robin Rice Lichtig

CHARACTERS
IBANNI*... 19. African-American. Free spirit. Kinfolk
family. Fiercely independent, but attracted to Peter.

PETER ... 19. Caucasian. Yuppie. Clean-cut. Infatuated with
Ibanni.
LACEY* ... 15. African-American. Ibanni's cousin. Surging
sexuality. Kinfolk family.
SIS* ... 17. African-American. Ibanni's sister. Salt of the
earth. Kinfolk family.

*The Kinfolk family ancestry is African, Jamaican, and
Native American. They have lived on a mountain apart from
civilization for 12 generations.
TIME
April, 1991.

PLACE
A forest in the Ramapo Mountains in northern New Jersey.
AT RISE: A stream in a forest. LACEY and SIS fish with
homemade poles, a pail beside them. THEY are barefoot,
their clothing rustic.

LACEY: Ew! Worm gunk under my nails!

SIS: You got a whine on you like a sick skeeter.

LACEY: Hate fishing.

SIS: Haint 'nuf of us to divvy up the chores no more.

LACEY: Divvied up mending the stupid wedding gown to me.

SIS: Sh!

LACEY: She haint nowhere near.

SIS: You done the mending?

LACEY: Not yet.

SIS: Better do it right after we catch supper. Tiny'll be mad if you don't do it good. He's been champin at the bit t'marry Banni since they was four years old.

LACEY: Don't talk on it. It might slip out afore he asks her. It's gotta be a surprise. I'm hopin she says "no."

SIS: Shut your mouf, Lacey DeVries!

LACEY: Here comes Mister doctor man.

SIS: Here comes trouble.

(PETER enters.)

PETER: That was an experience! I haven't used an outhouse since... Never. Okay, so let me --

SIS: Don't put your hand on me.

PETER: Your leader told me to examine you.

SIS: Nutting wrong wit me.

LACEY: Her husband Pud the onliest one sick for now.

SIS: Don't touch Pud neither.

PETER: If we catch it early he won't get worse.

SIS: He already worse.

PETER: What are his symptoms?

SIS: *(to Lacey:)* Hush.

LACEY: He kin help.

SIS: Auntie Fern say he caint.

LACEY: Miz Catalina say "mayhaps."

SIS: Tiny say "no."

LACEY: Ibanni say "yes."

PETER: Why do you hate me? Because I'm different from you?

(SIS and LACEY burst out laughing.)

LACEY: He is differ'nt!

SIS: *(laughing again:)* He is! I hate him!

PETER: Hey, jeez...

SIS: Tiny sees peoples at the K-Mart pay heaps of money for food that haint food color, water in bottles, winter clothes that haint even warm --

LACEY: They's differ'nt all right!

SIS: Peoples folding money, feeling money, counting money, handing money over like it a precious rainbow, changing money for tings what haint necessaries.

LACEY: A few not-necessaries okay, but --

SIS: But they go hog wild!

LACEY: Crazy tings they do, but it don't make Tiny like or not like them.

SIS: Don't make him wanna be wit them.

LACEY: But don't make him hate.

PETER: Is it because I look different?

LACEY: What he mean?

SIS: He taller.

LACEY: Don't like him 'cause he taller?

(SIS and LACEY are collapsing with laughter.)

You fatter than me. Mayhaps I shouldn't like you!

SIS: You got more hair! Don't like you.

LACEY: You got freckles!

SIS: You got owl eyes!

LACEY: You got a outtie belly-beamer!

(THEY laugh themselves out.)

SIS: Not liking somebody 'cause they look differ'nt. Never heard such a fool notion.

PETER: You live in a dream world.

SIS: You must have nutting to do, tinking up notions like "differ'nt."

PETER: You're the ones staying away from the rest of the world. Calling everybody else "foreigners."

SIS: We got reason.

PETER: You should join civilization. There's welfare, Medicaid, food stamps... Unless you like being poor.

(no reply)

Tell me Bud's symptoms.

SIS: Pud.

LACEY: His knees is bad.

SIS: *(warning:)* Lacey.

LACEY: Talk don't hurt. Got knee pain like Pig Head had. Talks tangled, like Dandora did. Swole head like Owlouda. Three circles like my Mama.

PETER: A rash?

LACEY: Hers on her back. Pud's on his leg. Red circles.

SIS: All what had the circles died.

LACEY: Some as didn't too.

(IBANNI enters.)

IBANNI: What's going on?

SIS: Wants to examine us.

LACEY: Do Banni.

IBANNI: *(smiling at Peter:)* Like to see him try.

PETER: Where's Tiny?

IBANNI: Why?

PETER: He's an awful big guy.

IBANNI: Don't worry 'bout Tiny. I got him up to the house making a bed for you. Hungry?

PETER: Yeah. Some.

IBANNI: I dished out a bowl of oatmeal left over from breakfast, but it haint too hard yet. Go on. Tiny won't bother. He's feared I'd holler at him.

SIS: Don't ask for nutting more than oatmeal. There weren't no lunch leftovers.

PETER: *(to Ibanni:)* Thanks.

(IBANNI smiles, watches PETER exit.)

SIS: *(calls:)* Examine Tiny!

LACEY: Like to see him try!

SIS: Don't need no doctor man. Still plenty-plenty life in my Puddy. When I tole him 'bout the wed -- (wedding)

LACEY: (interrupting quickly:) HUSH!

IBANNI: Tole him 'bout the what?

SIS: Nothin.

(a moment)

LACEY: 'Bout Peter bein here. Him bein a doctor man and such and mayhaps figure a cure.

SIS: When I tole Pud that.

LACEY: Pud sat up in bed and said:

LACEY + SIS: Well pluck me and call me "supper"!

(LACEY and SIS laugh. IBANNI looks in the empty pail)

IBANNI: Speaking of which, where is supper?

SIS: Gone belly-up.

IBANNI: You haint caught none? We got a guest for supper!

SIS: He should git afore suppertime. He should git away. Leave us alone. Git back to his own people.

LACEY: Don't listen t'her. She ate a bad pickle.

IBANNI: He can figure a cure, Sis. Mayhaps make Pud good as new.

SIS: That haint his main attraction.

IBANNI: What you mean?

SIS: You're acting differ'nt.

IBANNI: What's wrong with differ'nt?

LACEY: Nothin.

SIS: How you're acting haint a good kind of differ'nt or a don't-make- no-difference kind of differ'nt. It's a worrisome kind of differ'nt.

IBANNI: Like how?

SIS: You're all hot an' bothered since he came.

IBANNI: Me?

SIS: Flippin your eyelashes. Twitchin your hips.

IBANNI: I never --

SIS: He's a foreigner.

IBANNI: He picked wild roses and took off the thorns afore he give 'em to me. He ast about Momma and Daddy. He's interested in what I think about. He likes how I can swim acrost the lake with no stopping. He likes that I climb trees like lightning. He don't care that I want to travel to far places. He wants to travel too. He's been lots of places already. Places with no mountains. Places with the ocean! Places not in New Jersey.

LACEY: He haint hard on the eyes neither.

IBANNI: Plus -- he can read.

SIS: What you need readin for?

IBANNI: He's stayin for supper. Gimme that pole.

(BLACKOUT.)

End of Scene.

LIZZY, DARCY & JANE

By Joanna Norland

Originally published by Samuel French, reproduced with permission.

Act I   Scene 1

Evening, January, 1796. The ballroom at the home of the Bigg-Withers, a wealthy landed family. Dance music plays in the background, and fades as the scene begins. The actors playing MR. BINGLEY/HARRIS/MR. COLLINS, MR. DARCY/TOM LEFROY and MADAME LEFROY/LADY CATHERINE sit at a game table, upstage left. Each holds a hand of cards.

(JANE enters)

JANE: Impossible man. Intolerable man. I have walked by Mr. Lefroy's game table three times, and not once did he look up from his hand.

If I do not please him, why did he invite me to dance twice at the Heartleys' ball last week? And if I do please him, why does he insist on playing cards tonight? I wish that men at balls behaved more like men in novels. My Mr. Bingley always chooses dancing over cards. Is that not so, Mr. Bingley?

(louder)

I said, is that not so, Mr. Bingley?

(MR. BINGLEY rises from the game table and approaches JANE)

MR. BINGLEY: Most definitely. Particularly with so many lovely ladies assembled.

JANE: Thank you, Mr. Bingley. You always say the most enchanting things.

MR. BINGLEY: Miss Jane Austen is too kind.

JANE: Your charm should not surprise me. The moment I penned your name, I decided that you should be the most charming man in the world. And to settle the matter, I gave you an income of five thousand pounds a year.

MR. BINGLEY: Is that my income? I can never recall the exact figure.

JANE: It is in your nature to be affable, not precise.

MR. BINGLEY: It is in my nature to dance. I have been ever so impatient for a ball.

JANE: Shame on me! I promised you a ball to welcome you to your new neighbourhood!

MR. BINGLEY: On page seventeen, you mentioned that there was soon to be a gathering at the Assembly Rooms. Only then—

JANE: — I set my novel aside for days. My excuse was that my friends, the Bigg-Withers, had petitioned me to write a winter theatrical. But even that remains unfinished. Instead, I squandered my time flirting with my Irish friend. I am glad that Mr. Lefroy leaves for Lincoln's Inn next week— *(mimicking TOM)* "to devote himself to the mysteries of the law."

MR. BINGLEY: He will regret the wasted opportunity to dance when he is forced to burrow in the library.

JANE: *(inspired)* I will be avenged yet. That is what novels are for. I will give you a conceited, arrogant friend who always refuses to dance — A failing for which he will be universally derided.

(JANE approaches TOM, takes him by the hand and transforms him into MR. DARCY)

You are far too serious to dance, are you not . . . Mr. . . . . Mr. Darcy.

MR. DARCY: Dancing does not suit all tastes or moods.

JANE: Mr. Darcy has never cared for dancing. *(to MR. BINGLEY)* Even when you first met . . . at Cambridge.

MR. BINGLEY: In our first year. Michaelmas term.

MR. DARCY: It was I who first acquainted Bingley with the alarming intelligence that our college possessed a library.

MR. BINGLEY: If it wasn't for Darcy, I should never have known that our college even had a library, let alone that I was meant to be a patron. But he is a capital fellow, I assure you.

JANE: I do not think that all of Mr. Darcy's acquaintances would agree.

MR. DARCY: I consider their censure a relief, given the quality of their judgment on other matters.

MR. BINGLEY: Do not pay Darcy any mind. This is always his manner upon a first meeting.

JANE: His manners could not please me more. They accentuate your charm. Jane Bennet will notice the contrast between you when she meets you both at the ball.

MR. BINGLEY: Is it certain that the eldest Miss Bennet will attend?

MR. DARCY: I cannot imagine that she has any competing engagements.

JANE: Of course my pretty heroine will be there. Accompanied by her three sisters, Mary, Kitty, and Lydia.

MR. BINGLEY: The entire neighbourhood talks of her beauty.

MR. DARCY: The entire neighbourhood cannot supply many alternative subjects of conversation.

JANE: When you are introduced to Miss Jane Bennet, Mr. Bingley, you will not disagree with the report that she is uncommonly handsome.

(JANE assumes the role of Jane Bennet and curtseys)

MR. BINGLEY: Good evening, Miss Bennet.

JANE: Good evening, Mr. Bingley.

MR. BINGLEY: *(to MR. DARCY)*

Handsome? Why she is the most beautiful creature I ever beheld.

(MR. BINGLEY holds out his hand to JANE in introduction)

Miss Bennet, I am delighted to form your acquaintance.

(Music begins. MR. BINGLEY and JANE begin to dance)

JANE: We are honored that you attend our assembly this evening, Sir.

MR. BINGLEY: I am ever so fond of dancing.

JANE: *(as herself)* To be fond of dancing is a certain step towards falling in love.

MR. BINGLEY: What an enchanting evening, Miss Bennet!

(aside to MR. DARCY)

And what an enchanting lady.

JANE: *(resuming the role of Jane Bennet)*

I hope you will be happy in Hampshire, Sir.

MR. BINGLEY: Are balls in Hampshire always this lively?

MR. DARCY: And are they always this long, and attended by such tiresome company?

(The music ends abruptly. JANE breaks away from MR. BINGLEY, who joins MR. DARCY, and speaks as herself for the duration of the play)

JANE: Tiresome . . . Does Mr. Lefroy also thinks us tiresome?

MR. BINGLEY: Come, Darcy, I must have you dance. I hate to see you standing about by yourself in this stupid manner. You had much better dance.

MR. DARCY: I certainly shall not. At such an assembly as this it would be insupportable.

MR. BINGLEY: You jest!

MR. DARCY: There is not a woman in the room whom it would not be a punishment to me to stand up with.

JANE: Mr. Lefroy is of the same mind tonight.

(ELIZABETH BENNET enters)

I suppose that like Mr. Darcy, Mr. Lefroy prefers the fine ladies of London. Of course he does.

(JANE begins to cry)

And to make matters worse, young Harris Bigg-Wither ambushed me at the punch bowl and insisted that I save him a dance. If only my sister were here. Cassandra would know how to advise me.

ELIZABETH: I hope that she would upbraid you sharply first. Fancy making yourself wretched on account of a young bachelor who plants himself at the game table with his graying elders.

JANE: Obviously, Mr. Lefroy sees little else to tempt him.

ELIZABETH: Are you surprised? A woman weeping into her handkerchief can hardly expect to inspire admiration in the opposite sex let alone good sense in her own.

JANE: I am utterly ridiculous. Spurned by my would-be partner, I stand here alone and dream up suitors for my heroine. I wish I had never taken up novel writing. There is nothing more ridiculous.

ELIZABETH: That is a rather insulting thing to say to a character from a novel.

JANE: Oh. I beg your pardon. *(pause)* Which character are you? And from which novel?

ELIZABETH: I have not yet made up my mind. For now, kindly cease your sniveling so that we may follow the exchange between these two gentlemen.

JANE: Very well. I have no competing engagements.

MR. BINGLEY: I would not be so fastidious as you for a kingdom, Darcy! Upon my honour, I never met with such pleasant company, or so many agreeable ladies. And accomplished, too.

MR. DARCY: Accomplished?

MR. BINGLEY: It is amazing to me how young ladies have the patience to be so very accomplished as they all are.

MR. DARCY: All ladies accomplished?

MR. BINGLEY: They all seem accomplished to me.

MR. DARCY: I cannot boast of knowing more than half a dozen such women in the whole range of my acquaintance.

ELIZABETH: *(the gentlemen do not hear her)*

That man must comprehend a great deal in his idea of an accomplished woman. I suppose that a lady must have a thorough knowledge of music, singing, drawing, dancing, and the modern languages to deserve the word.

MR. DARCY: To deserve the word, a lady must have a thorough knowledge of music, singing, drawing, dancing, and the modern languages.

JANE: Does Mr. Lefroy also seek such a woman?

ELIZABETH: If he does, then he deserves to find her, for she is certain to be insufferable.

MR. DARCY: And to all this she must yet add something more substantial, in the improvement of her mind by extensive reading.

ELIZABETH: All these attributes united? In that case, I am no longer surprised at his knowing only six accomplished women. I rather wonder now at his knowing any.

JANE: Miss, your tongue is quick. But you would not be so gay if you were slighted by a gentleman of consequence.

ELIZABETH: Is that so?

JANE: Suppose my Mr. Darcy were to put you to the test.

ELIZABETH: I should like to see him try.

MR. BINGLEY: Well, whether the ladies at this ball are accomplished or not, you cannot deny that they are uncommonly pretty.

(indicating ELIZABETH)

Look! Here stands a lady in want of a partner. She is very pretty and, I dare say very agreeable.

JANE: Mr. Darcy, do your worst.

MR. DARCY: Which lady do you mean?

(MR. DARCY turns a critical eye to ELIZABETH)

Oh. She is tolerable.

ELIZABETH: Tolerable?

MR. DARCY: But not handsome enough to tempt me. I am in no humour at present to give consequence to young ladies who are slighted by other men.

ELIZABETH: Is that so?

JANE: You see. It is not so pleasant to be snubbed.

ELIZABETH: As Mr. Darcy is about to discover.

(ELIZABETH approaches MR. DARCY)
Dear Sir, pray do not admit that I am tolerable. Make no such concession.
JANE: *(taken aback by ELIZABETH's boldness)* Oh!
MR. BINGLEY: Oh dear.

ELIZABETH: Were I to believe myself worthy of being tolerated by a Mr. Darcy, the compliment would turn my head. I might even begin to aspire to dancing with the first valet to Mr. Darcy's second footman. And what an insult that would be to the house of . . . the house of—

JANE: *(constructing the story as she speaks)*

Pemberley. The house of Pemberley, in Darbyshire. Mr. Darcy is the master of Pemberley, with an income of nine . . . no, ten thousand pounds a year.

ELIZABETH: Perhaps he should invest some of his income in lessons on manners.

MR. DARCY: You expect me to be mortified, and to stammer a retraction. But why should I apologize to you for remarks spoken in confidence to another?

ELIZABETH: Why do you make confidential remarks where you are bound to be overheard?

MR. DARCY: My meaning was that I never dance unless I am particularly acquainted with my partner.

MR. BINGLEY: *(attempting to diffuse the situation)*
I can vouch for that. I have known Darcy to sit out dozens of dances because no lady of his acquaintance was present.

ELIZABETH: And of course, no one can ever become acquainted at a ball.

MR. DARCY: Acquainted, perhaps, if to be acquainted is to ascertain that we agree that the weather is uncommonly seasonable for this time of year, or to talk entertainingly of Kent and Hertfordshire, of traveling and staying at home. I cannot consider myself to be properly acquainted with a lady unless we have thoroughly exchanged our views on books—

ELIZABETH: I am sure we never read the same, or not with the same feelings.

MR. DARCY: As well as music—

ELIZABETH: I do not lay claim to any superior technique at my keyboard.

MR. DARCY: And we must also have discussed . . .

ELIZABETH: Yes?

MR. DARCY: In truth, what is of primary importance is not the subject matter but rather, the manner in which it is discussed. Any topic may be rendered ridiculous by a certain sort of lady, whose first object in life is a joke.

ELIZABETH: A certain sort of lady?

MR. DARCY: A certain sort of unmarried lady— Unmarried and, I dare say, unmarriageable, to any serious man.

JANE: Oh!

ELIZABETH: Unmarried and, I dare say, determined to remain in that state until she finds a man who warrants her serious attention. Until then, she makes no apology for laughing at follies and nonsense whenever she can.

(JANE bursts into applause)

JANE: Bravo! Bravo!

MR. BINGLEY: I so dislike arguments. If you would conclude yours, I shall be very thankful.

ELIZABETH: What you ask is no sacrifice on my side. The moon is full, the music is lively, and the night is short. Miss Austen, if your Mr. Darcy will not dance, I have no further use for him.

MR. BINGLEY: We had better join the game table, Darcy.

(MR. DARCY bows and repairs to the game table with MR. BINGLEY. JANE approaches ELIZABETH)

ELIZABETH: Impossible man! Intolerable man!

JANE: But he could not humble you, while I allowed Mr. Lefroy to reduce me to tears. Bravo to you! From now on, I will make you my model, Miss . . . Miss . . . But who are you? You could be one of my heroine's neighbours. Or one of her sisters. But which? You are too sensible to be Lydia, and you are no peevish Kitty or bookish Mary.

ELIZABETH: Lydia, Kitty, and Mary. Are any of them proper companions for your heroine?

JANE: The Bennet sisters provide comedy, not companionship. They are a rather silly trio.

ELIZABETH: How lonely your heroine must be.

JANE: I had not thought of that. A woman experiencing her first love ought to have a dependable sister to confide in by candlelight as they undress for bed. Do you volunteer for the role?

ELIZABETH: If I am to be a sister, I must be a younger sister. Too much is expected of the eldest.

JANE: Jane Bennet will be your senior by a year. I am delighted to form your acquaintance, Miss—

ELIZABETH: Elizabeth.

JANE: Miss Elizabeth Bennet.

ELIZABETH: You may call me Lizzy.

JANE: And you must call me Jane. So there are five Bennet sisters . . . Five unprovided for Bennet sisters at that. The whole lot of you are doomed to poverty and want unless you find suitable husbands, for your father's estate will be entailed away to a distant cousin upon his death.

ELIZABETH: You might have warned me of my incipient ruin before I agreed to join the Bennet family.

JANE: We have that in common, you and I, the threat of a destitute and miserable old age. Never mind. What fun we will have in the meantime. My sweet heroine requires a sister with spirit.

ELIZABETH: I shall enjoy being a heroine's confidante.

JANE: You will not begrudge your sister her leading role?

ELIZABETH: It is such a terrible responsibility to be a heroine, always setting an example. A heroine's sister can make an appearance when a scene wants enlivening. But no one misses her if she disappears on a solitary ramble on a rainy afternoon and returns three chapters later, her petticoats splattered with mud.

JANE: Petticoats splattered with mud . . . I must make a note of that.

End of Scene.

THE WEIGHT

By Steven Schutzman

Time: The present.

Setting: Eli's apartment. Early afternoon.

Characters:
Eli – 20, a rhythm guitar player and back-up singer
Laurie - 16, a talented singer

(ELI, sitting on couch, playing guitar, listlessly, things on his mind. A knock at the door. ELI rises and opens it.
LAURIE comes inside, dragging backpack behind her across the floor. She leaves pack, goes back out and reenters with a guitar case which she leans it against pack. She goes back out and a second or two later a rolled sleeping bag flies through the doorway to land next to the pack and guitar.)

ELI: This can't be good.

(LAURIE appears in doorway, holding a six pack of beer, two bottles short, one of which is in her hand. LAURIE is dressed in a sexy dress she doesn't fill out. She swigs on her beer. She is never drunk in the play but gets tipsier as the action proceeds.)

LAURIE: I have made four decisions, Eli. One, that I will not live at my Mom's house one day more or my Dad's house one day more.

ELI: You're not staying here. I've had it with your family.

LAURIE: Two, that I am dropping out of high school. Living in two stupid houses and going to stupid high school is so played out. Three that, look at me…

ELI: Why?

LAURIE: Just look at me.

ELI: No. Why should I? I have a question for you.

LAURIE: The answer is yes.

ELI: Have you seen your crazy brother? Because early this morning, he drives off in his truck. No note, nothing. And his cell phone's turned off again. Maybe he tossed it in the river like last time.

LAURIE: No. But I did get a text message from him, just two words, "The weight", W-E-I-...

ELI: I know what weight it is. The band's covering it.

LAURIE: *(Singing)*

'Take a load off, Annie/Take a load for free/Take a load off Annie, And put your load right on me'

ELI: You sound just like your mother. Look like her too in that dress.

LAURIE: Do not and do not.

ELI: Spittin' image.

LAURIE: Stop it.

ELI: What's with the dress, Laurie?

LAURIE: Four, that I am going to get out on my own as a singer and I need a dress like this to audition for certain, you know, clubs.

ELI: You skipped number three.

LAURIE: I know. Three that…Three that…

(She comes very close to him but he avoids her and starts walking around the room as he talks.)

ELI: Damn that brother of yours. I had to cancel band rehearsal today and we really need the practice. Been really trying to keep the guys organized, stay on top of the business end of things, professional, booking gigs, and we can't have this nonsense anymore. We have to be reliable, if we're going to make a living as a band. We're headlining at the Dell this weekend and don't even have our play list yet.

LAURIE: Headlining at the Dell. Nice.

ELI: It's a big deal for us but without our lead singer, I mean, damn it, if your brother bails again, we'll be banned from every club in the city. I thought we were done with that nonsense. What is with your family?

LAURIE: Wanderlust. *(She flops onto couch.)* Wander and lust. Sit down so I can tell you my third decision. *(He stays put)* New couch, huh?

ELI: Yeah, I just bought it, based on the money from this weekend's gig. Fix the place up, finally.

LAURIE: Does it fold out?

ELI: For some people.

LAURIE: If I sleep here, it won't be on any couch.

ELI: That's real funny, girl *(Beat)* God, your family is like an albatross around my neck.

LAURIE: The Rime of the Ancient Mariner.

ELI: What?

LAURIE: Rime of the Ancient Mariner by Samuel Taylor Coleridge, British poet. That's where the expression comes from.

ELI: What expression?

LAURIE: Albatross. Neck. 'Water, water, everywhere and all the boards did shrink. Water, water, everywhere and not a drop to drink.'

ELI: And you're gonna drop out of school. Smart as you are.

(Pause)

LAURIE: This here is a real comfortable couch. You can just sink right down, heavy and weightless at the same time, and never move again.

ELI: Oh no, you can't.

LAURIE: Everyone needs a place that'll take them in no matter what.

ELI: Normal people call that home.

LAURIE: Home is where the heart is, Sir, and you have mine.

ELI: I give up.

LAURIE: You give up? Surrender, finally, to fated love? Just like in Jane Austen, British novelist.

ELI: Like I don't know who Jane Austen is. You have always read way too many books for a girl with such an impressionable mind.

LAURIE: I will dress in white for you, my dress a piece of the moon on a moonless night. I will sweep my dark heavy curls slowly down your chest. Thomas Hardy, British novelist.

ELI: Sounds like a bodice ripper.

LAURIE: Wrong. It's British Lit.

ELI: What's with this British kick, all of a sudden?

LAURIE: I'm taking a British Lit. course over at the community college.

ELI: Yeah, I believe it. You were always smart as a whip, a pain in the ass but smart as a whip.

LAURIE: Eli, did you ever read Lady Chatterley's Lover by D.H. Lawrence?

ELI: No but I bet it's a British novel.

LAURIE: It's great. Hot and smart at the same time. Like in this scene I just read: After the gamekeeper, Mellors, makes love to Lady Constance Chatterley like she's never been made love to before, D.H. Lawrence writes, 'Connie thought a woman would have died of shame. Instead, shame died.' 'Instead, shame died.' In other words…

ELI: I get it. That's pretty good.

LAURIE: Good? It's better than good. It's deep, profound. Hey, I'll read the passage to you.

(She gets up, fetches book and bottle from six pack and sits back down on couch.)

Come and sit down. Come on, I won't bite.

ELI: Okay. Sure. Why not? If you want to read something. *(He sits but not too close.)* Don't you bite me.

LAURIE: Drink?

ELI: No. Put that thing away, Laurie. It's two o'clock in the afternoon.

LAURIE: Eli, I have made four decisions. One, that I'm not going to live with my parents anymore. Two, that I am dropping out of high school. Three, that I will lose my virginity to you this very afternoon.

(LAURIE unpins her hair and shakes it out.)

ELI: Way, way too many books.

LAURIE: I remember the summer I decided you'd be the one.

ELI: You see, those are the problems, right there, right there, you read way too many books and make way too many decisions.

LAURIE: I remember the summer I decided you'd be the one. My Mom was whaling on my brother, something awful, really smacking him, over some crack he made about her drinking, but he wouldn't defend himself, as usual, and you came in and lifted her off the ground from behind, arms pinned, legs kicking, and carried her out of the room. Remember that?

ELI: Sort of.

LAURIE: You were just fifteen but more of a man than anyone I knew. A real man. Handsome outside, good inside.

ELI: And you were eleven years old with a schoolgirl crush.

LAURIE: Twelve, just about. Compared to my crazy family and all the drama, you were so calm, so good, shining with the pure light of nobility.

ELI: Nobility? Normality, more like.

LAURIE: Your awkward goodness and shy eyes, your kind voice and those clever, funny words you made up. It happened in late summer and that night, that night, after I knew I loved you and would always love you, the sheets felt alive against my skin. I didn't know where I ended and where the world began. The frogs were croaking in the woods so loud they could drive a person out of her mind, remember, how they'd get in late August and what you called it, croakophony?

ELI: Don't remind me.

LAURIE: Croakophony. It was clever. Like a frog cacophony. My love feelings were so intense I just knew you were out there in the dark feeling them too, feeling this love with me like you were hearing the frogs with me, in the hot, croakophonous night.

ELI: Give me a break, girl.

LAURIE: My love thoughts were like a riot of frogs in my head. Our bedrooms like twenty yards apart. You in yours, me in mine. Where did I end? Where did you begin? It was torture and kept on being torture the whole time you lived next door to us. That's why I crept across the yards into your room, the night before your family moved away. But you'd never take advantage. Not you, shining with the pure light of nobility.

ELI: Because you were a mixed up thirteen year old kid looking for love in all the wrong places, after your parents' divorce.

LAURIE: I just wanted you to kiss me and feel my brand new parts. That's all.

ELI: I should've done it, just to scare you out of the idea.

LAURIE: Come on and try to scare me out of it now. Come on.

(LAURIE stands, pulls the dress over her head and sits down on couch, awkwardly trying to find a seductive position. She looks strangely fragile in her bra and panties.)

Come on. It might work this time. Because I'm real scared.

(ELI feints toward her. She flinches, cries out then composes herself.)

End of Scene.

"Moving On" from AT THE LINE

By Lynne S. Brandon

Background: Coach Cheyenne Pomeroy, an African-American lesbian basketball coach with an outstanding reputation, recruits players nationally to play for Carolina State. She has, then ends, a brief affairs with her friend and Assistant Coach Caroline. Hurt and angry, Caroline reports an alleged "impropriety" by Cheyenne with a former athlete to the university administration. Cheyenne chooses to resign rather than jeopardize the futures of her players and staff, and take her chances with an European professional team. But she can't forget her star guard, Almeida.

Scene setting: CHEYENNE Pomeroy's living room. A large screen TV is showing a basketball game, but the volume is off. Cheyenne is sitting in a recliner/sofa. It is early April in a southern US state. GENINE is her African-American friend. ALMEIDA is a Latina second-year athlete. Katy is another Assistant Coach.

CHEYENNE: *(at the TV)* For Christ's sake. A little pick and roll! *(leaps up)* Watch the corners! *(pacing)* Stupid coach. *(doorbell rings)* FINALLY!

GENINE: *(enters)* Hey girl. How's it going?

CHEYENNE: Ge-neen, baby! I'm about to kill somebody.

GENINE: Not in the immediate vicinity, are they?

CHEYENNE: Big ha-ha. I've been watching a semi-pro game, worst coaching since El Paso in '86.

GENINE: Weren't you the coach?

CHEYENNE: You got it. Really, really bad. You're late.

GENINE: Took me a while to get loose after dinner. As if my folks hadn't seen me ten times this year already. I've been dying to talk to you.

CHEYENNE: What's up?

GENINE: Did you watch the interview with Geno?

CHEYENNE: Nah. Too close, too soon. Why?

GENINE: He said the team won't be a contender now that you're gone.

CHEYENNE: No shit. That's not news.

GENINE: *(slightly indignant)* I know that. But. He did say it was a tough break. And I quote: "Working with these kids, you can't help but get real close. Things can be misinterpreted."

CHEYENNE: He said that?

GENINE *(pats her butt)*: C.Y.A., if you ask me, and he's got plenty to cover. *(they laugh)* But still.

CHEYENNE: Really. Nobody holding a gun to his head.

GENINE: Did you two talk at the tournament dinner?

CHEYENNE: Not about my situation. He was thinking two of his assistant coaches were getting a little close. He wanted to know what I'd do.

GENINE: And you said?

CHEYENNE: Hey, it's their lives. What they do off the clock is not his concern.

GENINE: So he knows.

CHEYENNE: Of course he knows. That's why he asked.

GENINE: Have you heard from Caroline?

CHEYENNE: *(beat) (cold)* How can you even say the name.

GENINE: She's gotta be hurting.

CHEYENNE: Good! I hope it never stops.

GENINE: Don't hang on to that shit, girl.

CHEYENNE: Hey, it's only been two months ... *(beat)* So tell me something new.

GENINE: Katy's going to Minnesota.

CHEYENNE: She hates the north!

GENINE: It was a great offer. They didn't grill her about what happened. Which was good, 'cause she wasn't going to tell, first of all, and second, she didn't want to go anywhere where they gave a shit.

CHEYENNE: I'm glad for her. Real talented.

GENINE: She wanted to know how you were doing.

CHEYENNE: You tell her?

GENINE: Not really.

CHEYENNE: Now what the fuck does that mean?

GENINE: *(they lock eyes)* I said it was like walking on glass for you. And that you missed folks.

CHEYENNE: "Folks"? I thought you were watching my back!

GENINE: That's just how I said it. No more, no less. And I always got your back, you know that.

CHEYENNE: *(beat)* Sorry. I just can't afford ...

GENINE: I know. Don't worry, everybody's being real cool.

CHEYENNE: *(pause)* Seen Almeida?

GENINE: You know I have.

CHEYENNE: And?

GENINE: I shouldn't be telling you.

CHEYENNE: Damn, Genine, give me some thing ...

GENINE: She's ...

CHEYENNE: ... dating a guy. *(long pause)*

GENINE: I didn't want ...

CHEYENNE: It's ok. Better from you. *(beat)* She all right?

GENINE: She's all right.

CHEYENNE: *(pause)* I need a drink.

GENINE: It had to happen, you know that.

CHEYENNE: Motherfucker! *(Genine moves to comfort her. Then Cheyenne gets drinks for them after she recovers.)*

GENINE: You talked to the lawyer today?

CHEYENNE: *(nods)* Hmmm. Nothing. She said it wasn't lies, as far as they're concerned. No matter that it happened TEN years ago after she left the team, <u>and</u> that she was totally into it, <u>and</u> would say so now! Oh no, "we have to protect our students." Well, how many profs do you know who are banging their sophomores?!

GENINE: You know it's not about the truth.

CHEYENNE: We knew that a long time ago. *(takes a good belt of her drink)* Who said, "good living is the best revenge?"

GENINE: George Herbert – died in 1633 by the time he was 40. *(beat)* You sure you want him for a role model?

CHEYENNE: Guess not! *(beat)* But there's other things I can do.

GENINE: In the revenge category?

CHEYENNE: Europe. The Czech team.

GENINE: You got it?! *(Cheyenne nods, big smile)* Hot damn! Get your sparkles on, girl. I'm taking you OUT!

End of Scene.

CAMELBACK CANYON

By Virginia (Ginger) Fleishans

CHARACTERS
WALT PETERS A real estate salesman in his early 30's.
Likable, assertive/aggressive and friendly, ALT is a
functioning alcoholic. HE is a womanizer, suffers with self-
esteem issues and has a jealous streak. HE is married to
PATRICIA.
PATRICIA PETERS A bright and attractive 26 year old.
Outwardly independent and but inwardly indecisive lacking
confidence. SHE has not worked outside of the home since
marrying WALT.
DEVORA GONZALES Quiet and pretty, DEVORA came to
Phoenix from Jalisco to marry RICARDO, a groundsman at
Camelback Canyon Estates in Phoenix, AZ. SHE speaks
formally with a heavy Hispanic accent.
RICARDO GONZALES Archetypical Hispanic man who
works as a groundsman at Camelback Canyon Estates.
Speaks formally with a heavy Hispanic accent.
MADINA DEVORA and RICARDO'S infant daughter.

SETTING
The Peter's kitchen/family room.

TIME
Midmorning, day three

SCENE 1-4

AT RISE: WALT pours himself a cup of coffee and puts some
whiskey in it.

PATRICIA: Isn't it kind of early for that?

WALT: *(WALT ignores her question.)* So, did Sheridan
bring her over?

PATRICIA: Yeah. Well, they didn't come together; they met here. Just a few minutes ago.

WALT: Did you know they were coming?

PATRICIA: He called first, yeah. Why?

WALT: I just hope he isn't going to start dropping in any old time he feels like it. He's so, … so, annoying.

PATRICIA: I think he's nice! Anyway, I'm sure he won't start "dropping by." He's a busy man and has other things to do you know.

WALT: You think he's nice, huh? And busy? What else do you know about him?

PATRICIA: All I know is that he's an investor and President of the HOA so I would assume he has plenty to do during the day!

WALT: Ooh--oohh, an important man. I see. Sounds like you're pretty familiar with his many, many responsibilities, eh?

PATRICIA: No, WALT, I haven't. I wish you wouldn't be so hostile.

WALT: Well... I just know that "things" can happen. And looking at all the makeup on your face, I'd say you were trying to look pretty hot for someone.

PATRICIA: I don't have any more makeup on than usual.

WALT: My point exactly. You know I think you look better without any. But no, you just can't stand to do something your husband likes, can you?

(WALT looks distastefully at the cup of coffee in his hand.)

This is cold.

(WALT strides over to the kitchen counter with the intention of reheating the coffee in the microwave. In reaching for the microwave, he accidentally knocks over a measuring cup of clear liquid on his sleeve.)

Damn! Damn it all!

(He brushes at his sleeve trying to clean it.)

How'd it spill? And what the heck is it anyway?

PATRICIA: Darn! I just used it when I started the laundry and set it down there when Dan and Wendy got here.

WALT: Laundry! What is it? Crap. It… it smells…

(WALT sniffs at the sleeve.)

Oohh, no! Don't, don't tell me it was bleach, for Christ's sake?

PATRICIA: I… it… Oh I'm so sorry! I'll try to—I'll make it right. Somehow.

(PATRICIA is dabbing and fussing at the sleeve while talking.)

WALT: One shirt, ruined! It was only $69, on sale. Why do you leave shit like that around, anyway? What were you thinking?

PATRICIA: It's for the laundry; the white clothes. And to clean the sink.

WALT: Maybe if you paid our bills you'd realize how much things cost! Last night you left the downstairs thermostat at 78° so the A/C was off and on all night long! And now, a shirt too. Damn it, Patricia!

PATRICIA: I'm sorry.

WALT: Jeez! Can't believe you.

(WALT pours more whiskey in the coffee cup.)

Nice, little outfit you're wearing, by the way.

PATRICIA: What?

WALT: I suppose you're going to say you put it on just hoping I would get home early.

PATRICIA: As a matter of fact, I...

WALT: Don't lie to me, Patricia! You knew Dan Sheridan was coming over.

PATRICIA: Yes, but...

WALT: As if the makeup wasn't enough! You had to look sexy for him too.

PATRICIA: No! I shouldn't have to explain, ...

WALT: Shut up! I don't want to hear it. I've got to make some calls. I'll be in the office.

(WALT drags his finger across a dusty bookshelf and holds up his finger for her to see the dirt on it with an accusing look on his face and leaves the room.)

(PATRICIA puts her head in her hands for a few moments. Then seems to pull herself together and walks over to the door. She opens it and breathes deeply. She smells something good and follows the odor outdoors and away from the house. In the community greenbelt near their house, she sees a man seated at a cloth-covered card table that has been formally set for one. He is dining; his shoes are set to one side. Nearby, a woman leans against a tree embroidering a piece of fabric. A baby lies on a blanket nearby. The man raises one hand and the woman walks over to the table and spoons more food on to his plate. PATRICIA watches for a few moments.)

RICARDO: More chilies next time.

DEVORA: It was not spicy enough?

RICARDO: No.

DEVORA: More iced tea?

RICARDO: Yes.

DEVORA: Churro?

RICARDO: Save it for later.

(DEVORA returns to the spot where she had been standing and is startled when she notices PATRICIA standing nearby.)

DEVORA: Hello there.

(RICARDO stands up abruptly as if to protect his wife.)

PATRICIA: Hello. I'm sorry. I didn't mean to interrupt.

DEVORA: That's all right. My husband is just eating his lunch.

PATRICIA: Oh. That's nice. It's a nice day to eat outdoors.

(RICARDO perceives that she is not a threat and busies himself lacing up his boots.)

DEVORA: Yes. Nicer than last week. There was rain.

PATRICIA: Yes. There was. Rain, that is. Your food smells delicious!

DEVORA: Thank you.

PATRICIA: What is it?

DEVORA: Tamales.

PATRICIA: Mmmm. You make them yourself?

DEVORA: Yes. Chicken, pork, beef, and corn.

PATRICIA: Oh. Do you ever sell them?

DEVORA: Sell them? No, I have not.

RICARDO: Sure she does. A dollar a piece.

PATRICIA: Okay. I'll take one dozen.

RICARDO: Pork?

PATRICIA: Sure. That's fine.

RICARDO: She'll deliver them tomorrow.

PATRICIA: Okay. I live right in that house, there.

RICARDO: She'll be there at 3 o'clock.

PATRICIA: That'll be fine. Oh, what is your name?

DEVORA: DEVORA. And this is my husband, RICARDO.

PATRICIA: RICARDO and DEVORA. Okay. I'll see you tomorrow.

DEVORA: Good-bye.

SETTING
The Peter's kitchen/family room.

TIME
Midmorning, day three
(Doorbell rings.)

PATRICIA: I hope that's my tamale lady!

(PATRICIA goes to the door and DEVORA is there.)

Hey!

DEVORA:

(DEVORA is wearing an infant sling with a baby in it and laboring under the weight a carryall full of tamales and a diaper bag).

I brought your tamales.

PATRICIA: *(PATRICIA takes the diaper bag from DEVORA.)*

Thanks for bringing them.

(PATRICIA notices that DEVORA has a very obvious black eye.)

Ooh! What does the other guy look like?

(DEVORA looks at the floor and does not make eye contact with PATRICIA. PATRICIA realizes that DEVORA is embarrassed so she changes the subject.)

PATRICIA: Oh! Is this your baby? What a beautiful little girl.

DEVORA: Yes. Thank you. Please, do you have something to put the tamales in?

PATRICIA: Sure! Right here in the kitchen. There.

(PATRICIA gets a container out of the cupboard and DEVORA busies herself putting the tamales into it. While she is doing that, PATRICIA stands behind her and indicates to WENDY with elaborate hand signals that there is something wrong with DEVORA'S eye.)

Would you like something? Coffee? Iced tea?

DEVORA: No thank you. I can't stay.

PATRICIA: What's his name? Her name?

DEVORA: She is Madina, after my mother. Since I come to Arizona and married Ricardo, I miss my family so much, so I named my baby for my mother so I would feel a little closer to home.

WENDY: Hi, Madina! Hello there, pretty girl.

(PATRICIA and WENDY fuss over the baby for a few moments and DEVORA beams.)

PATRICIA: And you're, Demora?

DEVORA: Devora.

PATRICIA: Ah. Sorry. That's nice too.

WENDY: *(Still fussing over the baby.)* She's a sweetheart.

PATRICIA: *(PATRICIA notices the carryall.)* Wow! This carryall is gorgeous. Where did you get it?

DEVORA: I made it. Myself.

PATRICIA: The embroidery is fabulous!

DEVORA: Thank you.

PATRICIA: I really mean that. You could sell these. You could sell them to that little boutique on Camelback and 24th Street. Okay then. Wow! Bags, embroidery, tamales! You do it all, huh?

(DEVORA looks somewhat embarrassed by the kind words.)

Thanks for bringing the tamales. And, for selling them! They smell so good I can't wait to eat them. They're a dollar each, $12 altogether, right?

DEVORA: Yes.

PATRICIA: I'll get it—my purse is in the bedroom.

(PATRICIA leaves to get the money.)

WENDY: *(WENDY picks up the empty carryall.)* This carryall is very nice.

DEVORA: Thank you. I'm glad you like it.

WENDY: Really? I wouldn't know where to start on

something like … oops!

(WENDY accidentally drops it on the floor. Both she and DEVORA reach to pick it up at the same time.)

Thanks. Oh my! That's quite a bruise you have there too.

(WENDY gestures to a bruise on Debora's arm.)

DEVORA: It is nothing.

WENDY: Really? And your eye? I suppose that's also "nothing?"

DEVORA: Oh! That? That. Well, I am very clumsy. I fell off my bicycle a couple of days ago. Silly. Stupid.

WENDY: *(WENDY speaks gently and calmly.)* You don't look a bit clumsy to me. I think you look very coordinated. Very graceful, as a matter of fact.

(DEVORA says nothing but looks uncomfortable.)

It'd be pretty hard to get a black eye from falling off a bicycle without knocking yourself out at the same time.

PATRICIA: Here's the… oh. Is something wrong?

WENDY: DEVORA was just telling me that black eye and the bruise on her arm are nothing.

PATRICIA: DEVORA! You weren't bruised yesterday!

WENDY: How did it really happen?

DEVORA: I… I was… I was riding along and I…

(DEVORA begins to cry.)

PATRICIA: Your bicycle? Did you fall?

WENDY: *(WENDY continues to speak gently.)* I don't think so. It's okay, DEVORA. Calm down.

PATRICIA: Yeah, it's okay. We want to help. What really happened?

DEVORA: My husband, RICARDO, is a good man. He works very hard but he gets tired. He is a good husband and a good father--most of the time. But sometimes, he...

(DEVORA sobs a bit and then pulls herself together and tells them the rest.)

Last night, I didn't have any queso blanco for the enchiladas so I made them with cottage cheese. Ricardo doesn't like them made with cottage cheese, but he had eaten a good lunch of tamales and beans, so I thought it might be okay. But it wasn't.

WENDY: And?

DEVORA: And it made him angry.

(DEVORA begins sobbing again and as she gulps in a breath of air, winces in pain and holds her side.)

PATRICIA: Are you all right?

WENDY: You didn't make him angry. He chose to get angry.

(DEVORA continues to hold her side)

What's wrong?

DEVORA: I just, I can't get a very deep breath.

WENDY: When did that start?

DEVORA: Last night. Right after RICARDO, … you know.

WENDY: Did he hit you, DEVORA?

DEVORA: No! Not really.

PATRICIA: Are you sure?

DEVORA: *(DEVORA speaks quietly, embarrassed.)*

No. He did not hit me--he, he pushed me. Across the room and I fell against the kitchen counter.

WENDY: I believe you just might have a broken rib to go along with that black eye.

(Doorbell rings.)

PATRICIA: Who could that be? *(PATRICIA looks out the window.)* It's RICARDO, your husband!

DEVORA: *(DEVORA moves around in panic.)*

Oh dear! I'm late! I knew he would be angry!

WENDY: Late? But, you've only been here five minutes!

(PATRICIA opens the door and RICARDO comes in.)

RICARDO: Where have you been? I've been waiting!

DEVORA: I'm sorry! I know, I'm sorry. The baby overslept and I --

RICARDO: I don't want your stupid excuses! I get off at

3:00 and I'm ready to go home! Get your ass out there...

WENDY: Don't talk to her like that!

PATRICIA: She didn't do anything wrong!

DEVORA: No, please don't--

RICARDO: You ladies in your fancy cars and fancy-pants! You think you can tell me how to talk to my wife?

(RICARDO grabs DEVORA roughly by the shoulder.)

DEVORA: They don't know what they're--

WENDY: Let go of her!

PATRICIA: DEVORA! Don't let him treat you like that!

RICARDO:

(RICARDO pushes DEVORA toward the front door.)

Get going. It's time for you to start my dinner.

(The baby starts to cry.)

PATRICIA: Watch out for the baby!

WENDY: In this country, men aren't supposed to push women around!

RICARDO: In my country, women are supposed to treat their husbands with respect! Hurry up, woman!

(DEVORA, crying, scurries around picking up the blankets, and diaper bag and secures the baby back into the sling.)

PATRICIA: You'd just lay off her!

WENDY: Devora! You don't have to go with him, you know.

PATRICIA: Stay here, Devora! Don't let him hurt you again.

RICARDO:

(RICARDO grabs DEVORA and pulls her across the room toward the door while threatening her in Spanish.)

Yo vamos!

WENDY: That's it! I'm calling the police right now.

(WENDY picks up her cell phone.)

DEVORA: No! No, please don't call the police. The police are no good!

RICARDO:

(RICARDO grabs WENDY'S cell phone and throws it across the room and it breaks; WENDY scrambles to retrieve it.)

My wife asks you do not call the police. The police come, the police find out she has no papers, they will send her back to Xalisco. But the baby stays here. With her father. With me!

WENDY: *(WENDY has retrieved the cell phone and tries to reassemble the broken pieces, but after hearing what RICARDO says, SHE tosses it aside.)*

So, you've got her right where you want her.

PATRICIA: He's got us all where he wants us.

RICARDO: So? We agree. Yes? Devora!

DEVORA:

(MADINA is back in the sling and DEVORA is carrying the diaper bag with blankets trailing behind as SHE scurries to the door.)

Coming. I am coming, Ricardo.

RICARDO: That's more like it.

(RICARDO stands to one side of the door letting DEVORA go through first in a sarcastic yet gentlemanly fashion, and then HE imperiously steps through the door after her. HE turns around and graciously bows to PATRICIA and WENDY with sarcasm before leaving.)

Adios, ladies.

End of Scene.

TRUCKER RHAPSODY

By Toni Press-Coffman

In this scene, RIOT 208 (18), a graffiti artist who lies in NYC, confronts DAMIAN "FOOTBALL" WILLIAMS (17), the young man who threw a concrete block at truck driver Reginald Denny's head during the 1992 Los Angeles Riots. The scene takes place near the end of the play.

RIOT 208: Looks like you've got something to teach me after all which is how brick-throwing, gangbanging and drug-smoking move us closer to justice. Enlighten me.

DAMIAN: You think you so funny? You think you so smart? All right, you enlighten me. What you gonna be teaching that baby when he comes? Watch daddy draw cartoons on the wall?

RIOT 208: Yeah, I'm gonna teach my baby to draw. Yeah, that's his legacy. I was painting since I was 12. I was running around the subways, I was throwing up on as many trains as I could, I was thinking of it as ruining government property and I know you know what I mean. I thought destroy the property, and at the same time make pictures of the beast in my daddy, expose his true self.

DAMIAN: Oh, you destroyed government property. So no matter about all that jabberin' you hidin' behind, you runnin' around Queens New York taking the law into your own hands.

RIOT 208: I create art. You created chaos.

DAMIAN: HOLD UP. I did not create that chaos. While you teaching that baby something, how about you explain to him what goes on out there?

RIOT 208: How about I teach him not to throw things at people?

DAMIAN: How about you teach him people gonna want to throw things at him, people gonna want to accuse him of shit he didn't do?

RIOT 208: How about I teach him violence begets nothing but more violence?

DAMIAN: Then you'd be teaching him a lie.

(RIOT looks at DAMIAN in amazement. This is certainly not the thing he expected to hear.)

DAMIAN: Suddenly you all quiet and shit.

RIOT 208: *(mostly to himself)*

A lie? Suddenly I'm gettin' flashes of 1776 with men throwin' crates of tea into large bodies of water and other men with muskets and even with rocks and truth be told – because I always always always attempt to tell the truth – those images are makin' me very uncomfortable.

DAMIAN: You gettin'' flashes of what?

RIOT 208: Do not dare say the words American Revolution to me.

DAMIAN: *(did I hear you right?)* Don't say – American Revolution?

RIOT 208: I am not going to believe you had one thought about this country's struggle for independence when you bashed Mr. Denny's head in.

(A beat. DAMIAN has no idea what he's talking about.)

DAMIAN: All right.

(RIOT 208 paints.)

DAMIAN: Explain to me what you're doing. I'm serious. What good is that? The police just going to cover it up anyway.

RIOT 208: They can cover it up all they want, but they can't stop me.

DAMIAN: Now I'm followin' you. *(indicating RIOT 208's graffiti)* Yeah, I think I finally got this figured out. You learned to protect yourself from what's going on around you by turning away from trouble and painting on the wall. You want to say I did what I did because I'm a punk, but brother, gangs had nothing to do with it. Anger just came up over me. You tell me anger never come up over you I will not believe that.

RIOT 208: You're right. When it happens, I paint.

DAMIAN: You paint. Mama prays. Me – I hear that verdict, then I see the police coming after my brother with viciousness like he was some kind of mass murderer – and we both know they would not think twice about killing him. *(a beat, then looking hard at RIOT 208)* We both know that right?

RIOT 208: We both know that.

DAMIAN: You keep tellin' me people can learn things. Those cops arrested me and they know I did not kill anybody - they learning things? What about those ladies on that police jury acquitted Rodney King? They supposed to learn things? How come we the only ones have to learn something?

RIOT 208: Brother, we can't control - . *(He stops himself from talking. Thinks for a beat.)* That's a good point.

(Pause, as RIOT 208 paints.)

DAMIAN: What's that you're painting?

RIOT 208: That's my baby. Any day now I'm gonna get lucky like you and become a daddy.

DAMIAN: There's a baby in there? (looking at the graffiti) How you know what he looks like already?

RIOT 208: Football. You got to use your imagination.

End of Scene.

NOT FOR THE FERRYMAN

By Donna Spector

CHARACTERS
THEA TOMADAKIS, 75, a Greek scholar
NIKOS TOMADAKIS, early 40's, THEA's son, a filmmaker
from Crete

SETTING
Single set. In real time, the sitting room between THEA's
and ORIAH's bedrooms in a treatment facility in the
Catskills, New York.
Also two scrims or projections--one of the mountains in
Crete, the other of the mountains in Appalachia—may be
used for the folktales of Crete and Appalachia.

SYNOPSIS
A comedy/drama about the meeting of two cultures, Greece
and Appalachia, this play is a love story that takes place in a
nursing home in the Catskill Mountains of New York. It is
here that two older women, THEA TOMADAKIS and ORIAH
PEABODY meet, and as their friendship develops, so does
the unexpected love between THEA's son NIKOS and
ORIAH's granddaughter TROUT.
Interwoven through the real time and place of this story are
the folktales of these two cultures. Each folktale—a journey
of the living to the land of the dead--springs from the psyche
of one of the characters. TROUT and NIKOS fall in love in
the folktales before they fall in love in our time.

The play has two acts, a single set (the sitting room in the
nursing home) with (or without) scrims or projections for the
folktales. Cretan lyre and Appalachian fiddle music is used
throughout.

SCENE: (A HOLLER IN THE APPALACHIAN
MOUNTAINS.)

NIKOS:

(Wears a battered black hat, an old coat and carries a shovel and a bag on his back. He starts digging and sings as he digs.)

I come from the mountains, Kentucky's my home.

TROUT:

(Tumbles in, wearing an old dress and wet apron.)

Damn, damn, damn an' hell!

NIKOS:

(Still digging, he doesn't notice her. He sings.)

Where the wild deer an' the black bear So lately did roam...

TROUT:

(Shaking water out of her apron.)

I fell down thet goddam well!

(NIKOS smiles but turns away so she can't see his amusement.)

TROUT: Thet'll fix me fer leanin' over so damn far! An' what was most undoubtedly peculiar was this river at the bottom... an' this fella in a boat with this ol' black hat like...

(To NIKOS.)

Hey! Yer thet very fella. How come you gimme a ride?

NIKOS: Oh, sometimes I he'p folks out.

TROUT: Yeah? Now what you doin'?

NIKOS: Diggin'.

TROUT: Diggin' what?

NIKOS: A hole.

TROUT: What fer?

NIKOS: I'm buryin' somethin'.

TROUT: What you buryin'?

NIKOS: Ain't goin' to tell.

TROUT: Come on!

NIKOS: Nope.

TROUT: I bet a hawg's left foot it's what's in thet bag.

NIKOS: *(Leaning on his shovel, smiling.)*

Yer right smart fer a girl.

TROUT: *(Daring him, she approaches bag.)* I'm goin' to look.

NIKOS: Well, go on, yer so interested.

TROUT: *(Opening bag.)* What the hell is this?

NIKOS: Oh, nothin'.

(Can't contain his laughter.)

But, frankly, I ain't surprised you don't reckanize it.

TROUT: Heh! Sure looks mighty familiar.

NIKOS: Don't it, though?

TROUT: Hey! Jes' wait a damn minute!

NIKOS: *(Returning to his digging.)*

Nope. I ain't waitin' fer nothin'.

TROUT: You got my soul in this here bag!

NIKOS: Do tell.

TROUT: You cain't take my soul.

NIKOS: *(Picking up bag.)*

Looks like I done it already, don't it?

TROUT: You got no right. Give it back.

NIKOS: Nope. It's mine.

TROUT: You got no use fer it.

NIKOS: Oh, yes, I most certainly do.

TROUT: What good it do you to put my soul down in the ground?

NIKOS: Well, you never do know what'll happen when you plant somethin'.

TROUT: Now, lissen! I got a ache right here in my chest alla the sudden. It's this empty place where my soul useta live.

NIKOS: Yer makin' thet up. You'll be a sight happier th'out it.

TROUT: *(Grabbing the bag and tugging at   it.)* Give it over!

NIKOS: Won't. Not 'less you willin' to wrestle fer it.

TROUT: What you mean? What kinda wrestle?

NIKOS: Jes' arms. I don't do no body wrestling with a girl.

TROUT: Who are you anyways?

NIKOS: Bet you can guess.

TROUT: Well, you look like the devil hisself.

NIKOS: *(Preening, he poses with his shovel.)*

Yep. I am the Old Boy.

TROUT: I knew it 'cause yer so damn ugly.

NIKOS: Now, wait jes' a damn minute!

TROUT: Ain't never seen nobody quite so ugly as you.

NIKOS: People said a lotta thangs 'bout me, but nobody never said I was ugly.

TROUT: Oh, they prob'ly was too polite to mention it.

NIKOS: Nope! I even got a reputation round these parts fer bein' han'some, in a oily sorta way.

TROUT: Yep. They're the kinda folks would say a possum that walked into a fan is han'some 'cause it ain't as bad as a road-kill.

NIKOS: Well, thet sure as hell is it!

(Points at her.)

Sit yerself down!

(Surprised, TROUT drops to the ground and sits, cross-legged. NIKOS sits facing her.)

Now. Put up yer arm!

NIKOS: *(They begin to arm wrestle, balancing their elbows on their knees.)*

Ugh! Who's ugly? Umpf!

TROUT: Oof! You are. Ack!

NIKOS: Yer pretty strong fer a girl. Gack! How come? Unh!

TROUT: *(Almost forcing his hand to the ground.)* Fought a lotta men in my day. Aark!

NIKOS: *(Almost forcing her hand to the ground.)*

Oog! Guess you oughta fought a few others.

TROUT: Glack! Urg!

(Back to a standstill, their arms quivering.)

Uncle?

NIKOS: Nope. Ain't tired a bit.

(More sweating and straining.)

Uncle?

TROUT: Ain't tired neither. Awk!

(Pushing so hard she can barely speak.)

Jes' bored, that's all.

NIKOS: Eh! Gettin' bored m'self. Wanna stop, gen'lman's agreement?

TROUT: *(Still pushing.)*

Ladies' agreement.

NIKOS: Fine.

(They both fall back on the ground, exhausted and stare up blankly.)

TROUT: Yer stronger'n my ol' boyfren'.

NIKOS: Who, him? He ain't strong. Anyways, I'm stronger'n anybody.

TROUT: 'Cept'n me. Guess you gotta give me my soul now, ain't you?

NIKOS: No, sir! This 'un was a draw, free an' clear, no

strings attached.

TROUT: Ain't thet like a man! I done all thet work fer nothin', an' now I'm punished fer bein' strong.

NIKOS: *(Raising himself on his elbows.)*

Yep. Even the Old Boy hisself don't take kindly to a tough woman.

TROUT: *(Raising herself on her elbows.)*

So what I gotta do next? Stomp on yer heart?

NIKOS: Haw! I ain't got no heart. But you can gimme yers.

TROUT: Lissen here. I'd ruther tie two cats' tails together an' hang 'em on a clothes line.

NIKOS: What use you got fer yer heart? Hit so bruised up, looks like a overcooked gizzard.

TROUT: Don't care. I'm still mighty attached.

NIKOS: Powerful good deal here: a used heart fer a simple soul.

TROUT: Nope, nope, nope! I'll give you sumpin' else. How 'bout my ol' cow, name a Ben Franklin?

NIKOS: Don't want no cow.

TROUT: Mebbe you need a ol' rooster name a Cain to wake you up mornin's?

NIKOS: Don't need no more Cains down here. An', 'case you ain't noticed, we ain't ezakly got no mornin's.

TROUT: Well, hell!

(She gets to her feet.)

I cain't think a nothin' would satisfy you.

NIKOS: *(Struggling to get to his feet.)*

Heh! Nope, guess you cain't. Oof!

(He's too stiff to make it.)

TROUT: *(Dusting herself off.)*

What you oofin' 'bout?

NIKOS: I got me a stiff laig here. I shouldn't ought to of wrestled.

TROUT: You mean you cain't get up?

NIKOS: *(Continuing to struggle.)*

Nothin' a the sort! I'm jes' takin' my time.

TROUT: Fine by me.

(Crosses to NIKOS' bag, rummages in it.)

I'll jes' take my soul outta here.

NIKOS: You mean you'd take advantage of a man when he's down?

TROUT: Yep. You'd do it yerself, wouldn't you?

NIKOS: Hell, yes! But I got a right. I'm the devil hisself.

Gotta keep up my reputation.

TROUT: So I'll jes'...

(Pulls a mirror out of the bag.)

Hey! This here ain't my soul! It's a lookin' glass.

NIKOS: Do tell.

(Grabbing his sore leg.)

Aaag! Guess I'm outta shape.

TROUT: *(Threatening him with the mirror.)*

What'd you do with my soul, you ol' buzzard?

NIKOS: Lissen, I'll give you a secret, free a charge. Nothin' ain't never what you think it is.

TROUT: I'm goin' to smash this right over yer head!

NIKOS: I got me a non-violent suggestion: Whyn't you look in thet glass 'fore you break it? Might find jes' what you want.

TROUT: I heard tell a yer sweet-talkin', I...

(But she is irresistibly drawn to look in the mirror.)

Oh! There I am! But I....sure am ugly! Damn, I look jes' like....

(Looking down at NIKOS.)

the devil hisself.

NIKOS: *(Nursing his aching leg.)*

You think so?

TROUT: Take a look.

(Holds the mirror down so he can see.)

NIKOS: I don't see nothin' but a pretty gal. Oh, she's kinda wild, but ain't no real meanness in 'er.

TROUT: Yer crazy.

NIKOS: Some folks think so. Say, how 'bout givin' me a hand up?

TROUT: You can jes' get up yerself.

NIKOS: No, I cain't. It's this bad laig here.

TROUT: If yer gettin' too ol' to be the devil, you oughta resign.

NIKOS: I cain't.

TROUT: Must be some home fer ol' devils you can go to.

(She turns to go.)

Bye, now.

NIKOS: *(A pitiful look on his face.)*

Take care a yerself.

TROUT: Oh, hell!

(She turns back and extends a hand to help him up.)

I got no damn will power.

NIKOS: *(Getting to his feet with her help, he removes his hat.)*

Thanks. I certainly 'preciate yer help.

(He sweeps off his hat and bows.)

TROUT: Th'out thet hat, yer not so bad-lookin'.

NIKOS: *(Putting mirror in sack, he hands it to her.)*

Don't fergit this.

TROUT: *(Taking sack, she moves a step closer, as though entranced.)*

Thanks.

NIKOS: *(Moving a step closer to her, his eyes on her eyes.)*

Ain't you goin' to look inside?

TROUT: *(Moving a step closer, she reluctantly looks away and peers into sack.)*

Well! My soul! How'd you do thet?

(Looking back into his eyes again.)

NIKOS: *(Shrugs, smiling, his eyes still on hers.)*

I got power.

End of Scene.

THE SEED SAVERS

By Katherine Koller

Characters:

SOLO. mid-twenties, farmer, has a few years of agricultural college.

TYLER, mid-twenties, local boy not but not always, salesman for a multinational chemical and seed company.

SKY, mid-twenties, of mixed race heritage.

ACT ONE, SCENE FIVE

TYLER offers SOLO a beer on a full moonlit night.

SOLO: Did you guys ever think of this?

TYLER: So Farmer Joe's got our genetics in his crop.

SOLO: All I know is he didn't put them there.

TYLER: Doesn't matter. I just gotta make a report. And you get this.

TYLER gives SOLO a leather jacket.

SOLO: What's this for?

TYLER: Comes with your phone call.

SOLO puts on the jacket. It looks great on him.

SOLO: Does it fit okay?

TYLER: The company says happy farming.

SOLO: I don't want Joe getting any flak.

TYLER: Joe? There might even be something in it for him.

SOLO: Like what?

TYLER: Did he give you any of his?

SOLO: Joe's the canola king.

TYLER: You got any leftover from last year?

SOLO: Didn't use it all, because I bought from you.

TYLER: I hear it's pretty good against blackleg. Clubroot, too.

SOLO: Yup, disease-free. But yours is weed-free.

TYLER: Yeah, see? We might be able to do a little tie-in.

SOLO: That would be taking what's his.

TYLER: He brown-bags it out anyway, right? And our lab docs are wicked at combining stuff. I mean, disease-free, weed-free, all we need now is drought-free.

SOLO: Frost-free.

TYLER: Storm-free.

SOLO: Yeah.

TYLER: Sorry.

SOUND of coyotes.

TYLER: Storm of the century.

Beat.

TYLER: I remember after, the moon hung down just like that. Quiet. Except for the flippin' coyotes.

SOLO: And me with a hammer, boarding up windows, and you in your work gloves, sweeping up glass. Ha! I didn't even know you had work gloves.

TYLER: Your folks let me hang out right through high school, no questions asked.

SOLO: We cursed the universe.

TYLER: When the sun came up we went fishing. Then got started on the harvest.

SOLO: What was left of it. Haven't been fishing since.

TYLER: No way!

SOLO: Who's got time for it anymore?

TYLER: How about this winter? Up north.

SOLO: Nah, I'll be driving all winter. Bills to pay.

TYLER: I'll do a promo deal with the company. We'll get a few new suckers, and show them how it's done, eh?

SOLO: Don't know if I can take the time off.

TYLER: All expenses paid.

SOLO: You can do that?

TYLER: When you get good yield you get the big fish.

SOLO: You're doing okay, then.

TYLER: You are. You got a pretty tidy return.

SOLO: How do you know?

TYLER: I checked.

SOLO: How'd you do that?

TYLER: A thing I got going with the fellas at the grain exchange.

SOLO: That's none of your business.

TYLER: Oh, but it is. You're my guy.

SOLO: You can't put your nose in my profit margin!

TYLER: I'm just making sure. That's all.

SOLO: Let me get this right. I'm performing for you?

TYLER: In spades, boy.

SOLO: Who's the customer here?

TYLER: I hand picked you! Just in time, too.

SOLO: You don't get my numbers. That's not part of the deal.

TYLER: Hey, buds. You're a company man now.

SOLO: Get outta here.

TYLER: First, I'm gonna put my feet in Joe's field.

SOUND of coyote choir.

TYLER whips out a zip-lock bag, and finds his way in the dark to the pole.

SOLO: Ha. Hey Ty, hear that? Yip, yip, yip!

TYLER: Shut up!

SOLO: They're coming to get you!

TYLER: Stop it!

SOLO: Yippy yap, yap!

TYLER: Funny. By the pole, right?

TYLER takes his sample and exits.

SKY enters, with her own zip-lock bag.

SOLO: Yip, yippy, yip, yip, yay. Gonna eat you up! Yippy, yip-yip!

SKY: Uh, what are you doing?

SOLO: Singing to the coyotes.

SOUND of the COYOTES.

SKY: Do they do that a lot?

SOLO: Just special nights. Change of the season.

SKY: You know about coyotes.

SOLO: Oh, yeah.

SKY: What about the wind?

SOLO: What about the bank.

SKY: I heard.

SOLO: Joe and Mindy don't have to worry.

SKY: They're worried about you.

SOLO: I've got to use technology.

SKY: But aren't you playing with Nature?

SOLO: No. I'm working with it. A new way.

SKY: To get out of debt.

SOLO: To keep my farm.

SKY: And pass it on. To your kids.

SOLO: I'm a long way from that.

SKY: I know.

Beat.

SOLO: Joe and Mindy are all I've got.

SKY: Me, too.

TYLER enters and hides his ziplock bag.

TYLER: Hey, Solo! Whoa, hey, hello!

SOLO: This is Tyler.

SKY: The salesman?

TYLER: Yeah.

SKY: I'm Sky.

TYLER: Haven't seen you in town.

SKY: I just got here, a few days ago.

SOLO: We've been working.

TYLER: Oh?

SOLO: Sky is Joe's granddaughter.

TYLER: Could've fooled me.

SOLO: Ty.

TYLER: So you're here looking for your roots.

SKY: I guess so.

TYLER: Black sheep of the family usually do.

SKY: Yeah?

TYLER: Takes one to know one.

SKY: Well. Good thing we're not plants, or you'd have to spray to tell us apart.

TYLER: A girl who gets chemicals!

SOLO: Hey.

SKY: I also get cross-pollination.

SOLO: Let's go, hey Tyler?

TYLER: The lady wants to discuss genetic drift! How about a brew?

SKY: I'm busy.

TYLER: Beer's like, organic.

SKY: I've got some digging to do.

TYLER: Hey, what have you got against me?

SKY: A degree in law.

SKY goes off to take specimens, taking out her own ziplock bag.

SOLO: Time for you to disappear.

TYLER: So that's who this is about.

SOLO: Hands off.

TYLER: I didn't think it was Joe.

SOLO: Just leave her alone.

TYLER: A lawyer? Get real.

SOLO: Now. Before she gets back.

TYLER: What's she doing?

SOLO: Getting a sample.

TYLER: Yeah? Maybe I should get lost.

SOLO: Out of bounds.

SOUND of the coyotes.

TYLER: Jacket looks good.

TYLER exits. SKY enters.

SKY: Solo? They're getting closer.

SOLO: Yeah. Cheering for us.

SKY: Us?

SOLO: For getting the harvest in.

SKY: Oh.

SOUND of coyotes.

SOLO: Just happy they're together.

SKY: Yeah?

SOLO: Yeah.

SKY: I'm not really a wild dog person.

SOLO: I'll walk you home.

SKY: Home. Huh. It got dark all of a sudden.

SOLO: Feel that air? First frost.

SKY: Smells almost sweet.

SOLO: Smells good to me only when it hits bare fields.

SKY: It's a lot colder than I thought.

MUSIC.

SOLO takes off his jacket, and puts it around SKY's bare arms, and they exit.

End of Scene.

COMPACT FAILURE

By Jennifer Farmer

COMPACT FAILURE tells the story of the fragile friendship that develops between two inmates; old-timer Chelle and ex-junkie Ruthie.

If there is no dialogue after a character's name, this indicates an active silence between the characters. This is where characters can also take a moment to make a transition.

SCENE 8
Dining hall.

MAYA: Come rockin' up in here. Like her shit don't stink.

CHELLE: Maybe it's coz she don't act the victim.

MAYA:

CHELLE: You guilty, I'm guilty, she guilty. And we all up in here.

MAYA: Ruthie's a criminal, Chelle. I committed a crime.

CHELLE: Ain't nobody innocent.

MAYA: Nah-ah. You see it in the way they look, way they walk. Tell me Chelle you ain't seen it. Do and you a liar.

CHELLE: That ain't Ruthie.

MAYA: What she did, she is in there with them.

CHELLE: In here with us, Maya.

MAYA: Criminals.

Chelle shakes her head, not wanting to hear.

Criminals, Chelle. With them, not with us. Some, like you and like me just got caught. Made the wrong choice and got caught. Maybe even thick a little bit. Then there's them lot. Criminals.

CHELLE: What about who she is now?

MAYA: You can't have a now without a then.

CHELLE:

MAYA: There's a gulf of difference. And you know it.

Ruthie enters.

CHELLE:

RUTHIE:

MAYA:

Ruthie sits down.

MAYA: Chelle; over here. This way.

CHELLE:

RUTHIE:

Pause. Chelle sits down. Beat.

MAYA: Chelle, what you doing? Get up. Stand up before you're seen.

CHELLE:

RUTHIE:

Pause.

MAYA: Sit there with the freak, then.

RUTHIE:

CHELLE:

When Ruthie stands to exit, Chelle stands as well.

RUTHIE:

CHELLE:

Silence.

RUTHIE: *(whispering)* You don't want this.

CHELLE: Don't I?

RUTHIE: *(whispering)* Chelle, you don't. 'Specially not here.

CHELLE: You don't know what I want.

RUTHIE: Handle, then. This is something you can't handle. Not up in here, you can't.

CHELLE: What is 'this' that I'm not wanting?

RUTHIE: They don't forget up in here, Chelle. Memory of elephants they got here.

CHELLE: Good, I don't want to get forgotten.

RUTHIE: You got no idea what this costs. This here Chelle, is something you can't afford.

CHELLE: There's fuck all I've got to lose, now.

RUTHIE: How about what I can't afford to lose? Spare a thought for me.

CHELLE: Family? Your kid?

RUTHIE: She, no she is off limits./

CHELLE: Freedom? Respect? You got no friends./

RUTHIE: You don't bring Rosie into this prison.

CHELLE: Pretty name. Rosie.

RUTHIE: Fuck you, Chelle.

CHELLE: Ruthie and Rosie.

RUTHIE: I don't see mates beating down your door.

CHELLE: Exactly. *(beat)* Seems to me losing is the only thing left for us both to lose.

RUTHIE:

Beat.

CHELLE: Don't you wanna know what I'm offering?

RUTHIE: I don't care.

CHELLE: But you do. Otherwise, you wouldn't still be sat here.

RUTHIE:

CHELLE:

RUTHIE: What they gonna do to you, you friending me up?

CHELLE: What?

RUTHIE: Friend up a nonce?

CHELLE: Hold up Ruthie, this ain't—

RUTHIE: I know what I am, but what does that make you?

CHELLE: This is not a friendship so don't worry about losing a friend.

RUTHIE: I've no fear in losing friends. I lose friends like I lose loose change through a hole in my pocket. It'll take much less than 30 pieces of silver for you to turn and run.

CHELLE: I said I'm not offering a friendship, so don't worry about your pocket money.

RUTHIE:

CHELLE: This is not a friendship. I don't want to be your mate, Ruthie. Mates can run.

RUTHIE: And they always run.

CHELLE: But I'm not going anywhere coz there's nowhere to go to.

RUTHIE: They always do.

CHELLE: I'm not interested in 'they.' Not interested in 'them.' 'They' and 'them' are not now; I am.

RUTHIE:

CHELLE: The only one to stand before you now is Chelle and I'm Chelle.

RUTHIE:

CHELLE: I'm Chelle. Not 'them'; not 'they.' Not 'Poor Chelle;' 'Victim Chelle.' Chelle who is a survivor. Survive with me. For the next 3 months, survive with me, Ruthie.

RUTHIE: What's in 3 months?

CHELLE: When I'm on the out. After that…

Beat. Ruthie laughs.

RUTHIE: You're not my first 'Chelle,' you know. 10-a-penny you lot. 'Chelle's' are 10-a-penny. My cup runneth over with 'Chelle's.

CHELLE: See I'm the only one that's here now; of this so-called overstock of 'Chelle's' you claim you got./Know why? No 'Chelle' like this 'Chelle' that's me; that's why.

RUTHIE: Clocked you within second three of walking up in here.

CHELLE: Coz you see in me what you never had with 'them's' and 'they's', don't you?

RUTHIE: Knew the softness of you by your shoulders. Knew by your hang-dog head. Beat down but with no visible bruises.

CHELLE: And words gonna bruise me now?/That what you hoping for?

RUTHIE: That's not true; bruises there./Just not black, not blue. Hang-dog head is a bruise./

CHELLE: Words, I can't be scared of them, not in the place I'm at./

RUTHIE: Stuck my thumb in the peach, not to test you, but to put my bruise in there amongst the bunch.

CHELLE: Last thing I gotta worry about, words.

RUTHIE: Could barely find room, so many bruises.

CHELLE: Always heal in time.

RUTHIE: Long time in healing: bruises. So why would I want to spend the next 4 months—

CHELLE: 3.

RUTHIE: —with my thumb in a peach?

CHELLE: Coz in these 3 months you know you can't bruise me anymore than those that came before you.

RUTHIE: That's what you want? Really, Chelle?

CHELLE:

RUTHIE: Mates with a sick bitch like me?

CHELLE: No, not mates I told you. Call it whatever else. Not friends. An 'understanding.'

Beat.

RUTHIE: I don't want this.

CHELLE: This isn't always about what you want. You need Chelle. Chelle needs us.

RUTHIE: Chelle needs a kick in the head, that's what Chelle needs. And that's what these elephants and their memories will give you, you keep this up.

CHELLE: What they can do—

RUTHIE: It pales—

CHELLE: —it doesn't scare me.

RUTHIE: It's got me bricking it, and I'm used to it.

CHELLE: I'm used to disappearing. I'm used to tucking myself away; tucking myself away in some tiny little corner. And I'm tired of it.

RUTHIE:

CHELLE: I'm tired of it and I want to stretch out and unfold.

RUTHIE: This is not a day out in Brighton.

CHELLE: But it is and I'm the towel. Mum's good towels, guest towels, she called them. Forever folded and the creases never get to see the light of day. Ain't unfolded until you laughed me into unfolding myself. Up and out. I'm not going to let you let me fold myself way again.

Maya walks over to them.

MAYA:

RUTHIE:

CHELLE: Go away, Maya. We're talking.

MAYA:

RUTHIE:

Maya spits at Chelle. Long pause.

CHELLE: I'm not going to let you let me disappear, coz you scared.

RUTHIE:

CHELLE: You don't want to keep on disappearing either. You don't want to be forgotten.

RUTHIE:

CHELLE: You're just as tired as I am.

RUTHIE:

CHELLE:

RUTHIE: Yes.

CHELLE: Yes.

RUTHIE: But there'll be no rest, Chelle. You do know that.

CHELLE: It's better than being tired alone.

RUTHIE: They'll turn their backs on you. Them that you claimed as a friend.

CHELLE: Backs been turned against me all my life.

Beat.

RUTHIE: What if you're ghosted out? What I do then?

Chelle shrugs.

CHELLE: Ruthie, I don't have any answers. *(beat)* I don't know if this is right, it's probably not.

RUTHIE: No. *(beat)* But.

CHELLE: Yeah. But.

Silence.

RUTHIE: Why me, Chelle?

CHELLE: You didn't let me look away. You looked me in the eye.

RUTHIE: How could I not, Chelle? How could I not?

CHELLE: Straight on you looked at me and made me to do the same. Knowing before I told you and still you looked me in the eye. Gave me the combination to my belly laughs, you did as well. *(beat)* I've stopped disappearing, Ruthie. My words come out, and now they're visible. I can see them now, not just hear them.

RUTHIE:

CHELLE: You see them too. The only other person to see them and I'm no stranger to myself anymore.

RUTHIE:

CHELLE: It wasn't them; it was you done the running. But not this time.

Silence.

RUTHIE: 3 months?

CHELLE:

RUTHIE: I don't know how to do this, Chelle.

CHELLE:

End of Scene.

CARRYING THE CALF

By Shirley Barrie

The play takes place in a self-defense class for women at a community centre.

Characters: INDIRA (16) South Asian, SHARON (16) West Indian, ANN, (pushing 40) white, FIROZA (mid-20's) South Asian, the instructor.

Scene 2

IT'S HALF WAY THROUGH THE THIRD CLASS. SHARON HASN'T TURNED UP. FIROZA IS DEMONSTRATING THE CROSS ARM GRAB WITH ANNE WHILE INDIRA WATCHES.

SHARON ENTERS.

SHARON: Hi everybody.

INDIRA: Where have you been!

SHARON: *(TO EVERYBODY)* Something came up.

INDIRA: I bet.

FIROZA: Don't worry about it. We're just glad you're here now.

INDIRA: What were you doing?

ANN: See. All that worry for nothing.

(ANN AND FIROZA BEGIN LAYING OUT THE MATS)

SHARON: I couldn't get away.

INDIRA: From what?

SHARON: Calvin wanted me to meet his cousin, Roy.

INDIRA: Why now?

SHARON: 'Cause he was driving back to Sarnia tonight, wasn't he.

INDIRA: Firoza was really worried. The whole class could've been cancelled. You let her down, not turning up.

SHARON: Is that why you're coming now, Indie?

INDIRA: What d'ya mean?

SHARON: *(SARCASTIC)* You don't want Firoza to lose her precious class. Well - I don't care that for Firoza. *(SNAPPING HER FINGERS)*

INDIRA: Sharon!

SHARON: It's you I was coming for.

INDIRA: Just cause I like Firoza doesn't mean I don't care about the class.

SHARON: Yeah? Well, I'll tell you Indie. I'm not gonna lose Calvin over this class. Not even for you. Got it. *(SHE IS TRYING TO GET OFF A NEW PAIR OF STRAPPED SHOES AND GET ON HER RUNNING SHOES. INDIRA GOES OFF ON HER OWN AND PRACTICES THE KATA.)*

ANN: *(GETTING UP FROM PLACING A MAT)* Ohhh. I seem to be full of muscles I never knew I had.

FIROZA: It'll get better.

ANN: Yeah. Sure. Last week I only ached for two days. First week it was seven. I was crippled.

FIROZA: *(JOKINGLY)* You haven't been getting enough exercise, Ann.

ANN: I'm a cleaner for god's sake.

FIROZA: Well, we are using different muscles here.

ANN: You don't have to tell me. I can feel every one of them.

SHARON: Doesn't bother me.

ANN: Yeah, well you're...

SHARON: Black!

ANN: I wasn't going to say that!

SHARON: Sure.

ANN: I was going to say young. Probably take gym or whatever they call it now.

SHARON: Not for long. Thank god.

FIROZA: My goodness, Sharon, you make it sound like you're leaving.

SHARON: Yeah. So.

FIROZA: Oh. Well....*(PAUSE)* Have you got a job?

SHARON: Haven't found the right thing yet.

FIROZA: Maybe you'd have more choice if you stayed on.

SHARON: What planet's she living on?

ANN: I don't think she wants to stay on.

SHARON: Wouldn't make any difference if I did.

FIROZA: But if she had a graduation diploma...

SHARON: When's the last time you talked to a guidance officer.

INDIRA: Do we have to talk about this?

SHARON: I didn't start it. Last month I went to see the Guidance. About what courses to take. I told Mrs. Gorman what I wanted and she spent half an hour trying to talk me out of it. Very subtle, like, you know. But I'm not stupid. I knew what she was doing. Going on about how good it was to be ambitious, but needing to be realistic and how important it was to have something to fall back on, if things didn't work out.

FIROZA: If you understood what she was doing, why'd you pay any attention to her.

SHARON: I ain't finished yet. Richard Bates goes in right after me, see. Now, I'm no brain, but he's a real dweeb. Stu...pid. And there was old Gorman, just slobbering with the effort to get him to take the same courses she'd been talking me out of because she couldn't bear to have him sell himself short on his potential.

INDIRA: How d'you know she said that?

SHARON: There wasn't nobody else around so I listened outside the door.

FIROZA: The important thing is why Mrs. Gorman did it.

SHARON: S'obvious. Richard's white, isn't he.

ANN: He's also a guy.

FIROZA: Sharon, we can't let other people's prejudices stop us from doing what we want. Indira's staying on at school. She'd be there to support you.

SHARON: Is that what she told you?

INDIRA: *(TRIES TO SHUT SHARON UP)* Isn't it time to get back to work?

FIROZA: Yes. *(PAUSE)* Well- Sharon's story has shown us pretty clearly that society still has lots of ways of making us think that we're inadequate. It doesn't mean we are. That's one of the things we're learning here.

SHARON: All we're learning is how to do rolls and falls an' hit the air an' stuff. That's nothing.

ANN: It is if you're not used to it.

FIROZA: Let's move on then. *(SHE GRABS SHARON'S WRIST)*

SHARON: Heyyyy!!! *(SHE'S REALLY PANICKED. SHE CAN'T BREAK AWAY)*

FIROZA: *(LET'S HER GO)* I'm sorry, Sharon. I didn't mean to frighten you. But that's how suddenly it could happen. Let's say.... I'm an aggressor. *(SHE MOVES TO INDIRA)* And I grab hold of you. *(SHE GRABS INDIRA'S WRIST)* What do you feel?

INDIRA: Scared?

FIROZA: What do you want to do about it?

INDIRA: I don't know.

FIROZA: Do you want to break away?

INDIRA: I suppose so.

FIROZA: Well, you must decide. If you're uncertain you give your opponent the advantage.

SHARON: Well, he's got the advantage, hasn't he. I mean, he wouldn't have grabbed her in the first place if he wasn't stronger than her, would he.

FIROZA: I guess we'd better review the old oriental recipe for victory in battle. First - Ann?

ANN: Oh, gawd. Um - uhh - eyes.

FIROZA: That's right. Be aware of your opponent. Two -

INDIRA: Legs.

FIROZA: For balance. Maybe even just to run away.

ANN: Guts.

FIROZA: Yes. Strength of will. You want to defend yourself. And what comes right at the bottom of the list, Sharon.

SHARON: *(PAUSE)* Strength.

FIROZA: Right.

SHARON: Why're you picking on me? This whole thing is just dumb. I don't need to learn all this stupid stuff.

FIROZA: Why not?

SHARON: 'Cause I can stick up for myself. Me 'n my friends. It's like I keep telling Indie, us West Indians, we stick up for each other. Your trouble is you don't help each other out. You're scared.

FIROZA: You know, you're partly right, Sharon. But only partly. South Asians have been taught that it's shameful to fight in public. That's not quite the same thing as being scared.

ANN: Could look the same.

SHARON: So what're you doing this for?

FIROZA: Because girls and women from whatever culture, are scared. And we limit ourselves because of that fear. I think it's important to know how to avoid dangerous situations and get out of them if they arise. Even you, Sharon - you can't go everywhere with a gang of friends, can you.

SHARON: Yeah - well I've got someone lookin' out for me.

FIROZA: A special guardian angel?

INDIRA: That's one way of describing Calvin.

FIROZA: A boyfriend!

SHARON: Yeah. And nobody gives me no trouble when he's around.

FIROZA: And when he's not?

SHARON: What're you getting at?

FIROZA: You sound a bit like my old uncle...

SHARON: Wha..!

FIROZA: ...when he found out I was taking self-defense. I should not be doing such a thing, he said. I should be content not to go out, especially at night, unless I had a man to protect me. What about coming home after working late, I asked. You should get married, he said.

SHARON: Yeah, well it's different for me.

FIROZA: What would you do if Calvin wasn't around?

SHARON: Look - that's not going to happen. I'm not gonna let it.

FIROZA: He could, by chance, get run over by a bus.

SHARON: That's really sick!

FIROZA: All I'm saying is people change. Circumstances change.

SHARON: You're just saying that 'cause you can't get anybody.

FIROZA: I don't want a man to have to look after me.

SHARON: Well, you're weird!

INDIRA: She didn't really mean that. You didn't, did you, Sharon.

ANN: I wanted somebody to look after me. Well, why not? I was working in a factory when I was 15. I nearly died of the boredom and my ears hummed all the time from the noise. Seemed to me it'd be heaven to get married, stay at home, have somebody look after me.

SHARON: See!

ANN: Trouble was it didn't last. I was home with the kids. He never was. Then he started getting laid off every job he got. Drank too much. I was cleaning out toilets to make ends meet.

SHARON: Yuk!

ANN: Smell, noise. What the hell. Life was shit whichever way you looked at it.

FIROZA: So doesn't it make sense to be able to look after yourself as well as you can.

SHARON: You don't give up, do ya. Hey - I'm not the brightest person in the world, but even I can figure out that some stupid piece of paper isn't gonna get me a job.

FIROZA: That isn't true. There are jobs.

SHARON: Yeah - well you won't catch me cleaning out somebody else's toilets. I'd rather get married and take my chances.

ANN: This Calvin got a good job then?

SHARON: He's self employed. He makes good money. And he's generous. He bought me those shoes.

ANN: I bet he's sexy too.

SHARON: Yeah.

INDIRA: Yeah. He is. And cool.

(INDIRA BEGINS TO 'PLAY OUT' CALVIN. SHE DOES IT VERY WELL. THE WALK. THE GESTURES, THE MONOPOLIZATION OF SPACE. THE INTENTION OF THE PLAYACTING AT THE BEGINNING IS TO RELEASE THE TENSION BUT IT TURNS INTO SOMETHING MORE SERIOUS. EVEN FIROZA GETS OUT OF HER WAY. BUT THEN, BOTH SHE AND ANN TAKE IT AS A JOKE AT FIRST)

Hey, man. *(IMAGINARY HANDSHAKES)* Gettin' trough? *(PRONOUNCED TRUE)* Magic. That little business, man. Soon come. No worries, man. Soon come. Trust me, bro'. Yeah.

(SHE MOVES AROUND THE AREA, FULL OF MASCULINITY, ENJOYING THE POWER SHE IS FINDING. SHARON GIGGLES. INDIRA GOES TO HER)

Looking good, woman. Yes, man. That's one good looking babe fer me to go out walking with. Get rid of your friend now.

SHARON: *(LAUGHS)*

INDIRA: Three's too many for what I got in mind. Hey, Indira, your books're waiting for you, girl. They're about the only hard thing you'll come in contact with. *(SHE LAUGHS)* Hey - ey - loosen up, woman. Too much up here ain't good fer you. Chuh! Can't take a joke, that girl. So - *(SHE PUTS HER ARM ROUND SHARON'S SHOULDER AND IN A VERY SEXY FASHION RUNS HER HAND ACROSS HER SHOULDER AND DOWN HER ARM. SHE STOPS AT HER WRIST, GRABS IT VISCIOUSLY AND TWISTS IT UP HER BACK.)* -what d'ya say?

SHARON: Please, Calvin, don't do that. You're hurting me. Please.

INDIRA: *(LETS HER GO)* Thass nice. Hey, let's see a big smile, now. *(STROKES HER CHEEK)* I'm walkin' out with my woman.

FIROZA: Indira. That's enough. Are you alright, Sharon?

SHARON: Yeah, yeah. She was just fooling around.
*(INDIRA IS VERY SURPRISED AND HORRIFIED AT
WHAT SHE HAS DONE)*

FIROZA: Was she?

SHARON: Calvin said you'd be trying to turn me against
him.

FIROZA: I'm not.

SHARON: Well, you're not going to. You don't even know
him. You don't know nothing.

FIROZA: So explain it to me.

SHARON: I can't. Why should I! Look - it's just the way
things are.

FIROZA: It's not the way they have to be.

SHARON: Chuh! I knew I shoulda stayed at MacDonalds
with Calvin and Roy. At least we were having a few laughs.
(SHE GOES TO HER COAT AND STARTS OUT)

ANN: Sharon.

SHARON: What?

ANN: Harry - that's my ex-husband, you know. Well he come
round to the house a few weeks ago. He was drunk as a skunk.
Pushed his way in saying it was his place. He smashed Mikey's
model. That kid spent hours building that plane and Harry I
just stood there. I was terrified. My older boy finally shoved the
jerk out the door. But I can't depend on him all my life, can I. In a
couple of years he'll be gone and there's the little ones to think
about...

(SILENCE. SHARON PUTS HER COAT DOWN.)

ANN: So maybe we can get back to work.

FIROZA: Right.   Partners.   *(SHE GOES TOWARDS SHARON BUT SHARON TURNS TO INDIRA.)*

ANN: Looks like you're stuck with me.

FIROZA: Let's review what we did last week.   Front choke hold.

(SHARON DOES A SUDDEN GRAB AND THROW DOWN OF INDIRA WHO LANDS HEAVILY.   SHE'S PAYING INDIRA BACK.)

FIROZA: *(NOT DARING TO DIRECTLY REPROVE SHARON, SHE POINTEDLY REPEATS THE CORRECT INSTRUCTION)* Front choke hold.   *(PAUSE)* Remember all the open spots you've got to choose from.   *(TO ANN)* Grab me.   *(SHE DEMONSTRATES)*   Hair, ear, floating ribs, solar plexis, groin, knee, instep, break away.

(SHARON AND INDIRA PRACTICE WHILE FIROZA WORKS WITH ANN.   SHARON IS VERY GOOD AT IT AND THERE IS A GROWING ENJOYMENT BETWEEN THE TWO GIRLS.)

FIROZA: *(TO ANN)* Ready?

ANN: Yeah.

FIROZA: *(GRABS HER)* Remember you've got seven places to choose from.   *(ANN BEGINS)* Good.   *(ANN PAUSES)* Solar plexis?

ANN: Where's that again?   *(SHE POINTS)*

FIROZA: Yes.

ANN: *(CARRIES ON)* And the top of the foot.

FIROZA: Good. Now push the attacker away. *(ANN DOES)* That's really coming, Ann. *(TURNS TO SEE SHARON DOING A VERY STRONG BUT AGGRESSIVE SEQUENCE ENDING WITH A BREAK AWAY)* That's really....coming. Let's finish now. *(SHE GOES INTO A FORMAL BOW. SHARON BARELY BOBS HER HEAD AND IS OUT OF THERE, INDIRA FOLLOWING)*

FIROZA: See you next week*? (NO REPLY. ANN BEGINS TO GATHER UP HER THINGS)* You're doing really well, Ann.

ANN: Yeah. I didn't know I had it in me.

FIROZA: I ....wanted to say thanks.   For helping me out earlier. You know...with Sharon.

ANN: Oh. That's okay.

FIROZA: She's so....difficult.

ANN: Oh, I don't know. I wouldn't wanta be her mum, but I kinda like her spunk.

FIROZA: You think I was too heavy.

ANN: You're the teacher.

FIROZA: That doesn't mean I'm always right.

ANN: So you were too heavy.

FIROZA: *(PAUSE)* D'you think they won't come back?

ANN: Hard to say.

FIROZA: I'm just not getting through to them.

ANN: I think what you mean is, you're not getting them to agree with you.

FIROZA: No! *(PAUSE)*   I just want them to understand...

ANN: Yeah, well....maybe it's you that don't understand.

FIROZA: What?

ANN: Ah, forget it.

FIROZA: No. You want the class to continue, so help me out here. Please.

ANN: You're just different from us. Even from Indira. You got answers to questions we ain't even asked yet. But I don't think you got a clue about how things are. Look, you come down here once a week with all these "facts" and "ideas". Most women have to work. Be strong. Well, you might be right. But you can't ignore love... and sex. You know the kind of stuff kids read. "How can Amanda get Kevin to notice her."

FIROZA: But they can't take that kind of thing seriously.

ANN: Why not? D'you expect something like 'How can Amanda get top marks in her finals' to turn them on?

FIROZA: Come on, Ann. You told Sharon the story about Harry coming back to your house. You know all this romantic stuff's a myth.

ANN: Some people think God's a myth. But plenty of them still believe in him anyway - especially when the chips are down. Haven't you ever been in love?

FIROZA: Well, yes, I suppose so, - but...

ANN: No. I don't think you have. Well, it's wonderful! I may be (getting) fat and pushing forty and divorced, but I haven't forgotten how fantastic it felt. Somebody loves you in spite of the fact that you don't look like Raquel Welch. You're the centre of his life. You count. And you relax because someone else is in charge now. *(PAUSE)* But then you wake up one morning and you realize that he might be the centre of your life, but he's not there when you need him, and feeding your kids is more or less up to you, and....

FIROZA: So the old myth's a fake.

ANN: It sucks you in.

FIROZA: You got out.

ANN: Yeah. But I'm not proud of it, Firoza. I'm not looking forward to spending the rest of my life on my own. But I haven't figured out what having a good relationship with a man really means. I don't think they know either.

FIROZA: How could they. They're too young.

ANN: Men I mean. The old myth whammies them too, don't it. They're supposed to be always in control. Never show they're weak. Well, that's impossible. Maybe that's why Harry drinks. I don't know. Gawd! I gotta go. I left the two youngest on their own. They're probably tearing the place apart. *(SHE LEAVES)*

(FIROZA IS LEFT ON HER OWN.)

End of Scene.

MAD LOVE

By Jennifer Maisel

CHARACTERS:
JACE - 13
KEN - 16

(7 minutes in heaven. The room is dark. Ken waits. Jace is pushed in and the door is shut and locked behind her.)

JACE: Hello?

KEN: Hi.

JACE: Who is it?

KEN: Ken.

JACE: Jace.

KEN: Oh.

JACE: Hi.

KEN: Hi.

(he reaches out and grabs at her breast)

JACE: What are you doing?

KEN: What?

JACE: Don't do that.

KEN: Don't you want me to?

JACE: Does it sound like I want you to?

KEN: Well, how am I supposed to know?

JACE: Figure it out.

KEN: Hey. You came in here with me. Not the other way around. You knew who you were getting into.

JACE: They pushed me in. I didn't know. I just got here. I didn't know anyone was choosing.

KEN: Great.

JACE: I'm sorry.

KEN: Sure.

JACE: I am.

(silence)

KEN: Do you want to make out?

JACE: No.

(silence)

KEN: Who would you have picked?

JACE: Not anyone, I think.

KEN: No one.

JACE: Becca brought me. I don't think I was really invited.

KEN: You don't say much to anyone -- I've never even really talked to you before. Everyone wonders about you.

JACE: Everyone talks about me.

(silence)

KEN: How's your mom?

JACE: Crazy.

(Silence.)

JACE: That was what you wanted to hear, wasn't it? My mother would rather be a snake. She tried to kill my father. My brother hung himself and my bra size, last time I checked, was a 34C and still growing. You've heard everything now.

(Silence.)

KEN: I'm sorry.

JACE: When are they going to let us out of here?

KEN: It hasn't been seven minutes yet.

JACE: Great...

KEN: I am sorry.

JACE: Tomorrow they'll probably be saying I fucked you on the top of the washer/dryer.

KEN: No they won't.

JACE: I don't care anyway.

KEN: Everybody's just curious.

JACE: Yeah...just tell them to read it in the Enquirer. Just tell them to leave me the fuck alone.

KEN: Don't you like anyone?

JACE: Becca.

KEN: Anyone else?

JACE: I don't know anyone else.

KEN: You don't have to know them. I don't know you.

JACE: No. You don't.

KEN: I'm sorry.

JACE: What for?

KEN: Just seemed like the thing to say.

JACE: What are you going to tell them happened in here?

KEN: Nothing.

(silence)

KEN: Adam was pretty cool -- I always thought your mom was...I don't know...nice.

JACE: I still don't want to make out with you.

KEN: I didn't ask.

JACE: I'm just saying.

KEN: Maybe I don't want to anymore.

(silence)

JACE: I might have picked you. If I had had to pick, I would have picked you.

End of Scene.

THE RASPBERRY

By Suzanne Bailie

CHARACTERS
Mary Elderly woman
Tyrone   Man, non-white late teen, early twenty.

SYNOPSIS
Shoved into a retirement home a feisty and angry octogenarian faces her birthday alone. It's a teenage worker and modern technology that shoves the resistant birthday girl back into embracing life.

(A chair center stage. Close by is table with a chair near it. MARY using a walker slowly moves across stage and eventually sits in chair. She pulls out a small package from her housecoat pocket.)

MARY: Happy birthday to me, happy birthday to me, I'm eighty-three and do what I please.

(Gives a raspberry to audience. Carefully opens package.)

Goodness.

(Reveals Blackberry phone.)

What in the world? How do? This is, where's the on button?

(Reads the card, fiddles with Blackberry unsure how to use it. Frustrated puts it down and picks up her crossword puzzle magazine. Distinctive quiet knocks on door, and then louder knocks.)

TYRONE: Ms. M. open up. It's Tyrone.

MARY: Come in Tyrone its open.

(TYRONE enters he wears jeans and an oversized t-shirt with a blue vest that is labeled Peaceful Gardens Retirement on the left side, on the right is a name tag that says "Hello my name is TYRONE".)

What's poppin' Ms. M.? Front office told me it's your birthday.

MARY: *(Continues to do crossword puzzle.)*

So it is. Bless their hearts, kitchen folk put a candle in my morning bran muffin. When Joe lit it, all I thought was, it's a good day to die. They'd forgotten Pearl May, at my table, uses an oxygen tank.

TYRONE: Hoping to start your birthday with a bang.

MARY: Sure enough. Got my paper?

TYRONE: You like chillaxin with it so I brought it over first. You kicken' it tonight? You know a little par-tay-ing for your birthday.

MARY: It's bridge night. They make a mean prune punch.

TYRONE: That's nasty. How you drink that stuff?

MARY: It gets me all jiggy so at bridge tonight it'll be crackin' I'll be steppin' out fitted like no other. I'll be hittin' all their bids, winning the tricks, showing my mad skills, the women be yelling "that's federal, take her away she's so good it's illegal". How'd I do? Am I getting better?

TYRONE: Ms. M. you keep talking like that your bridge partners gonna put you away.

MARY: That new bus boy is teaching some, off the chain, words to me. You going out dancing tonight?

TYRONE: It's a school night and I gotta be on my game tomorrow. Gettin' the hook up for the tech school I've been telling you 'bout. Anyway I'm not old enough to go clubbing Ms. M.

MARY: That's ridiculous you have to be at least fourteen to drive.

TYRONE: Yo, Ms. M it's not 1947, you gotta be twenty-one to go out clubbin'. Check it, boss lady has me delivering papers so I got to dip out.

MARY: Here can you take this out with you? (Hands wrapping to him.) My daughter sent me a present.

TYRONE: Surprised she sent you anything.

MARY: That was uncalled for.

TYRONE: Didn't security show up last time?

MARY: I know, I know I feel terrible about that. It was a hard adjustment from - you wait Tyrone, wait till you get shoved into a retirement home, then you'll understand.

TYRONE: Ms. M you can't be expectin' a call when you shouted, "listen sister, let me tell you when to call me again, never!"

MARY: Don't remind me. Take this to. *(Hands him Blackberry.)*

TYRONE: Dang! Is it hot? RIM BlackBerry Bold. Girl you sell that on E-Bay, you're gonna make some benjamins. *(Hands it back to Mary.)*

MARY: What do I need money for?

TYRONE: Listen to you. Everyone likes a little cheese in their pocket. Why you think I'm working here? It ain't cause I like cramming for school on a stanky bus making two transfers from the hood all the way to the a-fflu-ent Westside. All my cheddar gonna get me a ride.

MARY: I'll give you credit Tyrone.

TYRONE: A man do what a man gotta do. When I get my wheels I'll drive to tech and big boss lady told me I could work here nights and that's on the real.

MARY: I'm too old to figure out this new fangled stuff and that's on the real. Maybe I'm a wet rag; I can't even see the buttons without my glasses.

TYRONE: You sure Ms. M?

MARY: *(Hands it to Tyrone.)*

Of course I'm sure.

TYRONE: You're not going go Alzheimer on me and forget you gave it to me? I need this job and if someone starts saying I was jackin' stuff-

MARY: Alzheimer? Listen sonny, I might need hearing aides to hear, glasses to see, dentures to eat, a walker to get around, but I can still think my own thoughts. I know what I'm saying thank you very much.

TYRONE: This is off the hook! You're too much Ms. M profits from this baby are going straight to the Tyrone Bernard Jacob's ride fund. You hear me? Straight to it.

MARY: My hearing aid is on I hear you fine.

TYRONE: Thanks Ms. M.

(Bends down and gives her and awkward hug, leaves excited.)

MARY: She won't call she's too much like me.

(Same day, later that afternoon. MARY she struggles with using a pretend record player on the table. She gives up and slowly moves to her chair. Next to the chair is a small bag of garbage.)

MARY: Stupid thing probably scratched.

(Sits down and pulls out knitting. Distinctive signature knocks at the door.)

MARY: It's open Tyrone.

TYRONE: What's crackalackin' Ms. M.? Wednesday afternoon garbage run, got some?

MARY: *(Aggravated.)* Cock-a-doodle-do, cluck, cluck, cluck. This isn't a chicken coop Tyrone.

TYRONE: I come thru and you start getting all up in my ethnicity? Ok ok I know how to play it. *(Talks like a middle class white man.)* Good afternoon Ms. Mary, lovely to see you again. Ah, Spring, particularly nice weather today, wouldn't you agree?

MARY: Tickle your arse with a feather?

TYRONE: You playin' me? Don't be a hater, nobody likes a hater.

MARY: I'm teasing in a hurtful way, I'm sorry. I'm not a hater. You give spicy energy to this place

TYRONE: Truth that.

MARY: The player used to start automatically. It's breaking down just like me. I can't get the needle on it; I can't even listen to my music anymore. My world keeps getting smaller and smaller.

TYRONE: This janky thing belongs in a museum. How you listen to this scratchy thing?

(Places needle on record. "Too Fat Polka" starts to play extremely loudly.)

What the heck is that?

MARY: The Too Fat Polka.

TYRONE: It's wack that's what. Why you listening to that? Your mind and ears completely gone?

MARY: That's a classic, young man. We'd go dancing down at the Polish Hall. Jane and I would polka and schottische all night.

TYRONE: Makes me want to polka both my eyes out. This is crazy; I'm going fix you up.

(Turns off record player.)

MARY: I'm not interested in getting fixed up; I'm quite content being by myself.

TYRONE: You thought I was talking a date? Ha ha. Girl fix you up is, well here let me show you.

(Pulls out Blackberry from his pocket.)

MARY: That again.

TYRONE: Yes, that again.

MARY: I'm not a reneger.

TYRONE: A what?!

MARY: Renege to go back on what I said, it's a good crossword puzzle word.

TYRONE: That's cool. You can listen to music on this; you don't have to be getting up and listening to scratchy dusty music and then break something getting' back to your chair. Tell me what you want to listen to and I'll download it. How about some JZ or Beyounce, something old school. Ain't nothing to it.

MARY: Download. That's computer jargon I don't understand that type of stuff.

TYRONE: A song. I need the name or artist.

MARY: How about Sentimental Reasons or I Can't Give You Anything but Love.

(TYRONE types on Blackberry.)

TYRONE: Now you just plug in the earphones here and put them on. Ok. You use this little pearl here, ya it moves, ok you do it. Move it to the media icon or picture, push it, then push that arrow thing. You hear it? Here's the volume.

MARY: *(Hums and then sings along to Sentimental Reasons.)*

"I love you and you alone were meant for me. Please give your loving heart to me. And say we'll never part."

TYRONE: That's right Ms.M. you're feeling yourself now.

MARY: *(Removes head phones.)*

It's like Nat is right here. William and I used to play this and dance. It was so romantic. Perfect for –

TYRONE: I get it, I get it.

MARY: Who knew that thing played music; it doesn't have wires or anything. I see why you can get loads of benjamins for it. Here's my garbage, I've bagged it up.

TYRONE: It does lots of things. *(Grabs garbage.)* Heard from your daughter yet?

MARY: No, she's busy, always busy. She's a lawyer you know has a couple of real nice girls, my granddaughters.

TYRONE: Ms. M maybe I'd show you how to use it, you know, that way you could listen to music anytime you want.

MARY: Oh no, it's much too difficult. Anyway I gave to you.

TYRONE: Then I can do with it what I want.

MARY: Yes you can.

TYRONE: Let's make a deal.

MARY: I can't watch that anymore. It's just not the same without Bob Barker, he had class. Drew really should wear a girdle.

TYRONE: Ms. M you're wasting my minutes. How about I take that record player and give you this Blackberry, teach you how to use it? A trade.

MARY: What do you want with an old broken record player?

TYRONE: My brother fixes things later he sells 'em at the swap meets.

MARY: Well you can just take it and keep (Points to Blackberry.) that thing too.

TYRONE: Why you being like this?

MARY: Like what.

TYRONE: Like all difficult. Your world is getting smaller cause you're letting it.

MARY: Oh poppy cock.

TYRONE: Give me your daughter's digits, her phone number. She's paid for the service so you'd better use it once.

MARY: *(Hands Tyrone an address book.)* It's under Patricia.

TYRONE: *(Looks at address book and puts number in Blackberry.)*

Ok I'll put the digits in for her and your granddaughter, Lisa. After that you're doing it.

MARY: I can't the buttons are too small and my fingers hurt, arthritis.

TYRONE: Or you're just stubborn. Use the eraser end of a pencil to push the buttons. Now hold this.

(Hands Mary the Blackberry.)

MARY: I won't be able to remember how to do it. I think I should write this down, so I'll remember it later. What if I break it?

TYRONE: It ain't gonna break. Don't flush it down the crapper or put it in the washing machine. I got more trash to pick up so let's do this.

MARY: Alright, but I'm doing this under duress.

TYRONE: See that there. That's your daughter's number now push that green button. Now hold it up to your ear, it's a phone.

MARY: It's ringing.

TYRONE: Phones do that. When you're done push the red button.

(Grabs garbage and leaves.)

MARY: Tyrone wait what if - Hello, hello, Is this Patty? *(Beat.)* Oh Lisa, it's Grandma, you sound so much like your mother. Yes, I'm using my present, a blueberry? Blackberry. What? I wasn't too sure either. *(Beat.)* You got a car? Yes, I'd like to see it. Send me a picture. It'll be the phone?

MARY: *(CONTINUED.)*

Nice talking to you sweetie. *(beat.)* Oh Patty how are you? I'm so sorry about the awful things I said, please forgive me? Hearing your voice is the best present ever.

(Lights slowly fade as Mary continues talking to her daughter.)

(Next day. Mary is working crossword puzzle. Distinctive knock at door.)

MARY: Come in, I'm so glad you're hear.

TYRONE: *(Brings in her newspaper.)*

What's up Mary Poppins?

MARY: Do you know this phone does text messages and I can get pictures? Look, here is Lisa and her new ride. *(Shows photo on Blackberry to him.)* She's like you going to school and working. Stand there while I take your picture.

TYRONE: What you want my picture for?

MARY: Business cards. I'm getting all up in your business Tyrone. I got a plan; actually it was Lisa's idea. Do you know I can buy stuff on-line with this and it has a GPS, it knows where it is, so I know where I am. It is simply incredible.

TYRONE: Your granddaughter had an idea for me?

MARY: Listen it's brilliant. I'm going to pimp you out.

TYRONE: You gonna do what?

MARY: Pimp you out, sell your services, help you get that sweet slab you've been wanting.

TYRONE: How you gonna do that?

MARY: I'm thinking twenty dollars an hour. That's good money isn't it? What do you think?

TYRONE: About what?

MARY: About my idea.

TYRONE: Ms. M if you're thinking pimpin' me out means

some uh kinky stuff between me and the grandmas in this place, I gotta be truthful that ain't right.

MARY: Sexual services. *(Laughing.)* We can consider that if this doesn't work out, but I'm talking technical service. Get people's computers hooked up and running, set-up cell phones with speed dials get their personal digital doo-dads programmed, download music, stuff like that. What do you think?

TYRONE: That's cash-money for real.

MARY: Exactly. You have a customer base right here at the retirement center.

TYRONE: Is the boss lady ok with this?

MARY: She will be when we're done talking with her.

TYRONE: Tricked Out Tech by Tyrone.

MARY: Or Tyrone Tickles Your YaYas, *(chuckling.)*. I have your first tech customer lined up. Mr. Hosinski in 12B needs some Chopin and Polka music downloaded.

TYRONE: Still with that Polka. Planning on a little cupid shuffle with Mr. Hoskinski in 12B? Maybe get you a new boo?

MARY: You never know, Tyrone, you never know.

End of Scene.

GIRLS PLAY

By Masha Obolensky

Characters
MARTHA, 13 going on 14 years old, best friend to RUTH,
infatuated with Mr. Camargo, a new teacher recently
arrived
at her school from Italy.
RUTH, 13 going on 14 years old, coming to understand her
complex feelings for her best friend MARTHA.

While the characters of RUTH and MARTHA are 13 years
old,
the actors playing them should be in the range of 18 to 24
years old.

MARTHA and RUTH are in their secret fort in the woods.
They are
kissing.

MARTHA: Ouch.

RUTH: Sorry –

MARTHA: Mr. Camargo wouldn't bite my tongue.

RUTH: I know – I'm sorry! Let's try again.

MARTHA: I'm finished with this.

RUTH: What do you mean?

MARTHA: It's time.

RUTH: Time?

MARTHA: To tell him. About my feelings.

RUTH: You shouldn't do that.

MARTHA: Why not?

RUTH: It just … might not be a good idea.

MARTHA: I almost did - when we were at the pool.

RUTH: He's at the pool with you?

MARTHA: Sometimes.

RUTH: You didn't tell me that.

MARTHA: I forgot.

RUTH: So that's why you like swimming so much.

Beat

RUTH: I'm sure he likes you.

MARTHA: *(encouraged)* Have you noticed the way we look at each other in class?

RUTH: No. *(she notices MARTHA's disappointment)* Well, yes – I mean - now I think about it. I have noticed.

MARTHA: You have

RUTH: Yes

MARTHA: He looks

RUTH: at you – he does

MARTHA: I knew it. I knew it. That's it. I'm going to tell him.

RUTH: *(seizing the opportunity)* Do you want to practice what you'll say?

MARTHA: *(excitedly)* Maybe – okay! Yes – okay – yes - let's practice.

RUTH: You'll knock on his door –

MARTHA: His door is always open –

RUTH: *(She sets the scene in his house in order to gain more intimate access to Martha)* No, at his house.

MARTHA: Oh, I don't know if I'll go to his house.

RUTH: Might as well. He lives alone.

MARTHA: That's what we think –

RUTH: Well we've never seen him with anyone there –

MARTHA: Okay why not – we'll say his house for now. Maybe we walk there from the pool. That's it – I'll tell him – what –

RUTH: That – that the man on the bike – has been – watching you.

beat

MARTHA: That's – scary.

RUTH: You're afraid of him so you need Mr. Camargo to walk you home.

MARTHA: Okay - I'm afraid of Bicycle Man – yes! – so I ask him to walk me home and then as we near his house – I – I - tell him I'm not feeling well – that I swallowed too much chlorine or something -

RUTH: *(aware that she must set the scene up perfectly for Martha)*

All right – so– this is his couch. He – I – help you onto the couch – you are faint – or you're acting as if you are faint - *(as Mr. Camargo)* Let me help you, Martha.

MARTHA: Thank you, thank you very much – I'm feeling much better.

RUTH has sat MARTHA down in such a way that she is very close to her. She looks into her eyes. She is eager to turn the heat up.

RUTH: You know you have beautiful eyes.

MARTHA: *(to Ruth)* Wait. Move over. He wouldn't say that yet.

RUTH: Sorry.

RUTH moves over. She collects herself for a moment and readies for another attempt.

(as Mr. C) How are you feeling?

MARTHA: Better – like I said.

RUTH: Can I get you anything?

MARTHA: Just a glass of water would be fine.

RUTH: Okay.

Here you are.

MARTHA: Thank you.

(breaking character – to Ruth)

Comfort me.

RUTH: Oh! Okay!

RUTH rubs MARTHA on the back.

MARTHA: *(to Mr. Camargo)* No, really. I'm fine. You are
so kind to take me in. *(to Ruth, who is getting too involved
with the rubbing of her back)* Okay stop rubbing my back.

RUTH: Sorry. What should I do?

MARTHA: I don't know. What do you think Mr. Camargo
would do?

RUTH: Um. How about this?

She takes MARTHA's hand.

MARTHA is satisfied with this.

MARTHA: Mr. Camargo. I've wanted to speak to you
about something.

RUTH: Have you?

MARTHA: I've noticed our eyes have met several times –
at the pool – in class.

RUTH: I've noticed that as well.

MARTHA: You have?

RUTH: Oh yes. I cannot stop myself from looking at you.

MARTHA: So you – you have been – you do look at me.

RUTH: I can't keep my eyes off of you.

RUTH strokes MARTHA's hair – MARTHA brushes her hand away.

MARTHA: I'd like to ask you

RUTH: Yes

MARTHA: When you –

RUTH: When I?

MARTHA: When you look at me

RUTH: Yes

MARTHA: What do you see?

RUTH: What do I see?

MARTHA: Yes.

RUTH: I – I don't know what he sees –

MARTHA: Come on..!

RUTH: I see – I see – your eyes.

MARTHA: My eyes?

RUTH: *(Ruth says this from her heart, in her own voice)* I mean – I see in your eyes such... courage.

MARTHA: *(This is the best possible answer from Mr. Camargo)* Yes?

RUTH: You are courageous and ... alive – very alive. You are not afraid.

(MR. CAMARGO (RUTH) has spoken something that Martha could only have hoped for.)

MARTHA: Oh, Mr. Camargo. You're right. I am courageous. Mr. Camargo –

RUTH: Yes –

MARTHA: I've wanted to tell you –

RUTH: Go ahead

MARTHA: I have such feelings. Such big feelings. I see -in your eyes – something more – more than this – there has to be something more than this – is there? - something more that this - stupid – fort *(Martha tears off a piece of the ceiling of their fort. Ruth gasps and scrambles to put the piece back)* I want to know –

RUTH: what

MARTHA: I want to know what you've seen –

RUTH: ok

MARTHA: I want to see what you've seen –

RUTH: You can –

MARTHA: I can?

RUTH: Yes, I will show you. Come here.

RUTH pulls MARTHA to her. MARTHA is swept up in the imaginary circumstances. RUTH is swept up in MARTHA.

MARTHA: Oh, Mr. Camargo...

They kiss.

Then, RUTH takes it a step further and begins to unbutton MARTHA's blouse. MARTHA pushes her away.

RUTH: *(afraid she has ruined everything)* No?

MARTHA: No.

RUTH: He probably would.

MARTHA: Well...

RUTH: Remember what happened with Tom and Lilly.

MARTHA: Right.

RUTH: You have to be ready.

MARTHA: Okay. Let's try it.

RUTH returns to MARTHA's buttons.

But wait. Let me do it.

MARTHA stands before MR. CAMARGO. Ready to share

this gift with him, she unbuttons her blouse. With her back to the audience, she pulls her blouse down over her shoulders.

Here. Aren't they beautiful?

RUTH: Yes.

RUTH is overcome. She reaches out to touch. MARTHA, taken out of the fantasy, slaps her hand away.

MARTHA: I didn't say you could touch them.

RUTH: But I think he probably would!

MARTHA buttons up her blouse.

MARTHA: That's enough –

RUTH: Let's keep going – *(RUTH lurches toward MARTHA, trying to embrace her)*

MARTHA: *(pushing her away)* I said that's enough. I'm going to tell him. *(MARTHA gets ready to leave.)*

RUTH: *(desperate)* Are you sure?

MARTHA: What do you mean?

RUTH: That you should do this.

MARTHA: You said we look at each other -

RUTH: I think so – but.

MARTHA: But - ?

Beat

RUTH: *(intently, with weight)* Are you sure you are ready.

MARTHA: *(Martha looks at their fort, and then out at the world - with doubt)* I feel ready.

RUTH: You wouldn't want to ruin it - because you weren't ready.

MARTHA: We have to go home.

RUTH: Practice makes perfect.

Beat

Tomorrow.

Pause

MARTHA: Okay. I don't want to mess it up.

RUTH: Yes, you wouldn't want to mess it up.

RUTH impulsively reaches out to touch MARTHA's hair.

MARTHA: Don't do that.

RUTH: Sorry.

MARTHA: Tomorrow.

End of Scene.

"FOR SALE" FROM SQUARE

By Lene Therese Teigen

Square consists of four parts, "For Sale" being one of them. All the parts have different characters and settings, but the same ages and age differences for the four characters.

In this text we meet four sisters. Sara is the youngest, Mira the second youngest, Lea the second oldest and Eva the oldest.

They are trying to sell their house, but awful things have happened here, therefore some of them have a hard time to concentrate on the buyers (which can be the audience) and others use too much time trying hard not to remember. They breathe inwards to try to swallow their words and maybe also memories.

LEA: I'm Lea.
        This door is leading to my room.

MIRA: And this is mine
        I'm Mira.
        The door has some scratches
        I had a dog for a while
        a small one
        it died
        it –

SARA: Are you through?
        Sara, that's my name.
        This is my room
        You'll probably notice this by yourselves
        But the fact is I haven't lived here for a long time
        I stay in my moms room
        My sisters I mean
        And now he is dead

EVA: I'm Eva. This is my room, my door.

SARA: Ours

EVA: We have cleaned it
       Painted the door white, shining

LEA   It's cream

SARA: It smelled so bad for a while.
       Real oil-paint. The only thing in this house which
       has been painted lately
       It's beautiful, isn't it?
EVA: Yes, Sara, it is. Stop now.

LEA: We lived up here
       he on the main floor
       but now he is dead

MIRA: That's why we're selling
       We don't need it anymore

LEA: You have to stop that mom-crap

SARA: But where do I come from?
       I can't only have a father, can I?

MIRA: It is the same for all of us

SARA: But you do say I have another mother
       I know it's you.

EVA: I'm your sister

LEA: She is

MIRA: We don't exactly lie

LEA: It's complicated

EVA: Don't say any more

MIRA: It has to do with him

EVA: I'll kill you

MIRA: You didn't even manage to kill her

SARA: He is dead!
        We're all moving away from here

LEA: Sorry about their noise.
        See, that's why we want to sell the house,
        because he is dead.
        Tell them about the view, Eva.

EVA: The view is fabulous
        I used to stand by the window in the
        dining room and watch the sea
        could feel the house shake
        when the winds where heavy

LEA: Storm -

EVA: The grey wall of water
        came towards me,
        Asked me to come in a way –
        You're right, the windows are big, but solid,
        the sills must be painted, I'm afraid.

MIRA: It's a miracle there never was a flood

LEA: He talked about moving it
        in case –
        in case –
        the water came closer
        maybe
        The whole house
        with us inside

MIRA: He said all should be as it used to be
        we in our rooms
        and him downstairs

SARA: I –
        Look, the cats scratched me
EVA: I'll find some ointment afterwords
        Now we have to show the house, Sara
        We're about to the sell it, right?

MIRA: With the ongoing radio and the shouts

LEA: The kitchen needs to be redecorated
        that's for sure.
        It looks awful, we know
        but none of us like cooking
        there is something about the smells

EVA: Don't talk about it
LEA: It's just like –
        Like –

MIRA: The house just doesn't smell very well
        But it will change
        We thought of suggesting ammonia

LEA: Under the furniture, on small plates

SARA: You're my mother

EVA: Stop it
        Watch out for the dress
        You're dirty, Sara, where did you go?

MIRA: Ammonia works.

EVA: There has to be a real clean-up, don't you see?

LEA: We don't like to clean
        there's something about
        something about

EVA: He had his chair by the window with
        the view of the garden
        he used to sit there and watch the trees, I think
        I imagined that, anyway,
        he listened to the radio the whole day
        anything that was on
        shouted some times

LEA: And we came

They all keep their breath.

MIRA: I wish I had gone
        at least on a little trip
        always imagined -

LEA: Please be quiet

MIRA: What about a street
        maybe just –
        Something quite simple
        not any fancy stores or anything
        nothing expensive
        just a street with some stores
        I imagine walking upwards
        its a small hill
        and there on the right hand side

right next to the fabric-store with all
the buttons, there's a stationary
I walk inside
straight to the shelves with all the pens
pick out a green one
then to the boxes with stationary, cards
diaries
find some cards with flower decorations

LEA: Flowers

SARA: Can I have a diary

EVA: Hush

MIRA: White lilies perhaps
or hyacinths in a corner
quite simple, pale
and then to the counter
and I buy it
then out again
walking on upwards

SARA: You're my mother

LEA: Poor one, she's a little…
a little weird

SARA: But I recognize you
I know your inside
you can't fool me

LEA: We are sisters
all of us
you know that

MIRA: Sometimes I think how life would have been
without him.

LEA: Mira!

MIRA: He did need us.

SARA: We couldn't leave him

MIRA: But now we're selling - moving

LEA: You sound like you're looking forward

SARA: We all need change, don't we?
          I do
          I feel like choking
          Sometimes I wonder
          My heart doesn't beat
          I don't know
          Maybe it's not supposed to
          I feel so bad

EVA: You're right
          I'm your mother, I must be

LEA: What are you saying?

EVA: He was -

MIRA: But he –
          he was –

LEA: This is my room
          There used to be purple flowers on the
          white wallpaper
          Then the clothes turned too small
          There were a lot of fetuses
          They chopped off their heads
          Lots of crying
          Lots lots
          Little hands, feet

SARA: Stop it!

EVA: She's just trying to scare you
        She has this thing about making fun
        It's nothing
        Nothing to be afraid of
        Not now
        It's over, right

LEA: Right.
        We're selling.

MIRA: There once was a mother -
        I, –
        But she died too
        disappeared
        The smell was so strange

LEA: We all die

EVA: Lea!

MIRA: We cried

LEA: We're selling
        We will
        Moving

SARA: I didn't know a thing
        You understand?
        Nothing
        It's for the best

EVA: That's my girl.

LEA: We didn't know who he was

EVA: I did.
        I did.

SARA: He was our father, wasn't he?
LEA: Sara!

MIRA: He can't have been
        Not that
        Not the way he went on

LEA: Don't you read newspapers

SARA: They smell strange, and you get dirty from them

EVA: They write all weird stuff, Sara
        Lots you don't know if you can believe
        But it's useful
        A lot to learn

LEA: A lot to learn

SARA: Mom!

MIRA: No!

SARA: You're supposed to look after your children.

MIRA: Why didn't you kill her?
        She reminds me of –
        reminds me of
        Mother?

EVA: I can't remember her name.

LEA: She smells funny too.

EVA: We stink all of us.
        I'm sure there won't be any buyers if you go on -

SARA: We'll rot in here.
        All of us.

The other three laugh indulgently.
Sara drops a curtsey to the buyers.

SARA (contd.): This is my door. It leads to my room. My bed.
All keep their breaths.

End of Scene.

I CRY OUT FOR FREEDOM

By Patrizia Monaco – Translated by Kay McCarthy

PAUL: Sakuntala or The Abandonment. Station Nine.

Light on the neutral area of the stage representing a street in Paris. DEBUSSY in a waiting pose. He is very elegant. He is joined by a panting and disheveled.

CAMILLE wearing a little, black, worn-out suit.

DEBUSSY: Camille, at last! How did it go?

CAMILLE: Debussy, let's dance!

DEBUSSY: Here , in the middle of the street?

CAMILLE: I'm happy! So happy! My Sakuntala has received an honorary mention at the salon!

DEBUSSY: I was sure of it! *(CAMILLE obliges him to dance a waltz)*

CAMILLE: Soon I'll be famous, and I'm not yet thirty. Rodin has become famous only now, and he's old.

DEBUSSY: He's fifty. Where shall we be at fifty?

CAMILLE: My sculptures are appreciated , even if they continue calling me "Rodin's pupil" . . . but I'm used to that. *(At each whirl of the waltz she pronounces one line)* Rodin's pupil *(whirl)* the playwright Paul Claudel's sister *(whirl)* Rodin's lover *(whirl)* the ambassador, Paul Claudel's sister *(whirl)* friend… not yet lover of the musician Debussy *(DEBUSSY is embarrassed. they stop dancing)*. To feel myself a sculptress, that is, myself, I've had to change studios, rent one all of my own. This is my surprise.

They stop in front of the notice :

Camille Claudel, sculptress, 113 boulevard d'Italie.

He looks into her eyes.

DEBUSSY: Your eyes remind me of Ligeia's in Poe's story. "You're strangely lovely this evening. So lovely that you seem to be about to die".

CAMILLE: You're like my brother, quotations, always quotations. *(malicious)* Are these your orgasms?

DEBUSSY: *(thinking he hasn't heard properly)* What did you say?

CAMILLE: That I too read Edgar Allen Poe. What's that the crow said? Never again, never again. *(she stares at him)*

DEBUSSY: I know.

CAMILLE: No, you don't. Never again with Rodin, never again.

DEBUSSY: What!?!

CAMILLE: He's sucked my vital lymph.

DEBUSSY: But if you've just made a masterpiece, Sakuntala!

CAMILLE: Do you know what it's second name is? The Abandonment.

DEBUSSY: It's not true, it's impossible. A man and woman welded together, the two of you, the two Titans of sculpture.

CAMILLE: He's the Titan. He gets the commissions.
DEBUSSY: But a moment ago you said you'd received an important tribute!

CAMILLE: I don't want tributes, I want money, that is, bread. I'm always hungry. Marble is dear. Good Italian marble costs from 1,500 to 2,000 Francs a cubic metre and its takes two metres to make a life-size seated statue.

DEBUSSY: Everyone admires you. Nobody else has sculpted directly in marble for ages.

CAMILLE: Their admiration won't buy me a new dress. How many years have I been going to the Salon in this little dress? Black, a colour I hate! But suitable for all occasions. Red, I'd like a red dress! I've always wanted one , but my mother says only whores wear them. She didn't use that exact word. She prefers to say "hussy".

DEBUSSY: You should be more diplomatic. See, even Rodin puts on his Sunday best and frequents the right people.

CAMILLE: Who are the right people, Debussy?

DEBUSSY: *(after a pause)* Powerful people?

CAMILLE: My first real work was David and Goliath . We must always defend the weak against the strong. *(pause)* I'll leave the great Rodin and come out from isolation. I'll live, go out with you, we'll go to concerts, exhibitions . . . I'll sculpt a waltz and leave Rodin.

Darkness. PAUL appears.

PAUL: Tenth Station : The Red Umbrella, or Dialogue of Stones.

Light on the studio. CAMILLE, as usual, is sculpting frantically. RODIN enters with a package.

RODIN: I've brought you a gift. *(he unwraps the package and takes out a red umbrella)*

CAMILLE: *(turning around)* It's beautiful, I really needed something that superfluous.

RODIN: But you said . . .

CAMILLE: Exactly, a woman likes to receive the superfluous, it makes her feel, a woman . . .

RODIN: I'm glad.

CAMILLE: You're glad above all that I no longer ask you to live with me forever instead of with your scarecrow . . . above all, that I don't ask you to marry me .

RODIN: Well . . . I thought that, by now . . .

CAMILLE: By now, what? If she's given you a lot, I've given you everything! My youth, my talent, my very soul!

RODIN: You talk of soul?

CAMILLE: What we put into our sculptures! What's the use in people lining up like that for the Rodin Monet exhibition. They could come here, free of change, at least as far as the great Rodin is concerned! Your Eternal Idol is my Sakuntala, your . . .

RODIN: We've always known we had the same style!

CAMILLE: And this affinity . . . this extraordinary affinity . . . means nothing? *(she looks at him)* Hasn't all of this some sense?

RODIN: But you left me. *(as he leaves he turns around)* Ah, you can always come and take the blocks I don't need. *(exit)*

CAMILLE: *(taking up the red umbrella and brandishing it like a club she destroys everything around her)* Your marble! We communicate only through stones.

Darkness. PAUL on the proscenium.

PAUL: The eyes are the same as ever, but those who know her notice terrible flashes, a strange stare. Eleventh Station: The Giant Betrayed.

The study. DEBUSSY and CAMILLE. DEBUSSY watches her as she models the pedestal of an art nouveau lamp stand.

CAMILLE: *(ironic)* The English call these "bread and butter jobs".

DEBUSSY: The objects you make are lovely, are they not a minor aspect of your art, and yet, art? Like when they commission a piece of music from me. There's nothing to be ashamed of.

CAMILLE: Who said anything about shame? *(she models clumsily and makes a mistake)* Shit!

Silence

DEBUSSY: Where's Paul now?

CAMILLE: Consul somewhere. He sends me money, you know? My father too, unknown to the two Louises *(noticing DEBUSSY'S perplexity)* my mother and my sister.

DEBUSSY: Has something happened between you and Paul?

CAMILLE: No, why? He leads his life . . . I mine.

DEBUSSY: Perhaps you have never accepted his conversion.

CAMILLE: *(twisting the base of the lampstand)* No, not that! The 25th December, at Christmas Mass in Notre Dame! Now tell me, do people convert like that!

DEBUSSY: He's sincere, though, his works are permeated with Christianity. How can he find the time, conciliate his work as a diplomat . . . he says all he needs is to write an hour a day, if I don't practice for hours, I can't compose a note. And he turns out work after work, and they're staged everywhere, there's talk of a Nobel for him . . . they call him "the Catholic poet".

CAMILLE: Lucky him, he'll go to Heaven . . . while we . . . eh? We? *(provocative)*

DEBUSSY: Camille, have you been to the Universal Exhibition?

CAMILLE: To see the iron contraption? M. Eiffel's tower?

DEBUSSY: Rodin has finally exhibited his Balzac!

CAMILLE: *(taking off her smock; as dressed as she is; she prepares to leave)* Let's go, I want to see it. He's been working on it ten years.

DEBUSSY: It's impressive . . . almost three metres tall . . .

CAMILLE: The giant . . . *(to herself)* . . . please don't let it be the giant . . .

DEBUSSY: He wanted to leave it naked . . . then, he yielded to decorum . .

CAMILLE has already run ahead. She cannot be seen , but a blood-chilling howl is heard.

Darkness in the studio.

End of Scene.

BREATHE

By Kerri Kochanski

(The LIGHTS RISE on CHELSEA and MADDIE. They are 13-15 years old. They sit in MADDIE's living room, possibly near a couch. CHELSEA becomes scandalized, as she tells MADDIE her story.)

CHELSEA: She sleeps on the couch.

MADDIE: He told you?

CHELSEA: I was over there. And I saw her.

MADDIE: Late last night? You were –

CHELSEA: -- over there. At midnight. She was downstairs. Not upstairs. Not even between the upstairs and the downstairs. But the "basement." There on a "couch."

MADDIE: She was sleeping in –

CHELSEA: -- the "basement . . . "

(MADDIE begins to wonder.)

MADDIE: And where was "he?"

CHELSEA: In the bedroom, I guess.

MADDIE: You didn't even –

CHELSEA: -- I wasn't going to "look." Why would I "look?"

(MADDIE cannot believe it.)

MADDIE: She was "sacked" "out?"

CHELSEA: On the couch . . . Didn't even move when I touched her . . .

MADDIE: You touched her . . . ?

CHELSEA: Well it didn't look like she was breathing . . . What if she were dead, and I were in there –

MADDIE: -- you weren't s'posed to be –

CHELSEA: -- in there? No . . . But he said it would be okay, you see. 'Cause she was "sacked." "Sacked out . . . "

MADDIE: And she never heard you . . .

CHELSEA: He said his mother never hears -- Whomever he brings over –

MADDIE: -- oh . . . *(Begins to sour.)* So he's done this before then . . . *(Suddenly realizes. Is scandalized.)*
　　　You mean he's done this before!?

CHELSEA: With other "girls" . . . *(Arches her back, beginning to preen.)* Not that I am really a "girl," you see . . . I mean people who do things . . . Females who do things . . . The way that I do things . . . Well I really don't consider them –

MADDIE: *(intrigued)* -- you did stuff with him . . . You did stuff . . . *(Curious.)* What stuff . . . ? What kinds of stuff did you do . . .?

CHELSEA: Just -- Let's just say it was good.

MADDIE: "Good" "stuff." *(Stops. Wonders.)* For who?

CHELSEA: For both.

MADDIE: So he got in on the action, too?

CHELSEA: He'd have to get in on the action . . . You think I would just let him lie there . . . ? I mean, I know I work hard but – Not that hard . . . I mean, I'd like to get something, too –

MADDIE: -- so what did he give you . . . ?

(CHELSEA rolls down her turtleneck. Shows MADDIE her hickeys. MADDIE is not impressed. Actually, she is quite disappointed.)

MADDIE: Is that all . . . ?

CHELSEA: What do you mean "all?" There's two . . .!

(MADDIE frowns. She rolls down her turtleneck. Shows CHELSEA a string of hickeys.)

MADDIE: I get hickeys . . . I get hickeys, too . . . I mean, it's not like a big deal or anything. So "experienced . . . " I would think you'd've gotten more. Come away with something . . .

(CHELSEA is a little annoyed.)

CHELSEA: Do you want me to show you my privates . . . ? *(Begins to unzipper her pants.)* Because really, if you want to see –

MADDIE: -- I don't know . . . Wouldn't that make me "gay" or something . . . ?

(CHELSEA is suddenly uncomfortable.)

CHELSEA: I don't know . . . I mean, I'm not "gay," so how would I know . . . Know what "gay" would be . . . How a "gay" person would feel . . . What would make someone a "gay person . . . "

(MADDIE points to CHELSEA's pants.)

MADDIE: Well, you were the one who offered . . .

(CHELSEA begins to zip her pants up.)

CHELSEA: It doesn't mean that I'm gay . . . It just meant that I was – "Sharing . . ." *(She is suddenly curious.)* Why? Do you want to see it . . . ?

MADDIE: I've never seen anyone's – "you know" before . . .

CHELSEA: Well, then I guess you're not gay then . . .

(MADDIE begins to wonder.)

MADDIE: Do you think maybe I should see it . . . ?

CHELSEA: *(shrugs, secretly wanting to)* I don't know . . . Do you think that you want to see it . . . ?

MADDIE: Well obviously . . . Obviously I'm curious . . . I mean, your whipping it out . . .

CHELSEA: I'm not "whipping" it out . . . I've nothing to whip . . . !

MADDIE: Well you're unzippering . . . *(Begins to wonder.)* Is that what you did with him? Unzippered . . . ?

(CHELSEA thinks back. Becomes bored.)

CHELSEA: No . . . He unzippered me . . .

MADDIE: And then?

CHELSEA: Put his hand in . . .

(MADDIE moves up to CHELSEA.)

MADDIE: Like this . . . ?

(SHE puts her hand down CHELSEA's pants. THEY stand -- frozen, looking into each other's eyes. It is a very intimate moment. CHELSEA begins to feel something new and exciting. SHE is suddenly nervous, afraid. Trying to hide it --)

CHELSEA: I don't know if I like that . . .

(MADDIE takes her hand out. Pretends to be casual.)

MADDIE: Why? It's just a hand.

CHELSEA: But it's -- *(strangely uneasy)* I didn't look at him. . . While we were -- You know . . . We didn't look at each other . . .

MADDIE: Because your eyes were –

CHELSEA: *(becoming upset, distracted)* -- "dark." It was "dark . . . " And worrying about his parents! --

MADDIE: I thought you didn't have to worry about his parents . . . I thought you said –

CHELSEA: -- "sacked." She was "sacked" " out . . . " Still and all, we were sneaking around . . . I didn't want to – *(MADDIE suddenly kisses CHELSEA, then moves away. CHELSEA is confused.)* Why . . . ?

506

MADDIE: Just wanted to see what it felt like . . .

CHELSEA: *(lying)* I don't know if I liked it . . .

MADDIE: *(accusingly)* You liked it with Peter . . .
(CHELSEA doesn't answer.) So you didn't then. You didn't like it with Peter . . .

CHELSEA: Peter didn't really kiss me . . . Peter didn't really –

MADDIE: -- "kiss." You didn't "kiss . . . ?" Then what the hell'd you do . . . !?

(CHELSEA makes a squeezing motion with her hand.)

CHELSEA: "Groped . . . " We "groped . . . " There really wasn't time to –

MADDIE: *(softly)* Kiss . . .

(MADDIE moves toward CHELSEA. Kisses her again. CHELSEA is pleased. However, SHE doesn't want MADDIE to know. SHE pretends to evaluate --)

CHELSEA: It's okay . . .

MADDIE: Okay?

CHELSEA: Nothing spectacular . . .

MADDIE: Alright . . .

(CHELSEA begins to grow frustrated, confused.)

CHELSEA: It's just -- I've never done this before –

MADDIE: -- I haven't either . . .

CHELSEA: Why are you getting mad at me, Maddie? There's no need to get mad –

MADDIE: *(a little angry, embarrassed)* -- I'm not a "lesbian . . . " I was just trying . . .

CHELSEA: I'm not rejecting you . . .

MADDIE: A little enthusiasm then. For the effort . . .

CHELSEA: Okay . . . Okay, you get "kudos . . ." It was good, alright . . . ? I mean, if you were a boy -- Well, I guess it wouldn't have been so bad. If you were a boy – I mean, maybe, yeah. I could dig you . . . But you're –

MADDIE: I'm not a lesbian . . . (G*rowing soft, unguarded.)* The physicality. The kiss. The actual sensation of lip on lip. Cushion to cushion. Warmth on warmth . . . It has no boundaries . . . Just pure, unadulterated, lip . . . *(CHELSEA doesn't know what to say. MADDIE considers. Seeing CHELSEA is confused, she backs down. Pause. She decides to change the topic.)* So you didn't do –

CHELSEA: -- anything . . .

MADDIE: You just didn't do –

CHELSEA: -- anything . . . *(Grows distracted, thinking of MADDIE.)* He stood there . . . He unzippered my pants . . . He moved his hand in . . . *(Tries thinking of Peter.)* He kissed my neck . . . *(Notes significantly.)* But he didn't kiss me . . . No lip . . . *(Begins to remember.)* There was penis . . . There definitely was penis . . .

MADDIE: You like --

(CHELSEA is disturbed, confused.)

CHELSEA: I thought I -- Now . . . I don't know . . .
(Pause. Then suddenly – desperate, passionate, longing, afraid -- thinking of MADDIE –) She didn't HEAR us . . . !
She was sacked on the COUCH . . . ! If she HEARD! --

(MADDIE takes CHELSEA's hand. Matches her palm to hers. SHE moves their hands up into the air, sensually.)

MADDIE: Sometimes people are asleep . . . It takes a racket to wake them . . . A real racket . . . *(They stare at each other – energized and alive.)* There's no one on the couch . . .
(CHELSEA is overcome. She begins to lose her breath.)
Don't be afraid, Chelsea . . .

CHELSEA: I'm not afraid. I'm just --

(MADDIE places a hand on CHELSEA's chest.)

MADDIE: Breathe . . .

CHELSEA: I am . . . I am breathing . . .

MADDIE: You're alive then . . .

(BLACKOUT.)

End of Scene.

A BETTER PLACE

By Judy Chicurel

SCENE VI

INT. KITCHEN OF JASMINE'S APARTMENT - DAY
GRANDMA CEIL, 54, is serving cereal to Starr when
Jasmine comes in from the bedroom, dressed to go out.

STARR: They was a monster in the window and Mama made it go away.

CEIL: *(to Jasmine)* What she talking about, monsters? She having them bad dreams again?

STARR: Wasn't no dream! It almost come in the room with us.

JASMINE: You was dreaming, baby. They no such thing as monsters.

CEIL: There sure enough are monsters, living here on the streets right alongside the rest of us. Shooting down a pregnant girl like that in broad daylight--used to be you was afraid to walk around after dark. Now you got to be afraid to walk around 24 hours a day because these nappy-headed, nasty little niggers think they in the army or somewheres! And then they got the nerve to tell us crime is down--

JASMINE: Baby, whyn't you go inside and put on that new playsuit your daddy bought for you? Then Grandma gonna do your hair so you can go over to the church with her.

Starr gets down and runs into the bedroom.

JASMINE: *(to Ceil)* Why you got to talk like that in front of her?

CEIL: Child got eyes, don't she? She can see what go on around here. That's why she havin' them bad dreams. And why am I taking her to church with me? Where you running off to?

JASMINE: I got some business to take care of.

CEIL: That mean you going to see the big businessman ain't got time for his own family? The King of Bling?

JASMINE: Lay off that, Grandma.

CEIL: You right, he can't be the king; a mere prince be more like it. And girl, don't you be telling me to lay anywhere. We talking about the father of your child, and you none too happy about it either. I heard you fighting the other night--

JASMINE: How I'm supposed to have any privacy, you listening all the time when I'm talking to somebody?

CEIL: These walls ain't made of stone. You want privacy, maybe y'all better learn sign language. And I don't need ears to know that he never around when you need him. Or where he is when he ain't with you. Business--you think this was Wall Street, you didn't know no better.

JASMINE: Who you expect me to meet, living down here? You think it easy for me? I got to worry about Starr, I got my own mother buggin' out her brains, showing up at my window begging for money--

Jasmine stops abruptly; she hadn't meant to let this out.

Ceil slams her tea cup in the saucer.

CEIL: Why you didn't tell me? I told her never to show her face here after that last time--I can't afford to keep changing them locks--

JASMINE: Oh Grandma, you think she know what you saying? She don't remember nothing. I seen her on the street one day and she didn't even know *me*.

A few seconds of silence; Jasmine's mother is a source of deep sadness for them both.

CEIL: Well, when men lose they minds, it's up to the women to find a way back.

JASMINE: Women can't do nothing. Can't nobody do nothing about the way things is around here. The cops can't stop it, the city can't stop it, how I'm gonna stop it? Get a gun and challenge Corey to a show down?

CEIL: They's ways to put someone under the gun, girl. You got to find something they want and take it away from them until you get what you want, you see what I'm saying here?

JASMINE: No.

CEIL: I got to spell it out for you? You young'uns try keeping your legs closed for a spell, see how they like that.

JASMINE: Grandma, you trippin'! That the stupidest thing I ever heard!

CEIL: How you know you never try? Always work for me.

JASMINE: It work for you 'cause them old dudes you hang out with be desperate, but I tell Corey something like that, I probably never see him again.

CEIL: You watch who you callin' old, girl! And if that the case, good riddance to bad rubbish. You ain't the only unhappy heifer in the crowd--what about them other little girls you run with?

JASMINE: Don't do no good to talk about it, 'cause there ain't nothing we can do. Corey and the fellas, they think they in a movie or something; they say they don't have no chance in life.

CEIL: Chance! What chance they got acting like fools, shooting up the streets? It's like life don't have no meaning for them no more--they own or nobody else's. And you makin' him your only chance, where does that leave you?

JASMINE: Corey say we got to look at the big picture--

CEIL: Big picture, my sweet ass. This ain't no art gallery! People use any excuse to hide from the truth, and the truth is--

JASMINE: He only doing this 'til he got enough money so we can get away from here! Get someplace where you can walk down the street any time without having to be afraid.

CEIL: Yeah, I believe that when I see it. Don't look to me like he going nowheres, except prison or the graveyard--

JASMINE: So what I'm supposed to do? Tell Corey no more kicking it and everything be nice and peachy?

CEIL: You jumping ahead of yourself, girl. One thing at a time. There be strength in numbers, and with that little Spanish girl gone, your friends be ready to listen. They all got children. Ain't nobody want they own child layin' in the street in a puddle of blood. There's an old Italian saying that one woman, with just one of her hairs, could pull battleships across the ocean and rule the world.

Ceil turns and looks Jasmine dead in the eye.

CEIL: And that hair don't come off a woman's head, girl.

SCENE VII

EXT. CITADEL PARK - LATER

Jasmine is watching Corey and the fellas through the wrought iron fence of the neighborhood's notorious drug park. Corey looks up from a transaction with a wired white crack fiend and sees Jasmine at the fence. He completes his business and starts walking toward her. Their conversation takes place with Corey and Jasmine on opposite sides of the fence.

COREY: What you doing down here when I tole you this ain't no place to be at?

JASMINE: Hey, baby. Good to see you, too. Glad to know you missed me.

COREY: I didn't mean it like that. But I ain't got much time, you know what I'm saying?

JASMINE: Seem like you don't have time for nobody no more unless it be them bugged out dope fiends, or big boss Tyrone.

COREY: What that supposed to mean?

JASMINE: It means what it means! You was supposed to spend some time with Starr on Sunday; all day she ask me, `When Daddy coming? Where he at?' What I'm supposed to tell her? `He busy doing business?' She don't even know what you look like no more.

COREY: That ain't true!

He looks over his shoulder toward the fellas.

COREY: This what you came down here for?

JASMINE: I need to talk to you about something.

COREY: Can't it wait 'til later? I got to--

JASMINE: No it can't wait 'til later! You always saying later, and later never comes!

COREY: Damn, girl, I'm warning you, you keep dissin' me like you been doin'--

JASMINE: And what? What you gonna do? Hit me? Shoot me?

Corey is silent.

JASMINE: That the way it gonna be, now? It gettin' so I don't even know you no more, Corey! You gettin' farther away from me all the time!

Corey is quiet for several seconds.

COREY: You got something to say, say it.

JASMINE: It time, Corey. You said when I finished school we gonna bounce and never look back. I been waiting all summer--

COREY: Summer ain't over yet.

JASMINE: I want to leave now, Corey. If we don't, something bad gonna happen--

COREY: What that mean, something bad gonna happen? What brought this on?

JASMINE: I feel like everything closing in on me. I have nightmares about Starr getting shot up like little Malcolm and Tia Maria, and Starr--I don't know what scare me more, when she wake up screaming from the sound of gun shots in the street or she sleep right through it like she gettin' used to it. I don't want my child getting used to that sound, ever.

COREY: I feel you on that. But she won't have to, baby. I tole you, as soon as the time is right--

JASMINE: The time is right now, Corey. Last night my mama came to the fire escape again bugged out of her brains. She scare Starr to death; and with Lily getting shot up like that--

COREY: Girl, you mad confused! You talking about too many things at once! What Lily got to do with anything? She in the wrong place at the wrong time, that's all that was--

Jasmine fixes him with an icy stare.

COREY: Yo, why you looking at me like that?

JASMINE: 'She in the wrong place at the wrong time.' That what you gonna say when it happen to me?

COREY: Why you acting this way for? Everything I'm doin' I'm doin' for us, and you act like you don't know nothing about it.

JASMINE: I know enough. I know you so busy running errands for that evil Tyrone Savage you ain't got time to spend with your own daughter. I know I could get smoked like Lily 'cause I be in the wrong place at the wrong time, when the real problem is I be running with the wrong people!

She starts walking away, along the fence, and Corey follows her, on his side of the fence.

COREY: And just what that supposed to mean?

JASMINE: You so afraid of Tyrone, you do anything he want! What you gonna do if one day he tell you to smoke me?

COREY: He ain't never gonna do that! And I ain't afraid of Tyrone or nobody else!

JASMINE: Then why you got to stay here? Tyrone got all these other fools trained like dogs to they master, what he care if you here or not?

COREY: Tyrone don't have nothing to do with it!

JASMINE: Then why I can't tell nobody? `Don't tell nobody we going, baby, we got to keep it quiet 'til we way outta here,' that's what you tole me!

COREY: `Cause I don't want nobody knowing our business, that's why!

Jasmine stops walking and faces him.

JASMINE: Then what we still doing here? Why can't we leave like you said we was going to?

COREY: Because this our only chance to get somewheres, and I'm taking it. Time you started appreciatin' the fact that I do what I do so we can get some place better, and if you can't wait 'til the time is right--

JASMINE: We outta time, Corey. It now or never!

COREY: What you talking about, now or never?

JASMINE: I'm pregnant.

COREY: You WHAT?

JASMINE: You heard me the first time. And this one ain't gonna be born in no projects.

COREY: Why you didn't say nothing straight off?

JASMINE: `Cause I had other things on my mind.

COREY: You trippin', girl? What on your mind more important than this?

JASMINE: You ain't heard one word I said, did you? Not one word!

COREY: Damn, Jasmine! How you expect me to hear you when you talking in circles like you been doing?

JASMINE: I'm gonna ask you one more time, and I want an answer, Corey. We leavin' or ain't we?

COREY: I tole you we going, you just got to wait a little while longer.

JASMINE: I'm done waiting, Corey. It don't look like you going nowheres as long as Tyrone Savage around. But I got dreams for this life, and I'm gonna get them with or without you.

COREY: You ain't going nowhere with my child in your belly, girl! Especially if it's a boy--

JASMINE: Is that all I am to you now? Yo' baby mama? I thought you loved me, Corey. That's what you tole me all those times, and I believed you…and now you playing me for a chump!

COREY: I'm playing you? Look to me like it the other way around!

JASMINE: Whatever. I tole you I ain't having no more children in the projects. Especially with no stone-cold dope dealing killer for a father, raising them up with his blood money!

COREY: You wasn't talking that way when I bought Starr her clothes, or them diamond earrings I got you at Christmas! You never said nothing about no blood money then!

Jasmine yanks off her earrings, gold chains, and bracelets, and hurls them over the fence. They land at Corey's feet.

JASMINE: Here! Take them back! I don't want them no more! I don't want nothing offa you, ever! I'm leaving here, and I'm taking Starr with me, and I don't ever wanna see you again!

Corey slams the fence viciously.

Jasmine stalks off.

COREY: Girl, don't you walk away from me! You ain't going nowhere! We got business to settle! Jasmine! JASMINE!

Jasmine keeps walking. He slams his side of the fence again, then kicks the jewelry at his feet.

COREY: Damn!

ACT 2, SCENE II

CITADEL PARK - EVENING

Jasmine lays Starr down on the blanket and sits, gazing at her. Starr stirs sleepily.

STARR: Sing me a bed-time song, mama.

JASMINE: If you shut your eyes tight--

Jasmine starts humming a lullaby.

Felicia comes over and sits down on the grass.

She and Jasmine talk in whispers.

FELICIA: Everywhere I go I be trippin' over somebody's child. I feel like some kind of freak.

Opal comes over and sits down with them.

OPAL: Wassup, y'all?

JASMINE: Felicia sayin' she feel like a freak 'cause she ain't got no kids here.

OPAL: You ain't no freak, girl. Maybe you just smarter than the rest of us.

JASMINE: For real. Much as I love Starr--

FELICIA: You saying you sorry you had her?

JASMINE: Sorry the wrong word. It like--when things is bad, you want something gonna make you feel good. And at first, it like getting your favorite doll--but she ain't no doll. She a real, live person, same as you. And then you find out it's up to you to make things better for her--and when you don't know how--

OPAL: It worse with a boy. Growing up around here, you don't know how they gonna turn out. Kareem already wild; one minute he hate his daddy, the next he want to be exactly like him. When I think about what happen today, if y'all wasn't there--

JASMINE: Andre just tryin' to scare you, girl. Same as Corey was with me.

OPAL: Corey didn't pull no gun out. It different with Andre--it like he think Tyrone be God or somebody. He getting more like him every day. If I ditch him, it less money I have for Kareem. But when I think of him growing up like Dre, sometimes I rather see him--

She breaks off, not wanting to finish. They are silent for several seconds.

FELICIA: Y'all scared 'cause you have kids, and I'm scared to have 'em.

OPAL: Girl, that the first time I ever heard you say you was scared of anything! What you scared of?

FELICIA: Suppose something happen to 'em? I don't think I could stand it. I seen what it did to my aunt when my cousin got smoked--it like she don't wanna live no more. And you know Linda ain't been the same since Little Malcolm got killed. Kids supposed to give you something to live for. And if something happen to 'em, it's like it take away your reason for living.

OPAL: Don't talk that way, Felicia. Plenty of kids be alive and kicking in the projects; look at us. We survived.

JASMINE: That's just it. Sometimes--you get tired of just surviving.

FELICIA: Uh-huh. Not that I got to worry about having no babies--ain't nobody want to kick it with a fatso like me.

JASMINE: What you talkin' about, girl? They just more of you to love!

Jasmine puts her arm around Felicia. The girls laugh.

Dinisha comes over, carrying her two-year-old daughter, NASHOA.

DINISHA: What a time I'm having gettin' her to sleep. She ain't used to all this quiet.

FELICIA: Me neither.

OPAL: Make me nervous. You know it won't last.

DINISHA: Miss Doom 'n Gloom strikes again! Girl, you the most negative person on earth!

OPAL: You know the fellas be comin' back--

DINISHA: Oh hush up, girl. They gone now, ain't they? (*To Jasmine*) I got to hand it to you, girlfriend. I never in a million years thought we could pull this off. Thought you was mad crazy--

Nashoa starts crying.

DINISHA: Shit! I thought she finally asleep.

She begins rocking Nashoa. Jasmine resumes humming the lullaby, and the others join in.

End of Scene.

CRIME AND CHILDREN

By Kari Ann Owen

TIME: the present

PLACE: the locker of room of a high school in suburban New Jersey

CHARACTERS: Steve, a fifteen year old athlete
            Rose, a fifteen year old student
STEVE IS REMOVING HIS FOOTBALL CLEATS IN THE LOCKER ROOM. HE IS ALONE. HIS FACE IS BRUISED.

ENTER ROSE.

ROSE: May I come in? (TO STEVE'S SILENCE) May I sit down?

STEVE: This is a boy's locker room.

ROSE: Yeah, a real in-crowd place.

STEVE: Boys... boys only.

ROSE: Like your table in the lunchroom? You don't ask me to sit down there, either--

STEVE: Hey... I mean... it's nice to see you and all, but -- I gotta shower and--

ROSE: So go ahead and shower. I can still hear you.

STEVE: Hear... hear me?

ROSE: Would you stop looking at me like I'm Osama Bin Laden? Steve?

STEVE: Listen... Sue? No, Rhoda?

ROSE: Rose. But why would you know my name? All your friends ever call me is Blimp.

STEVE: I... I don't... But... *(HE REACHES FOR HIS SHIRT, AND BEFORE HE CAN GET TO IT, SHE SITS ON IT.)* Hey!

ROSE: I'm sort of on the school paper, and... did you know a reporter got an interview with a president this way?

STEVE: My... mom expects me home. If I'm late, she'll be really worried... Rose... My... my dad's in Afghanistan, and my mom wants... wants me home--

ROSE: Mine's at work a lot. You're really lucky you see your mom--

STEVE: Give that to me--

(SHE SITS ON THE SHIRT.)

Give me that back.

ROSE: Not until you stop it.

STEVE: Stop what? You're holding my shirt hostage.

ROSE: I'm sick of the Godzilla looks from your loudmouth sports gang. I'm sick of the "blimp" remarks when I stand in line to eat, go to class, sing in the Glee Club and face the audience.

STEVE: I'm getting out of here.

(HE GRABS THE SHIRT AND IT TEARS, AND ROSE IS KNOCKED TO THE FLOOR IN THE SCUFFLE.)

ROSE: You clumsy in crowd pig!

STEVE: I'm sorry. But you--

ROSE: Yeah, it's always my fault. If you guys harass me, it's my fault for being fat. If it hurts so much I can't concentrate in class, the teacher calls me lazy, even stoned, and everyone laughs at me. *(TO STEVE'S SILENCE)* My mother complained, and the principal said I "should lose weight or adjust."

STEVE: I'm not those kids, and I am not the principal.

ROSE: Don't you dare pretend you don't see them and hear them.

STEVE: I hear them. But if they're jerks, is it really that important what they say?

ROSE: Yes, when that's all they say. But what do you care? Kids look up to you just for hanging around with them.

STEVE: The team is supposed to sit together--

ROSE: And hate together?

STEVE: I don't hate anybody.

ROSE: Then you're the worst. You sit there while they torture me and know it's wrong and that lets them do it. What else have they done, Steve?

STEVE: *(to himself):* I didn't do it, but we're all dead.

ROSE: *(not hearing him):*

Even to the pretty girls, the cheerleaders, the other honor society kids if they're female or just not muscle freaks?

STEVE: What -- What do you mean? Listen, can't we discuss this elsewhere? Outside of school?

ROSE: Apparently not. I called your house and asked if I could talk to you--

STEVE: When?

ROSE: Last week.

STEVE: I never got the message.

ROSE: Sure.

STEVE: My mom doesn't lie and I never got the message.

ROSE: I left a message! *(YELLING)* I left a message!

STEVE: All right, you left a message. It must have got lost; I'm sorry-

ROSE: I am not on drugs, I work for my grades and I follow the rules. But you guys think it's all right to sit in the back in math class and cheat.

STEVE: I'm not in their math class. I'm in your math class, advanced math.

ROSE: But they tell you about it, right? Or you hear them talk about it?

STEVE: *(pausing)*: Sure.

ROSE: But no one ever gets suspended, much less kicked out.

STEVE: I didn't make the rules--

ROSE: What rules?

STEVE: May I have my shirt back? Rose, you're no angel, either, for doing this.

ROSE: You're going to see how it feels.

STEVE: Please -- please --

ROSE: I just want to talk to you.

STEVE: What are you carrying in that backpack?

ROSE: Want to see? You're scared, aren't you? *(TO HIS SILENCE)* I said, are you scared?

STEVE: Rose, my mom and I watch the news together every night at six and, believe me, I'm always scared. Please... give me my jersey and I'll never, ever tell anyone you were here.

ROSE: When it would get you points with the guys? To laugh at me? It's been done before.

STEVE: But I did not do it.

(ROSE STANDS UP.)

Sit down!

ROSE: I am not Osama Bin Laden!

STEVE: I didn't say you were! All right, I'm scared. Are you satisfied?

(SHE DUMPS THE BACKPACK AND THERE IS NOTHING IN IT BUT SCHOOL SUPPLIES.)

STEVE: Thank you, I see no Uzi. Now what the hell do you want me to do?

ROSE: Stop it. Stop it and stop them.

STEVE: I wish I could, before they do something really crazy and take the whole school with them. But I'm just another kid, Rose!

ROSE: You could talk to someone. Anyone! You're a hot shot jock!

STEVE: That only matters as long I'm producing. And believe me, I'm on trial every day. Have been since I started playing. You ever see athletes haze each other? You don't know a thing! Because it didn't stop for me til I got moved up to varsity.

ROSE: *(pausing)*: What didn't stop?

STEVE: The names. The wet towels dumped on my head. Speeches from Captain Pig in front of the other kids, telling me how I'd never be good enough. You're not the only one, Rose.

(HE STANDS UP.)

 It kept me up nights, and it did not stop til I gained eight inches and fifty pounds and tackled that loudmouth jerk during practice. He and the coach got the point. And I never, never did it to the newer, smaller guys.

ROSE PAUSES, THEN GIVES HIM BACK HIS JERSEY, THEN STARTS WALKING AWAY, THEN TURNS AROUND.

ROSE: I'm glad you know what it's like. A little of what it's like. And only a little, because you have letters and points and cheers. I get nothing for what I do. And I'm so scared that things will always be the same: I could be Einstein, but looking this way means smaller chances of everything: college, marriage. That's what the principal, the school nurse, even the college admissions and guidance counselors tell my mother, and studies say that on the Internet.

STEVE: But.. things change. My dad said Blacks weren't allowed in combat when his dad fought... Now we have Colin Powell--

ROSE: Supposed he'd been fat instead of Black? Steve, I've been dieting since age eight, and calculus is easier.

STEVE: I'm sorry. Rose, I'm sorry. I'll tell off the guys. I will.

ROSE: What will they do to you? Whatever it is, at least someday you'll be able to escape.

(SHE STARTS TO EXIT.) I'm sorry I--

STEVE: It's okay. You really needed to talk to somebody.

ROSE: Seen and heard, not like a blob.

STEVE: Have you really always been fat?

ROSE: Except when I was a baby. I had a disease that made me unable to eat anything except a special formula. My body conserves every calorie it gets, I think. Like a big animal.

STEVE: *(to himself)*: Suppose those guys can't help themselves, either? Oh, my God, what's going to happen to us? Columbine?

ROSE: I don't know about big animals, though. Have you ever seen a fat elephant or hippopotamus? I mean, they're big, not flabby.

STEVE: *(to himself)*: May I should open my big mouth?

ROSE: You... you really think things can get better?

STEVE: Sh... sure. Colleges aren't allowed to demand pictures of the kids who apply. Not anymore.

ROSE: I mean here in school.

STEVE: Not even Columbine changed anything, Rose. You keep studying, I'll keep playing and studying and we'll both get scholarships and get out of here. That's what's going to change. There are scholarships for the kids of active duty military. My dad hopes I can get into one of the service academies, on account of he never got to go.

ROSE: Good... good luck.

STEVE: Yeah. To all of us. *(AS SHE LEAVES)* Rose, next time you come in the lunchroom, sit where you want.

ROSE: Why?

STEVE: My dad's fighting for fat Americans, too. No one's any better than you are.

ROSE: I'll sit on their ugly, messy laps. *(SHE GIGGLES A LITTLE.)* During a food fight.

(EXIT ROSE.)

STEVE: Junior varsity tries out with varsity every year while the coaches sort... and we take everything the coaches say and do everything... (MOCKING THE COACHES'

PRIMARY VOICE) "Let's separate the hard shit from the soft shit. On this football field, you can either be a girl wuss, a half girl wuss or on your way to a man who is part of a team of predators. The Hollow Haven High School Predators. I do not care if I am hurting your feelings. I care if you show me I'm hurting your feelings." And we don't, and some of the guys are getting girls drunk to fuck them.

Cause if you have feelings, you're not a Predator, just a naked zero with nothing between your legs but a dangling tail, and nothing on your back. Dad, a man wears a uniform, like you, right, showing all your medals for your hostage rescues and kills. But your enemies are armed grown-ups! You didn't earn your green beret by torturing other kids. I don't mean at practice, Dad. I mean in the halls and in the lunchroom. And at parties. Dad, some of it's on video; we're all going to jail. I didn't...I didn't do it, but Rose is right: I didn't stop it and I didn't walk out because... I just feel too naked without them, and I have a really good throwing arm, Dad, and I think I can get this scholarship, and how can I bother you with the real truth when you have Osama Bin Laden to worry about and Mom needs me to be strong? She loves you so much. I wish... I wish you would come home and tell me to quit the squad and go to the cops just so I could blame it all on you. Then the guys wouldn't kill me, and I could still play. And why shouldn't I? I earned it. I'm good.

(HOLDING UP AND SCRUTINIZING HIS UNIFORM JERSEY)

So why can't I put this on now?

FADE TO BLACK

End of Scene.

THE SHAPE SHIFTER

By Rebecca Nesvet

Characters:
GILBERT CHESNET   A provincial doctor.
ALICE BARBIN A teenager: looks like a girl. Orphaned,
Alice attends a convent school. Alice has Androgen
Insensitivity Syndrome, a "hermaphrodism" condition. In
2010, the South African athlete Caster Semenya was
disbarred from competing as a woman on the grounds that
as she has AIS, she is a "hermaphrodite."

The Shape Shifter is based on an historical occurrence from
nineteenth-century France. "Abel" Barbin's memoir and
Gilbert Chesnet's medical reports were discovered by
Michel Foucault in the 1970s.

Place/Time:
France, 1970s.

(DR CHESNET has been called in by the Abbess of the
convent to determine whether rumours that ALICE is "a boy
in disguise" are true. Here, he is alone with ALICE in a
classroom with a chalkboard. On the tray is chalk and a
ruler.)

CHESNET: I need to ask you a few questions, Alice. You
must answer truthfully and completely. In return, I promise
that everything we say in this room will stay in this room.

ALICE: What do you mean?

CHESNET: No one will know what you tell me. I won't tell
anyone else and there are no witnesses.

ALICE: God witnesses everything.

CHESNET: With the exception of God, no one outside this room will hear our conversation. Have we an agreement, Alice?

ALICE: All right.

CHESNET: Good. Now, Alice, have you ever thought about what it might be like to be a boy instead of a girl?

ALICE: No.

CHESNET: Have you ever wanted to be a boy instead of a girl?

ALICE: Why would I want that?

CHESNET: There are plenty of reasons. I wanted to change what I was, once. I found it very frustrating to be a second-year student with hands reeking of chloroform when I thought I could be an actor. All the girls were obsessed with the Paris actors. Of course.

ALICE: Did you ever want to be a girl?

CHESNET: No.

ALICE: Never?

CHESNET: Never. Of course.

ALICE: May I go now?

CHESNET: Not just yet.

(On the board, he draws a woman's body. It is somewhat anatomically correct. The face is a blank.)

That, Alice, is what a normal human female looks like. Do you look like that?

ALICE: Like a chalkboard, Monsieur?

CHESNET: Alice, human animals are not as incredibly complex organisms as we've been led to think. They come in a limited range of styles: This and Not-This. You must at least consider the possibility that you are male, that you have been since beyond the reach of your memory. And if the two of us can produce sufficient medical and legal evidence of this, then you can take your rightful place.

ALICE: I have a place.

CHESNET: Alice, there are girls—women—who would give so much for this opportunity.

ALICE: Maybe some women.

CHESNET: Extend your hand. Palm up.

(measures it with a ruler)

Fifteen centimetres from wrist to index fingertip.

ALICE: What does that mean?

CHESNET: Your hands aren't very large.

ALICE: What is the point of this?

CHESNET: I need to take measurements in order to determine your true sex.

ALICE: "And Pilate said unto them, behold: Man!" For him that was obvious, but was it the truth?

CHESNET: Can we dispense for a moment with theology?

ALICE: Why?

CHESNET: Because theology is the application of logic to a

system whose basic tenets are inherently illogical.

ALICE: How long exactly is a man's hand supposed to be?

CHESNET: There's a continuum.

ALICE: What's the minimum before it becomes a woman's hand?

CHESNET: It doesn't work that way.

ALICE: Then how does it work?

CHESNET: In order to make a formal report I'll have to examine rather more of—

ALICE: No.

CHESNET: To make a report.

ALICE: Your words make no sense.

CHESNET: Then I can show you.

ALICE: All right. Show me.

CHESNET: Take off your clothes.

ALICE: What?

CHESNET: Take off your clothes. That dress. I can't show you if you're wearing a dress. If you want to see what you look like—

ALICE: I know what I look like without my clothes.

CHESNET: I mean, to answer your question—

ALICE: You are a man, Doctor Chesnet, isn't that right?

CHESNET: Of course. What a question. Now—

ALICE: Take off your clothes.

CHESNET: What?

ALICE: I know what I look like, and you know what you are. But I've got no example for comparison. You take off your clothes, and if when I look at you I see a body like myself in the mirror, then I'll see I am like you. And if you look different—

CHESNET: I can't do that.

ALICE: Everything that happens in this room is witnessed only by ourselves and God. Are you ashamed of your nakedness?

CHESNET: No.

ALICE: To be afraid or ashamed is a sign one has fallen.

CHESNET: I am a doctor of medicine. A professional. It's not allowed.

ALICE: Then I can't either.

CHESNET: Alice, circumstantial evidence and hearsay cannot be submitted to the Prefecture as medical fact. If I am going to write a report that will be taken seriously and used to your advantage then you have to let me complete the physical examination.

ALICE: Why are we talking about writing a report now? If there is anything to write about I want to see it proven to me first.

(Pause.)

CHESNET: I'll show you what you need to see if you'll show me what I need to see.

ALICE: I want to see first. Then if you're wrong you won't be wasting your time.

CHESNET: I seriously doubt I am wrong.

ALICE: But you don't know yet.

CHESNET: All right, Alice. We will each turn around, 180 degrees, and walk ten paces in the opposite direction, over a count of ten. At ten, we will take off enough of our clothes to answer our respective questions and then immediately we will both turn around. Will those terms satisfy you?

ALICE: This sounds like a silly game. Do you play it with a lot of patients?

CHESNET: You've got to understand this case is not typical of what I usually see.

ALICE: All right.

CHESNET: Good. Let's begin, then. One, two, three—

ALICE: I want to say the numbers.

CHESNET: If you insist.

ALICE: One, two—

CHESNET: You know, Alice—you're right. This is a stupid game. And it's unprofessional. I can't allow—

ALICE: We agreed on the rules.

CHESNET: We did. Continue.

ALICE: I'll start again. One. Two. Three. Four. Five. Six. Seven. Eight. Nine. Ten.

End of Scene.

THE PROM DRESS

By Lea Galanter

Characters
Annie: High school senior
Marvin: Annie's grandfather

Scene
Marvin's dress shop

Props
Store counter
Dresses on rack

Annie and Marvin at Marvin's dress shop.

ANNIE: Please. If you only knew how important this was. Please!

MARVIN: I'm sorry, kiddo. It's too late. Try Romano's.

ANNIE: I did. They don't have it.

MARVIN: Well, then, neither do I.

ANNIE: But if I don't have this dress, I won't be able to go to the prom.

MARVIN: So, wear another dress.

ANNIE: I don't have another dress! I saved up two years for a dress. And I have to have this one. Please!

MARVIN: But someone came in and put it on hold. They put down half for it.

ANNIE: But I have the entire amount. Right here. See?

MARVIN: I can't just sell it out from under someone else. It's just not right.

ANNIE: But it's for me, grandpa!

MARVIN: I know. But that still doesn't make it right. I gotta think of my business reputation.

ANNIE: But I just have to wear this dress to the prom. I just have to! It's the biggest night of my life. I've been waiting forever.

MARVIN: Listen, you're young. There'll be lots of other dances.

ANNIE: Not like this one! The rest of my life depends on this prom.

MARVIN: One night! You young people.

ANNIE: I just know if I wear this dress, Justin will want me. I saw it in a dream. It was so real. He's the love of my life.

MARVIN: Does he know this?

ANNIE: Not yet. But he will.

MARVIN: You saw the dress in a dream?

ANNIE: Yes.

MARVIN: This dress?

ANNIE: Yes. This dress. There's no other dress like it.

MARVIN: Listen, if you were meant to have this dress, the lord would have given it to you. And maybe you weren't meant to have Justin either. Did you ever think of that?

ANNIE: No. It can't be true!

MARVIN: It certainly can be. A lot of things you don't want to hear can be, and are, true.

ANNIE: But I just know that we're meant to be together.

MARVIN: You do, eh?

ANNIE: Yes! He's just so...so...

MARVIN: Justin?

ANNIE: Yes!

MARVIN: And I suppose he's handsome, this Justin?

ANNIE: Oh, yes!

MARVIN: And charming?

ANNIE: Yes, how did you know?

MARVIN: And the most popular boy in school?

ANNIE: Well, nearly. He's not on the football team or anything, but he's really smart, and funny, and he's got the greatest blue eyes.

MARVIN: Listen, let me give you a piece of advice. Stay away from guys like that.

ANNIE: Why?

MARVIN: They tend to peak too early. I know. They stay in town, marry their high-school sweetheart, get any old job, and then spend their lives pretending it's the good old days. They never go nowhere, never do nothin'. You deserve better than that.

ANNIE: What's wrong with that? Even Dorothy said you shouldn't go looking for your heart's desire past your own backyard.

MARVIN: But what about in 10 years when you have three kids, and you're tired 28 hours a day, and Justin ain't lookin' at you the same way he did on prom night.

ANNIE: But I want to have Justin's children. I've even picked out the names.

MARVIN: You really got it bad, kid. If I were your mother, I wouldn't let you out of the house.

ANNIE: Well, you're not my mother.

MARVIN: Does she know about this Justin? That you're even here?

ANNIE: No. Not exactly.

MARVIN: Oh boy.

ANNIE: She doesn't care what I do.

MARVIN: I'm not surprised. Anyway, you should care. You got the rest of your life ahead of you. Why do you wanna go and tie yourself down now for? What a waste, pretty girl like you. You should go to college...date every boy who asks you. Find the best one. The one who will treat you right.

ANNIE: But I'm so tired of studying. It's all too much work.

MARVIN: The best things in life are worth working for.

ANNIE: That's why I've worked so hard to get the money for this dress, don't you understand?

MARVIN: That's not what I meant.

ANNIE: Besides, I don't have the money for college.

MARVIN: You're a smart girl...and I know you're determined...you could get that scholarship. Easy.

ANNIE: What's the use? So I can be an "independent woman"? Which really means "lonely".

MARVIN: That scholarship could be your ticket out of here.

ANNIE: I don't want a ticket anywhere.

MARVIN: Don't you want to be something when you grow up? Go places?

ANNIE: I never really gave it much thought.

MARVIN: Yea, too much time thinking about this Justin.

ANNIE: He's all I've ever wanted.

MARVIN: You gotta have a plan B. And C. Maybe this Justin already has his eye on someone. Someone who ain't you.

ANNIE: I just know the universe is waiting for him to realize that I'm his soul mate.

MARVIN: You watch too much TV.

ANNIE: But what if the universe really does want Justin and I to be together? And I ignore the signs?

MARVIN: Oh, Tommy rot! Signs are for highways and toilets. *(Pause.)* Have you thought about what you'll do if this thing with Justin doesn't pan out?

ANNIE: I can't allow myself to think about things like that. I'm willing the universe to make it happen!

MARVIN: I see. Well, when you get a chance, can you will the universe to give me a winning lottery ticket?

ANNIE: Oh, silly. You know what I mean. If you really, really want something, and you focus all your energy on that, then it has to come true.

MARVIN: Is that so?

ANNIE: Oh, yes. I read about it in a book. It's called visualization.

MARVIN: Sounds like prayer to me.

ANNIE: I guess it's sort of like prayer. But different.

MARVIN: Not all prayers come true.

ANNIE: Don't say that!

MARVIN: Sorry to disappoint you. Just thought you oughta know. *(Pause.)* You know Mick Jagger?

ANNIE: You mean that old singer? From, like, the Rolling Stones or something?

MARVIN: Yea, that guy...he said it pretty well back in the day. "You can't always get what you want."

ANNIE: I bet he didn't know about visualization.

MARVIN: *(Sigh)* I give up. You can't talk sense to a crazy person.

ANNIE: I'm not crazy.

MARVIN: It's love. Same difference.

ANNIE: Grandma used to say, don't underestimate the power of love.

MARVIN: No offense against grandma, may she rest in peace, but all the love in the world can't make something out of nothing.

ANNIE: You know what you are? You're just a mean, spiteful, stingy old man. You don't know anything about being in love.

MARVIN: Now you just hold your horses, young lady. You can't go talking to your grandfather like that. And it sure as hell ain't gonna get you any closer to wearin' that dress.

ANNIE: I'm sorry. It's just that if you knew what it was like...

MARVIN: I know what it's like. At least, I used to know.

ANNIE: Then sell me the dress!

MARVIN: I told you, I can't do that.

Annie starts to cry hysterically.

MARVIN: God damn it! You are not going to turn out like your mother!

ANNIE: I won't! I promise!

MARVIN: You don't know that. You don't know anything!

ANNIE: If I don't get this--

MARVIN: Christ all mighty! Okay, okay, here's what I'll do. IF I sell you the dress--

ANNIE: Oh my god, oh my god!!!

MARVIN: I said IF...oh, jeez, I'm gonna get into so much trouble for this...IF I sell you the dress, you gotta promise me something.

ANNIE: Anything!

MARVIN: You gotta apply for that scholarship.

ANNIE: What? The whole idea is for me to be with Justin! I don't want to go to college.

MARVIN: Just promise. Now. It's your backup plan.

ANNIE: Okay, okay, I promise.

MARVIN: Cross your heart.

ANNIE: I cross my heart.

MARVIN: Swear on the Virgin Mary.

ANNIE: All right! I swear on the Virgin Mary!

MARVIN: Good.

ANNIE: You have made me SO happy!

As Annie jumps around with glee. Marvin shrugs.

MARVIN: Love. Sometimes you just can't fight city hall.

End of Scene.

GEOGRAPHY

By Shirley King

CHARACTERS
HANNAH -- seventeen, separated from her mother by
Hurricane Katrina.
ALBERT -- nineteen, living in Lakeland, Mississippi when
Hurricane Katrina struck.
ANITA -- thirties, forties. Television reporter.
VOICE -- a commentator.

Diversity in casting is appreciated.

GEOGRAPHY -- When Hurricane Katrina separates
Hannah and Lisa, Hannah seeks urgently needed help in
finding her mother.

ACT ONE   SCENE SIX

HANNAH and ALBERT are waiting in line at a service
station.

HANNAH: How long do we have to wait?

ALBERT: Till I fill this gas can. There's people ahead of
us.

HANNAH: Duh.

ALBERT: I said you could ride to Galveston with me, but
you gotta stop bein' so negative.

HANNAH: Okay, we take off for Lakeland and then my
auntie has a stroke and dies. She leaves us her house and
then like, poof Hurricane Katrina strikes. The house is gone
and so is my mom --

ALBERT: That's my fault?

HANNAH: -- and now I'm with a guy who passes out all the time-ALBERT: I never pass out when I drive.

HANNAH: And if we ever get to Galveston I still have to hitch a ride to Houston, so yeah, I should be really up about all this. Look, mostly my mom's the positive one and I'm not. That way we balance each other out.

ALBERT: Hey, our house is gone too. You don't hear me fussin'.

HANNAH: But you know your parents are okay.

ALBERT: My dad's got lung problems and can't work. Mom cleans for people. The house was all they had.

HANNAH: Okay. I guess things aren't so good for you either.

ALBERT: Duh.

HANNAH: Why isn't this line moving?

ALBERT: I dunno.

HANNAH: I'm gonna run up there and ask. Give me that can. *(HANNAH tries to grab the gas can, but ALBERT won't let her.)*

ALBERT: That's not how we do things here. This isn't California, you know, where people get what they want all the time.

HANNAH: Obviously you've never been to California.

ALBERT: Never been and no desire to go.

HANNAH: Right. Because this is such a great place to live. Some people might say, you know, since my house keeps getting totaled maybe I might think about living somewhere else, somewhere nice. Okay, I didn't mean that. How come this line's not moving? The fumes are making me sick. Doesn't it ever cool off here?

ALBERT: We're all leavin', that's why this line's so long. We gotta leave. No food, no place to stay, but I'm comin' back quick as I can. I was born in Lakeland.

HANNAH: Well, I was born in Turlock, but that doesn't mean I had to stay there, like, forever.

ALBERT: Could you just be quiet for a while?

HANNAH: So how come you do wrestling? What's with that?

ALBERT: You ever slam anyone to the mat?

HANNAH: No way. I'm a non-violent.

ALBERT: Okay, so that's what I get to do and nobody puts me in jail. I might be able to make a livin' at it.

HANNAH: But that stuff's all fake.

ALBERT: Entertainment. Like the movies. Pro wrestlers, they're just puttin' on a good show.

HANNAH: You fake killing each other and everyone knows it's fake but they pay to see it anyway. Got it. You know, that's really weird. So what do you do for fun? Hunt possum?

ALBERT: I don't hunt any more. You want to go to Galveston or not?

HANNAH: Not really. Maybe we could go to Houston instead.

ALBERT: Maybe you could be quiet. You don't even know what Galveston's like.

HANNAH: Galveston: located in Galveston County on the East Texas coast. Named after Bernardo de Gálvez. Worst natural disaster in U.S. history was caused by a hurricane that hit Galveston in 1900. Are you sure you want to go there? Houston's much safer.

ALBERT: So you know Geography. I know stuff too. Mud devils? They look like giant salamanders. In Missouri they call 'em hellbenders. Gets hot there too. Hotter'n hell in the summer.

HANNAH: What?

ALBERT: Mud devils. You asked, remember? I know stuff too.

(ANITA enters.)

ANITA: Holly, where are you going?

HANNAH: It's Hannah. To Galveston, if we ever get this gas can filled up.

ANITA: I'm afraid they just ran out of gas here. Ah, but here's a solution. You ride with us to Houston while our viewers track your desperate search.

HANNAH: What about the wrestler?

ALBERT: Albert.

HANNAH: Can he come too?

ANITA: Can he? Hmmm. Let me think. All right, I'm seeing a story unfolding here: Hurricane Katrina unites two lost youngsters: the wrestler and the orphan. All they have is each other and the will to survive, one day at a time. Yes! I think people need to know about this.

HANNAH: I am not an orphan!

ALBERT: And I'm not lost. (To HANNAH) You go on and ride with her. She's goin' where you need to be.

HANNAH: And you won't have to put up with me all the way to Galveston.

ALBERT: Right. Well, good luck. Hope you find your mom.

HANNAH: Were you punkin' me about the mud devils?

ALBERT: Maybe.

ANITA: Albert, no buildings in Lakeland are intact. My sources report at least fifty people dead, and that's not the final body count. The National Weather service predicted this, but nobody listened. Your comments?

ALBERT: I don't care about your sources. We're gonna rebuild and they can't stop us.

ANITA: That's the spirit! Hannah, let me run to the van for a quick minute and call my producer. I'll be right back.

(ANITA exits.)

HANNAH: Omigod. Fifty people in this town died? Look, maybe I act negative, but I'm actually trying to be hopeful.

ALBERT: Don't seem like it.

HANNAH: This morning I think I saw God, or maybe not --
maybe I just have a fever. But what she said was I needed to --

ALBERT: God's not a woman. Don't you read the Bible?

HANNAH: Why can't God be a woman?

ALBERT: One thing I know, God has a plan for us. That's
why he spared some folks. I volunteered for Search and
Rescue but they said I wasn't trained. I'm thinkin' they don't
want me findin' bodies of people I know.

HANNAH: I keep wondering, did God actually have a plan
for all those people who didn't make it?

ALBERT: He called 'em home to Heaven.

HANNAH: All of them? Even the sinners?

ALBERT: Don't you ever stop?

HANNAH: I'm like really stressed -- you know? Okay,
here's the deal: you don't get in my face, I don't get in
yours. We could try that.

ALBERT: How about you stop tryin' to be so cute? If you
know Geography, you gotta know Galveston's not too far
from Houston.

(ANITA enters.)

ANITA: Okay, good news, bad news. Good? A truck just
delivered more gas. Bad? We're not going to Houston. The
story's in New Orleans. I need to get back there, so good
luck, Hannah. Good luck, Alvin. You two take care of each
other.

(ANITA exits.)

HANNAH: Hey, this line's actually moving.

ALBERT: I keep wonderin', when's the president gonna get here? We'all voted for him.

HANNAH: We'all didn't. Not that I could.

ALBERT: Well, y'all shoulda. He took action when the terrorists struck, got the troops mobilized to go over there and hunt down WMDs, put a dictator in prison. He's a righteous man.

HANNAH: I'm not going there, Albert, but one thing I know for sure, this country's in like, major trouble and the hurricane didn't help. I don't get this. How come our government's not doing anything?

ALBERT: The government's gonna help us. Okay? We're gonna rebuild and so is New Orleans and we'll go on just like we always do.

VOICE: Today House Speaker Dennis Hastert said this of federal assistance for hurricane-devastated New Orleans: "It makes no sense to spend billions of dollars to rebuild a city that's seven feet under sea level,"

End of Scene.

WHERE THE SIDEWALK ENDS

By Meg Haley

Sorbelia……………….mid 20s. "Femme". Civilian.
Winnie…………….…..late 20s. " Butch". Soldier.
Place: The relationship of Sorbelia and Winnie
Time: Now. And earlier.

A camouflage jacket is folded and is laying far down center stage. SORBELIA enters, sees it, and collapses onto it. She stands, her back to the audience, and Picks it up, revealing a rainbow flag folded into a triangle.. A moment passes. She breathes deeply. She holds the jacket out, dances with it as her partner. She attempts a spin, but can't get it right.
Beat.
She puts on the jacket. It does not fit. After a moment she shrugs off the jacket, and leaves it on the floor. She turns to face downstage and looks around the still empty space.
There is a lighting shift wherein SORBELIA takes a backwards step upstage and WINNIE enters but keeps her distance. They are talking over the phone.

WINNIE: Have you been going out with the girls?

SORBELIA: Yeah, they make me.

WINNIE: They shouldn't have to make you.

SORBELIA: I know. And I still can't spin.

WINNIE: You should practice. I'm going to want to go two-stepping when I get back.

SORBELIA: I am practicing! Step by step, it'll be perfected by the time I see you. I promise.

There is a lighting shift wherein the two take a backwards step upstage, towards one another. They are still talking over the phone.

WINNIE: You still have my mom's number, right?

SORBELIA: Yeah.

WINNIE: Ok. And I emailed you the numbers to call if you need to get a hold of me. Use my last name. Just tell them you're Sorbelia. They'll know who you are.

SORBELIA: What if you need to get a hold of me?

WINNIE: Oh, don't worry about me. I'm a sergeant in the United States Army. If I'm not resourceful enough to contact you when I want to, I should just get out right now.

There is a lighting shift wherein the two take a backwards step upstage, and are now standing together.

SORBELIA: Maybe if he wins the election they won't have to send you.

WINNIE: It's not that simple.

SORBELIA: Why not? If he's the president, he could make it happen. Just put a total halt to the surge in Afghanistan and bam! The deployment list goes away.

WINNIE: Honey.

SORBELIA: Sorry. A girl can dream, though, right?

Beat.

What?

WINNIE: It hurts to hear you talk like that. Have you still not made your peace with this?

SORBELIA: We'll walk a walk that is measured and slow.

WINNIE: What?

SORBELIA: A line from the Shel Silverstein poem. It goes something like that. It was always soothing to me. But we can never get to where the sidewalk ends.

WINNIE: I don't understand.

SORBELIA: I'm trying to say you're right. I'm sorry. Let's take it one step at a time. I just felt so powerful voting for him; like it might really make a difference in my life. Make it so at least I can stand up next to you in uniform and be present and proud.

WINNIE: I know, I want that too, God do I! You have been doing an amazing job of supporting me. Well, most of the time. I just can't live my life hoping someone's going to change their mind again and let me stay home.

There is a lighting shift wherein the two take a backwards step upstage.

SORBELIA is crying.

SORBELIA: I don't know if I can do this.

WINNIE: A fine fucking time to tell me this!

SORBELIA: I'm sorry! I need your help! I need to figure out how people do this!

WINNIE: I gave you an out. You didn't take it.

SORBELIA: Just tell me how to do this!

WINNIE: I don't know! You have to do that on your own.

Beat.

I'm out of here.

SORBELIA: No, no you can't just leave like this. We have to talk about this. Come back!

WINNIE: I have to go! I told him I would be on post in 20 minutes. I have to leave.

SORBELIA: If you walk out that door right now…. Just wait. Just wait, we have to talk about this. I don't know what else to do! I go out when you want me to, and I don't complain about you not even being able to hug me. I'm learning the acronyms, and the ranks, and I want to know about it. I want to wear the sweatshirt and be able to tell people about you when they ask. You. Not your secret male identity. I know that this is your life, and I want to be the good Army girlfriend, but I have no support here. I don't have anyone to talk to about this. You have a go-to person, who knows what you're going through. I don't. I'm floundering.

WINNIE: I don't know what to tell you.

SORBELIA: You've done this before. I haven't.

WINNIE: No I haven't. I've never been in your position. I've only been the soldier. That's easy. I have a job. I get to leave and just do my job. You have the hardest job in the Army. And you told me you could do it.

SORBELIA: I want to, I just don't know how. I don't know if I'm strong enough.

WINNIE: Don't sell yourself short.

Beat.

Get dressed. We have to finish this in the car.

SORBELIA: What?

WINNIE: We are going to talk to Sgt. Clancy. I don't have the answers. He's my chain of command. It's his job to have the answers.

SORBELIA: What? What are you going to say? 'My roommate doesn't want me to stick her with the rent'?

WINNIE: No. I don't know what I'm going to say but we need help. He'll talk to you.

SORBELIA: No way. This is not worth you getting fucked over. We'll figure it out.

WINNIE: Trust me.

There is a lighting shift wherein the two take a backwards step upstage and WINNIE exits.

SORBELIA is on the phone.

SORBELIA: Hey it's me. I know you're working, but I was just calling to say I love you. And I'm in this. I'm in it for the long haul.

There is a lighting shift wherein SORBELIA takes a backwards step upstage. WINNIE calls from off stage.

WINNIE: Seriously?

SORBELIA: Yup.

WINNIE: Where have you been?

SORBELIA: I needed to go be by myself for a while. Is that ok?

WINNIE turns on her heel.

I didn't ask you to leave.

WINNIE doesn't move.

In fact I asked you not to.

WINNIE turns around again to face SORBELIA.

WINNIE: That's not fair.

SORBELIA: I know.

Beat.

I'm not sorry.

WINNIE: You knew this was a possibility.

SORBELIA: Yes, but you can never really know how you're going to react to a thing like a name on a list that changes your whole future.

WINNIE: It just changes your idea of what the future was going to look like. Adjust your idea. Or don't. But I need you to tell me what you're going to do before I leave.

SORBELIA: Give me a minute, baby, damn.

WINNIE: I'm going back inside. Make your decision.

WINNIE starts walking forward, towards the audience. SORBELIA turns her back to the audience, but it is as if she is getting pulled backwards by WINNIE. They remain equidistant apart, as if a string connects them.

They get stuck on pause for a beat before there is a lighting shift and country music plays. The two take a step upstage.

WINNIE: Let's go.

WINNIE pulls SORBELIA into a dancing position.

SORBELIA: I don't know how!

WINNIE: I know. I'm going to teach you. Just count to two.

SORBELIA: Oh my God. Ok…

The pair two-steps around the stage, talking and laughing for the length of the song. WINNIE tries to spin SORBELIA, to no avail. When the song ends, SORBELIA exits.

There is a lighting shift wherein SORBELIA re-enters. She is wearing only an apron, and is surprised to see WINNIE who has taken another backwards step upstage.

SORBELIA: Hey! Hi! Dinner's ready, I just have to get dressed.

WINNIE: What's wrong with what you're wearing?

SORBELIA: I was just cooking and I didn't want to splatter anything on the dress, so…

WINNIE: Oh damn… are you sure we have to go?

SORBELIA: Baby, yes…

WINNIE: Let's go another time, let's stay here…

SORBELIA: I planned this whole thing! We have to go…

WINNIE: Fine, fine…Go get dressed, I'll put the stuff in the car.

There is a lighting shift wherein SORBELIA puts pants and shirt back on, and the two take a backwards step upstage and sit.

SORBELIA: Ok, if you could vacation anywhere, where would it be?

WINNIE: Ireland.

SORBELIA: Did I ever tell you that I lived there? Well, studied abroad for a semester.

WINNIE: That's awesome. Did you love it?

SORBELIA: Absolutely. I'll have to show you pictures. I would move back in a second if I thought I'd actually be able to support myself.

WINNIE: Right on. But where would you like to visit?

SORBELIA: Italy. Pasta. Mmmm. Your turn.

WINNIE: Right. Ok, um, God I'm bad at games like this. How long have you been out to your family?

SORBELIA: Just a couple of years. You?

WINNIE: Um, eight. Years.

SORBELIA: Wow, you were young.

WINNIE: Yup.

SORBELIA: Ok, so a related question. What are the things your mother warned you about?

WINNIE: Oh God, I was a crazy child. And we lived in a rural area so there were lots of rules like staying away from the road, don't play Evil Knevil on your bike, don't miss church, don't get pregnant.

SORBELIA: Well that's not so much of an issue now, is it?!

WINNIE: Don't kiss on the first date.

SORBELIA: Oh.

WINNIE: Yeah that one never really stuck. But as I've grown up she really only lectures me about being irresponsible and spending too much money.

SORBELIA: That's legit though. I'm so anal about bills, my folks think I'm responsible.

WINNIE: Ok, so where did they have to set your limits?

SORBELIA: What limits?

WINNIE: Oh really?

SORBELIA: Don't cheat, don't lie, and don't sell yourself short. But mostly it was dos. You can do anything. And when she was moving me across the country and I was 16 and angst-y they wanted to move me into a planned community where all the houses looked the same and I freaked out. She told me that a house is just a building; it's the people that matter. She spends much more time reminding me of positive things than adding any more negatives.

WINNIE: Yeah, I could see that.

Beat.

SORBELIA: You're really done with this game, aren't you?

WINNIE: I'm just bad at coming up with questions!

SORBELIA: There's nothing you want to ask me?

WINNIE: I figure I'll learn it all in good time.

There is a lighting shift wherein the two take a final backwards step upstage.

WINNIE: What does your ring say?

SORBELIA: Oh, I'm married to my work.

WINNIE: Yeah? Me too. I'm in the military.

SORBELIA: I always did have a thing for uniforms.

Blackout.

End of Scene.

TREE MAN

By Steven Schutzman

Time: The present.

Setting: A kitchen looking out on a backyard.

Characters
Helen – late 30's – 40's
Charlotte – a bit younger and a good deal taller

Scene 2
(Some wine later.)

CHARLOTTE: Now here's something weird, really weird, I did the other day. Did you ever try to get yourself stuck in traffic?

HELEN: What do you mean?

CHARLOTTE: I mean: Did you ever like try to get yourself stuck in traffic? Last Monday, I was going to pick Larry up from the sitter's and I heard about this bad tie-up on the radio and I drove right into it on purpose so I'd have a legitimate excuse for a few more minutes alone. It's just been terrible lately. Really bad. I'm so worn out dealing with his teacher and the principal. Everybody trying to get rid of me.

HELEN: One more pain-in-the-neck parent blaming the school for her kid's disruptive behavior.

CHARLOTTE: Won't sit still, fidgets, fidgets...

HELEN: Fidgets...

CHARLOTTE: Leaves his desk, touches other kids, fidgets, fidgets...

HELEN: Fidgets.

CHARLOTTE: God, I know he fidgets. You're the experts: Tell me something I don't know.

HELEN: The alphabet soup.

CHARLOTTE: Right. And all these developmental things he's got. This whole mess of developmental things they say, the authorities who are supposed to know about this stuff but don't know crap and are just hanging on a few years more so they can get their full retirement packages.

HELEN: He'll settle in eventually like Ricky when he's ready.

CHARLOTTE: If he's not totally screwed up before that thinking he's a bad person. Whenever he gets in trouble, and it's a lot, he says "I'm so stupid, I'm so stupid. What's wrong with me?" I know he brings these things on himself. I mean he did bite Nicholas but he didn't break the skin and they were wrestling which is not a good situation for Larry because he can't control his impulses...if he's fighting...so we just have to make sure...

HELEN: Charlotte...

CHARLOTTE: I'm just hoping to get him through the next few years until he can catch up with everyone else.

HELEN: Listen Charlotte, I have to say this: I know how rough it is. I know all the doors that get slammed in your face. And I'm willing to see how things go but I'm not going to let it go too far for the sake of trying to do the right thing.

CHARLOTTE: Trying to do the right thing? What right thing?

HELEN: Let me just finish okay? So we know where we are here.

CHARLOTTE: I don't want anyone's pity. What right thing do you mean?

HELEN: I mean that I'm willing to hold the door open to see if something good can happen between our kids but I'm not going to sacrifice Nicholas for...

CHARLOTTE: Sacrifice, Nicholas?

HELEN: Don't take the word wrong okay? Let's just see how it goes. Fair enough?

CHARLOTTE: Fair enough. *(Beat)* Larry's not an easy kid to like I know that but he's my kid and he can't take any more losses...
(CHARLOTTE almost breaks down.)

HELEN: Listen Sweetie...

CHARLOTTE: Sorry. That was inappropriate. A person's nice to us and I just want to collapse. That's all I want really. To collapse. To completely collapse. But I won't. Don't worry about it.

HELEN: I said what I had to say and it doesn't need to be said again.

CHARLOTTE: I'm just so exhausted from the effort to get other people to see what a wonderful, loving person he can be because I'm the only one who sees it.

HELEN: I can tell he's very intelligent. And verbal. Some of the sentences that come out of him really turn my head around.

CHARLOTTE: And that makes it worse. The way he can argue. Mrs. Delaney has been trying to get him out of the class but I've been fighting it and fighting it and that's why he has that young aide with him half the day. Last week, he convinced the aide that he'd learn to spell better if he read his spelling words out to her and she wrote them down instead of the other way around.

HELEN: Really?

CHARLOTTE: Larry hates to write.

HELEN: A con artist eh?

CHARLOTTE: You know it. He's turning the aide into his personal slave. (Beat) Your other son how long did it take for him to settle in?

HELEN: Ricky was around twelve.

CHARLOTTE: Twelve? I won't make it.

HELEN: Sure you will, Hon. One day at a time.

CHARLOTTE: One new drug at a time.

HELEN: One meltdown at a time.

CHARLOTTE: One behavior report at a time.

HELEN: One weird play date at a time. You want more wine?

CHARLOTTE: Sure. Why the heck not?

(HELEN pours two glasses.)

HELEN: Here's to weird play dates.

(They clink glasses.)

End of Scene.

THEY MET IN A BAR

By Shareen Knight

CAST:

SAMMY: A gay woman.

CHARLIE: Sammy's partner.

They are in a relationship. Will they stay together?

Or, is this the final break up?

SET: 2 Chairs. A small table, a pile of flowers, a pair of scissors, and a vase for the flowers, which SAMMY is arranging. CHARLIE is sprawled in a chair.

SAMMY: (musing) We met in a bar.

CHARLIE: A gay bar.

SAMMY: WAY GAY. How could I forget?

CHARLIE: Just making sure.

SAMMY: (ignoring her) Through the curious situation of (pauses) one's future sister-in-law being there.

CHARLIE: Amazing.

SAMMY: For what purpose was not entirely clear.

CHARLIE: I have a pretty good idea.

SAMMY: (ignores the comment) Her fiancé not being present.

CHARLIE: Exactly.

SAMMY: Well, she DID get married.

CHARLIE: That's what was amazing.

SAMMY: Do you think it was fate?

CHARLIE: Not damn likely.

SAMMY: You seemed (pause) overly interested.

CHARLIE: So, we danced. Big deal.

SAMMY: Well, something happened.

CHARLIE: Indeed it did. But, not what you think.

SAMMY: Are you now going to admit that you spent the night with her? My own sister-in-law?!

CHARLIE: We just talked.

SAMMY: Until four in the morning!

CHARLIE: Yes, until four in the morning. So? She wasn't sure she wanted to get married.

SAMMY: You seemed enchanted. Bewitched, even.

CHARLIE: Bewitched?

SAMMY: Yes, bewitched. Even at their wedding for god's sakes.

CHARLIE: She's an amazing girl. Woman.

SAMMY: You're supposed to say they are an amazing couple.

CHARLIE: Couple, then.

SAMMY: There was someone else, she said.

CHARLIE: She said that? When?

SAMMY: Last night. She called me. She's thinking about leaving.

CHARLIE: I know.

SAMMY: You know? Exactly when were you going to tell me?

CHARLIE: I didn't want to upset you, or hurt you.

SAMMY: So, I have to hear it from my own sister-in-law?

CHARLIE: I'm sorry. Do you know how it is when you want to see someone so bad that...

SAMMY: That you're willing to break up a 10 year relationship?

CHARLIE: I tried. Believe me when I say I really tried... (pause) to not let this happen.

SAMMY: I'm cold.

CHARLIE: I'm sorry.

SAMMY: Are you sure about this?

CHARLIE: You mean leaving?

SAMMY: Yes.

CHARLIE: We've stuck it out through worse.

SAMMY: (sarcastically) Through worse? I think this is about as "worst" as it can get.

CHARLIE: I just want to do the right thing. (pause) And, I can't. There is no right about this, no way I can make it right. To you or her or anybody else.

SAMMY: Anybody else??? Like her husband??? My own brother for Christ's sakes!

CHARLIE: I know. It's not good.

SAMMY: Not good is miniscule to what I'm feeling. (brandishing the scissors) I'd like to kill you right now.

CHARLIE: I'm not too happy with myself. But, if you kill me you'd wind up in prison.

SAMMY: It might be worth it.

CHARLIE: You're not the killing kind.

SAMMY: You think you know me that well?

CHARLIE: I do.

SAMMY: (begins walking around the room) There was a time when that would have made me happy.

CHARLIE: I know.

SAMMY: Stop saying "I know", "I'm sorry".

CHARLIE: What do you want me to say? Do you want me to leave?

SAMMY: Leave, stay. It makes no difference. I wish I was dead.

CHARLIE: Don't say that.

SAMMY: I'll say what I damn well want to say. God-dammit! God-dammit! God damn YOU!

CHARLIE: I'm sorry.

SAMMY: OK, enough of this shit! First, you slept with the house painter, and now…ARE YOU SLEEPING WITH HER?

CHARLIE: I did not!

SAMMY: Which? Which one didn't you sleep with Charlie?

SAMMY: Which? Which one didn't you sleep with Charlie?

SAMMY: So, you did sleep with my sister-in-law.

CHARLIE: She has a name.

SAMMY: Answer me!

CHARLIE: What? What do you want me to say, Sammy? That I love her? What difference does it make whether I slept with her or not? I love her.

SAMMY: You love her.

CHARLIE: Yes.

SAMMY: But, did you SLEEP with her?

CHARLIE: Not really.

SAMMY: Not really? What the hell does "Not really" mean?

CHARLIE: It means no. Sort of.

SAMMY: Sort of. Sort of? Oh, that's good. So, you "sort of" "not really" slept with her?!

CHARLIE: This is going nowhere fast.

SAMMY: You got that right.

CHARLIE: I wish it were easier.

SAMMY: Easier? For you, maybe. No way in hell will this ever be easy.

CHARLIE: I'm sorry.

SAMMY: Stop saying, "I'm sorry"!!!

CHARLIE: I'm sorry. I mean. Okay.

SAMMY: Oh my god, this is crazy!

CHARLIE: I didn't want this to happen. Believe me when I say this. I DID NOT WANT THIS TO HAPPEN!

SAMMY: But, it did happen. And, it doesn't even really matter whether you slept with her or not. It's too late for that. Beyond that. Is there any going back Charlie? Any chance?

CHARLIE: I wish I knew.

SAMMY: But, you do know. You KNOW, Charlie. You know. Just tell me. I'm tired. I don't want to hurt anymore. I want to sleep. I want to GET DRUNK. And, I want you to LEAVE!

CHARLIE: It's late.

SAMMY: So? What does that mean? You want to sleep here? Why?

CHARLIE: I'm tired, too.

SAMMY: Well, you should have thought of that….oh never mind. Just get out.

CHARLIE: I don't have anywhere to go.

SAMMY: (laughs crazily) YOU have nowhere to go?

CHARLIE: Not really.

SAMMY: You are making me crazy!

CHARLIE: I could sleep in the closet.

SAMMY: No! You can't sleep in the closet!

CHARLIE: I'll leave tomorrow.

SAMMY: Let's see. YOU have nowhere to go. YOU want to sleep in the closet. Well, hear this, Charlie! FUCK YOU! You can sleep in the street for all I care.

CHARLIE: Let's be rational. The street is dangerous.

SAMMY: (mimics) Let's be rational. YOU are dangerous!

CHARLIE: I wasn't dangerous yesterday

SAMMY: Oh, but you were. I just didn't know it.

CHARLIE: I still love you, Sammy.

SAMMY: But, you're not in love with me, is that it?

CHARLIE: Yeah, I guess.

SAMMY: You guess? Oh, you are too much. Pack your bags kiddo. And, you can sleep on the couch.

CHARLIE: Thanks, Sammy. I appreciate that.

SAMMY: (softly) Unbelievable.

CHARLIE: It's pretty unbelievable to me too.

SAMMY: I don't want to hear any more. Do you hear me? NO MORE.

CHARLIE: Just one thing. What did she tell you?

SAMMY: Actually, she didn't tell me anything.

CHARLIE: She didn't? What do you mean?

SAMMY: She didn't call.

CHARLIE: Then, how did you…..?

SAMMY: I made it up.

CHARLIE: You made it up?

SAMMY: Yeah, I made it up. I guessed something was going on. And, I was right, wasn't I?

CHARLIE: (shocked) Oh my god

SAMMY: Be gone by the time I get home from work tomorrow.

(SAMMY exits)

End of Scene.

THESE PEOPLE

By Martha Patterson

CAST OF CHARACTERS
MELINDA   American, 50 years old, works in publishing in sales
SUSHILA   25, Eastern Indian, originally from Mumbai but speaks fluent English, very sweet-natured, lives down the hall from Melinda, works in business
TOMMY   American, 30, lives next door to MELINDA, shy and awkward, runs a bike messenger service

(Lights go up on MELINDA's apartment. There is a loaf of banana bread on the counter. MELINDA is curled up on the sofa reading a letter from SUSHILA, who is in India. SUSHILA's voice is heard as a voiceover, over a speaker, while MELINDA reads in silence.)

SUSHILA's VOICE:

Dearest Melinda,
I am curled up on the settee in my apartment, having just gotten home from work at Bain, the same company I worked at when we knew each other in Boston. Work is going well and I expect to keep my job for a long time. You asked when you wrote when we would be getting married. I believe it will be in another year. He is a wonderful man and works in business, as I do. It is summer now, and I sleep in the garden outside as it is warm. The scent of the flowers is lovely. I know sleeping in the garden is not done in America, but it is quite common here. I think fondly of the dinner you and your friend Tommy and I had just before I left the States.

I will send you a cookbook so you can learn how to cook Indian food. I am very happy with my fiancée, and I do hope your work is going well and that you are not depressed about not moving on at your company. You are very intelligent, Melinda, and I wish you the best of all things.

My love to you,
Sushila.

MELINDA: How sweet! An Indian cookbook!

(Smiles. There is a knock on the door. MELINDA folds the letter up and puts it on the coffee table, then answers the door. It is TOMMY.)

Hi! Tommy! How've you been?

TOMMY: Okay.

MELINDA: I was just reading a letter from Sushila, the girl from India who used to live down the hall.

TOMMY: Oh, yeah, I remember her. She was nice.

(Looks at countertop.)

Banana bread! Mind if I have a piece?

MELINDA: Help yourself.

(He does. She beckons him towards the sofa.)

Well, what's new?

TOMMY: I'm leaving again, in another week, to tour the Midwest.

MELINDA: *(Smiles.)* Excellent!

TOMMY: Yeah, it seems like this music thing is taking off.

MELINDA: Oh, Tommy, I'm so happy for you!

(Kisses him on the cheek and gives him a hug.)

TOMMY: I wanna say, though, I miss you sometimes.

(He seems shy.)

I think about you a lot.

MELINDA: Oh, for Heaven's sake, Hon, I'm just a middle-aged woman by your standards.

TOMMY: No, really, I like you a lot. And I always wanted to see you again.

MELINDA: You mean, for sex?

TOMMY: *(Hanging his head.)* Well, maybe. But not just for that.

(Crosses to counter for another piece of banana bread.)

MELINDA: Oh, sure it is, Hon. You just need to get out there and meet some girls! I'll bet you do meet them, on the road.

TOMMY: *(Munching.)*

Not that much.

MELINDA: Really?

TOMMY: The guys still tease me 'cuz I don't know how to talk to people.

MELINDA: Well, dish it right back!! Tell them you've been with an older woman and there's nothing like it!!

(Grins.)

TOMMY: It's not just that. I really, really like you, Melinda. You're not like the other girls I meet. You're not empty-headed.

MELINDA: *(Thinking.)* Somehow that reminds me of something Sushila said once.

TOMMY: Well, if you ever want to get together again, I'm right next door. And I think you're just the greatest.

MELINDA: *(Leading him to the sofa.)*

Now, I'm going to tell you something, Tommy. Listen to me. I'm too old for you. We have a good time together, but you should be with someone younger. And not every girl is a jerk, you know? For the longest time I thought all men were jerks. But they're not. You're not. And you need a little confidence. I'm not the only women for you. What happened between us just happened. And you're a beautiful lover, and kind, and sweet, but I really think you should be with someone closer to your own age.

TOMMY: Well, what about you? You're alone, just like me.

MELINDA: Oh, I'll probably always be alone. I don't like people that much. Most of them drive me crazy, the people I work with, folks I deal with on the phone. I like you, though. And I think you deserve a good future. So don't dwell on memories of me. We aren't fit for each other. I'm telling you the truth. No man would ever put up with me. I'm such a slob. I probably won't give a man kids. And I like spending time by myself, reading the New Yorker.

TOMMY: *(Getting up from sofa.)*

I didn't want to bother you. I was just hoping we might be able to…..to…..

MELINDA: Sleep together again?

TOMMY: *(Helps himself to another slice of banana bread. MELINDA looks at him sternly.)*

More than that! Hang out, spend our time together.

MELINDA: *(Watching him eat.)*

Take two, they're small. Tommy, my dear, you're barkin' up the wrong tree. I could do it, it might even be fun, I would just feel as if I were taking advantage. So don't look to me. Find someone who's 27 and really, really loves you. That's your best bet.

(Takes his hand.)

But you're a real sweetie pie, Tommy. I'll always value your friendship.

TOMMY: *(Kisses her on the cheek and heads towards the door.)*

Thanks, Melinda. I'll burn a CD of my band's music for you soon.

MELINDA: *(Smiles at him.)*

Thanks!

(TOMMY exits.)

What a case!! Maybe not even him, maybe it was me. Why did I sleep with him? Charity? No. I thought he was a nice kid.

(Sits down on sofa and picks up SUSHILA's letter again.)

And Sushila said once that I was an ignoramus. She didn't really mean it. ….. They sleep in the garden in India?

(She looks up at the ceiling.)

"The scent of the flowers is lovely." Sounds nice.

(She starts to re-read the letter, and lights go down.)

(Lights go up, a few weeks later, on MELINDA making coffee in the kitchenette. She is holding a letter from SUSHILA and reading it as she makes coffee. She brings the coffee cup and the letter to the sofa and sits down, reading the letter.)

SUSHILA's VOICE:

Dearest Melinda,

I just got back from a seaside vacation with my fiancée and family. It was quite lovely; we had rooms in a small hotel and nobody bothered us. We had our laundry done by people you would call peasants, for whom this is a common occupation. They pick one's clothes up in the morning, mark them with different colors of thread, and return them to you the next day, freshly washed. By the way, I keep meaning to send you my recipe for Parantha, a flaky Indian bread. Here it is:

Ingredients:

2.5 cups chappati flour

1 cup water at room temperature

1 cup chappati flour in a large plate for dusting the dough

while rolling it out

ghee for brushing the bread

Ghee, Melinda, is the clear part of the butter after you have melted it in a pan.

MELINDA: *(Dropping the letter at her feet and daydreaming.)*

I would love to go to India.

(Lights go down.)

(Lights go up on MELINDA, snoozing on the sofa. There are cheese and crackers on a plate on the coffee table. The doorbell rings and she gets up and answers it. It is TOMMY.)

TOMMY: Hi Melinda! I just got back from Wisconsin!

MELINDA: *(Letting him in.)*

I just had another letter from Sushila. She sent me a recipe for Indian bread.

TOMMY: Indian bread! Will you make it for me?

MELINDA: Oh, Tommy, give it up. We're not having a relationship, you and I aren't anything at all. But, sure, I'll make you some bread.

TOMMY: *(Suddenly stiff.)*

You're kind of mean, you know that?

MELINDA: I'm not trying to be mean.

TOMMY: I wasn't asking for anything except your company. Don't misunderstand me.

MELINDA: Oh.

TOMMY: *(Kisses her on the cheek.)*

Can I at least do that?

MELINDA: Well, yes, certainly, and by the way you are getting more forward with me as time goes on. Have you been meeting women?

TOMMY: *(Smiles and helps himself to some cheese and crackers.)*

A few. I had a one-night stand with a girl last weekend.

MELINDA: I hope you didn't take her virginity.

TOMMY: *(Eating.)*

Oh, no, I would never do that! She was married once, and she divorced him a year ago. It was nothing like what you imagine. She was nice, sweet, even, but I wouldn't take advantage of a woman, for God's sake!

MELINDA: Well, I don't suppose I thought you would. Have a seat and I'll pour you some lukewarm coffee.

(Goes to kitchenette.)

TOMMY: Guess what? My band might be getting a record deal, from a very small label!

MELINDA: No kidding!

(Brings two cups of coffee to the coffee table.)

TOMMY: I'm not! If this goes through I might be able to leave the bike messenger service forever!

(Takes another cracker and some cheese.)

MELINDA: Cool!

(Sips her coffee.)

TOMMY: *(Pulling a CD from his pocket.)*

I brought you a copy of our CD. Maybe you'll like it. I know you like some of the bands from the '60s and '70s. We kind of have that sound.

MELINDA: *(Looking at the CD cover.)*

You're in the cover shot.

TOMMY: *(Shyly.)* Yeah.

MELINDA: You look very cute. Very star-worthy, I might add.

TOMMY: Thanks.

MELINDA: I'll look forward to listening to this. Tell me, you have gotten over us, haven't you?

TOMMY: *(A little cocky.)*

Oh, yeah. You don't have to get egotistical about it. You just seemed so.....wise, and kind. And that dinner we had with your Indian friend was nice. It made me think I should try to do things like that more often, you know, initiate, and offer invitations to people to do stuff, even go out for a beer.

MELINDA: I'm all for that.

TOMMY: *(Softly.)*

I have to tell you something. For a month I was in the hospital. My father put me there. I was depressed, I had to stop working, and touring.

MELINDA: Oh, Tommy! I am so sorry!

TOMMY: It's okay. I'm better now, and I've been taking meds.

MELINDA: That's good. We all have problems. For years, off and on, I had a pretty severe anxiety disorder.

TOMMY: Really?

MELINDA: Yeah! I am the world's worst worry-wart, and I carry more anger in me than you would believe.

(TOMMY laughs.)

And now I have a good job, some nice friends, a nice place of my own to live in. But for Heaven's sake, do you know that one out of 100 people in the U.S. either have or will develop schizophrenia? I read the papers!

TOMMY: I don't have schizophrenia.

MELINDA: Well, it wouldn't be the worst thing in the world if you did. People are just ignorant of how very common these disorders are.

TOMMY: *(His head in his hands.)*

I thought I'd never see the light at the end of the tunnel.

MELINDA: *(Motheringly.)*

Tommy, I'm telling you, you can hardly find a family in the United States that hasn't been touched in some way by mental illness. That's a big part of the reason why there's such a health care crisis in our country.

TOMMY: You're really smart, you know that?

MELINDA: No, I'm really NOT. But I read a lot. Look at these newspapers all over the place.

(Gestures with her hands to the mess in her living room.)

You're okay, Tommy. You're gonna be okay. You've practically got a record deal, for Heaven's sake! And you can always, always knock on my door. Even bring a girlfriend over someday.

TOMMY: *(Getting up.)*

Well, thanks. For a being a good friend and neighbor.

MELINDA: *(Walking him to the door.)*

Don't mention it.

(She pats him on the back.)

I'll listen to your CD tonight.

TOMMY: Let me know what you think. And don't worry, you can be honest.

(Exits.)

MELINDA: Bye, Tommy.

(Closes the door and walks to the bed, lies down with a sigh, and starts reading the New Yorker. Lights go down.)

(Lights go up. It is a month later. MELINDA is coming home from work, closes the door behind her and sets her bag down on the floor. She has a letter in her hand. It is from SUSHILA. MELINDA stands next to the sofa, reading it.)

SUSHILA's VOICE:

Dearest Melinda,

It was so good to get your letter a week ago. I am glad to hear you and Tommy are still friends, even though he seemed to want something more from you than you could give. You are a very giving woman, Melinda, do you know that? Very kind and sweet. And – I must tell you - I am coming back to the States next month! My company is sending me to be there for a meeting for Bain, and because I have lived in Boston they wanted me to be their emissary. I hope to visit you, perhaps we can have dinner at a restaurant. It will be my treat. They are putting me up at the Four Seasons. Can you meet me?

All my love to you,

Sushila.

MELINDA: *(Smiles and drops the letter on the coffee table.)*

Well, that's nice. Really, really nice. I've missed her.

(She kicks off her shoes and lies down on the sofa and starts to snooze. Lights go down.)

End of Scene.

SUCKLED BY WOLVES

By Pat Montley

SYNOPSIS
Steve and Rick—with varying motivations and degrees
of resolve—prepare to confront their former abuser,
now a bishop, with an ultimatum.

CAST OF CHARACTERS
Steve: 40's, once Rick's best friend. Man with a
conscience and a mission. A realist.
Rick: 40's, once Steve's best friend. Sensitive. A
romantic.

SETTING
A room with an Oriental carpet and a few pieces of stiff
Victorian furniture
(OR...bare stage with two chairs)
The present
STEVE and RICK wait in a room with an Oriental
carpet and a few pieces of stiff Victorian furniture.

STEVE: What's taking him so long?

RICK: He was never very...punctual, Steve. Don't you
remember?

STEVE: No. *(Beat.)* I try not to.

RICK: I thought you went through years of remembering.

STEVE: That was a long time ago.

RICK: Right after?

STEVE: Not right.

RICK: Later, then.

STEVE: Much later. You?

RICK: Right after.

STEVE: Oh.

RICK: My parents.

STEVE: Of course. *(Beat.)* Rick, we do have an appointment, don't we? I mean you called and talked to him.

RICK: Well, not to him. But we have an appointment. *(Pause.)* How's Sharon?

STEVE: Fine. Up for tenure at St. Mary's this year.

RICK: A shoo-in.

STEVE: We hope.

RICK: And the Vunderkind?

STEVE: Good. Great.

RICK: Show me.

STEVE: *(Taking out wallet.)* Prepare to be dazzled. *(Shows picture.)*

RICK: Wow! Cap and gown time already.

STEVE: Only grade school.

RICK: What're you saying—that we're not that old?

STEVE: What about your twins?

RICK: *(Getting out wallet and showing.)* Child prodigies, both. I think they actually look like Mike, don't you?

STEVE: *(Looking.)* Wow—you're right. Amazing resemblance. Considering. *(Taking photo for closer look.)* A mighty pair.

RICK: Regular Romulus and Remus.

STEVE: *(Taking photo back.)* Don't.

RICK: I was only...

STEVE: I hated when he called us that.

RICK: Sorry. *(Referring to photo as he puts it away.)* They're just the age we were... *(He trails off. STEVE pats his arm. Beat.)* Do you...can you ever forgive him?

STEVE: For starters, he'd have to repent.

RICK: You think he hasn't?

STEVE: In the confessional where it's easy and anonymous, sure.

RICK: He has publicly apologized.

STEVE: For the sins of *(Imitating the bishop's tone)* "all those priests in my dioceses who have committed such heinous crimes." But not for his own sins. And not to us.

RICK: Perhaps he will...tonight.

STEVE: And what about restitution? What about the obligation to restore what was stolen.

RICK: How can he give us back our innocence?

STEVE: He stole our sense of worth and dignity. And now he has to give them back.

(Beat.)

RICK: But you have those things.

STEVE: You don't—not in the eyes of the world.

RICK: Is that his fault?

STEVE: His church's fault!

(Beat.)

RICK: What time is it?

STEVE: Quarter after.

RICK: What if he says no?

STEVE: *(A determined reminder.)* Like we decided on the phone after I saw the article...we go to the paper.

RICK: Are you sure you're ready to do that?

STEVE: If we have to.

RICK: It won't be pretty. Aren't you concerned about...what about Sharon's job?

STEVE: We've talked it through.

RICK: I can't tell you how much it means to me, Steve, that you're willing to put everything on the line like this.

STEVE: Aren't you?

RICK: Yeah but I have more to—

STEVE: *(Interrupting.)* No. You don't. Not really. Not in the grand scheme of things.

RICK: How did he used to put it...? "In lux aeternitatis." All moral decisions should be made "in the light of eternity." Sounds grand, doesn't it?

STEVE: Maybe that was the problem. It was too grand. Maybe something less ambitions would have worked. Like the Native American idea of considering the effects of your actions on seven generations.

RICK: Seven's a good number.... Seven sacraments...seven last words of Jesus...

STEVE: Seven sorrows of Mary...seven gifts of the Holy Spirit...

RICK: Seven deadly sins.

STEVE: I would've settled for one.

RICK: Sin?

STEVE: Generation.

RICK: Was it a sin?

STEVE: For us?

RICK: For him.

STEVE: Are you kidding? How much did our families spend on therapy?

RICK: I know, I know. But maybe...if things had been different...I mean if people...if the Church hadn't...if the culture didn't...

STEVE: What are you saying...that it could have been possible for him to do what he did without fucking up our lives?

RICK: I'm just saying...I'm saying that he loved me. All right?

STEVE: *(Sarcastic.)* Yeah, right.

RICK: He did! I know he did!

STEVE: Okay, okay. He loved you. Short-term love. Not seven-generation love. Because it's clear he doesn't love you now. Or he wouldn't have said what he said in the pulpit and in front of the state legislature, and we wouldn't be here now insisting that he take it back.

RICK: Do you think he will?

STEVE: I think he'll say he's duty-bound as a bishop to uphold the teaching of the church, that same-sex marriage is a threat to the family, that the bible says yadda, yadda, yadda, and anything else he needs to say to get his cardinal's hat.

RICK: How'd you get to be such a cynic?

STEVE: Life.

RICK: Well, here's what I think. I think when I show him the picture of my boys and explain what good parents Mike and I try to be, and what hopes we have for our sons and what we're doing to make those hopes a reality, he'll understand that we're just like any other family and need the same—

STEVE: *(Interrupting.)* No, Rick. He won't. He won't let himself understand and he won't change his story. You need to be prepared for that.

RICK: But when he sees me...when he sees that I'm no threat to anybody...

STEVE: Don't you think he's seen hundreds of you? Don't you think he has sat in the confessional—and probably in this very room as well—listening to Catholic homosexuals spill their guilty little guts in paroxysms of despair. And what do you imagine he has said to comfort them—or to ease the shame of their heart-broken parents? Do you really imagine he has told them that tolerance is the only solution, that love is the only answer?

RICK: The point is that—

STEVE: *(Interrupting.)* The point is that we can't let him see us as "no threat to anybody." He has to see us as a threat to him!

RICK: This is so...not-me. I don't do ultimatums. It's not the way I deal with people.

STEVE: Don't think of him as a person. Think of him as an institution. An institution that has raped you—stripped you of dignity, honesty, respect, the right to a happy life—and must not be allowed to keep doing it.

RICK: It wasn't rape. I told you he loved me.

STEVE: And you're here to...?

RICK: Remind him of that. *(STEVE shakes his head in amazed disbelief.)* What's the matter? Isn't that why you're here too? Didn't he love you?

STEVE: Yes....

RICK: But?

STEVE: But I didn't love him back. That's the difference between us.

RICK: Oh.

STEVE: So I...

RICK: You what?

STEVE: I gave him you.

RICK: You what?!

STEVE: I...I didn't like what he was doing to me, so I...I introduced him to you.

RICK: Because...

STEVE: I thought...I thought you might like it. *(RICK looks away.)* Did you?

RICK: *(Beat.)* How did you know...about me?

STEVE: I just...guessed.

RICK: How?

STEVE: By the way you.... You were in love with me, weren't you?

RICK: *(Beat. Nods.)* My first "falling." But...you didn't love me back.

STEVE: You were my best friend...

RICK: Your best friend who understood "No, thank you" when I saw it.

STEVE: Which is more than he did.

RICK: Did you tell him "No, thank you."

STEVE: In a hundred ways. But he ignored it. What did you tell him?

RICK: That I was afraid. But he said he would take care of it. That if I just didn't say anything, it would be okay...that God would understand.

STEVE: Do you think he believed that?

RICK: Yes.

STEVE: Then why doesn't he still believe it—that God understands? *(RICK shrugs. Beat)* Rick...can you...can you forgive me?

RICK: For not wanting me or for giving me away?

STEVE: Both.

RICK: No. *(STEVE looks away.)* If I didn't have Mike and the boys...if I didn't have that family, my life with them...the answer might be "no." But...in the "light of eternity," I suppose...what you did is forgivable.

STEVE: Then why can't I forgive myself?

RICK: Is that why you're here?

STEVE: Yeah...I guess so. But I like to think I'm also here for the same reason you are—because I want a saner, kinder world for all our children to grow up in.

RICK: And you think he can single-handedly give us that?

STEVE: Let's just say his vote goes a long way. That's why we have to...do whatever we need to get it.

RICK: Threaten? Intimidate? Blackmail? Be as cruel as he was?

STEVE: His victims were innocent. Ours isn't.

RICK: So our revenge is justified?

STEVE: It's not revenge to punish a hypocrite.

RICK: Then punish me too...if I betray someone I love.

STEVE: Still?

RICK: He didn't mean to hurt me, Steve. I know he didn't.

STEVE: Then why did he say the things he—?

RICK: He just didn't understand. But now he will. He has too. You wait. When he really sees, really sees...he'll understand. He'll change.

STEVE: You're dreaming, Rick.

RICK: *(Beat.)* Dreaming in the light of eternity.

(Lights.)

End of Scene.

I HOPE ITS RAINING IN PARIS

By Molly Hagan

*DOTTY sits on a park bench in front of the Louvre on a
rainy late afternoon. She holds a red umbrella.
NARRATOR 1, in a yellow poncho, stands to her right,
slightly behind the bench. To her left, sitting next to
her on the bench, is NARRATOR 2, who is wearing a
business suit. He is completely drenched. Dotty does
not acknowledge either narrator.*

NARRATOR 1:
Dotty enjoys visiting the Louvre because Dotty is a painter.
Were it the case that Dotty were not a painter, this narration
must note, she would also, probably and most likely enjoy
visiting the Louvre as well - as most find it to be a
transcending cultural experience. However, in this particular
circumstance, the character in question, Dotty, is in fact an
artist and - very much accordingly - enjoys her frequent
visits to the Louvre museum in Paris, France. Dotty was
born in White Oaks, Wisconsin, but that is neither here nor
there.

NARRATOR 2:
Dotty shifts her weight and looks at the people passing by.
Or what we assume to be the people passing by. We do not
see them.

NARRATOR 1:
Dotty would tell you, if you were to ask of course, that she
also enjoys walking along the Seine in the evening or
sunbathing in the French Riviera in the summertime or
obscure French wines or Monet. Or Les Miserables by
Victor Hugo. People pass by unseen to the audience. Dotty
smiles and nods.

NARRATOR 2:
Dotty reaches into her purse and takes out a thin package of
French cigarettes. She pulls out a long, sleek cigarette, and

puts it in her mouth. It appears she has forgotten a light. She roots around her purse trying to find her box of matches. She finally retrieves it, but alas, it is empty.

NARRATOR 1:
However, these things would not be true. Well not entirely true, anyway. Dotty has never walked along the river Seine although she has seen it from her apartment window above the Boulangerie. It seems like it would be a lovely river to walk along, she muses. As for the French Riviera, she has never been at all, in summertime or otherwise, nor has she the view from her tiny apartment to see it, of course. She has never finished Les Miserables in its literary form, although she has tried, but she has seen the musical – she cried. This was quite an admission for Dotty – she doesn't even like musicals. And as for Monet – she never liked Monet. In fact, she doesn't even know why she tells people that she likes him at all. Dotty waits for her boyfriend, a man who owns a Monet. Something with lilies.

NARRATOR 2:
The passers-by don't seem to have matches either. Dotty examines her unlit cigarette.

NARRATOR 1:
No. Dotty's pleasures are much more simple than these. She enjoys smoking long, thin French cigarettes and letting the smoke roll slowly out of her mouth. But what kind of thing is that to tell people, she wonders. Dotty doesn't read books very often, but she keeps a notebook of sketches. She calls it "Le Notebook de Pretty Things" or "Le Notebook de Fantasie" or "Ma Vie en Paris." Jean-Luc adores her notebook, amused that one can have so many names for one thing.

NARRATOR 1 (cont'd):
Dotty tries to explain that they do not represent the same thing – the name depends on her mood, much like the content. *(Beat.)* Dotty also enjoys champagne. In her

notebook she drew an abstract interpretation of a man popping the cork on a bottle of Dom Perignon in a Paris hotel room on a girl's first night in Paris. The man was Jean-Luc. The girl was Dotty. And she drew that abstract interpretation exactly eight months, 2 weeks and 3 days ago tonight – the night Dotty moved to Paris to be with Jean-Luc. But then again, everybody enjoys champagne, especially Dom Perignon, so she doesn't bother to tell people. Nobody ever asks, anyway.

NARRATOR 2:
The path before her is empty. Dotty dejectedly lets her cigarette die in the rain. Then in a sudden inspiration, she sets the soggy remnant down carefully on the arm of the bench. She reaches into her purse and pulls out her notebook and a pen. She begins to draw furiously.

NARRATOR 1:
As an Artist, that is, an Artist with a capital "A," as it is her profession, Dotty finds it necessary to appreciate the smaller things. She draws an abstract interpretation of a damp cigarette bending in the rain in her "Notebook de Pretty Things." Perhaps the shape could serve as the soft curve of a smile in a portrait or the arc of a finger accepting a diamond ring. That would be pretty wouldn't it? Especially if the accepting finger were Dotty's. She expects it any day now.

NARRATOR 2:
Dotty sits back and smiles. She puts her notebook away. She looks around and pulls her coat a little tighter.

NARRATOR 1:
He said 5 o'clock, it's only a little after. No matter, Dotty enjoys the Louvre after all. She could wait here all day. Besides, Jean-Luc is never on time, but he always makes it up to her.

NARRATOR 2:
Dotty taps her foot gently on the ground. She twirls her umbrella. She drums her fingers on the arm of the bench. She still wants a cigarette.

NARRATOR 1:
Dotty imagines Jean-Luc coming to meet her.

DOTTY:

(Her voice low to imitate Jean-Luc's...)

Ma cherie, it was raining all over Paris. I was on my way to meet you – walking down the rue from Montmarte with the red umbrella you bought me for my birthday – but the cobblestone streets were slick. I wanted to be on time to prove to you that I can keep commitments as you so wisely advised, Dotty, but I tripped in front of a cart where an old woman was selling pink roses. I hit my head on the stones and upset the cart. A thousand pink petals rained down on me, ma cherie, and before I went unconscious, my last thoughts were of you.

NARRATOR 2:
Dotty pauses to absorb this touching admission.

DOTTY:
(Still as Jean-Luc.)
I awoke in a room in the back of a small grocery with a family of gypsies. I didn't remember who I was or where I was from. They took me in as their own –

NARRATOR 2:
Dotty stops abruptly. She looks at her watch. For a moment she is quiet.

NARRATOR 1:
Dotty dislikes white canvas tennis shoes, tardiness, and cognac. And that Monet that hangs in Jean-Luc's living room - something with lilies. She really detests Monet. Jean-Luc's money would have been better spent on a portrait. Dotty thinks people are infinitely more interesting than expensive landscapes.

NARRATOR 2:
Dotty glances ruefully at the museum, at Paris, at her pack of cigarettes and empty matchbook. Her shoulders slump a little as she folds her hands in her lap, holding the umbrella in the crook of her arm.

NARRATOR 1:
Dotty's favorite painting in the Louvre is Da Vinci's La Belle Ferroniere or Portrait of an Unknown Woman, as it is often called. Jean-Luc doesn't like it very much. It is an oil painting of a woman who sits and waits. She wears a "ferroniere" – a jewel on her forehead tied on a string. Her face is calm, but her eyes are shrewd and purposeful. Dotty always wonders what the Belle Ferroniere is thinking.

DOTTY:
(As the Belle Ferroniere.)
'Dis jewelle, 'dis jewelle it is too tight! I sit in this picture and I watch the people pass by but I do not see him. Five-hundred years I wait! Da Vinci, paint me this man, paint him into my picture with me.

(Beat.)

'Dis jewelle, 'dis jewelle. It is too tight.

NARRATOR 2:
Dotty twirls her umbrella and adjusts her beret. She finds half a match lying wet on the ground. She picks it up.

NARRATOR 1:
Dotty also dislikes cubic zirconium. She wonders if the Belle Ferroniere's jewel was real. She also wonders how big a jewel you can get for a Monet. *(Beat.)* Sometimes Dotty likes to imagine that the Belle Ferroniere is feisty and European, and today Dotty decides to imagine that she is waiting for her love who, much like Jean-Luc, is running very late.

NARRATOR 2:
Dotty is no longer smiling, her eyes are shrewd and purposeful. Exasperated, she tries to light the dead match.

NARRATOR 1:
It's not like Dotty wouldn't settle for cubic zirconium because she would. She would settle for a plastic ring out of a vending machine or a Ring Pop or a little piece of string at this point. But that's not saying she wouldn't prefer a real diamond because of course she would. Anyone would. But she doesn't bother to say it. Nobody ever asks anyway. *(Beat.)* It's not like he can't afford it. She imagines his reaction to this admission.

DOTTY:
(As an exasperated Jean-Luc.)
A Ring Pop? I have never heard of this. I give you pink roses, champagne, Paris, the Louvre. What more do you want?

NARRATOR 1:
Jean-Luc did not give Dotty Paris, au contraire. Dotty discovered her own Paris. It was she who found her apartment above the Boulangerie with the leaky pipes and the water faucet that usually runs cold. She loves that apartment. She loves waking to the smell of fresh bread and looking out her window to watch the French women carefully distinguishing the cheeses that the grocer sells across the street. Dotty, our Wisconsinite, is mystified by the sheer number and variety of cheeses that inhabit the grocer's

stand. Dotty just knows that she likes Camembert, which she now knows comes from the north of France. And Jean-Luc didn't tell her that. The grocer did.

NARRATOR 2:
Dotty tosses the match, defeated. She watches a group of children pass. None of them have a light either.
NARRATOR 1
So Dotty doesn't know a lot about cheese. Or wine. Or the French resistance. Or any of the other terribly important things that French people are supposed to know about. Yes, she may not know a lot about these things, but she certainly doesn't depend on Jean-Luc to tell her about them. No, Dotty is perfectly capable of figuring these things out on her own.

NARRATOR 2:
Dotty, determined, puts an unlit cigarette in her mouth and pretends to smoke it as she again whips out her notebook.

NARRATOR 1:
Dotty draws another abstract interpretation in her "Notebook de Fantasie." It is a French woman sitting on a park bench in front of the Louvre museum in Paris, France. She smokes French cigarettes and holds a red, French umbrella and wears a French beret. She draws in a little French notebook. She has a serene French expression with a knowing, French smile because she knows all about the French resistance and she has read Les Miserables and not just seen it on Broadway and on her finger is an enormous, glittering French rock. And she likes French painters like Monet too, but it is only an abstract interpretation so you wouldn't actually know that, but just by looking at her you could tell that she probably does.

NARRATOR 2:
Dotty stops drawing, and looks quietly at the sketch for a moment.

NARRATOR 1:
Dotty suddenly wonders if Jean-Luc would prefer the abstract interpretation to Dotty.

NARRATOR 2
Dotty puts her notebook away. It's still raining and she still has an unlit cigarette dangling from her lips. The lights of the Louvre's glass pyramid behind her illuminate the sunless sky. The clouds are getting darker, but you can see the first few stars of evening beginning to appear behind them.

NARRATOR 1:
Dotty smokes when she's nervous. She likes to paint in her bare feet in the middle of the night, she knows that bottled water is a scam yet drinks it anyway, she almost never answers her cell phone, she doesn't like to be alone although she would never admit it and sometimes when a thought occurs to Dotty that she doesn't like, she simply ignores it.

Pause.

NARRATOR 2:
Just as Dotty is about to give up hope *(for a light, that is)* a stranger passing by lights her cigarette for her. Her body relaxes.
Narrator 2 pulls a match from his pocket and lights Dotty's cigarette.

NARRATOR 1:
That's better isn't it, Dotty? *(Beat.)* Dotty likes Paris when it rains. It reminds her of a movie. Dotty likes movies. Sometimes she likes to imagine her life as a movie. She imagines this moment as a scene in a movie and pictures how it would end. It would be in black and white. Except for her umbrella, that might still be red. Rhapsody in Blue would be playing softly in the background because An American in Paris is too cliché. Besides, Dotty doesn't like musicals. Dotty sits back lost in thought.

NARRATOR 1:

And in this movie we would see Jean-Luc. He would have just escaped a wild old woman selling pink roses and a family of gypsies and have overcome a mild case of amnesia. His expensive suit would be torn yet he would look as handsome as ever. He would also be in black and white. Except for the single rose he would carry, that might still be pink. And although you wouldn't see it, in his pocket he would carry a small box, but we wouldn't yet know what was in it. Jean- Luc would be walking or running rather, as suavely as a Frenchman can run, down the rue to meet his love, Dotty, where she would be waiting for him on a park bench on a rainy early evening in front of the Louvre museum in Paris, France. He would be late, as usual, but he would make it up to her because he always does. Dotty is an Artist, and she particularly enjoys the Louvre as well as Paris, her home and Jean-Luc, her future husband. And when the two finally reunite, Dotty would sketch an abstract interpretation of their reunion in a notebook that she would fondly refer to as, "Ma Vie en Paris" or "My Life in Paris."

NARRATOR 2:

The Louvre dims as Dotty sits serenely on the park bench clutching her red umbrella and letting the smoke roll slowly out of her mouth. Dotty smiles, still waiting as the lights fade to black.

End of Scene.

HARRIET'S HOUSE

By TARA GOLDSTEIN

Characters:
HARRIET: A school teacher and mother of three daughters,
the first two adopted from Colombia. She ages from 44 to 45.

LUÍSA: Harriet's eldest daughter, adopted from Colombia
at the age of 10. She ages from 17 to 19.

ANA: Harriet's middle daughter, adopted from Colombia
at the age of 7. She ages from 14 to 16 and is lighter-
skinned than Luísa.

CLARE: Harriet's youngest daughter, not adopted. She
ages from 11 to 13.

MARTY: A school teacher and Harriet's girlfriend/partner.
She ages from 35 to 36.

ANITA: Harriet's friend and founder of Global Family, an
international adoption agency. She ages from 50-51.

Place
Harriet's kitchen, Toronto, Canada.
An orphanage, Bogotá, Colombia.

Time
The present

Scene 6
(That night)
(HARRIET's kitchen. ANA and LUÍSA are at the island
drying pots and pans. The music fades.)

LUÍSA: Estas cambiada. *("You're different," in a*
fundamental way.)

ANA: You think?

LUÍSA: Y no para bien *("And not in a good way.")*

(ANA shrugs her shoulders.)

Ya no hablas español. *("You don't speak Spanish anymore.")*

ANA: So what?

LUÍSA: Es nuestro idioma. *("It's our language.")*

ANA: Speak Spanish with Clare.   She can count up to a thousand now.

LUÍSA: ¡ Caramba muchacha! *["Jesus, girl"!]* No quiero hablar español con Clare. Lo quiero hablar contigo. *("I don't want to speak Spanish with Clare. I want to speak Spanish with you".)*

(ANA shrugs her shoulders.)

Quiero que no lo tierdas. *("I don't want you to lose it.")*

ANA: You've been home for less than twenty-four hours and already you're bossing me around. I don't need it here.

LUÍSA: Aquí no vas a pasar toda la vida. *("You're not going to be here all your life.")*

ANA: *(Grounded)* Yes, I am.

LUÍSA: *(Switches to English)* No, you aren't. You're going to go back someday.

ANA: How do you know?

LUÍSA: You're going to be curious.

ANA: About what?

LUÍSA: About how people in Colombia live. What our culture's like, what our music's like.

ANA: *(Puts down the pot she's dried)* I know what Colombian music's like. I've heard it. Lots of times.

(She takes her dishtowel and snaps it against LUÍSAS's backside playfully. It doesn't hurt.)

LUÍSA: Ow!

(She takes her dishtowel and tries to snap it against ANA's backside, but ANA moves away too quickly. Ana laughs.)

There's more to Colombian music than Shakira, you know.

ANA: *(Picks up another pot, still grounded)* I like Shakira.

LUÍSA: *(Excited)* You need to hear some Reggaetón.

ANA: Shakira sings Reggaetón.

(She begins to sing Hips Don't Lie from Shakira's Oral Fixation CD.)

LUÍSA: I mean real Reggaetón. (Puts down the pot she's dried) I want you to come back with me next summer.

ANA: I already have plans.

LUÍSA: What plans?

ANA: *(Puts down the pot she's dried and picks up a third one)* I'm going to work at Brian's camp.

LUÍSA: Brian, Brian, Brian. All I hear about is Brian. *(Beat)* He's a bad influence on you.

ANA: *(Puts the dried pot down)* No, he isn't.

LUÍSA: Yes, he is. He's the reason you don't speak Spanish anymore. He's the reason you act white.

ANA: You're behind, I've done four you've done one.

LUÍSA: *(Picks up another pot)* Three. You've done three. (Beat) Don't you want to meet her?

ANA: Who?

LUÍSA: Our Mamá.

ANA: *(Puts down the dried pot and picks up another one and waves it in LUÍSA's face)* I'm way ahead of you.

LUÍSA: *(Starts drying again)* We have to find out what happened to her.

ANA: If you haven't found out by now, she's probably dead.

LUÍSA: But there's no record of her death in our files. The Sisters looked.

ANA: So?

LUÍSA: So, there's a chance that she's still alive. And that one day I'll find her and we'll get a chance to meet her.

ANA: I don't need to meet her.

LUÍSA: I don't believe you. *(Puts down the pot.)* You look just like her.

ANA: *(Suddenly angry)* Even if I do look like her, I'd never act like her. Every single thing inside of me comes from living here. In this family. In this country. *(Raises her voice)* If you want to go back to Colombia, go! You want to look for a woman who left us alone at the orphanage and who is probably dead, go! Go look for her. But I'm staying here.

(HARRIET enters.)

HARRIET: What's going on?

LUÍSA: Nothing.

HARRIET: *(To ANA)* Why are you shouting?

ANA: She made me mad.

HARRIET: *(Light)* Just like old times.

LUÍSA: All I did was ask her to come to Colombia with me next summer and she freaked out.

ANA: I didn't freak out.

LUÍSA: Yes, you did.

(Puts down the pot she's drying, picks up another one.)

ANA: *(Angry)* No, I didn't. I told you that I'm not going because I've got other plans. You just can't take no for an answer.

HARRIET: *(To ANA)* You don't want to go?

ANA: *(Trying to be calm)* No.

HARRIET: *(Trying to buffer the tension)* Well, there's no rush. Most of the other Global kids don't go back until they finish high school. You have plenty of time.

LUÍSA: *(Exasperated, puts the pot down with a bang)* You shouldn't try and influence her that way.

HARRIET: I wasn't trying to influence her. I just said there's no rush.

LUÍSA: Yes, there is a rush. She's not speaking Spanish anymore. She's losing it. *(Accusatory)* She's being robbed of our heritage.

HARRIET: And that's my fault?!

(CLARE, who has been standing in the doorway, quietly enters.)

LUÍSA: She doesn't have a chance to practice. She spends all her time with Brian. She doesn't see any of the Globals anymore. Anita says you didn't go to Seder and you haven't been to any of the events since Passover. What's that about?

HARRIET: *(Worried now)* That's a long story … Let me make some tea and we can –

(CLARE enters, happy to join the family.)

CLARE: I can do it.

HARRIET: No, that's okay. Honey. I'll do it.

LUÍSA: What happened?

ANA: It's because of Marty.

LUÍSA: Marty? Who's Marty?

HARRIET: You remember my friend Marty. From school?

ANA: She's my new hockey coach.

CLARE: And she's Harriet's –

HARRIET: Clare, honey, could you go next door and ask to borrow some milk for the tea? We're all out.

CLARE: Okay. Luísa, do you want to come with me?

LUÍSA: No. You go. I'll stay here.

CLARE: Okay. ¡hasta luego!

(CLARE leaves.)

LUÍSA: So what's the problem with Marty? Anita doesn't like her?

HARRIET: Anita has never even met her.

LUÍSA: So then why – ?

HARRIET: Marty's gay.

LUÍSA: So?

HARRIET: *(Brave, defiant)* And so am I. She's my partner now and Anita doesn't approve.

(There's a second or two of silence while Luísa absorbs the news.)

LUÍSA: She's your partner?

(HARRIET nods.)

You're with a woman?

(HARRIET nods.)

Why didn't you tell me? I called every Sunday. You could have said something!

HARRIET: I wanted to … but you were so full of stories of what you were doing in Colombia … they seemed more interesting than my … I don't know. I should've told you. I'm sorry.

LUÍSA: Sorry's not good enough.

HARRIET: Sorry's what I have to offer.

ANA: There's nothing to be sorry about. Marty's great. Everyone likes her. I like her, Clare likes her. She's even got Clare coming to our games.

LUÍSA: Are you planning on moving in together?

HARRIET: Someday.

LUÍSA: Someday soon?

HARRIET: I don't know. Maybe.

LUÍSA: With Ana and Clare still living here?

HARRIET: Maybe. Why not?

ANA: Marty's great!

LUÍSA: Sshh.

ANA: Don't sshh me! This isn't Colombia. I'm not one of your orphans who you can sshh.

LUÍSA: *(Ignores ANA, to HARRIET)* I don't think she should move in here.

HARRIET: Well, it's not your decision to make.

LUÍSA: Fine. I'm not staying anyway.

HARRIET: You made a promise that you'd go back to school if I let you go to Bogotá. You promised to give it a year. All your registration material is sitting here, waiting for you. I want to see you back to school next week. Just like you promised.

LUÍSA: I don't care about what you want or don't want. I'm done listening to you. I'm done hearing what you want me to do and not do. I'm eighteen now and I am going to do what I want. I'm not interested in going back to school. There's only one thing I'm interested in. Finding out what happened to my real mother.

(LUÍSA leaves. ANA and HARRIET look at each other in dismay and then ANA goes over to give HARRIET a hug.)

HARRIET: What am I going to do about your sister?

ANA: What can you do? You have to let her go.

(Dan's Luisa's Ballad-2 closes the scene and opens Scene 7).

End of Scene.

TOSS

By Pam Calabrese MacLean

SCENE I

Late evening on a small balcony. Two women sit in a chair swing. Grace is 55ish and plump. Her mother Eleanor is 80ish.

ELEANOR: I don't know how to make this kind of decision.

GRACE: At least you've got it narrowed down to two places. One in the country and one right her in Antigonish.

ELEANOR: I've lived in this house my whole adult life. Your father....You...

GRACE: Mom you know you have to move! If I lived closer...

ELEANOR: I don't have to move! Two little fires in 80 years!

GRACE: Two fires in a month!

ELEANOR: I don't like making choices. And Grace, neither place will take a dog!

GRACE: You don't have a dog!

ELEANOR: Listen to you. What do you call Percy?

GRACE: Dead. Percy's been dead for 40 years.

ELEANOR: Well Rocky then?

GRACE: Twenty!

ELEANOR: Whatever the dog's name is!

GRACE: Mom they're all gone. There is no dog. There hasn't been a dog for years.

ELEANOR: Oh God, everything I love is dead.

GRACE: I'm not dead. Oh Mom I'm worried about you. Every time I call you tell me how much you hate eating alone.

ELEANOR: Well Miss Smarty Pants, will I be eating at all in some 4 by 4 upright coffin with no stove? If you were half as smart as you think you are, I couldn't stand you.

GRACE: You can't stand me anyway.

ELEANOR: I'd be better off dead! Just take a bunch of pills and be done with it.

GRACE: That **is** a choice **you'll** have to make.

ELEANOR: But you'd gladly hand me a glass of water! You're a cold fish Grace.

GRACE: And you're trolling for sympathy. You're not going to kill yourself. And we both know it. You've never taken the easy way out.

ELEANOR: Not that you know of, anyway. Have I been a good mother?

GRACE: *(W.C. Fields)* Best mother I ever had!

ELEANOR: That's a clever way of not answering.

GRACE: I don't know if I can say what you need to hear.

ELEANOR: And what would that be?

GRACE: That we're the best of friends and you made sacrifices for me your whole life and I wouldn't change a minute...

ELEANOR: I have made more sacrifices than you'll ever know! We are the best of friends, aren't we?

GRACE: We're the best friends we can be. We're not very good at it.

ELEANOR: My fault no doubt!

GRACE: No, but… you've always been too critical.

ELEANOR: I only criticize you for your own good. For all the good it's done.

GRACE: Oh Mom, let's not do this. We're both tired and we have a lot to do tomorrow. You promised the new owners. I've been here a week – we've packed nothing.

ELEANOR: I haven't said one critical thing since you got here.

GRACE: *(Mimics Eleanor)* "Oh Grace, look at the size of you. I **will** have to take the bigger apartment!"

ELEANOR: Constructive criticism!

GRACE: Jesus Mom, you're the fat Nazi. You've been telling me how fat I am since I was ten years old. How is it constructive? Do you really think I don't know? Do you think if you tell me just one more time, I'll wake up the next morning, thank you, start a crash diet, and become that perfect daughter you always wanted!

ELEANOR: One lives in hope!

GRACE: It's not working Mom.

ELEANOR: You're too sensitive.

(Grace goes into the apartment. One of those motion-sensitive birds chirps. Tweet Tweet.)

GRACE: And I'm too sober!

ELEANOR: See if the dog's ready to come in Grace.

(Grace sticks her head through the door to the balcony. Tweet Tweet.)

GRACE: Mom we really really don't have a dog. It's just me, you and a plastic bird.

ELEANOR: I love that bird.

GRACE: Rum and coke Mom?

ELEANOR: It's awfully fattening, dear.

GRACE: Rum and diet coke then?

ELEANOR: There are beer nuts in the cupboard over the fridge.

GRACE: No thanks, not hungry.

ELEANOR: And there are chips.

GRACE: No, I'm good.

ELEANOR: Cheese and crackers.

GRACE: Do **you** want something to eat, Mom?

ELEANOR: Oh no, I never eat between meals. It really puts the pounds on! Maybe something you should...

GRACE: Do you want a Goddamn drink or not?

ELEANOR: Talk about a rock and the deep blue sea!

(Grace sits by Eleanor and picks up some brochures).

GRACE: Remember Jameson House? It was unique, and like they say here, cozy, rustic, nestled in a 50 acre wooded compound with all the amenities…

ELEANOR: Translation: run down, ramshackle old barn, so far into the woods I'll never be found.

GRACE: I'll send out the search party. And they offer round the clock nursing care, home-style meals served in the comfort of your room.

ELEANOR: Lots of nosey nurses. And YOU NEVER GET TO LEAVE YOUR ROOM! Slide your meals in through a slot.

I could afford to live there for the rest of my life! Because after a month I wouldn't want to live!

And that delivery cart - wouldn't be surprised if they wheel the visitors in on it. Squeak, squeak, squeak a hundred times a day, up and down that corridor and it as long as a wet Sunday with a toothache.

GRACE: The residents seemed nice, happy.

ELEANOR: The inmates?

Do you mean the ones that met us at the door quacking or the ones tied in their seats who haven't lifted their heads for years? Waiting for the big 100 so a loved one, if they bothered to visit, could stick a cake under their face and take a picture for the local paper. The Casket. Now there's a forerunner for you!

GRACE: Maybe the other place would be better. One bedroom assisted living apartments. Maybe even a two bedroom?

ELEANOR: So you can move in when you leave you latest bozo! I don't believe that boat is going to fly.

GRACE: The apartment is right here in town, beautiful gardens, a lifeline.

ELEANOR: I don't remember a stove…

GRACE: You only have a week left to decide.

(Grace disappears inside, Tweet Tweet)

ELEANOR: They are more expensive. I'll have to plan to die in a year or two.

There will be nothing left for you when I die.

GRACE: Doesn't matter.

ELEANOR; Oh Grace don't talk so wooden! You've screwed your chances. That many husbands you'd think one might have worked. And I don't mean the marriage, I mean the man.

GRACE: Ted works!

ELEANOR: Is that his name? I must have missed that one! Imagine forgetting… I'm afraid to move. What if I never find the room again?

(Grace sticks her head through the door, Tweet Tweet.)

GRACE: There'll be lots of room there. More importantly at the moment, I can't find the rum …

ELEANOR: Grace? What are you doing here? How did you get in?

GRACE: I came last week. To help you pack. \

ELEANOR: Pack? Are we taking a trip?

Grace: You have to move Mom…

ELEANOR: Why do I have to move? Because **you** think I'm lonely! I'm perfectly fine here.

Not having a stove is not going to make me feel less alone.

I'll have you know that at least a dozen people came to see me last week.

GRACE: Firemen don't count!

ELEANOR: Besides all the people I want to see are dead or gaga.

And the dog Grace.

GRACE: No dog, Mom. Wait, I think I know what we can do. Don't go anywhere.

(Grace ducks so she won't set off the bird and disappears into the apartment again.)

ELEANOR: Like there's somewhere I could hide!

(Grace comes back holding a coin. Tweet Tweet.)

GRACE: Remember what Dad used to do when I was having trouble making up my mind.

ELEANOR: I miss your Father. Why did he have to die? My life would have been so different.

GRACE: We can't know how it would have been different, Mom.

ELEANOR: It had to have been better!

GRACE: You can't know that Mom. The only thing that's certain is that life's uncertain.

ELEANOR: I know, I know, eat dessert first. That's three quarters of your problem.

GRACE: Do you remember what you said to me the time I lost all the weight?

ELEANOR: No, but I'm sure you do!

GRACE: *(mimics Eleanor)* "What Grace, you came home to die?"

ELEANOR: You did look awful.

(Grace shows Eleanor the coin.)

GRACE: Dad always did this with a big flourish!

ELEANOR: You're going to decide my fate with the toss of a coin? You know Grace, you have to live with your choices your whole life. What if I make another mistake?

GRACE: Picking the wrong place to live has to be better than burning the house down!

ELEANOR: It's my god-damn house and I'll burn it down if I want. You are not deciding my life for me.

GRACE: I'm not going to decide anything. You are. Heads you go to Jameson House in the country and someone looks after you. Tails, you stay her, in town, at Colonial Towers and someone helps you a little.

ELEANOR: This is stupid!

GRACE: Dad didn't think so.

ELEANOR: He loved me Grace, but he didn't really know me. Didn't know what I'd done.

GRACE: What did you do?

ELEANOR: Let's get this over with. Heads I live long and miserable in Jameson House. Tails, I die quickly in poverty.

(Grace tosses the coin, catches it and keeps her hand covering it.)

GRACE: What do you **want** it to be, Mom?

ELEANOR: Tails. But what is it?

GRACE: Doesn't matter. You've decided. It's assisted living in Colonial Towers.

ELEANOR: You tricked me, Grace.

GRACE: And no doubt, I'll rot in hell for it!

ELEANOR: We could get a double room.

GRACE: Come on Mom, let's go find the rum.

(Lights down. Tweet Tweet.)

End of Scene.

THE PINK PARLOR

By Susan Lieberman

In 1953, United Nations economist Grace Ellers – four months pregnant after many miscarriages – finds her world collapsing. The witch-hunting Senate Sub-Committee on Internal Security has infiltrated her department and subpoenaed her. Grace's writer husband Cliff is conducting an affair with a bookshop owner, Florence Dunn, despite his wife's delicate pregnancy. When Grace learns that her FBI file includes information on her husband's affair with Florence, she goes to see her sister Helen for advice.

Cast:
Grace Ellers – 31-year-old economist, pregnant
Helen Branhill – 39-year-old Park Avenue matron, Grace's sister
Wendy Waldman – 45-year-old science teacher, Helen's friend

ACT II, SCENE 2

HELEN'S APARTMENT

HELEN sits in the living room with WENDY WALDMAN, a grammar school science teacher.

HELEN: ...There's no shame in doing repairs.

WENDY: That's what I told Aunt Sadie. I'm a science teacher, after all. If there's one thing I know about it's electricity -- that was my best unit for the kids. They'd rush home afterwards and try to rewire their mother's bedroom lamps.

HELEN: Did anyone electrocute themselves?

WENDY: Not that I know of. That was always a problem -- explaining to twelve-year-olds that what makes for a good experiment at school can be a disaster at home. Well, it's not a problem anymore, is it? No one's about to let me near young people.

HELEN: It can't possibly last forever.

WENDY: If I did private tutoring at home instead of "manual labor," it'd be less embarrassing for Ted. That's what Aunt Sadie said. So I said, no thanks, I do much better repairing radios and TVs. People who wouldn't let me in the same room as their child are very happy to slip me their broken radio through the back door. I can't make a Communist out of an RCA, can I?

HELEN: Oh, Wendy!

WENDY: If you ever have a problem with your set, just call. I'll be over in a second, no charge.

HELEN: We don't have a television.

WENDY: You don't?

HELEN: No.

WENDY: You're missing Ernie Kovacs.

HELEN: We're sort of backwards.

WENDY: Ernie Kovacs is marvelous. So is *The Arthur Murray Party*. I'd be lost without them. The TV set is great company now that no one comes to see us.

HELEN: What about your Aunt Sadie?

WENDY: She calls from the pay phone.

(Doorbell rings.)

HELEN: Excuse me.

(SHE lets in GRACE.)

GRACE: I just had to see you. Fred met me up in Washington Heights --

(sees WENDY)

Oh, excuse me. I should have phoned first.

HELEN: Wendy Waldman -- my sister Grace.

GRACE: Yes, of course. Nice to see you.

(There is an awkward pause.)

HELEN: Oh what's the use pretending! Grace has been subpoenaed by the McCarran committee.

WENDY: Welcome to the blacklist.

HELEN: She's not on the list at the moment.

WENDY: You'll get there, just wait.

HELEN: Wendy, I think it'd be better if we didn't jump to conclusions.

WENDY: Whether you rat on your best friend or let yourself get raked over the coals, there's no getting out of trouble. Everyone avoids you.

HELEN: We've found a very good civil rights attorney...

WENDY: Lot of good that'll do you.

HELEN: Wendy, if you don't mind, you're upsetting Grace and right now --

GRACE: I can speak for myself. There's much truth in what you say, Mrs. Waldman.

HELEN: But you don't need it hammered into you.

WENDY: Was I hammering?

GRACE: No.

HELEN: Yes.

WENDY: I think you girls need some privacy.

(WENDY gets up and puts her hat on.)

HELEN: I'll be in touch. Stanley wants to see Ted one of these days.

WENDY: His days are certainly open.

HELEN: If anyone needs their radio repaired, I'll call you.

WENDY: Be sure to use a pay phone.

HELEN: I will.

WENDY: I'll let myself out.

(to GRACE)

I didn't mean to hammer. Your sister's a good egg.

GRACE: Yes, she is.

(SHE leaves. GRACE waits a moment before speaking.)

GRACE: Why is she going into the kitchen?

HELEN: She's using the back stairs.

GRACE: Why?

HELEN: I don't want the doorman spreading the word that she's been here.

GRACE: I thought she's your friend.

HELEN: You know it's not easy. Stanley could lose his job if the bank finds out the Waldmans visit us.

GRACE: What a terrible, terrible way to live.

HELEN: I hate it, Grace.

GRACE: Nothing's comfortable anymore. Riding the subway, I thought, why am I doing this? Why am I going all the way up to Washington Heights to talk to my boss? Why are Fred and I so afraid of being seen? That was the best part of going to work every morning -- being with people who fit together like an old worn-out puzzle.

HELEN: What did Fred say?

GRACE: Cliff and Florence are in my file. Her bookstore is an alleged Communist front. And Cliff is still seeing her. It was in the file too.

HELEN: Damn him!

GRACE: Fred thought that if I say who was at the book signing, I might be able to get out of testifying.

HELEN: Naming names?

GRACE: He says I ought to do it.

HELEN: I suppose he's right.

GRACE: You do? But...what about Ted Waldman? Someone named his name to the FBI.

HELEN: Ted is an honest, loyal human being. You can hardly say that about Florence.

GRACE: True.

HELEN: Somebody else will point the finger if you don't.

GRACE: What about the other people at the book signing?

HELEN: Don't be a fool, Grace. If you take the Fifth to protect a few groupies who'd sell you out in a minute, you'll look guilty as hell. No one will publish Cliff --

GRACE: But he's not --

HELEN: He's your husband. When your face ends up in the papers, only the lefty publishers would look at his work and then you'll really be ostracized.

GRACE: I hadn't thought about his career.

HELEN: He won't have one if this thing explodes. He'll lose classes -- and that means he won't be able to support you and the baby.

GRACE: We'd go to North Carolina. Cliff can always get a teaching job.

HELEN: I wouldn't count on it.

GRACE: But he's got family there.

HELEN: Don't underestimate how much damage can be done by that subpoena!

GRACE: It's not even for anything real.

HELEN: Real or imaginary, it doesn't matter. A wall of cardboard casts as big a shadow as a wall of brick.

GRACE: You're not going to make me use a pay phone to call here, are you?

HELEN: Don't be ridiculous.

GRACE: The way you're talking --

HELEN: I wouldn't do that to my own sister. Just give that stupid committee what they want, all right?

GRACE: If I don't, will I have to use the back stairs?

HELEN: Florence Dunn is destroying your life!

GRACE: But if I don't name names --

HELEN: Destroying it, do you hear me? Jeopardizing your pregnancy! Your baby and your family come first!

GRACE: You're screaming.

HELEN: *(lowering her voice)*

A little boy was asked to leave Pammie and Andrew's school because his father got dismissed from the State Department...

GRACE: So, it ruins everything for the children, too.

HELEN: That's what happened at my son and daughter's school.

GRACE: It's for the best, then, that I use the back stairs. Isn't it?

HELEN: We're not at that point.

GRACE: I need to understand the rules.

HELEN: You'd ask the same of me, wouldn't you? Wouldn't you?

GRACE: I think it's time for me to go.

HELEN: I'd never do anything that would be dangerous for you.

GRACE: I understand.

HELEN: Not in your heart you don't. I can tell. I'm not your sister for nothing. I know what's going on in your heart --

GRACE: Right now, my heart is so full of holes, I'm surprised it's still beating.

(GRACE goes to leave the room in the same direction that WENDY did.)

HELEN: What are you doing?

GRACE: I'm taking the back stairs.

HELEN: Don't do that! Nothing's happened yet!

GRACE: A wall of cardboard casts as big a shadow as a wall of brick.

HELEN: Grace! Wait!

GRACE: There's nothing to wait for.

(SHE leaves out the back. LIGHTS out.)

End of Scene.

PATIENT HM

By Vanda

CAST of CHARACTERS
YOUNG H.M.: In the beginning H.M. is an exuberant boy
filled with life, ready to charge into adult life. Later he
becomes embittered, angry, disappointed. He wears glasses.
BEV : HM's girlfriend. She is a coquettish teenaged girl
who only wants to get married and have babies like most
teenaged girls of her generation. (1940's)
DAD: Dad is a hardworking electrician with the values of
working class people of the 1940s, 1950s.
MOM: A working class housewife with the values of that
class in the 1940s, 1950s.

Setting/Time
The play takes in the HM's family's home in the fifties.

MOM and DAD sit at the table, having a cup of coffee. DAD
reads a book. MOM studies a collage of cards depicting
different places: Wisconsin, Miami, etc. She's trying to
figure out where to put another card.

MOM: He's not getting any better.

DAD: Uh, huh.

MOM: The pills aren't helping at all.

DAD: Uh, huh.

MOM: He's completely stopped adding any cards to this
collection. Mrs. Walker gave him this new one from
Vermont and he just threw it on his dresser like he didn't
care. I thought maybe if I glued it on for him he'd get
interested again. He never talks about the places he wants to
see anymore. Oh, Gus, what's gonna become of him?

Gus keeps reading with no sign that's he's heard.

Will you listen to me!

DAD: I am listening! What do you want me to say? You think I don't know he's not getting better. You think I don't want to do something to make him get better? But what, Mommy? What? What am I sposed to do about it?

MOM: I heard about a doctor.

DAD: Another one? How much is this one gonna cost?

MOM: I'll get a job.

DAD: No, you won't. No wife of mine is gonna work. I can take care of my own.

MOM: Maybe we could take out a loan and…

DAD: This family does not buy on credit! We pay our bills or we go without! What kinda father would I be if I let H think buying on time was okay? I'll get a second job.

MOM: But, Gus you already work so hard at the plant. I heard they were hiring over at the high school cafeteria. I could….

DAD: No! And I don't wanna hear no more about. It's settled. I'll start looking for a second job tomorrow. Take him to the new doctor. Maybe he can do something.

He goes back to his book. MOM pats his shoulder, lovingly

MOM: You're a good man, Gus M. And a good father.

H storms into the house wearing an open graduation gown; Beverly follows behind him.

BEVERLY: Don't worry about it. It's gonna be okay.

YOUNG HM:

Tears off the graduation gown and throws it in the garbage

There! That's where that thing belongs!

To BEVERLY

Okay? Nothing's gonna be okay ever again.

MOM: What happened?

YOUNG HM: They're not letting me walk with my class for graduation. I have to sit with the audience.

BEVERLY: I'll sit with you.

MOM: But why?

YOUNG HM: Why? You know why? Because they're afraid I'll have a "fit" on their stage and mess up their pretty ceremony.

MOM: Oh, honey, I'm so sorry.

DAD starts to leave.

Where are you going now? It's Saturday.

DAD: Bowling. Some of the boys and me…

YOUNG HM: Why don't you come right out and say it, Dad. You can't stand even being near me. You can't stand having a mental for a son.

DAD: *Moving as if he's going to reach out to his son.*

H…

He exits.

BEVERLY: Don't worry, H. It's gonna be okay.

YOUNG HM: It will not be 'okay'? Don't you get that? It'll never be okay again. What are you still hanging around me for?

MOM: H…

YOUNG HM: Don't you know I can never marry you? Ever.

BEVERLY: What?

MOM: H don't.

YOUNG HM: Freaks like me can't get married.

MOM: Well, there's this doctor and…

YOUNG HM: Stop it, Mom! There is no doctor! There's never gonna be a doctor.

BEVERLY: What are you saying, H?

YOUNG HM: I can't give you no babies. We can't risk having any more of me around. I'm a mental. I can't do nothing. I can't make babies. I can't drive. I can't graduate. I can't do nothing.

MOM: Beverly, he's just upset. He doesn't mean it.

YOUNG HM: I do so mean it. Get outta here! Run, run! Before you catch it. Go find someone normal to have babies with. You're never gonna have babies with me.

HE runs at her playing the part of a crazy person.

Never! Never! Never! I'm a mental! I'm a mental! I'm a, a...

Suddenly his body begins to shakes. He falls. He has one of the worst seizures he's ever had. MOM goes into action, moving furniture out of the way, putting the spoon into his mouth, loosening clothes. BEVERLY stands watching becoming more and more disturbed by the sight.

BEVERLY: I'm sorry, Mrs. M. I can't do this. I can't spend my life doing this. I can't. I can't.

She runs out

End of Scene.

SMOKE

By Helen Shay

Synopsis
This one-act play is based on the experiences suffered by a
woman playwright in Indonesia. It focuses and distils such
experiences into an interrogation encounter. Whilst echoing
the actual politics, which were in question, it also seeks to
explore issues of idealism and freedom of speech.

Characters:
Vinya, 40, former academic, writer and mother, now
incarcerated for producing subversive drama.
Yawud, 50, interrogator and rising star in new political
order. Also a former academic.

Setting:
Room with two chairs at each end of a table. Vinya is seated
on one, staring at the table. Yawud is pacing round her and
the table.

YAWUD: Must I ask again? Play?

VINYA: Play what?

YAWUD: Not games. Not with me, Vinya.

Yawud sits down, takes out a packet of cigarettes. Vinya
looks up. He takes one out, places it in his mouth and is
about to light it, as Vinya watches him intently.

YAWUD: Some things you miss, don't you, Vinya?

Yawud takes the unlit cigarette out of his mouth and rolls it
across the table to Vinya. Vinya picks up the cigarette and
stares at it.

YAWUD: Light?

Yawud laughs and walks round the front of the table to Vinya. He crouches beside her.

YAWUD: You don't have to miss everything, Vinya.

Yawud lights the cigarette, still crouching beside her. Vinya takes a long drag.

YAWUD: See, I can be kind to you. *(Strokes her cheek)* But you must be kind to me.

VINYA: What kind of `kind'?

Vinya blows smoke in Yawud's face. Yawud suppresses a cough, rises then laughs and walks round the back of the table to his seat.

YAWUD: Oh, they all say you're a very kind woman, Vinya. Your international reputation. Your compassionate soul. How does it go? `Full of the milk of human kindness'. No, that's wrong. `Too full of the milk of human kindness.' You see, I like theatre as well, Vinya. We have a lot in common, you and I.

Vinya snorts.

VINYA: A few lines from Shakespeare and we're soulmates? Still, it's a novel chat-up line, at least. 'Do you come here often?' is rather wasted on someone nine months in prison.

YAWUD: That's it, Vinya. Relax. Make a few jokes. It's what I always admired about you. Your spunk. Others would not see it in so *(Beat)* endearing a light. But me, you can talk to.

VINYA: Only it's very bad luck. (Beat) To quote 'Macbeth', I mean.

YAWUD: No such thing as luck, good or bad, unless you make you're own. But luck is not hard work or talent, Vinya. You've tried those. Look where it got you. In here. Such bad luck. Good luck, my luck, is pragmatism.

VINYA: Like joining the New Order?

YAWUD: If it takes me up.

VINYA: And pushes others down. Follow the blood-brick road.

YAWUD: Better than the red-brick to mediocrity, I was stuck on. Not that that was ever your way, Vinya. Golden girl, darling of the dons. Book after book, play after play. Only it wasn't all play, was it, Vinya. Especially your last play.

VINYA: I couldn't stay forever, cosy inside some drawing-room drama. So suitable for a woman., of course. I had to go outside. I couldn't ignore what was happening there.

YAWUD: You think I could? So many years in an office, no bigger than your cell. Back-room boy, reader, researcher, non-doer. Like I said, we have a lot in common, you and I. We both had to do something. You wrote plays. I acted.

VINYA: You mean you joined in the 'action'. The disappearances? The cover-ups?

YAWUD: *(Bangs table)* You're the one being interrogated here.

Vinya starts smoking the cigarette quickly and intensely, as he continues.

YAWUD: *(Softening)* You know this was my old table? I rescued it. It was when they sacked the university to burn the books. It's a sort of souvenir of when I was the prisoner, in that old life. Ideals and pig-shit. *(Beat)* But we're here for you to talk, Vinya, not me. Talk, Vinya. You must be very lonely. Your daughter visits what? Just once a month? You know I arranged that for you.

VINYA: Thank you, Yawud.

YAWUD: That's better. `Yawud'. We're becoming friends already. You need a friend, Vinya.

Vinya stubs out the end of the cigarette, on the table.

VINYA: I need a cigarette.

Yawud goes to give her another cigarette, repeating the same fondling actions as before. As he walks back to his seat, he lights himself a cigarette.

YAWUD: Where were we, my friend? Ah, yes, plays. *(mock posh)* The the-atre. *(ordinary voice)* You see, when you love it as I do, you get to recognise a certain *(draws on his cigarette)* style.

Vinya is smoking quickly again.

YAWUD: In a writer, I mean. You know? `The play's the thing, wherein I'll catch ....' Well, what do you think, Vinya?

VINYA: *(drawing on cigarette, then stubbing it out)* I think it's a good brand.

YAWUD: *(Sharp)* I told you, no games, not with me. *(Soft)* Here.

Yawud passes her the cigarette from his mouth.

YAWUD: This is not a good place for a nicotine addict.

VINYA: Where did you get such a good brand?

YAWUD: Would you like black coffee and cocaine too?
All the trappings of creativity, for my little artist.

VINYA: Where did you get -?

YAWUD: I'm asking the questions. *(Softer)* Oh, come,
come, Vinya. I've turned a blind eye long enough. Your
daughter's little packages. You must expect the odd routine
search of a detainee's quarters.

VINYA: Quarter? Not even an eighth. A four by four cell.
A blanket and a bucket. *(looking at cigarette)*   You stole
these from me. When? That day the guard made me -

*She stubs the cigarette out hard, crushing and twisting it into
the table, long after it is already out*

YAWUD: Yes, I'm sorry about the guard, Vinya. That
shouldn't have happened. A woman of your intellectual
standing. That's why you need a friend.

*Yawud walks over and lights her another cigarette, in semi-
tender manner as before. This time he stays crouched beside
her.*

YAWUD: Let me be your friend, Vinya.

*Vinya blows smoke in his face again. He coughs, but does
not laugh this time, then walks back to his seat.*

YAWUD: You are weak, Vinya. Look at you. Desperate
for your `ciggies'. Weak, like all you intellectuals. But the

New Order will cure you. `Too full o' the milk of human kindness.' Or nicotine in your case. But we shall `catch the nearest way'. Such decadence, Vinya. Nicotine and theatre have no place in the New Order.

VINYA: I thought you liked *(mock posh as him before)* the the-atre.

YAWUD: Some theatre.

VINYA: Official theatre.

YAWUD: Of course. I am a discerning critic. For instance, your last play interests me greatly.

VINYA: Ah but that was not `official' or I wouldn't be here.

YAWUD: Your last play, Vinya. Quite an artistic development. From mere subversive to outright revolutionary. But I would argue that your heroine was fatally flawed.

VINYA: I wrote about abuse of workers' rights.

YAWUD: Rights don't belong to those who have to work.

VINYA: Why should I be in here for stating the law?

YAWUD: In here, I am the law. *(Beat)* 'Everything starts with the individual.' Now where have I heard that line? 'Fighting is always personal – as personal as sex.' Now that has a certain style, way beyond the drawing-room. 'And war, politics and repression are the most personal of all.' How many times did I see that performance? Couldn't stay away from the sound of your words. 'To loose courage is –'

VINYA: 'to loose everything.'

Vinya starts to smoke in an agitated manner.

YAWUD: Good words, Vinya. Did your pen shake as you wrote them? *(Pause, then softer)* I wrote once, you know, *(sighs)* upon a time and upon this table.

Yawud strokes his hand over the table surface.

VINYA: What happened?

YAWUD: Like you, I looked outside. I saw too much. Not the pen, but the very words shook. 'To loose courage'

VINYA: Perhaps we can be friends, Yawud. I could show you how to push through words and fear. *(Beat)* Why isn't this table your desk anymore? Why make it into an interrogation tool?

YAWUD: *(Bangs table)* I told you, I ask the questions. Let's get back to the 'personal', your 'personal. *(Beat)* Let's discuss your last play.

End of Scene.

Author Bios

Suzanne Bailie is an award winning playwright with works performed throughout the United States. She has a Masters Degree in Education and frequently uses her writing skills to build interest in subjects and creatively engage her students. Suzanne enjoys creating experimental abstract art, playing her ukulele, drinking good coffee and contemplating Seattle rain.

Shirley Barrie co-founded the Tricycle Theatre in London, England and Straight Stitching Productions in Toronto, which first produced *Carrying the Calf*, earning awards for both writing and production. Recently: Shoestring Opera toured schools with her libretto, *Bozo's Fortune* and she has written two plays for 4th Line Theatre. *Beautiful Lady, Tell Me...*, a vaudevillian, musical murder mystery, was produced in 2007 and *Queen Marie*, a play about Marie Dressler, will be produced in 2012. www.shirleybarrie.ca

Lynne S. Brandon has an MFA in Playwriting, Smith College, 2008. *Bare Chested* monologue, SAS Playfest, Atlantis Playmakers, Lowell, MA, 2006. *Bare Chested* staged-reading, Smith College, 2007. ISOSCELES, Smith College, 2008. Scenes from THE RANDOMNESS OF NATURE, Playwrights' Platform, Boston, MA 2008. AT THE LINE staged-reading, Boston, 2010. Member, Dramatists Guild of America, Inc.

Hindi Brooks writes for stage, page, television, and has written the book, <u>Writing the Ten-Minute Play</u>. She is translated into other languages and has won awards. Member: The Dramatists Guild, The Writers Guild, PEN, Alliance of Los Angeles Playwrights, Who's Who of American Women. She has taught playwriting at UCLA, various workshops, and privately.

Emily Cicchini is resident playwright at The Pollyanna Theatre Company, which has produced many of her plays, including *Edward, the Owl, and the Calico Cat* (published by Dramatic), *A Christmas Rose, A Dragon's Happy Day*,

Pattern Nation, and *Just Bee*. Other titles include: *Art Beat, Becoming Bronté,* and *Mays and Terese*.

Christina Cigala is originally from San Antonio, Texas. She holds a BA from Baylor University where she studied with Horton Foote and is currently completing her MFA in Playwriting at the Actors Studio Drama School. Her work has appeared in New York, San Antonio, Houston, Dallas, Waco, and Los Angeles; primarily representing the American South with empathy, but mostly making people laugh.

Anita Chandwaney is a performer, playwright and director. Her first full-length play, *Gandhi Marg*, won 2nd place in Writers Digest's 75th Annual Stage Play Competition and was a finalist for Chicago Dramatist's Many Voices Project. She and MEH Lewis co-wrote *Thirst*, which is a semi-finalist for the 2011 O'Neill Playwrights Conference and an Honored Finalist for the Collaboration Award given by the New York Coalition of Women in Arts & Media. Her short plays and monologues include, *2020, Instant Recall, Helpline, Judging Jaya,* and *On-Track*. Anita is the recipient of a 3Arts Fellowship, Ragdale Residency, Neighborhood Arts Project grant, and serves on the Artist Advisory Council for the Ragdale Artist Retreat. Her Chicago acting credits include, Pulitzer Finalist *Miss Witherspoon* by Christopher Durang at Next Theatre, and work with Lookingglass, Organic, Remy Bumppo, Pegasus, Collaboraction, Stage Left, Silk Road, Strawdog, Live, Center Theatre and Rasaka - for which she was Founding Executive Director and co-producer of Jeff-winning *The Masrayana*. In NYC she worked with Ensemble Studio Theatre, Playwrights Horizons and Open Eye New Stagings. You can catch Anita in *Enemy of the People* at Stage Left, where she is an Ensemble Member.

Judy Chicurel's work has appeared in national and regional publications, including The New York Times and Newsday. Productions and readings of her plays have taken place at the Cherry Lane Theatre, Sage Theater, Metropolitan Playhouse, and New Perspectives Theatre, where she was a Women's

Work Playwrights fellow. She is a member of the New York Writers Coalition and currently a fellow at the City University of New York Graduate Center Writers Institute. Judy lives in Brooklyn, N.Y.

Natalya Churlyaeva was born in a military prosecutor's family (Novosibirsk, 1955), graduated from the Institute of Nonferrous Metals and Gold (Krasnoyarsk, 1977), defended her first doctoral thesis in Mathematical Economy Studies at the Institute of Industrial Organization and Management (Novosibirsk, 1983), and since then worked as a lecturing professor at the Siberian Aerospace University (Krasnoyarsk). Here she developed another thesis on the Maintenance of Quality Education of Engineers at the Market Conditions from the Competence Point of View, and in 2008 defended it to become a full-doctor of pedagogical sciences.

Cecilia Copeland is the Founder and Artistic Director of New York Madness. Her Full Lengths Include: Light of Night Developed at New Dramatists, upcoming production with IATI Theater. BIOLIFE Semifinalist for The O'Neill Playwright's Conference, Finalist for Mabou Mines Residency, and workshop at TerraNOVA. 'The Wicked Son', named one of the "Top Three Best New Jewish Plays," by the JPP. Courting SLP's New Play Winner and reading in the undergroundzero festival. One Women, winner of the Lennis J. Holm Scholarship. One Acts: Amusement Bomber adapted into a short film with Metro Screen Australia. BILLBOARDS GREATEST HITS Commissioned and Produced by The Performing Arts High School. Velvet Eggs presented along with, KCACTF Finalist, Playing by IATI Theater. Other short plays have been produced by the Anarchist Theatre Festival of Montreal, Culture Project, CAPSLOCK THEATRE, and The Disreputables. She participated Write Out Front as featured in the New York Times and the 31 Plays in 31 Days Project. With New York Madness her plays have been presented at Ensemble Studios Theatre, The Cherry Lane Theater, INTAR Theater, and ESPA Primary Stages. Cecilia is an Alumna of the Writers

Workshops at University of Iowa BA with Honors and Ohio University MFA.

Trina Davies is an actor, writer, and director. Trina's award-winning plays include *Multi User Dungeon* (Alberta Playwrights Network Discovery Award 2000), *Shatter* (Alberta Theatre Projects 24 hr Playwriting Competition 2003, Short List for International Prism Residency Prize 2003, Short List for New Works of Merit 13th Street Repertory Theatre NYC 2004, Short List for International Dramatic Literature Prize Media Arts Literature and Sound San Francisco), *The Auction* (Alberta Writer's Guild Short Play Award 2002), and *Waxworks* (Alberta Playwrights Network Award 2007). For more information access www.trinadavies.com

Jessica DiGiacinto is a playwright and screenwriter currently living in Boulder, Colorado. She received her MFA from the Tisch School of the Arts in 2008.

Jennifer Farmer is a native of Chattanooga, Tennessee who currently lives and works in London. Jennifer was named one of the UK's newest theatre talents by The Guardian in 2004. Compact Failure premièred to critical acclaim in 2004 and Bulletproof Soul was shortlisted for the 2008 Brian Way Award. Her work includes *Clean* (BBC Radio 3, 2003), *A Million Different People* (BBC Radio 4, 2005), *Stutter* (Hotbed Festival, 2008), *These Four Streets* (Birmingham Rep, 2009), *.54* (Stour Space/ViewTube, 2011).

Colette Freedman is an internationally produced writer who was voted "One of 50 to Watch" by The Dramatist's Guild. She has had over 15 plays produced including her critically acclaimed adaptation of *Iphigenia at Aulis* (Hayworth Theatre), *Deconstructing the Torah* (Odyssey Theatre), *Ellipses...* (Grand Prize Winner – Palm Springs Fest), *Rock, Paper, Scissors* (Finalist Harrogate Festival UK), *First to the Egg* (Grand Prize Winner), *Serial Killer Barbie* (Brooklyn Publishers). Her play *Sister Cities* was the hit of the 2008 Edinburgh Fringe and earned five star reviews: It has been produced around the country and is gearing up for productions in Paris (*Une Ville, Une Soeur*) and Rome (*Le Quattro Sorelle*). She has won over 60 awards for her commercial writing and directing, including the International Summit Award, Telly, and Communicator Awards. She received a B.A. in English from Haverford College, where she was an All-American lacrosse player and voted Philadelphia Player of the Year in field hockey. She also attended Colgate University, where she earned a Masters Degree in Teaching with an emphasis on Drama and Literature. She has just co-written, with International bestselling novelist Jackie Collins, the play *Jackie Collins Hollywood Lies*. Freedman and New York Times best selling author Michael Scott, have just sold their thriller *13 Hallows* to Tor/Macmillan. Member of the Dramatist's Guild. www.curtainrise.com

Catherine Frid's recent plays include *GuineaPigging* (Alumnae Theatre), *Solitary* (InspiraTO Festival), *Homegrown* (SummerWorks, Toronto District School Board/Ontario Justice Education Network), *Dead Cat Bounce* (Toronto Fringe, Unhinged Festival), *Buff* (New Ideas, Arts & Letters Club), and *Over the Edge* (Arts & Letters Club, Eastbound Theatre). *Us and Them* was published in Thirtysomethings: Mother-Daughter Monologues, ICWP Press (2009).

Lea K. Galanter is a Seattle-based playwright with a writing career spanning three decades. She is a member of two playwriting groups and has performed with numerous Seattle theatre groups. By day, Lea is a technical editor and writer.

Cheryl Games' plays include: *Augusta* (Paul T. Nolan One-Act Play Award, Writer's Digest Award), *Half-Baked, Little Death* (Actors Theatre of Louisville National 10-Minute Play Contest finalist), *Trip Twenty* (CATCO/Greater Columbus Arts Council Fellowship, Fred & Howard Best-In-Fest Award, Tears for Sale, One Practice Round, To Be Confirmed, Onus On Us (ID America Festival, Future Tenant Play Festival). Her plays have been produced in New York (Circle in the Square Downtown, St. Clement's

Church, Connection Theatre Company, Quo Vadimus Arts), Los Angeles (The Attic Theatre, The American Renegade Theatre, Cypress College), Greenvile, SC (Warehouse Theatre), Pittsuburgh (Future Tenants) and Columbus, Ohio (The Enjoy Theatre, CATCO).

Tara Goldstein is a playwright based in Toronto and the founder of Gailey Road Productions, which produces women-centered research-informed theatre (www.gaileyroad.com). Tara's latest project Harriet's House, a contemporary drama about international adoption in a same-sex family, was produced at Hart House Theatre during the Toronto Pride Festival in July 2010.

Evan Guilford-Blake is the author of 18 published plays, available through neoNuma Arts, Playscripts, Eldridge, Heartland, and others. His work has been performed internationally. Evan has won 33 playwriting competitions including the Tennessee Williams Competition twice, the only playwright to do so. More information is at www.guilford-blake.com/evan.

Molly Hagan is a graduate of Ohio University. Her short works have been performed on the Kennedy Center Stage and can be read in "North Northwest," an anthology published by the Northwest Playwrights Alliance.

Meg Haley is a graduate of St. Olaf College in Minnesota where she studied English and Theatre. Meg currently spends her mornings writing and works, in the afternoon, with 3-6 year old children at Austin Montessori School. Meg is a member of ScriptWorks, a local Texas playwrights' organization, where her work is produced regularly.

G.L. (Geralyn) Horton has acted in NYC, at the Edinburgh Fringe and in the American premieres of contemporary Irish plays at Boston's Sugan Theatre. Her web-published scripts have had productions in theatres all over the world and in 200 high schools and colleges in the USA.

R. Johns - Rosemary has a First Honours degree in Drama from Manchester University, UK. She received a one year scholarship to Tulane University New Orleans and a two year scholarship to UCR in the USA. She now lives in Australia where all the influences of many wonderful countries inform her work. She works as a writer, actor and director. This play and other work can be found at The Australian Script Centre (Hobart) www.ozscript.org and through Currency Press Australia.

Vivien Jones started writing drama as a mature student, has had rehearsed readings at The Traverse, Edinburgh in their Fringe programme, and has had site specific historical drama performed at Whithorn and various renaissance locations. She has done short plays and monologues with the Swallow Theatre and often works with early musicians; very much likes working with actors.

Inkeri Kilpinen has had the courage to tackle difficult subjects that most of her contemporaries would not be willing to touch.In her plays, Kilpinen explores a wide range of topics such as the treatment of mentally ill patients, weaknesses of municipal democracy, communicational barriers between generations, and the fear of narcotics. The scope of her focus is equally diverse, with some of her works exploring international politics and fates of entire ethnic populations, while others concentrate on the lives of individuals. Throughout her work, the role of women has also been prominently featured in Kilpinen's output.This enormous variety, combined with the constant quality of her work, has earned her much accolade not only in Finland, where many of her works have had a direct impact on the public discourse, but also abroad.

Shirley King's first play won a California Arts Council contest. Since then more than 60 of her plays have been performed in the United States, Canada, the UK, and Korea. She lives in Benicia, California.

Jean Klein's "Unreasonable Possession" was a semifinalist at Reverie Productions and will be workshopped at the Earl Hamner Theater. A one-act, "Snapshots," was the winner in the 2010 Kernodle competition. She is co-owner of

HaveScripts.com and ScriptWorks Press (www.havescripts.com), a dramatic publishing company marketing to high schools, universities, regional, and community theaters. She teaches playwriting in the MA/MFA program at Wilkes University in Wilkes-Barre, PA, and has taught at Carnegie-Mellon University and at the University of Iowa.

Shareen Knight is an artist, playwright, and photographer, who, after an earlier life in California, now lives in a remote part of British Columbia with her dog and cat, where she is renovating a 1910 farmhouse, writing plays and trying to keep the bears out of her orchard.

Kerri Kochanski's plays include: "The Food Monologues," "The Pink Plays," "Penis Envy," "The Marriage Plays 'Til Death Do Us Part," "Myth," "Spitting Daisies" and "Communicating Through the Sunset." Her short plays and monologues are published by Dramatic Publishing, Meriwether, Smith & Kraus, Applause Books, and Original Works Publishing. www.kerrikochanski.com

Katherine Koller lives in Edmonton, Alberta, and her one-act plays have been produced across Canada. *Coal Valley: the Making of a Miner* is included in *The Alberta Advantage* (Playwrights Canada Press, 2008). *The Seed Savers* premiered at Workshop West Theatre in Edmonton and is included in her collection, *Voices of the Land: The Seed Savers and Other Plays* (Athabasca University Press, 2012). Katherine also writes fiction, and for dance, ballet, opera, radio and film, and teaches in the Department of English and Film Studies at the University of Alberta. Her website is www.katherinekoller.ca.

Robin Rice Lichtig magical realism is my paintbrush. My plays tap into the imagination and create new worlds. Reoccurring themes: environment, creativity, diversity. Produced worldwide, most recently: LISTEN! THE RIVER in South Africa and THE POWER OF BIRDS in New York City. Available scripts (10 minutes to full length) at: www.dramamama.net.

Susan Lieberman A resident Playwright at Chicago Dramatists, Susan Lieberman received a Jeff Citation for *Arrangement for Two Violas* and Jeff Award nomination for *Prairie Lights*, as well as two regional Emmy nominations. Her work has been produced by Stage Left, Visions & Voices Theatre, Chicago Dramatists, Bloomington Playwrights Project, Pandora Productions, 20% Theatre, Jerusalem English Speaking Theatre and elsewhere. *Car or Quince?* developed with American Theatre Company, will be produced by Clockwise Theatre in 2012-13.

Joan Lipkin A playwright, lyricist, director, educator and social activist who writes about disability, class, sexuality, gender and language, Joan Lipkin's other plays including *Some of My Best Friends Are...*, *He's Having Her Baby, Small Domestic Acts, Crab Cakes* and *The Girl Who Lost Her Voice* have been produced throughout the US and Europe. Her work may be found in *Mythic Women/Real Women, Amazon All Stars, Best American Short Plays, Out & Allied*, and other publications. For more info, see www.uppityco.com.

Pam Calabrese MacLean has published two books of poetry: *Twenty-four Names for* Mother (Paper Journey Press 2006); *The Dead Can't Dance* (Ronsdale Press 2009). Her first play, *Her Father's Barn*, garnered awards across Canada and Sunnyside Café, received rave reviews in the 2009 Atlantic Fringe Festival.

Jennifer Maisel's plays have been hailed as "inventive and sophisticated" and "human and eternal" with a "formidable flair for the mysterious" and have been produced nationally and internationally. MAD LOVE received the Roger L. Stevens Award from the Fund for New American Plays. THE LAST SEDER received the Fund for New American Plays award from the Kennedy Center. THERE OR HERE, produced by The Hypothetical Theatre Company in New York, was a PEN West Literary Award finalist. She workshopped her new play, OUT OF ORBIT, at the Sundance Theatre Lab at MASS MoCA. www.jennifermaisel.com

Felicity McCall is a career journalist with the BBC, now a full-time writer. Ten professional plays, 2 Meyer Whitworth nominations, Tyrone Guthrie Award and Arts Council and Irish playwrights awards. Co-founder of the NW of Ireland based artist/activist company Handful Productions, and its professional sister Postscript. Author of nine published works.

Patrizia Monaco, Italian playwright, is graduated in History of the Theatre. She has worked for a while at UCD, Dublin, Ireland. After her return to Italy, she has been teaching playwriting and history of theatre. Since 1976, her plays and radio plays have been staged and broadcast in Italy and abroad. She has been awarded many prizes.

Pat Montley, a Dramatists Guild member, has had 14 plays published (Samuel French, Playscripts, Inc., Meriwether, Heinemann, Applause, Dramatic Publishing, Prentice-Hall, *Dramatics Magazine*). Her plays have been given readings at the Kennedy Center, Baltimore's Center Stage, and the Abingdon Theatre, and productions at The Nebraska Repertory Theatre, the Manhattan Theatre Source, the Harold Clurman Theatre, the Nat Horne Theatre, and Baltimore's Theatre Project. Her work has been supported by residencies at the Millay Artists' Colony and the Djerassi Resident Artists Program, and by grants from the MD and PA Arts Councils, the Shubert Foundation, the Mary Roberts Rinehart Foundation, and Warner Brothers. She has taught playwriting at Chatham University, Goucher College and the Johns Hopkins University.

Joanna Alexandra Norland, a UK-based lawyer-by-day/playwright-by-night has had work produced off Broadway, New York, throughout the United Kingdom, and in Australia. "Lizzy, Darcy & Jane," published by Samuel French Ltd., is the first in a series of plays in which she dramatizes the clash between her protagonists' internal and external world.

Masha Obolensky's plays have been produced by TimeLine Theatre (Chicago, Joseph Jefferson-nominated "Best New Work"), The Nora Theatre (Cambridge), Arts Emerson (Boston), the Kennedy Center (D.C.), Access Theatre (NYC), Here Arts Center (NYC), Source Festival (D.C.), and the Boston Theatre Marathon. She has an M.A. from Emerson College and an MFA from Boston University. Masha is currently a Huntington Theatre Playwriting Fellow and recently received the 2010 Pen New England Discovery Award and was a 2011 Massachusetts Cultural Council Fellowship Finalist. She is also an actor and director.

Martha Patterson has been published in four anthologies by the International Centre for Women Playwrights. Her work has been produced Off-Off-Broadway and by Changing Scene Theatre Northwest, Washington, the Seoul, Korea Players in Asia, and the Pink Banana Theatre in Milwaukee, as well by SWAN Day at the Boston Playwrights Theatre and Write On at the Boston Center for the Arts, and a Performance & Advocacy Event in Cleveland, Ohio. She has also been produced by Thespian Prod., Florida, Shoestring Radio Theatre in San Francisco, the Short + Sweet Festival in Sydney, Australia and by the Paw Paw Village Players in Michigan. She has had several works published by JAC Publishing. She earned her B.A. from Mount Holyoke College and an M.A. from Emerson College, both degrees in Theatre. She is a member of the Dramatists Guild of America, the International Centre for Women Playwrights, Screen Actors Guild, and Actors' Equity Association.

Toni Press-Coffman has lived in 14 cities in the United States and done artist residencies in 11 more. She wrote her play about Richard III (Two Days of Grace At Middleham) at Hawthornden Castle outside Edinburgh from where she traveled to Richard's birthplace, to Middleham Castle where he grew up, and to Bosworth Field where he died. With a grant from the Arizona Commission on the Arts, she wrote Touch at coffee shops and motels along the Pacific Coast as she traveled to and from the Oregon Shakespeare Festival.

She wrote La Sangre Llama in Indianapolis in collaboration with that city's Santeria community and Coyote y Culebre in collaboration with second, third and fourth graders in Tucson public schools. She wrote That Slut! during an NEA/TCG Playwright Residency at the Phoenix Theatre in Indianapolis, where it premiered. All told, she has written 20 plays, which have been produced throughout the country, including in New York, Los Angeles, Indianapolis, San Francisco, Portland

(OR), Tucson, Columbus, Miami, and Baltimore. She has had work developed at the Sundance Institute (All Ye Faithful), Playlabs (Trucker Rhapsody), the Minneapolis' Playwrights Center (Touch), and the Eugene O'Neill National Playwrights Conference (Stand).

Aiste Ptakauske is a film and theater maker from Lithuania. A winner of numerous awards including a national prize for the best fiction debut of the year and a Fulbright fellowship, she had her plays presented at national and regional theaters in Lithuania as well as international festivals in Russia, Turkey, and the U.S. Recently, she started writing and producing narrative television series for a Lithuanian television network.

Steven Schutzman is the author of dozens of published plays and plays produced at such theatres as New Jersey Repertory, Circus Theatricals, Cleveland Public, Rochester Repertory and Baltimore Theatre Project. He is a five-time recipient of Maryland State Arts Council Individual Artist Grant Awards. His long one-act "Tree Man", excerpted in this book, won the First Stage L.A. One-Act Play Contest, 2004. His full-length play "A Question of Water" was named the unanimous winner of the Across the Generations New Jewish Play Festival, 2010. Find out more about his work and learn how to get copies and reproduction rights to all his plays at http://mysite.verizon.net/stevenschutzman/

Helen Shay is an English dramatist and also a spoken word performer. Other hats include wife, mother, lawyer, poet and non-fiction writer. She currently works at the University of

York, where she teaches some play-writing. Her plays have been performed at Edinburgh Fringe, Ilkley Literature Festival, Harrogate Theatre and other UK regional venues. In 2004, she won first prize in the radio play competition by the International Playwrights Forum of International Theatre Institute. (Play published and translated.) She holds an MA in Creative Writing from Manchester Metropolitan University (Distinction awarded.) Helen has also performed poetry, including at Glastonbury Festival. Helen is currently serving on *Authors North* committee of Society of Authors and as UK rep for IWPC, plus is an 'ambassador' of *SWWJ* and an active member of *Script Yorkshire*. She is author of *Writer's Guide to Copyright, Contract and Law*, 4th ed (ISBN 9781845283216). More info at www.helenshay.originationinsite.com.

Faye Sholiton, who develops her work at the Cleveland Play House, has seen her plays performed all over the U.S. and in London. Winner of three Ohio Arts Council grants, she has also been published in multiple anthologies. She is Ohio's regional representative to the Dramatists Guild of America. Visit www.fayesplays.com.

Lojo Simon is a playwright, journalist, MFA student, and mother of two daughters. Lojo Simon writes plays with roles for strong women of all ages. Learn more about her and her writing at www.lojosimon.com.

Donna Spector's play GOLDEN LADDER (*Women Playwrights: Best Plays of 2002* , Smith & Kraus) was produced Off Broadway, as was her first play, ANOTHER PARADISE. She has written 17 full-length plays that have appeared Off Off Broadway, regionally and in Canada, Ireland, Scotland and Greece. She received two N.E.H. grants to study theater in Greece and production grants from Geraldine R. Dodge Foundation and New York Council for the Arts. Winner of Acrosstown Repertory's 2008 Sunwall Comedy Prize and the 2009 Eileen Heckart Senior Drama Award, she was a finalist in the Beverly Hills/Julie Harris and Mill Mountain Theatre competitions, Reverie' Productions' Next Generation Contest and the Theatre

Unbound Competition, a semi-finalist for the O'Neill Playwrights' Conference, Chesterfield Writer's Film Project and short-listed in the BBC/British Council International Playwriting Competition. Her play SHORT-TERM AFFAIRS (*35 IN 10: Thirty-Five Ten-Minute Plays*, Dramatic Publishing) won the Palm Springs National Short Play Fest and was produced at Playwrights Circle in Palm Springs, Gallery Players, Brooklyn, and Actors on the Verge, NYC. Her poems, stories, plays, scenes and monologues have been published in many literary magazines and anthologies. Her poetry book, *The Woman Who Married Herself,* was published in 2010 by Evening Street Press as a Sinclair Poetry Prize finalist. Her agent is Carolyn French at Fifi Oscard Agency.

Jennie Staniloff-Redling is the 2007 winner of BMI's Jerry Harrington Musical Theatre Award for Outstanding Creative Achievement as a librettist, is the national recipient of the Stanley Drama Award, the Arlene R. and William P. Lewis Playwriting Award for Women and the 18th Annual R. Joyce Whitely Arenafest of new plays at Karamu Theatre in Cleveland where a staged reading of her play, *Gone Astray*, was performed in May 2010. Ms. Redling's plays have been read or produced at Soho Rep, Ensemble Studio Theatre, the Mint Theater, West Bank Downstairs Theatre, Mefisto Theatre Company, the New York Fringe Festival, the Sage Theatre, Abingdon Theatre Company, Urban Stages, The Barrow Group, the Globe Theatre, Hudson Stage Company, Stamford Center for the Arts, the Organic Theatre Company, the Alleyway Theatre, New Jersey Rep Lumnia Theatre and others. Her monologues and scenes are published in Smith & Krause's "Audition Arsenal for Women in Their 20's; 101 Monologues by Type," 2010 JAC Publishing Monologue Compilation the upcoming Smith & Krause release, "Award-winning 90 Second Comic Scenes."

D. Stirling has previously had work commissioned for television and theatrical productions in London, Edinburgh, and Glasgow.

Bara Swain serves as the Playwriting Outreach Coordinator at Abingdon Theatre, NYC. Her plays are anthologized in Best 10-Minute Plays 2007 ("Prized Begonias") and 2009 ("Critical Care"), Mother/Daughter Monologues: Babes and Beginnings (JAC Publications), and Contemporary Monologues for Young Women (Meriwether Publishing). Her plays have been produced in thirteen states.

Lene Therese Teigen (1962) lives in Oslo, Norway. She has worked as a writer, director, and dramaturge since 1989, mainly in theatre, but also in film, television, radio drama, and as an author of fiction. She has broad international experience, both as a director and as a playwright. Teigen has a Masters degree in Theater from the University of Bergen, Norway. www.houseofstories.no

Lucy Tyler is a playwright and poet. Her plays include *The Measurements of a Murderer*, *Claudia Schiffer's Mind*, *The Operators*, and *Saviours*. Her new play *Current Regimes*, about the Spanish Civil War, is currently in development and will receive its public debut in June 2010. Lucy has just completed an M.Phil in playwriting studies at Birmingham University.

Vanda is a Lambda Award Finalist and an Edward Albee fellow whose play *Why'd Ya Make Me Wear This, Joe?* was a winner or finalist in the following: New Play Contest at Celebration Theatre, the Ashland New Plays Series, Reva Shriner Contest, Panowski Playwriting Award, Play Labs at the Playwrights' Center, the O'Neill Playwriting Conference, and the Cherry Lane Mentor Program. Her play, *Patient HM*, was workshopped by Emerging Artists Theater in NYC. It subsequently was invited to be performed at the Conference for the Society of Neuroscience in Washington, DC.

About the International Centre for Women Playwrights (ICWP):

ICWP is a non-profit membership organization with a mission to support women playwrights around the world. The movement to create **ICWP** began at The First International Women Playwrights Conference was held in Buffalo, NY in 1988. The Buffalo conference brought together more than 200 women playwrights from over 30 countries. A sister organization, **Women Playwrights International**, continues to plan tri-annual conferences. The **ICWP-L** email discussion List was started in 1994, and since 1997, the group has operated continuously as a virtual centre, providing ongoing online networking opportunities, professional development grants, periodic writing retreats, and funding for public events and readings. The group is a 501 (c) 3 organization managed by a Board of Trustees elected from and by the membership. Membership is open to all people who support women playwrights. Join us at:

http://www.womenplaywrights.org.

About the Diversity Scenes Project:

Editor/Project Coordinator: Karin Diann Williams

Readers and volunteers: Donna Kahwaty, Sally Patricia Smith, Paddy Gillard-Bentley, Roberta D'Alois, Nicole Kearney, Mary Reinhardt, Lucille Beatty, Bernadette Vanburen, Mary-Ann Greanier, Kiesa Kay, Teleah Scott, Kristine Bauske, Prudence Holmes, Alicia Grega, Jewel Seehaus-Fisher, Roz Cannon, Sophie Dowllar, Heidi Decker, Elena Kaufman, Shirley Tucker, Diane Baia, Elisabeth Feltaous, Ellen Kaplan, Kelly

Burnett, Tabitha Keast, Laura Pfizenmayer, Lauren Bies, LaChris Jordan, Kellie Bean, CJ Ehrlich, Virginia Goncalves, Thyme Shieh, Meghan Sharer, Katherine Burkman, Rhea MacCallum, Deb Magid, Tee ONeill, Donna-Michelle St. Bernard, Kisha Emanuel, Kay Cook, Sam Mitschke, Avery Leonard, Elizabeth Whitney, Sara Lampert Hoover, Theresa Pine, Mary Steelsmith, Marsha Sheiness, Jacklyn Janeksela, Farzana Datta, Karen Mueller Bryson, Xiaoyan Lu, Kevin Six, Jacquelin Hedeman, Ching-In Chen, Claire Braz-Valentine, Elise Geither, Sofia Etcheverry, Saundra Lee Words, Lisa Leaverton, Val Valdez, Sherlene Humphrey, Catherine Aselford, Jacklyn Janeksela, Rebecca Nesvet, Kisha Emanuel, Celeta McCall, Natalya Churlyeva, Alicia Grega, Mona Curtis.

Special Thanks To: Margaret McSeveney, Emily Cicchini, and all the members of ICWP who made these books possible.

All proceeds from the sale of this book benefit the collective membership of ICWP.

Made in the USA
Las Vegas, NV
02 December 2023

81969587R00386